T0314124

BORDERLAND CAPITALISM

BORDERLAND CAPITALISM

*Turkestan Produce, Qing Silver, and
the Birth of an Eastern Market*

KWANGMIN KIM

STANFORD UNIVERSITY PRESS

Stanford California

Stanford University Press
Stanford, California

Library of Congress Cataloging-in-Publication Data

Names: Kim, Kwangmin, author.
Title: Borderland capitalism : Turkestan produce, Qing silver, and the birth of an eastern market / Kwangmin Kim.
Description: Stanford, California : Stanford University Press, 2016. | Includes bibliographical references and index.
Identifiers: LCCN 2016012979 (print) | LCCN 2016020368 (ebook) | ISBN 9780804799232 (cloth : alk. paper) | ISBN 9781503600423
Subjects: LCSH: Xinjiang Uygur Zizhiqu (China)—Economic conditions. | Capitalism—China—Xinjiang Uygur Zizhiqu—History. | Xinjiang Uygur Zizhiqu (China)—Commerce—History. | Agriculture—Economic aspects—China—Xinjiang Uygur Zizhiqu—History. | Xinjiang Uygur Zizhiqu (China)—Relations—China. | China—Relations—China—Xinjiang Uygur Zizhiqu. | Xinjiang Uygur Zizhiqu (China)—History. | China—History—Qing dynasty, 1644–1912.
Classification: LCC HC428.X56 K56 2016 (print) | LCC HC428.X56 (ebook) | DDC 330.951/603—dc23
LC record available at https://lccn.loc.gov/2016012979

Printed in the United States of America on acid-free, archival-quality paper. Typeset at Stanford University Press in 10/14 Minion.

Contents

Acknowledgments   vii

Introduction   1

1   Beg, Empire, and Agrarian Developments in Central Asia,
1500–1750   19
2   Capitalist Imperatives and Imperial Connections, 1759–1825   47
3   The "Holy Wars" of the Uprooted, 1826–30   90
4   The "Just and Liberal Rule" of Zuhūr al-Dīn, 1831–46   126
5   Global Crises of Oasis Capitalism, 1847–64   156
    Conclusion   184

Appendixes

A. Population and arable land in Eastern Turkestan, 1759–1950, 201.
B. Muslim Notables Submitting to the Qing, 1697–1760, 203.
C. Muslim Aristocrats in Hami and Turfan, 208.
D. Private Land Transactions and *Waqf* Donations in the
Oasis, 1750–1911, 216.   E. Oasis Rural Settlements in
Yarkand, 1770s–1870s, 221.   F. Yarkand Tax Register: Population
and Land, 223.

Notes   225
Bibliography   263
Index   287

Acknowledgments

I incurred many debts while writing this book. I would like to thank my teachers who helped me to become the historian I am now. At the University of California, Berkeley, Professor Wen-hsin Yeh patiently guided me in articulating the ideas presented in this book. This would not have been possible without her unfailing support and encouragement, as well as her probing and enlightening questions, which often took years for me to answer. The late Professor Frederic Wakeman, Jr., also generously shared his deep knowledge and insights on Qing history with me. At Sogang University in Korea, Professor Han-kyu Kim first inspired me to study the history of the Chinese frontiers and international relations with his eye-opening scholarship.

Professor Mark Elliott of Harvard University taught me Manchu, a language that played a crucial role in shaping the narrative of this book. Professor Morris Rossabi of the City University of New York and Professor Engseng Ho of Duke University kindly showed interest in the book project from its early stage, and shared their insights on Muslim societies in Eurasia.

The vibrant intellectual community of the History Department of the University of Colorado at Boulder influenced the book's evolution in a direction that I had not imagined before joining the department. Professor Tim Weston, Marcia Yonemoto, John Willis, Marjorie McIntosh, Mithi Mukerjee, Miriam Kingsberg, Fredy González, and Celine Dauverd read many early, poorly articulated versions of its chapters, and provided numerous constructive comments. Professor Fred Anderson has guided me in every possible way since my joining the department. Also, his insightful comments on the similarities and differences between eighteenth-century North America and Qing Central Asia have urged me to think about the Qing Empire within a broader, world historical context.

Generous support from the following institutions also helped me to complete the book. A postdoctoral fellowship at the Council on East Asian Studies at Yale University, 2013, provided a one-year research leave, which was critical in developing the book into its present form. The Kayden Research Grants from the University of Colorado at Boulder provided subvention for publication costs. The following institutions invited me to give presentations on various parts of the material over the past years: UC Berkeley, Institute of East Asian Studies; University of California, Los Angeles, Asia Institute; Stanford University; Harvard University; Yale University, Council on East Asian Studies; Duke University; Brandeis University; and the National University of Singapore.

Some material in Chapter 1 appears in "Profit and Protection: Emin Khwaja and the Qing Conquest of Central Asia, 1759–1777," *Journal of Asian Studies* 71:3 (2012), and is used by the permission of the publisher, Cambridge University Press.

Finally, I would like to thank my parents in Korea, who supported me through the long years of my education, although they will not be able to read this book written in English. Especially, I am grateful to Sungyun Lim, my wife and colleague, who has always stood by me through the good and bad times. This book could not have been finished without her support, sacrifice, and steadfast faith in me.

BORDERLAND CAPITALISM

Introduction

In 1754, when the British entered into a fight with the French in the Ohio Valley that would become the Seven Year's War (1754–63), halfway around the globe the Qing Empire launched an attack on its archrival, the Zunghar Mongols. To their surprise, the invading Qing army found a group of Muslim natives who were eager to offer their assistance to the "Chinese" ruler in the desert oasis terrain of Central Asia. The Qing were fortunate to acquire their alliance. As the major landlords in the Qing-controlled region, these individuals, called begs, wielded the political power that could dictate the fortunes of any empire or state seeking to establish itself in the region. They developed land, moved goods, organized capital, and, most important, controlled human labor in the oases. Their families produced secular leaders called *hākim* (a governor or head of local civil administration) and religious leaders called *akhūnd*s (spiritual leaders) and *mullā*s (Muslim scholars) for the Islamic establishment.[1] They became the lifelines of the Qing Empire in Central Asia (see Map I.1).

This book examines the beg alliance with the Qing within the broader context of the expansion of global trade in the sixteenth century and the emerging interconnections and coherence of the early modern world facilitated by it. Because the begs had been well connected to the rhythm of expanding world trade through China since the sixteenth century, this book argues that they allied and supported the Qing in order to promote the agenda of the capitalist transformation of the oasis political economy in response to expanding global commerce. This partnership also helped the begs to weather the social, demographic, and political volatility inherent in the capitalist transformation. In this way, the Qing Empire became the patron of the borderland capitalists and their interests in Central Asia.

This view from the periphery, or bottom up, opens up a vastly expanded historical horizon for understanding the Qing imperial expansion into Central

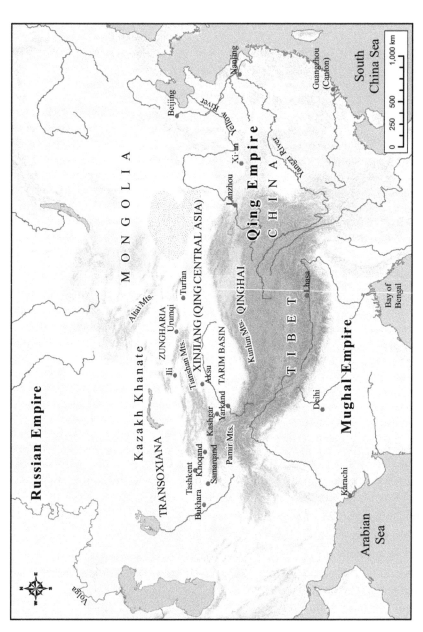

Map I.1. Qing Central Asia (Xinjiang) in Eurasia, ca. 1800.

Asia. No longer a merely parochial event in Chinese history, it rather reflects a global event at large—an event embedded in the capitalist transformations of local societies occurring all over the world from the time of the expansion of world trade in the sixteenth century, and a development occurring simultaneously in many parts of the world, from Europe to the Americas and Eurasia, if in different fashions. The needs of Eurasia's borderland society undergoing such significant change contributed to the success of Qing expansion into Central Asia, as much as, if not more than, did the Qing state's security forces. Chinese expansion was the story of "borderland capitalism."

What is at stake in this book in terms of broader implications is a fundamental question—namely, the location of Qing history or early modern Chinese history within the broader sweep of the global history of imperialism and capitalism in the early modern period. This book challenges the "European exceptionalism" model that considers the interconnected development of imperialism and capitalism as a fundamentally unique European phenomenon, one that paved the way to European hegemony in the world beginning in the sixteenth century. By showing the Qing Empire as a quintessentially early-modern empire that emerged at the crossroads of world-scale commercialization and agrarian and imperial expansion from the year 1500, this book seeks to deprioritize the European experience in the historical narrative of global capitalism and imperialism. Especially by highlighting the pivotal role of the Qing state in agrarian development in Qing Central Asia—a pattern that had strong parallels in British North India in the eighteenth and nineteenth centuries—this book articulates the simultaneous (even coeval) paths to imperialism and capitalism in the colonies and borderlands taken by the European and Chinese empires.

Commercial Agriculture in the Oasis: Stage and Actors

The home of oasis capitalism was southern Xinjiang, or Eastern Turkestan, a 350,000-square-mile area, about two times the size of California. It comprised eight major oasis systems (from Turfan in the east to Kashgar in the west), located on the rim of the Taklamakan Desert. The Zungharia steppe to the north, also in Xinjiang, remained a world apart, one dominated primarily by Chinese settlers and merchants, although it was never completely isolated from the southern oases. This book examines the political dynamics of agrarian development in Muslim Xinjiang, but in no way comprehensively studies the economic history of Qing Xinjiang. Rather, it concentrates specifically on the

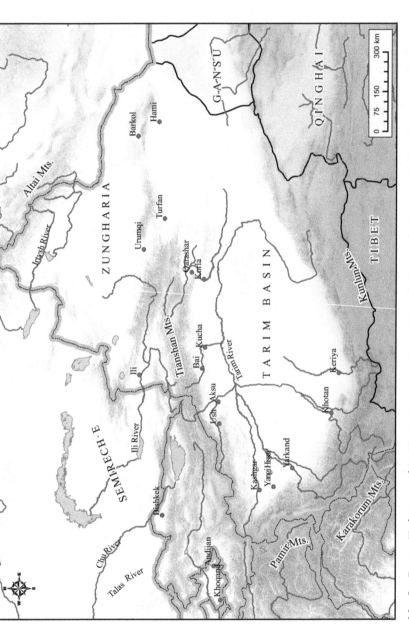

Map I.2. Eastern Turkestan and Its Mining Resources. Source: Forsyth, *Report of a Mission to Yarkund*, pp. 32–62; GPYSA; MLZZ, QL49/4/12, DG1/7/8, DG5/10/23, DG11/4/21; MW, vols. 156, 241, 247, 252, 265; SYD/XF, vol. 8. *Note:* Mining resources: Yarkand, jade; Kashgar, copper; Khotan, jade, gold; Aksu, lead, copper, sulphur, coal; Kucha, copper; Qarashar, lead, copper, silver; Tarbagatai (in northern Xinjiang), gold

events occurring within the geography of the oases in southern Xinjiang, where the majority of the Muslim population resided (see Map I.2).

Each oasis system constituted an expanding constellation of agricultural settlements, organized around the nucleus of a central market (*bazaar*), which in turn was closely linked to the web of international trade connecting the Chinese, Central Asian, Indian, and Russian markets. In the aggregate, each system linked into the regional and long-distance trade nexus penetrating Eurasia. Surrounding each *bazaar* were a cluster of suburban settlements and rural villages, interspersed with vast spreads of dry wildlands. The people residing in the urban centers included merchants, handicraft workers, and officials. The oasis people in the suburbs and rural villages maintained their livelihoods by farming and cultivating cash crops, including fruit, vegetables, and cotton. They also raised livestock for the consumption of the urban population. In theory, this oasis system could expand endlessly, as long as the waterways carrying water to the farmland likewise expanded. However, in reality, in Eastern Turkestan, geographical features of the land curtailed such progress sharply. The high mountains of Tianshan, Pamir, and Kunlun enveloped the Tarim Basin on the north, west, and south. And the Taklamakan Desert, at the center of the basin, would set another fierce physical boundary, also inhibiting new development profoundly.[2]

In the mountains and foothills lived various nomads such as the Kirghiz, also known as the Burut, and the Kazakh, raising sheep and horses. Also present were hardy small polities of Tajik (mountain people of Persian descent), who cultivated various crops suitable to high-altitude agriculture. These various mountain nomads and farming communities interlinked with the oasis people in the Tarim Basin through trade, usually buying cotton and selling livestock. The mountain enclaves also engaged with the oasis economy through underground means as well. They often enriched themselves by preying on the caravan merchants traveling through the mountain passes.

Water, or the lack thereof, predetermined the scope of all economic activity in this region. Annual rainfall on the oasis of the Tarim Basin ran a scant 100 mm, or four inches, a degree of aridity extreme even by the standards of Central Asia and the Middle East, known for their dry climates. Iran and Afghanistan, for instance, receive 300 to 500 mm of rainfall annually.[3] Even worse in the basin was the absence of good rivers, unlike the Fergana Valley on the opposite side of the Tianshan from Kashgar, which benefited from the flow of the Syr Darya and Amu Darya rivers. Any effort to develop oasis agriculture then would rely heavily on artificial irrigation, to secure water resources from either inadequate river systems or mountaintop water melt during the summer. Major canals (*ustāng*) were built to pull water from main rivers to farming areas; branch canals were built to carry water from the major canals into homesteads. Therefore, basic rural communities (*mahalla*) comprising four to eighty farming households were formed along each branch canal. In turn, several *mahallas*, established along the branch canals originating from the same major canal, formed a larger rural community called a *yaz* (village). Above the *yaz* was the *känt* (rural settlement), a conglomeration of two to three or more *yazs*.[4]

Development and upkeep of such artificial irrigation systems required substantial investments of capital and labor. This outlay in turn prompted the development of high-profit commercial agriculture ventures, so as to garner as much profit as possible per unit of cultivation. Also found in this region were a few highly coveted mineral resources: gold, copper, and lead, scattered across the oasis valley floors and the mountains of the Tarim Basin, as well as the Zungharia steppe located on the north. The most important mining commodity, however, was jade, concentrated in sites on the two westernmost oases of the Tarim Basin, Khotan and Yarkand. Khotan was the larger center of the two. The jade market in China and Central Asia was huge, and the deposits made these two destinations an important node of the Eurasian trade network (see Map I.2, above).

The begs, by initiating the development of commercial agriculture, ranching, and mining in the Tarim Basin, walked tall in the desert oasis region of Eastern Turkestan. In fact, the name itself literally translates as "lords," and these figures would head various oasis settler communities scattered in the oasis towns and countryside (comprising, for example, Sufi migrants, former nomadic tribesmen, and caravan merchants). These heads of settler communities began to emerge as a new group of commercially oriented entrepreneurial landlords from the sixteenth century onward, and especially under Qing rule (1759–1864). The begs built a highly diversified commercial enterprise comprising three major interlocking sectors—revenue farming, mining, and agriculture—aimed at local, regional, and international markets (China, Russia, India, and the Middle East). They invested capital to expand their production. They built canals and dikes and organized new land reclamation and mining enterprises. In order to facilitate this development, they purchased land, slaves, and wage laborers. They also aggressively expanded their private domination of formerly common resources such as wildland and water, in spite of resistance from the rural village communities.

Distinctive to the begs' initiative to expand commercial enterprise was the heavy reliance on their political connection to the Qing. The latter could and did provide stable access to the vast China market. As the ultimate owner of all the undeveloped resources in the oasis, the Qing emperor provided the begs privileged access to untapped land and mines. Because the local Qing administration needed the begs as much as the begs needed the administration, in order to develop resources and raise military revenue regionally, the Qing state willingly shared the fruits of the development, leaving the begs substantial surpluses to be reinvested in local agriculture and commerce.

The Qing emperor's land grant played an especially crucial role in the begs' development. The Qing emperor awarded the begs who served him grants of wildland, cash, and *yanqis*. The latter were oasis farming households required to pay certain dues to the begs to which they were assigned, not the Qing. These grants helped the begs to secure the right to develop vast wildlands into large-scale commercial farms and the necessary labor forces to cultivate them. Often the begs claimed more wildland and *yanqi*s than were officially awarded by the Qing. They recruited wealthy farmers as *yanqi,* legally and illegally, by promoting the benefits the Qing allowed to *yanqi*s—namely, an exemption from the onerous tax and corvée labor obligation owed to the empire. The begs utilized the recruited *yanqi* farmers as partners in their land development projects.[5]

The size of these enterprises was substantial to say the least. For instance, one prominent individual amassed at least 8,459 acres (200 *batman*) scattered across the oasis region by the time of his death in 1778; that is approximately the size of Stanford University's campus.[6] He also had conducted a thriving jade smuggling business, which had sent fifty tons (76,000 *jin*) a year into China.[7] Another notable beg family was able to invest 6,560,000 taels (*liang*) of silver in trading with China in the late nineteenth century. This family stationed their own commercial agents in various locations there and also held trading relations with India, the Mongols, and Russia.[8]

The begs' growth in commercial enterprises elicited a political reaction from the oasis farmers, the second major actor on stage in the political and social history of Qing Central Asia. The development of commercial agriculture provided opportunity and danger to this group simultaneously. Taking advantage of the opportunity provided by the increasing commercialization of the oasis economy, some oasis farmers thrived; others, who experienced bad luck, however, increasingly could barely sustain a livelihood, and desperately hired themselves out to the begs. Moreover, as the latter encroached on their communal dominion over the wildlands and waters in the rural hinterland, the village communities, the units that retained customary rights over such common resources, spiraled into serious trouble. This pressure, in large part, contributed to the dislocation of oasis farmers in the eighteenth and nineteenth centuries.

Many, facing personal disaster of various sorts, chose to flee into the surrounding high mountains to form outsider, refugee communities. From there they would threaten the security of the begs and their protector, the Qing Empire, throughout the nineteenth century, attacking caravan merchants passing through the mountain recesses and developing a lucrative smuggling business. They would eventually organize a menacing war against the begs and Qing in the early nineteenth century, feeding off the oasis villagers' constant discontent with the begs' agrarian development. The tension and contention between these rural and mountain refugee communities, on the one hand, and the oasis begs and their "Chinese" protector, on the other, informed the trajectory of Qing imperial politics in Central Asia.

In the midst of the mountain refugees were the *khwaja*s who could provide the political capacity to organize these motley elements into concerted action.[9] These *khwaja*s descended from an influential branch of the Naqshbandī Sufi Order, which had dominated the politics, economy, and religion in the oasis region in the sixteenth and seventeenth centuries (the Āfāq faction, or "White Mountaineers"). When the Qing conquered the Xinjiang oases, the majority of the Sufi leaders and *khwaja*s made a decision to join the Qing, primarily because of their interests in the agrarian development of the region; they became a central constituency of the pro-Qing begs. However, these "White Mountaineer" *khwaja*s made a different political choice. Taking advantage of the transfer of overlordship from the Zunghar to the Qing in the mid-eighteenth century, they had tried to wrestle independence from the Qing but failed and consequently were expelled from the oasis. On the run, dispersing to northern India and various Central Asian cities (such as Samarqand, Bukhara, and Khoqand), the sons and grandsons of these dead *khwaja*s traveled far and wide. They would finally find a home and a similar calling in the Tianshan and Pamir mountains, among the mountain refugees and Kirghiz. There they would lead the refugees' attacks on the oasis valleys.

Global Capitalism and the Qing Empire Reconsidered

The oasis economy of Eastern Turkestan was capitalist, this book argues, because it featured the expansion of the class relations and rural production relations that were characteristic of capitalist economy. Begs, the center of agrarian production in the oasis, were the commercially oriented capitalist landlord gentry. They invested *capital* to bolster production. They expanded their *private* claims over rural resources, and utilized *hired laborers*, whether they were wage laborers or slaves. They accumulated land and recruited resources through expanding the capitalistic institutions of private property and wage labor. They even managed to appropriate the nomadic "feudal" institution of the ruler's land grants for their commercial purpose, and developed large-scale commercial farming and ranching operations. This book, therefore, contributes to a non-Eurocentric view of the formation of global capitalism, by exploring the expansion of capitalist commercial enterprises in the most unexpected of places—landlocked Central Asia.

For the past few decades, historians have pushed for a global understanding of capitalism. Historians in various parts of the world have explored whether capitalism, understood as the fundamental essence of modernity, had local roots in the historical trajectory of non-European societies, implying that the modernity of the European model was not merely derivative on the local end—that is, a simple transplant transferred from Europe at the time of nineteenth-century European imperialism. Drawing upon empirical dates from China, Japan, Southeast Asia, and the like, these scholars persuasively show that the trajectory of local economies of non-European societies displayed strong similarities with the European one until the watershed moment of the "great divergence" in the eighteenth century. At that time, the expansion of commercially oriented European imperialism and the origin of opportunistic industrial development happening in Western Europe catapulted the latter into a hegemonic force in the global capitalist world order.[10]

Obviously, these studies tremendously enrich our understanding of capitalist development on a world scale. However, the comparative approach employed by these works may unintentionally tempt scholars into the fundamental methodological pitfall of Eurocentrism. If one defines the existence of capitalism with indexes drawn from the specificity of Western European development and institutions, such measures conceptually elevate the relative European mode of economic production as well as its social and political formations into a universal mode of capitalism, one that is categorically bound to fail in identifying the presence of capitalism in the non-European world. There will always be a "defect" or "absence" in capitalist development in different parts of the world that makes it imperfect at best, or an utter failure at worst. European development was historically specific, and can not be found with exactly the same parameters in other parts of the world. Therefore, by narrowly defining capitalism as a specific mode of production existing in the European core historically, one is likely to forfeit a global interpretation.

What is needed is a more organic and historical definition of capitalism that takes serious account of European experience but does not conceptually privilege it. If the specific historical form of European capitalism of the sixteenth century and onward was a mode of response of local society to maximize profit from the expansion of world trade, it is for us more profitable to examine whether other parts of the world displayed similar development in orientation, if not in institutional specificities, and to capture the complex realities of the transformations as different but interconnected forms of global capitalism. Indeed, Fernand Braudel, one of the prime theorists of the origin of modern capitalism, suggested such a broad, global definition of capitalism—namely, an interconnected system of expansionist, transformative commercial enterprises that re/organized local economy and society in order to make maximum profit from the emerging global trade. At the heart of such capitalist enterprises was the commercial class (landlords, merchants, and industrialists) who considered as their ultimate goal the accumulation of profit vis-à-vis, say, accumulation of power. To achieve their goal, they appropriated every possible resource—commerce, agriculture, and industries—and every kind of preexisting social formation including slavery, feudalism, and even an "Asiatic mode of production." The existence of specific institutions and social structures similar to those of the West was not essential, as long as the local political economy transformed itself in a way to secure advantage in the growing commercialization of the world. This book adopts and tests this global and interconnective definition of capitalism in an Eastern context, and explores whether the expansion in world trade also resulted in the formation of such capitalist enterprises in the greater Chinese world.[11]

The beg enterprise fits this description of capitalism very well. It was expansionist, because it insatiably absorbed available resources and labor into the ever-expanding agrarian production in the oasis. It was transformative, for the begs' efforts set the oasis economy on the path of unprecedented economic growth. Arable land doubled during Qing rule, even using a conservative measure. In 1772, land under cultivation was recorded as 3.4 to 3.5 million *mu*. By the 1850s–60s, that had expanded to 6.8 million *mu*. The actual figure was larger, though, because the official number excluded land belonging to the religious facilities (*mazār*s [shrines], *khanqa*s [Sufi meeting places], *madrasas* [Islamic schools], and mosques), bestowed as religious endowments (*waqf*)—a prominent portion of property holdings in oasis society. During the same period, the oasis population increased more than threefold, again using a conservative measure.[12] While the population estimate of 1772 stood at a little under 200,000, it rose to 1,015,000 in the 1850s–70s (see Appendixes A-1 and A-2).[13]

And the beg enterprise was a part of the interconnected developments of commercial agriculture then occurring across the world; it was stimulated by the expansion of global trade—the same commercial growth that contributed to the rapid multiplication of New World plantations, for instance. In the global trade occurring in Chinese Central Asia, the Ming (1368–1644) and Qing (1644–1911) empires, respectively, played a significant role. The two dynasties facilitated the flow of New World silver and globally circulated Chinese goods (such as tea and silk) into Central Asia from the east through their operation of the tribute system, a scheme of ceremonial gift exchanges and trade, and their financial investment in military ventures in the region.[14] The availability of silver and the opportunities for tribute trade with China had prompted many of the beg families to migrate to and settle in Eastern Turkestan in the first place. Furthermore, the eighteenth-century Qing occupation of the area consolidated the area's Chinese connections on a firm ground, providing the region a constant supply of silver as well as new Chinese market outlets.

The beg enterprise in turn made the post-sixteenth-century oasis economy radically different from the earlier one. Located on the Silk Road, the oasis economy had long been well connected to the rhythm of global trade even prior to the period. However, the earlier Silk Road trade did not stimulate local production in the earlier trade. Xinjiang oases had served as nodal points for long-distance transit trade between China and the Middle East/India, organized by transregional "intermediary merchants," who transported Chinese luxury goods such as silk and ceramic but did not have production bases in the oasis.[15] However, locally based beg capitalists, who emerged as the new organizers of commerce and agriculture in the oasis, produced local goods (jade, horses, livestock, cotton, and grain) to meet the increasing demands of the Chinese state and market.

In the broad picture, then, this book highlights a remarkable but often ignored development during the age of global commerce—namely, the expansion of a China-centered eastern market and the formation of an indigenous capitalist venture in the greater Chinese world. Emergence of China as a major anchor of global trade—the biggest consumer of silver and the provider of globally traded goods such as ceramics and tea—from the sixteenth century helped the inland Eurasian frontier to be integrated into the circuit of world trade and influenced the trajectory of economic development in broader Eurasia. This formation of Eastern capitalist ventures in Chinese Central Asia was in turn a part of the widespread emergence of commercial agriculture across Muslim Eurasia in the seventeenth and eighteenth centuries as well. From the Middle East to South Asia, commercially oriented landlord gentries, known respectively as *ayan* in Ottoman and *zamindar* in Mughal contexts, conducted energetic agrarian development within the context of the growing commercialization of their societies. These *ayan* and *zamindar* also made significant progress in bringing new lands into commercial cultivation, and augmenting their private domination over once commonly held resources, all the while causing conflict with rural village communities, as did the Xinjiang begs.[16]

Most interesting, though, this book's finding regarding the begs' reliance on their political connections to an outside empire—Qing—and its state (military) building prerogative in advancing their capitalist agenda, has a strong parallel in British northern India, a point that will be explained in more detail in the Conclusion.[17] Notably, the symbiotic relations between the beg capitalists and the Chinese empire, so to speak, also provides a fresh new insight into the fundamental interconnection between early modern imperial expansion and capitalism from the perspective of Eurasian borderlands. Scholars have been making a causal linkage between the capitalist transformation of society and imperial expansion from a metropolitan perspective. Kenneth Pomeranz argues that capitalist development caused major ecological pressures in the major economies, which became the metropoles of the European empires, such as that of Britain; such ecological pressure in the Western European metropole from the time of the sixteenth century encouraged the metropolitan states to increasingly expand their search for land and resources, as well as sites of migration to relieve overcrowding in metropole populations vulnerable to the Malthusian trap. This development created the metropolitan vector of imperial expansion.[18]

What the story of oasis capitalism highlights is another aspect of the liaison between capitalism and imperialism. Not only the European metropolitan society but also the frontier society, becoming the colony of the Chinese empire in the eighteenth century needed imperial power in its midst to address economic and ecological needs. In addition to constant access to the market in the metropoles, state military power, more importantly, would assist the borderland capitalists to secure new resources and weather the social tension inherent in the capitalist transformation of their underdeveloped economy and ecology. In other words, the same capitalist transformation that created the metropolitan vector of the European imperial expansion may have forced the borderland elites to ally with the expanding Chinese empire, thus creating the periphery vector of the imperial expansion as well.

This discovery also radically revises our understanding of the Qing imperial history of Central Asia. Previous scholarship has explained the Qing expansion into Central Asia from a distinctively Chinese point of view, focusing on the dynamics of Qing state-building and Chinese migrations.[19] The standard narrative chronicling these events starts in the late seventeenth century, when the Kangxi emperor (r. 1661–1722) dispatched his elite force, the Banner Troops, to the Central Asian frontier to respond to threats from a new Mongol state, the Zunghar. The Qing troops subjugated them in spite of all odds and with much difficulty, in 1754. Eastern Turkestan also fell to Qing rule because it had been a former Zunghar domain. After overcoming initial local Muslim opposition led by *khwajas* in 1759, the Qing then implemented a set of partially successful policies to ensure the peace and security of its rule in the oasis. The first measure taken was a military buildup. The Qing stationed tens of thousands of troops in Xinjiang to defend its western regions and adopted innovative fiscal policies that would transform the frontier economies by allowing them to provision the troops.[20] The second measure set up a semblance of multicultural representation in the administration of Qing imperial authority in the oasis. The Qing emperors did not present themselves as alien "Chinese" conquerors but posed instead as patrons of the Islamic faith—that is, as the sultan and as the Mongol grand khan—two familiar modes of political legitimation in local culture.[21] Additionally, the Qing rulers opted the institution of indirect rule, permitting a degree of ethnic autonomy. Under this system, the Qing entrusted civil administration of the oasis to local secular authority and the legal decisions for intracommunal affairs to the local Islamic establishment, while handling military and foreign affairs themselves.[22] In spite of initial reluctance, Qing rulers also decided to encourage Chinese migration to Xinjiang and to utilize the financial and political support of these settlers and merchants to sustain their rule in

Eastern Turkestan, especially from the early part of the nineteenth century.[23]

At this time Qing rule started to decline when its military power weakened under increasing pressures from Central Asian powers such as the Khoqand and Russia, as well as the Muslims' rising uneasiness with the growing Chinese presence.[24] Descendants of the resistant *khwaja* who had been expelled by the Qing troops at the time of the initial conquest would lead a series of revolts against the Qing Empire, a development that weakened Qing power decisively over time. It failed to respond adequately to the uprisings because of its weakening military power and, more important, its failure to develop a successful ethnic and religious policy toward Muslims and Islam.[25] In this sense, the Qing rulers' problem in Central Asia became fundamental. Elsewhere the emperors might pose as patrons of Tibetan Buddhism without themselves becoming *lamas* (high priests of Tibetan Buddhism), but it was impossible for infidels truly to become Islamic sultans, at least in the eyes of local Muslims.[26] Eventually, the Qing fell in 1864 amid an Islamic religious war, a "holy war (*jihad*) in China" that swept across all of Eastern Turkestan; in its wake Yaʻqūb Beg (1820–77), a military adventurer from the neighboring Khoqand country, established an "Islamic state" that replaced the Qing Empire in Central Asia.[27]

However, this China-centered narrative is not sufficient to fully explain the success and tenacity of Qing rule in the oasis. In spite of the intensifying challenges to their military power in this region from the early nineteenth century, the Qing did survive until 1864 and would subsequently resurrect their power in 1877. And the strength of Han Chinese migration cannot explain that phenomenon, simply because the massive Chinese influx to the area would not begin until the early twentieth century. Furthermore, in contrast to the northern part of Xinjiang, Han Chinese settlers were never a major force in Eastern Turkestan during the Qing Period. Even the adroit deployment of multicultural political symbols by Qing rulers, the answer favored by the most recent scholarship, does not explain the success. As scholars admit, the Qing rulers' cultural representation as sultan, the protector of the Islamic faith, was weak at best.[28]

This book will show instead that the borderland begs played a critical role in both the consolidation of the Qing Empire as well as its later unraveling, and will highlight the embeddedness of the empire within the local political, social, and economic oasis nexus. The Qing Empire sustained itself as long as it did because the local begs extended their support to it in direct proportion to the benefits that the empire offered them; the empire broke down as the social tensions caused by the begs' agrarian development intensified. In the broader scheme of events, then, the Qing Empire thus reflected a network of power that was itself integrated into the warp and weft of commerce and agriculture that local begs wove across the vast tapestry of desert terrain in Eastern Turkestan.

In other words, Qing rule was as much drawn into the social and ecological disorder of the borderlands by the expanding trade as it was by the extension of its frontier territories. The unstable dynamics of the reorganization of the oasis economy into a capitalistic agriculture provided the conditions for its initial success in the region in the eighteenth century, as well as its temporary fall in 1864. At the same time, through its involvement in the process of the capitalist transformation of the oases, the Qing state transformed itself into an integral element of the borderlands' local political economy as well. Its rule thus became a necessary structural factor in the emerging relations of capitalist production in oasis agriculture, with or without intending it.

Source Materials

This book's task of exploring the borderland view of Qing expansion required locating new, local, multilingual source materials, in addition to employing Chinese-language government publications, the latter commissioned and sanctioned by the Qing court. Thus, local Turki materials, both in the original and translation (Chinese and Russian), have been utilized. The most important work cited in this category was Mullā Mūsa Sāyramī's *Tārīkhi Hämīdī* (History of Hämīd), the first local history narrative of Eastern Turkestan published late, at the turn of the twentieth century. Although scholars have mined this work thoroughly for the study of the Ya'qūb Beg era (1864–77), they have yet to peruse it systematically for the study of the Qing rule. This history provides an invaluable local perspective on the politics and society prevalent there under the Qing, in both the eighteenth and nineteenth centuries. Hagiographies (*tazkirah*) of the Sufi holy men who migrated to the region in the fifteenth and sixteenth centuries have also been referenced. Although those works rarely discussed directly the topic that this book is primarily concerned with—namely, local economic development—they did contain material offering insights into Sufi involvement with the oasis economy. However, the data that became essential for this book's narrative and analysis have been local Turki contract documents. Currently available primarily in Chinese translation, they include deeds for land transactions, renting and labor contracts, and records of religious donations, among others, and thus show the social, economic, and religious relations at work within oasis society in the eighteenth and nineteenth centuries.

Another local source utilized was Chokan Valikhanov's (Wali Khan, 1835–65) works on the history of Eastern Turkestan. A Russian military officer, he visited the area personally to collect information on its history and geography. Although he served in the Russian military when he visited and wrote primarily in Russian, his narrative, however, of Eastern Turkestani history during the Qing rule can be read as a local or Central Asian narrative, at the very least. Inasmuch as he was originally a native prince, descendant of a Kazakh khan, he inevitably applied a Central Asian perspective to his writing. For that reason, this book relies on his information and narrative heavily to place the Qing sources in some perspective, particularly where a local Muslim narrative is lacking.

Arguably, however, the most important primary sources relied upon have been the Qing government documents written in Manchu, the official language of its frontier administrations. They come primarily from *Manwen lufu zouzhe* (Manchu language memorial copies from the Grand Council reference collection, hereafter, MLZZ), housed in the First Historical Archives in Beijing, China. The Qing in Xinjiang retained Manchu military governors (Chinese: *cancan dachen, banshi dachen*) stationed in each major oasis; they were obliged to produce reports about current events and conditions, including criminal investigations and routine administrative procedures entailing tax collections, appointments of begs to posts in the oasis districts, harvests and fluctuations in grain prices, smuggling and illegal mining activities, local unrest, espionage on domestic and foreign development, and diplomatic relations with neighboring Central Asian states.[29]

Given that local Turki materials are not abundant, these Manchu-language materials constitute the best primary sources for the reconstruction of the local history of Chinese Central Asia under Qing rule. However, to date only Laura Newby has used these materials extensively. Especially valuable for this book have been the records of criminal investigations and depositions made by offenders in front of Manchu military governors regarding homicide cases among oasis farmers, robberies of caravan merchants by Kirghiz mountaineers, various smuggling and illegal mining activities, and oasis villagers' accusations of corruption and exploitation by oasis begs. These records unexpectedly revealed vivid illustrations of the lives of the oasis people that would otherwise be unavailable, and opened up new possibilities for studying the social, economic, and religious conditions prevalent in Eastern Turkestan under Qing rule. As such, these Manchu-language materials constitute by far the most important primary sources providing the empirical basis for this book.

Chapter Overview

This book comprises five chapters, each narrating in chronological order the story of the begs, their reorganization of oasis political economy, and their relations with the Qing Empire since the sixteenth century. Through the family history of Emin Khwāja, arguably the most important Turkic local ally to the Qing conquest of Central Asia in 1759, Chapter 1, "Beg, Empire, and Agrarian Developments in Central Asia, 1500–1750," examines the foundation of the beg alliance with the Qing Empire. This chapter argues that the begs, as agromanagers of the oasis region, invited and sustained the Qing rule because of their interest in developing commercial agriculture.

Chapter 2, "Capitalist Imperatives and Imperial Connections, 1759–1825," analyzes the structure of the begs' commercial enterprises and the social tensions they created in the oasis society. Through the lives of Ūdui and Osman, a prominent father-son duo who served as powerful native governors in the oasis districts, this chapter argues that the beg took advantage of the Qing Empire's utter dependence on them for revenue development and expanded the scope of their commercial enterprises based on capitalistic principles.

Chapter 3, "The 'Holy Wars' of the Uprooted, 1826–1830," examines the careers of Jahāngīr and Yūsuf, two Sufi *khwaja*s who led two rounds of local resistance against the Qing-beg state in the early nineteenth century. Their perspective shows that the violent process of beg-initiated agrarian development contributed to the emergence of a rapidly expanding community of refugees in the rugged mountainsides of Pamir and Tianshan, surrounding the oases.

Through the examination of Zuhūr al-Dīn, a powerful *hākim* of Kashgar District in the early nineteenth century, Chapter 4, "'The Just and Liberal Rule' of Zuhūr al-Dīn, 1831–46," discusses the ironic result of two rounds of *khwaja* wars—namely, the emergence of new prosperity and wealth in Kashgar and other Eastern Turkestani cities. This new prosperity for the begs resulted from the Qing's decision to increase residential troops in the oases, to finance military reinforcements by increasing silver imports from the Chinese metropole, and to invest in a state-sponsored land development project, or "agricultural colony" *(tuntian)*.

Chapter 5, "Global Crises of Oasis Capitalism, 1847–64," examines the eventual fall of the beg regime in the late nineteenth century. Through the career of Ahmad, a governor of Kashgar District during the last decades of Qing rule, this chapter shows that the Opium War (1839–42), a war that took place some 2,000 miles southeast of Xinjiang, contributed to the fall of the Qing Empire. By causing discontinuation of the silver imports flowing into the oasis from the Chinese metropole, the war undermined the fundamental structural foundation of the success and stability of oasis capitalism generally and the Qing Empire in Central Asia.

1 Beg, Empire, and Agrarian Developments in Central Asia, 1500–1750

In the summer of 1731, Yue Zhongqi, the highest-ranking field commander of the Qing troops fighting a difficult war against the Zunghar Mongols in Central Asia, had a surprising piece of good news for his emperor: "2,000 Zunghar enemies surrounded the wall of Lukchun [a small town of Turfan]. They fought for 20 days, day and night. Local Muslims of Turfan showed courage and made raids, and killed 200 enemies, and hurt many more."[1] The leader of the Turfan in this remarkable battle between the Muslims and the formidable Zunghar forces was Emin Khwāja (d. 1777). The Qing record identifies him simply as the "headman" of the Muslims of Lukchun. However, Emin Khwāja was a quintessential oasis notable. A "grand *akhūnd*" of Turfan, the Khwāja was an important leader of the *'ulamā,* when he surrendered to the Qing in 1732. For this heroic battle, Emin was awarded the lowest-level imperial aristocrat title, *fuguo gong,* by the Qing in 1732. By this act, Emin became the second of the Eastern Turkestani elites who joined the Qing side during the Qing-Zunghar War (1696–1759).

Emin Khwāja was one of the hundreds, if not thousands, of oasis notables, begs, who joined the Qing Empire during the latter's conquest of Chinese Central Asia from 1754 to 1759—and arguably the most prominent. Originally a leader of the local Islamic establishment of Turfan, Emin went on to have an influential career under the Qing rule, even working as the imperial superintendent of the entire Muslim domain, a post that no other Muslim assumed after him.[2] His descendants also remained as the most reliable allies to the empire throughout its rule in Eastern Turkestan, working primarily as the powerful Muslim governors of the strategic, affluent oasis districts of Yarkand and Kashgar.[3]

Offering an examination of Emin's career and his family background, this chapter examines the foundation of the beg alliance with the Qing Empire. Commercially oriented landlords sensitive to the fluctuations of global commerce, this chapter argues, the begs joined the Qing Empire because of their interests as agromanagers in the oasis region. They pledged their alliance to the empire in order to overcome the fundamental crisis of the oasis agriculture that they had been presiding profitably over since the sixteenth century. That crisis was caused by the downward fluctuation of the rhythm of China trade—the trade that was most critical to the success of the agrarian developments in the oasis. The begs saw the alliance with the Qing Empire as a viable solution to the crisis of the oasis economy.

Qing expansion in the eighteenth century was thus an event embedded in the expansion of trade and agrarian developments across Eurasia. In Muslim Eurasia from the Middle East to South Asia, the economic expansion resulted in a synchronous "decline" of central political authority of the Ottoman, Mughal, and Safavid empires over their provinces, and fostered the decentralization of political authority within each empire during the eighteenth century.[4] In the eastern part of Eurasia, in the Sino-Central Asian borderland, on the contrary, the same expansion of trade resulted in the unprecedented expansion of the Qing Empire. Behind these different patterns of political realignment emerging in the east was the agency of the commercially oriented begs. Their choice to seek patronage of the infidel Chinese ruler who could provide stable access to the China market and political protection of their agricultural interests made the difference.

Muslim Eurasia and the Beg Context to Qing Imperial Expansion

As the Qing Manchu extended the arm of their empire into Central Asia to defeat the Zunghar Mongols in the late seventeenth and early eighteenth centuries, large numbers of Turkic Muslim leaders from Eastern Turkestan joined the Qing side. The first to submit was the ruler 'Ubayd Allāh of Hami, an easternmost town on the border to China, in 1696. Subsequently, numerous Muslim leaders from all over the oasis would offer their allegiance as well, in 1754—and later, against the resistant Naqshbandī Sufi leaders who rose in revolt against the Qing in 1758 and 1759.[5] The Turkic Muslims served as field commanders, led vanguard forces, and handled logistical support for the Qing troops during the wars (see Appendix B-1).

Eventually, six families and their associates emerged as dominant figures under the cloak of Qing rule, achieved by their military contribution and political influence in local society. They were (1) ʿUbayd Allāh, (2) Emin Khwāja (Turfan), (3) Ūdui (Kucha), (4) Gadaimet (Ush/Bai), (5) Setib Aldi (Ush), and (6) Khwāja Si Beg (Ush). Not only did these people go on to acquire various prestigious Qing aristocrat positions, from *junwang* (the second-highest Qing aristocrat title), *beile* (third-highest Qing aristocrat title), and *beise* (fourth-highest Qing aristocrat position), to *gong* (lowest-rank Qing aristocrat title), but their families achieved virtual autonomous rule of their hometowns, and virtually monopolized the governor positions in the major oasis districts (Kashgar, Yarkand, Khotan, and Aksu), which had not been their original domains (see Appendix C-1).[6]

These Muslim collaborators came from the beg. According to local definition, they were the headmen of the settler communities, large and small, scattered across the oasis towns, villages, and foothills, although the settled community led by them could be often mobile, if not tribal. Khwāja Si Beg's son, Modzapar, would define the term as "chief" (Manchu: *da*; a word referring to a chieftain of nomadic tribe), or a "leader of a small place" (Manchu: *buyasi ba i dalaha niyalma*), if a Qing inquirer asked. The same beg would describe *hākim* (Manchu: *akim*) as "manager" (Manchu: *jakirukci*), or a "leader of a big city" (Manchu: *amba i hoton i dalaha niyalma*). In this definition, beg was different from *hākim* in terms of the size of the domain controlled. More important, the nature of the former's relations with the people and place under their control was also different from latter's. The beg was the leader of the community "chief," while the *hākim* was the official appointed by a sovereign to manage a certain domain. Indeed, the original meaning of the word, "beg" was nomadic noble, a Turkic equivalent of Persian *amīr*, and Mongolian *noyan*. However, the meaning of the word was broadened to include other kinds of leaders of settler communities in Eastern Turkestan in the eighteenth century. This change occurred in the seventeenth century as the nomadic nobles gradually became landed elites in the oasis and thus largely indistinguishable from leaders of other settled communities.[7]

They reflected diverse backgrounds, including both nobility and commerce. For instance, the Ūdui descended from a prominent nomadic noble.[8] Some were also heads of caravan merchants. However, by far the most prevalent source of the pro-Qing begs were the Sufi leaders and their descendants. ʿUbayd Allāh, for example, traced his ancestry to a Sufi named Muhammad Shah Khwāja. Emin Khwāja claimed his lineage from a rather famous Sufi *shaykh* (chief), Khwaja Muhammad Sharīf. Khwāja Si Beg's genealogy extended back to Jamal al-Din, a saint associated with the Kucha *khwajas* and a Sufi order known as the Qadiriyya.[9]

The *Tārīkhi āminiyä* explains the foundation of the beg alliance with the Qing Empire from a borderland perspective: seven rulers of the Seven Cities (*Yättishahr,* meaning Eastern Turkestan) comprising the domain of Eastern Turkestan decided to petition the "Chinese emperor" to help them solve the local people's hardship—trouble caused by the Zunghar and *khwaja* rule in the seventeenth century. Hearing their petition, the emperor decided to grant them soldiers. Thus, these rulers subdued the seven cities even without waging a war. And the emperor gave the seven begs Chinese aristocrat rank, designating them as the governors of their respective towns. He also bestowed land and water, as well as several families of *yanqi* farmers as sources of revenue. The emperor additionally decided to grant the begs large amounts of silver as salaries.[10]

The story emphasizes the agency of local Muslims in this process: it was their invitation to the "Chinese" to the region, and it was they who ruled the oasis domain under their protectors. Equally intriguing, this passage provides an explanation of a surprisingly materialistic foundation to the begs' alliance with the Qing. That loyalty was circumscribed by the provision of land, water, the *yanqi* to draw revenue and silver. This exchange would incur such a depth of loyalty that the conquering emperor's successors would find even the begs' descendants still collaborative when the Chinese later resurrected their power in the region after a short hiatus in the late nineteenth century, at that time extending to them "salaries" to resume relations.

Previous scholarship in the field has considered the beg alliance as derived from a series of political actions taken by traditional (noble) nomadic ruling elites to preserve their political, social, and economic privileges—most importantly their right to extract revenue from the oasis population without engaging in production—in the face of the rapid Islamization of oasis society in the sixteenth and seventeenth centuries.[11] This explanation is not necessarily contradictory with the explanation provided by the *Tārīkhi āminiyä,* above. However, the problem is that the begs were not exclusively, or even primarily, descendants of nomadic nobles. The mainstay of the pro-Qing begs were the Sufi leaders that the begs supposedly struggled against to protect their interests. Thus, one should not understand the begs' economic interest in allying with the Qing as that of nomadic nobles of the old days. Rather, a better approach is to consider the interest as that of the oasis society itself and of its Sufi leaders in particular.

Recent scholarship on the Sufis in Central Asia sheds new light on the Sufi's role as the agromanager in Central Asia in the post-Mongol period. During the Timurid Dynasty (1370–1507), Sufi *shaykh*s had the reputation of being managers and developers of agriculture in the wider area of Central Asia. As constant tribal war threatened political and social stability, the Sufi institution was the most stable one to manage the oasis agriculture in the Timurid domain—both as the institution for managing large scale landholding and as the transmitter of the technological knowledge for agrarian development. Its shrines and meeting places, which had substantial landed property holdings from religious endowments, emerged as centers of management and development of the oasis agriculture as a whole. The Sufi *shaykh*s and the managers of the shrines and meeting places organized irrigation works and sponsored land development. For this reason, even the reigning khan donated much desolate land under government control to the Sufi-affiliated facilities—not only to show religious support but also to procure the development of the land as a potential revenue source.[12]

Indeed, the evidence confirms that the Sufi descendants among the pro-Qing begs were the major agrarian developers in Eastern Turkestan. For example, Khwāja Si Beg's father, Azziz Khwāja (Manchu: Ashūji), established a new agrarian settlement in the oasis district of Ush for the Zunghar ruler sometime in the late seventeenth and early eighteenth centuries. Azziz Khwāja even renamed the new settlement in Ush as "Turfan"/"Turman," because the landscape reminded them of his hometown.[13] In Eastern Turkestan, which suffered from a severe scarcity of labor, perhaps the most fundamental base of the Sufi leaders' position as the agromanager was their ability to recruit and manage the human labors. They were able to mobilize oasis farmers by offering the believers various incentives including protection from the rulers' arbitrary taxation, as well as a chance to cultivate their private estates and land donated as religious endowment.[14] Mobile Sufi leaders also often moved with their disciples and new converts into new locations in the region. If we are to believe one legendary account, 'Ubayd Allāh's father, Muhammad Shah Khwāja, a Muslim missionary, captured the city of Hami with the aid of one thousand Muslims as well as Mongols, and became governor there.[15]

Notably, the Sufi family's ability to control and organize the collective labor of the settlers was the most important feature the Sufi leaders held in common with other pro-Qing begs. The descendants of the former nomadic tribal leaders still firmly controlled the mobility of the settlers they led. Thus, for example, when Ūdui relocated from a southern oasis district, Kucha, to Ili Valley under pressure from the Zunghar Mongols in the early eighteenth century, he moved together with his settler community. When he surrendered to the Qing from Ili in 1756, he was accompanied in his surrender by twenty-five hundred households, fifteen thousand Muslims altogether.[16] Likewise, the heads of caravan merchants also organized mobile labor groups. Caravan merchants in Central Asia at that time were not like those in the contemporary sense—that is, professionals specializing in the transaction of moving goods in the marketplace. The term *bederege,* which we translate as "caravan merchant" for the lack of a better word, refers actually to a group of traveling people who work in a common productive endeavor. Given that the most prominent item of trade in Central Asia during the period was livestock, including horses and sheep, one can easily discern that they were in fact a traveling cohort of ranchers constantly moving across the vast oasis terrain. *Bederege* were also known to have developed agriculture in Ili Valley for the Zunghar ruler in the seventeenth century.[17]

In this regard, it is important to note that moving logistical supplies to the Qing troops was the most crucial among the many contributions that the begs made for the Qing. For instance, as early as 1718, Hami rulers developed agricultural colonies (*tuntian*) in Hami to supply grain to Qing troops stationed nearby in Barkul.[18] In addition, in 1758, Ūdui provided military supplies to a division of Qing troops heading to Kashgaria to fight against the *khwaja* there. On three separate occasions within a month in early 1759, he and his wife supplied the Qing troops with two hundred sheets of cloth made of lambskin, three hundred bolts of cotton cloth for making winter clothing, one hundred horses, as well as a thousand foot soldiers and cavalries, along with the provision of lamb and grain.[19]

One can easily see why the Qing Empire, or any state or empire builder for that matter, would have been eager to acquire the beg allegiance.[20] With the ability to manipulate the flow of goods and manpower, the begs could dictate the political fortune of any ambitious state builder. The begs' motivation in allying with the Qing during this period also relates to the exchange they received—for example, not only did the Hami rulers and Ūdui received remuneration for the supplies in silver and satin; they also received various kinds of "rewards" for their contributions, in the form of gain, silver, and cotton clothes.[21] In other words, the begs engaged in profitable trade with the Qing troops.[22]

The realization puts the formation of the beg alliance within the broader and long-term context of agrarian development in Central Asia. The pro-Qing beg family shaped their political, religious, and migration strategies, in order to remain viable as agrarian developers under the changing conditions of global trade post sixteenth century. They migrated into Eastern Turkestan in the first place in order to take advantage of the unprecedented expansion of the China trade into Central Asia after the sixteenth century. In the eighteenth century, the begs entered into the alliance with the Qing to cultivate the imperial connections that would help them expand their commercial agriculture enterprises in the oasis, and to gain access to more resources ("land," and "water") and labor ("farmers") in the oasis countryside, and to "silver" circulated globally to achieve that goal. The illustrious careers of Emin Khwāja and his esteemed ancestor will illuminate this history.

Emin Khwāja and His Legendary Sufi Ancestor

In the late nineteenth century, one of Emin's descendants informed a Russian ethnologist that he was a scion of Khwaja Muhammad Sharīf (1473/74–1565), a legendary Sufi master who migrated to Eastern Turkestan in the mid-sixteenth century.[23] Having migrated from Samarqand to Eastern Turkestan, Muhammad Sharīf became the leading political and spiritual guide to the second khan of Yarkand khanate, 'Abd al-Rashīd Khān (r. 1533–60). According to Emin's family, they were the children of this venerable Sufi holy man. Indeed, even prior to this declaration, Emin's family cultivated connections to the venerable Sufi for a while. The family had built a *madrasa* dedicated to the *khwaja* in Yarkand in the early nineteenth century.

One may raise some doubt on the family's claim, for there is no concrete evidence to support it. However, at minimum, it seems certain that Emin Khwāja had a Sufi ancestor. As late as the early twentieth century, his family appointed a *khalīfa* (Sufi master's representative) in Yarkand—an act that only Sufi masters could do.[24] In this light then, their claim takes on new meaning. What it shows is the specific content of the social identity, fictive or not, the family wanted to project as offspring of a Sufi master. A brief examination of the hagiography of Muhammad Sharīf, the work that Emin Khwāja's descendants must have referred to when they made the claim, indicates a dual identity for the man both as a zealous proselytizer and energetic agrarian developer.

Upon arriving in Yarkand, the *Khwaja* built a *khanqa* (Sufi meeting place) as well as a *mazār* in the rural village where he settled. He then bought and donated land and water to the facilities as a religious endowment. He further announced the intention to establish a market town and a new village around the Sufi meeting place and shrine; both efforts were met by less than enthusiastic support from the local residents. They objected to his plan to build a market town on moralistic grounds ("If a market comes here, our children would become gambler[s]"). And they were skeptical about its feasibility: there simply was no water there. The *khwaja* responded to this cold reception with prayers and a miracle. He dragged a stick on the ground, and its trace filled with water, subsequently flowing over the distance of one *tash* (five miles).[25] Hence, the wildland came to be cultivated and several villages sprang up; people from nearby vicinities came to settle; the market flourished and the Monday market came to be established.[26]

Sifting through the embellished layers of this tale, we see then in its simplest outline that Muḥammad Sharīf was characterized not only as an Islamic missionary but also a land developer. The Sufi master brought the desolate, dry land of the oasis to life and gave new spiritual life to the pagan idol worshipers among the villagers. He provided water to the barren land at the margins of oasis agriculture, and it bore fruit. Notably, this powerful image of Muḥammad Sharīf as the founder of a new agrarian settlement in the oasis was a pervasive motif appearing in many Sufi hagiographies from Eastern Turkestan from this period. Mawalana Arsiddin, the legendary Sufi master who first brought Islam into the land of Moghul nomads in the mid-fourteenth century, had a similar episode, depicted in his *tazkirah*. One day he dispatched his son, also a *khwaja*, to a place that later became Aksu, "to make it prosper." Located in the area of a steep cliff, the original market had become desolate and buried under sand. The *khwaja* blocked the valley of Aksu and, as a result, it filled with water. In a fashion reminiscent of Muḥammad Sharīf, Mawalana Arsiddin also pulled a stick on the ground while walking; the water flowed from the end of the stick. The *khwaja* also dug a spring. Then he established three markets: "Khwaja City," "Sayyid City," and "Mongol City." The news circulated widely that a saint had come and made it possible for the people to survive in the area. Groups of five or six relocated from all directions and poured in. Within a year, the population had leapt to one thousand households, and later increased to fourteen hundred. The *khwaja* built a Sufi meeting place in the area and lived there. He taught the order of the Sacred Law and its prohibition.[27]

Sufi Settlement in the Oasis and the China Trade

In the sixteenth and seventeenth centuries, large numbers of Sufi developers like Muḥammad Sharīf pioneered their way into Eastern Turkestan primarily from the former Timurid domain of Bukhara and Samarqand. The prominent

families of the Sufi leaders who later graced the pages of the political and religious history of the region had mostly arrived in the region during this period.
Indeed, this period became the high point of Sufi migration in the area.

First, the specific dynamics of nomadic politics in the region contributed
intensely to this development. For the better part of the sixteenth and seventeenth centuries, Eastern Turkestan was ruled by an Islamized Chinggisid
Khanate (referred to by modern scholars as the Yarkand Khanate [1514–1680]),
established by Sultān Said Khān, a cousin of the first Mughal emperor of India,
Babur, in 1514.[28] As was typical with TurcoMongolian nomadic polities, this
regional Moghul regime had been unstable almost from the start because of
the endemic internal political struggles between the khans, princes, and other
powerful nomadic nobles. The khans' five reigns over a span of thirty years
during the late sixteenth century clearly testify to this structural instability. In
order to overcome the political weakness, the Yarkand khans pushed seriously
to centralize power.

In such a context, they welcomed and encouraged the Sufi migration to
Eastern Turkestan. Receiving the blessing of prominent Sufi masters, who
commanded immense prestige in Central Asia, would lend significant political
legitimacy to any reigning khan seeking an edge to outmaneuver the challenges
of rival Mongol princes and nomadic nobles. The Sufis also provided a new
pool of human resources from which the khans could select loyal administrative representatives (*hākim*) to govern the major oasis districts as well as military commanders and soldiers for the battlefield, all useful tools with which to
man their fight against their rivals. Most important for the prospect of agricultural development in the oasis, the Sufis also developed new financial resources
for the rulers.

A khan would grant his affiliated Sufi masters tax-free grants of land and
economic resources. For example, they personally received a revenue assignment or fief (*soyurghal*), the same revenue assignment that the nomadic khans
provided to princes, subordinate nomadic nobles (*amīr*), and meritorious subjects in his domain. Occasionally, the Sufi masters would also receive *waqf* (religious endowment) and *khanqa*s.

However, in the case of the Sufis, a khan's grant of land and resources was
as much a gift of a secure income source for their favorite subjects as a call to
develop the resources for the khanate's sake, particularly so for jade mining in
Yarkand and Khotan. Jade was arguably the most profitable local commodity,
with markets in Central Asia as well especially as in China, and could enrich

Table 1.1. Yarkand Khan's Land Grants to the Sufi *Shaykh*s

Name	Land	Others	Size
Mawalana Arsiddin's descendants	Undisclosed (Ku, A, T)	Workshops, fruit garden, and ships	
Mu'in Khwāja		Jade mining (Kh)	
Muhmmad Sharīf	*Waqf* (K, Y); personal grant (Y)		10 slaves; 60 *batman* of *waqf* to a *khanqa* (Y)
Khwāja Ishāq Walī	Undisclosed (Kh/1 village; Y/9 villages)	Jade mining (Kh)	
Āfāq Khwāja	*Waqf* (K)		

Sources: Zhongguo Xinjiang diqu Yisilanjiao shi bianxiezu, *Zhongguo Xinjiang diqu Yisilan jiao shi* [History of Islam in Xinjiang, China], pp. 268–70, 274, 301–2, 324, 342; Churās, *Khronika*, pp. 32, 178, 301–2.
Note: Ku = Kucha, A = Aksu, T = Turfan, K = Kashgar, Kh = Khotan, Y = Yarkand.

a khan's coffer significantly. The second ruler of the khanate, 'Abd al-Rashīd Khān, granted river jade from Khotan and, consequently, the income from the sale of this stone to a Sufi master (Mu'in Khwāja) from Western Turkestan. However, these were usually temporary contractual mining rights, renewable year to year.[29] Muhammad Khān (r. 1591/92–1609/10) granted a prominent Naqshbandī *khwaja*, Khwaja Ishāq Walī, who had removed Muhammad Sharīf from power, the right to mine jadestones from Khotan's river and mines.[30] In this relationship, the khan's land grants to his favored Sufi leaders functioned much like a partnership agreement between the state and resource developers. The former granted the resources, and the Sufi *shaykh*s, using their own capital and labor to develop the resource, enriched themselves and their sovereign at the same time.

A closer look at land grants sheds new light on their scope. Throughout the khanate's existence, the Yarkand khans implemented various kinds of land grants to particular Sufi masters and associates in the religious facilities. Some grants constituted entire villages, gardens, or manors, or merely certain tracts of land. Some land grants reached 60 *batman* (approximately 2,538 acres) (see Table 1.1).

However, the ecological conditions of each land allotment made their value uneven. Some land and villages were already prosperous parcels with substantial numbers of residents, well served by irrigation canals and ditches. In this case, the Sufi masters merely needed to collect dues from the people. However, less-developed lands, half-dry terrain located at the margins of the oasis or in the foothills, or even sections of wildland, would allow only small-scale towns and rural settlements to thrive. Under the right handling, however, such areas might still be made to improve with judicious application of "development." The story of Khwaja Muhammad Sharīf's initial settlement in Yarkand mentioned above sheds some light on the conditions of such a land grant circumstance. Officially, the *khanqa* that he established in the area was the gift and grant of a khan. However, the *khwaja*'s hagiographical records show that it was actually he who established the *khanqa* and the rural settlement surrounding it. Between this official account of land grant by the khan and the reality of the actual land development undertaken by the Sufi master, we see how the Yarkand khans seriously needed the Sufis as resource developers.

At the most fundamental level, however, the Sufi migration to the oasis region in the sixteenth and seventeenth centuries reflected a part of a much broader process underway in the expansion and reconfiguration of the commercial network emanating from the center of the Central Asian trade of Transoxiana—Bukhara and Samarqand—since the sixteenth century. It would become the turning point of Central Asian politics and economy. Since Vasco da Gama's first arrival in Calicut in 1498, European empires (Portuguese, French, and British in India; Dutch in the East Indies; Spanish in the Philippines) had expanded their trade network in maritime Asia. The previously predominant overland trade route of Eurasia saw its transit network disturbed. As many scholars have convincingly argued, that did not necessarily signal a "decline" in Central Asian trade. Its volume remained strong or even increased as a result of the relevance of local and regional trade. And significantly, Central Asia remained closely connected to global trade, carrying the bulk of the long-distance trade and able to complement the new maritime trade routes. However, it is also certain that Central Asian trade and politics were never the same after 1500.[31]

Their trade disrupted, the caravan merchants from the centers of the overland trade newly ventured to the east beginning in the sixteenth century. The merchants from Bukhara, for example, moved eastward into Eastern Turkestan first and eventually to the northwestern border of China and Tibet. "Bukharan merchants" emerged as the dominant force of trade in Eastern Turkestan during this period. These adjustments happened through the Sufi networks. Most of them were associated with various Sufi meeting places that were known to belong to a Sufi order called the Bukhariyya. Most of that network also belonged to the Naqshbandī, the dominant Sufi order originating in Bukhara, but not exclusively so. Some constituents in this network were associated also with the Qadiriyya.

Whether Muhammad Sharīf and his followers associated with this Bukharan merchant network is unclear. However, the two branches of the Naqshbandī Order that were transplanted into Eastern Turkestan certainly were, so much so that it gained the nickname of "Little Bukhara."[32] At the time of the Qing conquest of the oasis region in 1759, a military commander mentioned that the *bederege* who follow the Naqshbandī *khwaja*s that rose against the Qing were all from Bukhara and Andijan.[33]

The migration then of Sufi leaders from Transoxiana to Eastern Turkestan in the sixteenth and seventeenth centuries was not merely the development of a religious network. These Sufis and their merchant associates formed essentially a vanguard of individuals seeking new opportunities in the landscape of global trade beginning in the sixteenth century. The merchants may have defensively reacted to the competition of the maritime trade occurring in the Indian Ocean, but they also aggressively sought positive opportunities. In the east was Zungharia and western China, which could provide passageways to the Russian settlements also increasing rapidly since the sixteenth century.

However, the most important trading opportunity that the vanguard Sufis were looking for in the east was arguably direct trade with China.[34] Ming China's tribute trade with Central Asia, which the Yongle emperor (r. 1402–24) initiated in 1402, reached its highest point then. Numerous Central Asian merchants reached the frontier market in Suzhou, Gansu, to trade; some of them were granted a permit by the Ming court to proceed to Beijing. There, the Central Asian merchants acquired coveted Chinese goods such as silk and ceramics as well as New World silver. As events on the ground unfolded, tribute trade was the venue by which global trade and circulation of New World silver expanded into Central Asia.[35]

Sufi migrants were active in the tribute trade with China. Many had visited the Ming capital as the tribute envoys of the Yarkand khans and princes since its beginning in the early fifteenth century.[36] Some even engaged in the China trade and agriculture while fighting a "holy war" against China. Khwāja Tāj al-Dīn of Turfan (d. 1524), a descendant of the aforementioned Mawalana Arsiddin, participated in a Mongol Muslim ruler's war against the Ming in the early sixteenth century; however, during the same period he also many times traveled to Beijing as the envoy of three Moghul rulers. The engagement in China trade made him wealthy. "The khwaja occupied himself also with commerce and agriculture," one Muslim source noted. "And from these occupations, he accrued, by the blessing of the Most High God, great wealth."[37]

Thus, the Sufi had a compelling reason to settle in the domain of the Yarkand Khanate and enter into close relations with its khan. During the Ming Period, the oasis of the region emerged as the center of the China–Central Asian tribute trade. The oases—especially the two easternmost ones, Turfan and Hami—dispatched the tribute missions most frequently and on the largest scale. If the Sufi developers wanted to take advantage of the growing tribute trade, they needed to be settled in one of the oases of Eastern Turkestan.[38]

It also helped that the Yarkand khans held the ownership of the coveted jade mines and had the power to award the right of development. A Portuguese Jesuit, Benedict Goës, who spent time in a Yarkand khan's court in 1603 on his way to China as a member of a merchant caravan delivering a tribute mission, noted that "there is no article of traffic more valuable, or more generally adopted as an investment for this journey," than jade. Central Asian caravans carried the commodity to the "Emperor of Cathy," "attracted by the high prices which he deems it obligatory on his dignity to give." The Jesuit priest quickly added that the Yarkand khan owned the right to mine the jade in his domain. He then sold the right "at a high price to some merchant, without whose license no other speculators can dig there during the term of the lease."[39] The merchant that Goës mentioned as "buying" the right to conduct jade mining might possibly have been one of the Sufi masters-developers at the court of the Yarkand khan.

However, the impact of the tribute trade on the politics of the Yarkand Khanate cut in the opposite direction as well. The dynamic of the tribute trade also worked to undermine the stability of the Yarkand khans and princes. The competition among the Sufi leaders for spiritual influence over the reigning khans who could offer them political and economic privileges became increasingly intense, as the profits of the China trade grew larger. This development introduced a new source of political conflict within the khanate.[40] More important, as the China trade boomed in the late fifteenth and sixteenth centuries, some of the oasis elites relocated closer to China (to places like Gansu) to gain direct access to the China market outside of the monopoly venue of tribute trade. This development could undermine the political vitality of the khanate, by depriving the khans of an important source of political support. This change was most intense in Turfan and Hami, the towns closest to China, and the most avid Central Asian participants in the Ming tribute system. The oasis people belonging to the two oasis polities defected in large numbers to Suzhou and Ganzhou, where the Chinese frontier market was located. Some of them even changed their surnames, clothing, and appearance to facilitate their resettlement in Gansu and Shaanxi.[41]

All in all, however, the two opposite impacts of the tribute trade on the internal politics of the Yarkand Khanate—the stabilizing and destabilizing forces—balanced each other out, as long as the tribute system worked. It was only in the late sixteenth and early seventeenth centuries when it finally collapsed that the tension-filled equilibrium broke. The new begs finally became alienated from the Yarkand Khanate.

Disruption of the Chinese Tribute Trade and the Crisis of the Oasis Economy

Disrupting the security of the Yarkand Khanate was the constant decline of the tribute trade in the late sixteenth and early seventeenth centuries. The number of tribute missions from Central Asia allowed to arrive in Beijing and the frontier market in Gansu, as well as their size, became radically reduced during the late sixteenth century. The Qing conquest of Ming China in 1644 exacerbated even further the decline of the tribute trade. The Qing court intentionally reduced the number of the missions as much as possible from the beginning. In 1681, the Kangxi emperor eventually abolished tribute trade with the Yarkand Khanate altogether. Five years later, the Yarkand khan sent another mission in 1686, but that was the last. The tribute trade between Eastern Turkestan and China then ceased.[42]

The financial difficulty that bedeviled both the late Ming and early Qing governments as a result of their constant military spending did not leave any funds with which they could maintain the tribute trade.[43] The sudden reduction in the import of overseas silver into China from its peak in the early seventeenth century (10 million *pesos*/250 tons), which was one-fifth to one-third of the total silver circulation in the world, and the consequence of the reduction of production in the New World and Japan, also contributed to the decline of the tribute trade.[44]

Its sharp decline exercised a catastrophic impact on the domain of the Yarkand Khanate, whose prosperity and security had been sustained by the tribute trade since the previous century. Turfan and Hami reacted most violently. In 1649, the locals of the two oases joined the local Muslims of Gansu, a significant portion of whom were migrants from Hami and Turfan, in open revolt against the Qing. They first brought in the Hami ruler, Ba-bai Khan's son Tu-lun-tai, as their "king," and, later, an alleged heir of the fallen Ming Dynasty, to set up an independent Muslim regime in Suzhou.[45] These were known as the rebellion of Ding Guodong and Mi-la-yin, taken from the names of the leaders designated in the Qing record. Notably, the rebels aimed to restore the Ming, the operator of the heretofore thriving tribute trade system, from which they had benefited so much; they rebelled against the new ruler of China, the Qing, who apparently showed no inclination to sustain the tribute system.

When the revolt failed to revive the tribute trade, the Hami and Turfan Muslims relocated to certain locations in China's frontier in efforts to open a new private trade route with China, outside of the official system of tribute trade. Xining in current-day Qinghai Province thus emerged as the new hub of Sino-Central Asian trade, replacing Gansu, the center of the defunct tribute trade system. It was not that Xining was never an official frontier market for the Ming trade. It simply had never been designated as such for Central Asia, even though Xining was used by Tibetan traders and others. In the early seventeenth century, Central Asians flocked to the place to conduct private trade outside the formal constraints of regulation in collusion with Tibetans, Mongols, and Chinese merchants.[46]

One of the new markets was situated in a town called "White Pagoda" (Bai-ta'er). After the Ding Guodong Rebellion, its former participants from Turfan and Hami fled to the Xining area and built this new town. There, the migrants from Hami and Turfan endorsed land reclamation, engaged in artisanal production, and engaged in private trade between China, Central Asia, and Tibet (along with Chinese refugees from the Manchu conquest of China in 1644) under the protection of a local Mongol prince.[47]

The Turfan and Hami Muslims were not the only ones who left the oases of Eastern Turkestan during the course of the seventeenth century. From the political center of the Yarkand Khanate in Kashgaria, a leader of the White Mountaineers faction of the Naqshbandī Sufi order also left, when he was edged out by a rival faction (the Black Mountaineers) in their mutual struggle to gain the patronage of the khan's court. The Sufi leader, named Āfāq Khwāja, made two extended sojourns in Xining—first in 1632–38 and the second in 1670–78. During his stays in Xining, the Sufi married a woman of Persian descent whose ancestors had migrated to the area during the Yuan Period; reportedly, his son (Ma Shouzhen) later founded a Sufi order called Muftī (mu-fu-ti) Menhuan in Gansu. Āfāq Khwāja even made a third trip to Xining to see his son but to no avail.[48]

There is little concrete evidence to corroborate the specificity of this local Muslim story. However, it seems that the kernel of the narrative—that Āfāq Khwāja and his followers left Kashgaria after his defeat by a rival and then relocated to Xining—is indisputable. Otherwise, one cannot easily explain the sudden, unprecedented spread of Muslim Sufi orders that claimed ties to Central Asian Sufi orders in Xining and its neighboring regions of Gansu and Ningxia during the Kangxi and Yongzheng periods.[49]

In other words, the Sufis' relocation from Eastern Turkestan to Xining and other locations in China's northwest frontier to open new access to the China market reflected a widespread phenomenon. They did not hesitate to move—not only from the eastern fringe of the Yarkand Khanate in places such as Turfan and Hami but also from its political center in Yarkand and Kashgar—either by being edged out by a rival in competition to offer the khan spiritual guidance or to secure his political and economic patronage. However, notably, the Sufis did not journey randomly in their travels. They moved pointedly to Xining, the center of the newly emerging private China trade that flourished outside of the official tribute system. What this means is that their relocation was not merely a passive response to their losing religious influence in Kashgaria but was also a proactive effort to open access to the China market during a time of constant decline in the tribute trade.

In Xining, the *khwaja* found an improbable patron for his quest for spiritual, political, and material power—it was the new hegemonic Mongol force in Central Asia, the Zunghar Khanate. In all probability, Āfāq Khwāja saw an alliance with the Zunghar as an effective way to revive the official China trade from its long hiatus.[50] Around the time of his alliance, the khanate was busily pressuring the Qing to reopen the defunct tribute trade with Central Asia and in Xining.[51] Also, in 1683 the Zunghar finally forced the Qing to reopen a frontier market in Suzhou (in Gansu), which had been a major frontier market in the Ming tribute trade between China and Central Asia. By this, the Zunghar successfully reconstituted the official tribute trade with China under its sole monopoly. What made this plan feasible was the Zunghar's military strength, which continued to threaten the security of the Qing's northwestern border.[52]

From his sojourn in Xining, Āfāq Khwāja saw all of this firsthand and became impressed by the Zunghar ruler Galdan's ability to reopen the tribute trade. If the *khwaja* could be the handler of the new tribute trade between the Zunghar and China, he would profit significantly. During Galdan's rule, the Eastern Turkestani merchants ("Bukharan merchants") dominated the Zunghar tribute trade with Qing China; they headed several tribute missions to China sent out by the Zunghar ruler. No doubt, Āfāq Khwāja's merchants were the mainstay of the "Bukharan merchants."[53]

Their developmentalist nature put the Zunghar relations with oasis settlers on an odd footing, however. The Zunghar Mongols conducted a new kind of Mongol power. Unlike the earlier Mongol ruler, who accumulated wealth by merely collecting taxes and tributes from farmers and traders, or by looting them, the new Zunghar rulers came to be directly involved in agrarian production to exploit available commercial opportunities in trade with China and Russia. In order to do so, they became proactively involved in the development of the regional economy, constructing a series of urban centers in their bases in Ili Valley and Urumqi and developed state farms, ranches, and mining across Central Asia.[54]

To fuel this effort, the Zunghar required manpower—skilled artisans and farmers and agrarian and mining laborers. Thus, in their relations with the oasis settlers, the Zunghar did not want merely to collect taxes and loot goods, although those were still important. Ultimately, what they wanted most was the systematic forced mobilization of human labor. For this reason, after Galdan conquered the Yarkand Khanate in alliance with Āfāq Khwāja in 1680, the Zunghar not only extracted an annual payment of 100,000 *tangga* of silver from the oasis,[55] they also captured and transferred the Muslim farmers themselves from the oases of Kashgaria to Ili Valley and on a forced scale that had never before been seen.[56] The Zunghars also moved the oasis Muslims from the eastern towns such as Turfan and Hami to work in agrarian development in Urumqi.[57]

This establishment of Zunghar power, therefore, added a new dimension to the crisis of the oasis political economy that had been caused by the decline of the tribute trade—the new Zunghar state did not want only to tax and collect tribute; it wanted the muscle and sinew of labor as well. Such seizures undermined the very foundation of the Muslims' agrarian production and threatened the security of the oasis community at large. Indeed, this aspect of the Zunghar rule—its forced labor acquisition—emerged as the most deplored aspect of its rule. Thus, one Muslim historian, a follower of Āfāq Khwāja's rival faction, severely criticized the *khwaja* on this front in his history of the *khwaja*s of Eastern Turkestan. He did this in a roundabout way by inserting an improbable episode in his recounting. By the power of a prayer, a *khwaja*, belonging to Āfāq's rival faction, killed Tsewang Raptan, the Zunghar ruler who took numerous Muslims from the oasis area with the help of Āfāq Khwāja. Then, God turned the "infidel heart" of the next ruler of the Zunghar "so that he allowed all the captive Musulmans to return to their home."[58]

This was certainly one of the most dramatic episodes in the entire history. To debate the correctness of this record is beside the point. What is important is that the liberation of the captive Muslims was described as the most important heroic miracle performed by the rival of Āfāq Khwāja. As the incessant attacks to secure laborers from the oasis undermined the communities' ability to control their own labor contingent, as well as maintain overall security, the begs desperately needed a solution to this problem.

Emin Khwāja's Surrender to the Qing

In 1731, Emin Khwāja came up with a new solution to the deepening crisis prevalent in the oasis, caused by the double threats of the decline of tribute trade and the voracious Zunghar manhunts. The solution was an alliance with the Qing Empire, which was then expanding to Central Asia to contend against its archrival, the Zunghar. In that year, Emin surrendered to the Qing Empire, as was shown at the beginning of this chapter. A local history of Turfan, written sometime after 1741 (probably much later) upon the commission of his family, described the pivotal episode of Emin's surrender to the Qing within the context of his long-standing fighting against the Zunghar attacks on the Turfan Muslims.

Long before 1731, the latter had endured fierce Zunghar assaults. Emin had to lead "100,000" Turfan people to migrate into another town in 1722–23. For twelve years they gained many victories, killing some Zunghar attackers and arresting others; however, in the process they suffered greatly from other various catastrophes "that broke forth as if on the Judgment Day." When the superiority of the unbelievers became too much to overcome for the Turfans, as the local history goes, Emin Khwāja, for the sake of safety and mercy, asked the Chinese emperor (*Cin padashah*) for "protection" (*penah*) upon the advice of his political advisors (*vazir*) and *amir* as well as venerable Muslim scholars (*'ulamā*) and judges (*qādī*) of the community.[59]

Looking back from the vantage point of the late eighteenth century, various Turfan historians described Emin Khwāja's pivotal decision to join the Qing as a communal decision based on a consensus among the secular and spiritual leaders of the community for the greater good. They used the notion of *penah*, which was a concept of vital concern for the Central Asian Muslims in the articulation of their relations with the nomadic state builders.[60] In other words, as the Turfan historians saw it, Emin surrendered to the infidel Qing ruler in order to save the Muslim community from the formidable threat posed by a nomadic Buddhist destroyer.

Certainly, while the Turfan historians used the notion of protection in a religious context, their notion held a social, economic, and political connotation as well—the protection was against the threat of the Zunghar's pursuit of Turfan labor. In other words, the Zunghar attacks represented not only the Buddhist nomadic rulers' threat to the survival and integrity of the Turfan as an Islamic community. It was also a structural threat to the economic reproduction and enrichment of the *khwaja* family and the oasis community. Joining the Qing side in the Qing-Zunghar War (1696–1759) could remedy this problem. And the Qing military protection did give the oasis community the expected relief from the relentless attacks of the developmentalist Zunghar state.

At the same time, the alliance with the Qing also provided a solution to a more fundamental structural problem that the begs faced in the eighteenth century. This was none other than the disconnection from having direct access to the China market, which was also a most fundamental cause of insecurity in the oasis community, along with their constant mobility. The fix came in the wake of the wartime economy created by the Qing-Zunghar War. As Qing troops marched deeply into Inner Asia's territory against the Zunghar in the early eighteenth century, they needed to mobilize logistical support locally for that pursuit (especially in supplies of grain, cotton cloth, and horses). Although the Qing spent significant time and resources to develop its northwestern agriculture and commerce, it turned out that the court was never satisfactorily able to solve its problem of logistics support in the Central Asian battlefront. The Qing needed to mobilize the logistics locally through trade with the encountered agrarian communities.

By entering into alliance with the Qing, local Muslim communities were able to participate in this wartime economy. Its size, thus created in the Sino-Central Asian borderland in which the eastern cities of Eastern Turkestan, Hami, and Turfan were located, was huge. The Qing spent 137 million *liang* of silver in Chinese Central Asia during the Qing-Zunghar War in total, 23 million *liang* for the Dawachi Expedition (1754–55) and the Khwaja Campaign (1758–59) alone.[61] The local oasis community supplied the Qing troops with horses, grain, lamb, and the like and received in turn the coveted Chinese goods of silk, tea, and, most important, silver. It was as if the Sino-Central Asian tribute trade disconnected a half-century ago was totally restored and amplified under the new wartime economy. The difference between the two eras was that while, during the Ming, it was the Central Asian merchants who traveled to the China market for trade, now in the early eighteenth century the China market came to Central Asia. Even prior to his official surrender to the Qing in 1731, by 1727 and 1730 Emin Khwāja was already producing grain for the Qing army in Turfan and receiving satin and silver in return.[62]

Muslim Agriculture "Under the Feet of the Divine Lord's Horses"

Although Emin Khwāja fended off the initial Zunghar attack in 1731, the leader of the Turfan Muslims lacked military power and resources to withstand successive Zunghar battles in the following year, even with the help of the Qing troops. As the Yongzheng emperor retracted Qing troops from the Turfan area, Emin Khwāja decided to follow them to Gansu. In 1733, he and 8,113 people/2,387 households of Turfan Muslims, who survived the arduous journey from Turfan to Gansu, settled in a place called Guazhou, the site of ancient Dunhuang. They began farming land that had lain largely uncultivated until then.

A Qing source described the emperor's decision to relocate Emin Khwāja's group as one deriving from his (the emperor's) mercy regarding the miserable fate and plight of the Turfan people. However, the fact of the matter is that the Qing also needed Emin Khwāja and the Turfan community. As the Zunghar badly needed the oasis Muslims for the development of agriculture in the Sino-Central Asian borderland, so did the Qing. It engaged in full-scale agrarian development in the northwestern frontier to facilitate effective military mobilization during the time of the Qing-Zunghar War.[63] In its effort, the Qing also had the same structural problem that the Zunghar faced. The Qing state builders needed agrarian labor to put the development project into effect. However, such labor in this sparsely populated area was hard to come by. Surely, the Qing were better positioned to solve this problem than the Zunghar. After all, the emperor commanded the Chinese population. However, he found it not easy to persuade Chinese farmers to relocate to this remote part of the empire—it was much too remote, at least from their perspective.

The Yongzheng court must have taken into account this need for labor when it welcomed the Turfan Muslims into the Gansu frontier. There, the Qing settled them near Anxi zhen—a crucial military outpost that badly needed agricultural production, and under attractive conditions. While Emin Khwāja and his followers provided the labor, the Qing state provided the incentive. The *khwaja* and the Turfan people initially received cattle, household utensils, and grain, upon arriving in Guazhou. From 1735, the Qing lent seeds to the Turfan refugees to be used in their land, which was supposed to produce 1,685 *shi* and 4 *dou*.[64] Emin Khwāja and the Turfan Muslims were exempted from tax for a while. Most important, the Qing provided a ready market for their production. The Turfan refugees began supplying grain to the Qing troops from 1736.[65] Anxi zhen, the westernmost Qing military outpost before Barkul and Hami, to which Emin Khwāja supplied grain, had sixty-five hundred foot soldiers and cavalry by 1737, and annually sent one thousand soldiers to Hami on duty.[66]

Indeed, the Turfan refugees in Guazhou occupied a significant portion of the total agricultural labor force, which the Qing government transplanted in the Gansu Corridor to produce grain for the Qing troops. In addition to the Turfan refugees, the Qing recruited Han Chinese farmers from China to work in the *tuntian,* located west of Jiayuguan Pass, or Guanxi, from the time of the late seventeenth century. According to a 1742 estimate, these Han Chinese constituted 4,293 households. In the meantime, the Turfanese refugee farmers comprised 2,389 households. In other words, the Turfanese refugees accounted for 36 percent of the total farmers who worked on the production of grain supplied to the Qing troops in this significant location.[67] When the refugees left Guazhou to return to Turfan in 1756, twenty-three years after their migration into Guazhou, they left behind 20,450 *mu* of reclaimed farmland that the Chinese migrants inherited.[68]

Another aspect of the Qing contribution to the Turfan Muslims' agriculture in the Gansu frontier was their active investment in Muslim agriculture at a time of crisis in production. For instance, the Turfan Muslims in Guazhou borrowed seeds and food grain, 12,000 *shi* in 1735. Emin Khwāja's group was scheduled to repay the grain as well as the silver used for its transportation, 2,271 *liang,* over six years beginning in 1736.[69] In a similar instance, the Qing awarded 10,000 *liang* of silver to the Hami Muslims, another major pro-Qing oasis polity, in order to replenish the livestock that the Zunghar had stolen from them at the time of their attack on Hami in 1732.[70] This kind of state investment in Muslim agriculture must have helped the oasis Muslims significantly; they had always been under threat of uncertainty regarding agriculture and pasturing under harsh ecological conditions and constant threat of robbery by their nomadic neighbors. The Qing even established a new official in Guazhou to manage the affairs of agrarian colonies and the irrigation works, when they settled Emin Khwāja's group in Guazhou in 1733.[71]

In the Sino-Central Asian borderland, in other words, the Qing established themselves as the patron of the oasis Muslim begs and their agrarian and commercial interests. The emperor provided land and capital to them and was a major force behind the agrarian development of Central Asia, in order to develop undeveloped lands. On their part, the Muslim begs provided what their protector desired, to enhance their own agrarian interests. Thus, land development became the social basis for the alliance occurring between the Qing Empire and Muslim begs. If land development was important for the Qing state for its military mobilization in the remote frontier region, it was important also for Muslim notables and the social and economic base of the Muslim way of life. In other words, the Qing rulers established themselves as a patron of Islam and oasis Muslim elites—if not of their religious ideas, then certainly their social and economic interests as landowners and developers.

At the most fundamental level, the relations that Emin Khwāja had with the Qing ruler were reminiscent of the patronage between the Yarkand khans and the migratory Sufi. The Qing provided the protection and support of the Muslim begs' agriculture because of its own military and revenue needs, as had the Yarkand Khanate in providing the Sufis with land, water, and other resources for the same purpose. As the Yarkand khans provided the Sufi access to the important China market, the Qing offered access to the China market directly through the wartime trade. The only difference was that the Qing did so more generously and proactively in their support and protection of the oasis agrarian development, and the access given to the China market was much more secure. Moreover, the Qing could provide Emin Khwāja something that the Yarkand Khanate was never able to give: protection against the Zunghar, the biggest menace to the security and economy of the oasis Muslim community.

Furthermore, quite unexpectedly the political alliance with the Qing enhanced the fundamental base of Emin's capacity as an agrarian developer—his control over human labor. Since 1741, the Qing had continued to settle in Hami and in Beijing, under the control of Emin Khwāja in Guazhou, Muslim deserters from the Zunghar side, whose numbers had continued to increase during the time of the Qing-Zunghar War. The Qing were suspicious of the political loyalty of the deserters and placed them under the control of a reliable political ally. Of course, this added responsibility made the Emin Khwāja's control over this labor contingent more difficult. Obviously, occasional deserters would drift back to the Zunghar side from Guazhou. However, the arrangement did not negate the fundamental advantage he received for his agrarian development: the gain of a substantial number of additional laborers.[72]

By the 1730s and 1740s, the eighteenth-century crisis that had been caused by the long decline of the tribute trade seems to have been over, as far as the leader of the Turfan Muslims was concerned. Its solution had come in the form of the Qing troops, which provided the oasis begs land, capital, as well as military protection, and finally access to the China market locally. The tribute trade was replaced by the military economy. The Qing troops stationed in the Sino-Central Asian borderland provided a fresh new demand for the Muslim community's agricultural products (grain and livestock) in exchange for coveted Chinese goods (silk, ceramic, and tea) and, most important, the ever-demanded global good, New World silver.[73]

The Begs under the Umbrella of Qing Protection

In 1761, Emin Khwāja arrived in Turfan as part of the triumphant Qing forces, twenty-three years after leaving the town in a hurry. In his home district, he and his family replicated a new economy, which they had found in the frontier district of Guazhou. He received an investment of 1,000 *shi* of barley from the Qing military commander of the area to resettle in Turfan, in exchange for a promise of repayment of the initial Qing investment within a year, and an annual payment of 4,000 *shi* beginning in the third year. The Qianlong emperor showed a keen interest in Emin Khwāja's agrarian development. The emperor ordered that the Qing military commander should provide "the gifts" of cotton cloth and tea leaves to show the *khwaja* "encouragement," when the latter paid their promised annual payment.[74] Also, in 1761, the emperor decided to award the Turfan Muslims the land of the former agricultural colonies scattered in the Turfan region that had been cultivated by the Qing troops. These lands had been left idle when they had moved out of Turfan after the war.[75] The size of the land was 3,000 *mu* in one area in Pichan.[76] The emperor ordered this action for the reason that it would help the Turfan pay the default payment of grain to that point. However, it seems that he actively tried to use Emin Khwāja's group in the development of agriculture in strategic locations. Again, the Qing state proved itself to be the new investor, protector, and built-in market for the Turfan Muslims' agrarian development.

Emin Khwāja's story shows that gaining Qing state support was critical for the oasis begs' success in agriculture and trade in Eastern Turkestan in the eighteenth and nineteenth centuries. Indeed, the fate of a Muslim beg who did not succeed in obtaining Qing protection illustrates how important it was in the scheme of beg enrichment under the court. The Qing sources, such as the *Qinding Waifan Menggu Huibu Wanggong Biaozhuan* [Tables and Biographies of Mongol and Muslim Princes] recorded only the most prominent Muslim allies of the Qing Empire, and did not relay the story of unsuccessful people. However, one corruption case broke out in the late eighteenth century, and it does refer to such stories.

In 1781, a certain Tu-er-du-shi, son of a Niyas Sufi, came to the Qing military governor's office in Turfan (Pichan); he accused both of its rulers (identified with their Qing titles, *taijis*, sons of Emin Khwāja) and the Qing military governor of bribery and corruption. The gist of the charge was that Emin Khwāja's sons had bribed the military governor with seventy animal and lamb skins, and 400 *liang* of silver. The real force behind this accusation, however, was Tu-er-du-shi's father, Niyas Sufi. Tu-er-du-shi did not have firsthand knowledge of the situation but merely relayed his father's words. The subsequent investigation found the accusation to be without ground. However, the information revealed in the process of the investigation provides interesting insights into the relations between the begs and the Qing state.

At the time he brought the accusation forward in 1781, the Niyas Sufi was fifty-seven years old and living in the town of Lukchun with his family and his son Tu-er-du-shi's family, a total of twelve people. The family subsisted as farmers at the time, working on the government land of the Qing administration. They were poor. His other son (Tu-er-du-shi's brother) had to work as a hired laborer. However, formerly the situation had been different. Previously, Niyas Sufi had been a beg of a small town in Turfan, called Han-du. He then had land that produced agricultural products annually and he controlled thirty-two households of Muslims. These people had a long history with the Sufi. When he had originally moved to the Turfan area in the 1760s, these thirty-two households also migrated into Lu-bu-qin with him. Emin Khwāja provided them with land to be settled and appointed Niyas Sufi as the beg of Han-du.

The process of his move into Turfan had been remarkable in many ways. Niyas Sufi first surrendered to the Qing general Bandi, when the commander of the Qing army led the troops to conquer Ili in 1755. Niyas Sufi, with a certain La-ke-ji Sufi, leading the thirty-two households of Muslims—altogether 552 people—surrendered. Afterward, he and ten Muslims followed the Qing campaign and captured the Zunghar ruler, Dawachi. Later, when an ambitious Zunghar noble, Amursana, rebelled and massacred all the Qing troops stationed in Ili Valley almost immediately after the Qing conquest, Niyas Sufi managed to hide twenty-seven Qing soldiers in his house. When Qing reinforcements arrived in 1756, he again surrendered to them, and sent the hidden soldiers to the commander. For this contribution, the latter awarded Niyas Sufi silk and satin as well as grain. Later, Niyas told the Qing commander, "I had already surrendered [to the Qing], and I wanted to move to the interior of the Qing territory (*neidi*) and reside there." However, the Qing commander objected and persuaded him to stay in Ili and cultivate land there instead. But noting that their number was small, and the Zunghar rebels many, Niyas Sufi pleaded to go to Turfan. The Qing commander immediately permitted it. He gave him the seal of the Turfan governor (Da-er-han Beg) as well as seeds with which to cultivate land. The commander then sent Qing soldiers to escort him to Urumqi, from which Niyas Sufi and his group proceeded to Turfan alone.

Six months later, Emin Khwāja also moved from Gansu to Turfan. Niyas Sufi told Emin the reason he had come to Turfan; however, Emin did not respond. Later, when the Qing established a *banshi dachen* in Pichan, Niyas tried to report his prior service to the Qing administration. However, Emin Khwāja obstructed his attempt, and the Qing did not learn of these circumstances. Finally, in 1780, Niyas Sufi attempted to report his situation to the Qing military governor. Upon making further inquiry into the story with the Turfan *taiji*s, the latter bribed him. The Qing military governor then declared that Niyas Sufi's claim was false and had him flogged thirty times and put in a cangue for three months. Then the Turfan *taiji*s scattered all the Muslims that had accompanied Niyas Sufi throughout Turfan; they deposed him of his beg post and made him a "small Muslim." Niyas Sufi complained, "We contributed to the Qing, along with the prince of Turfan [meaning Emin Khwāja]. Now our sons and brothers are hired by other people to cultivate land. Thus, we became poor. Because of this, I plead to Daren [meaning the current Qing military governor]."[77]

This had been an extraordinary accusation in many ways. As Niyas Sufi also confessed later, the details of his charges may well have been fabricated. However, there was also certainly some truth in them. Large parts of his basic story were not challenged by the Qing investigators. First of all, as his name suggested, Niyas Sufi was a small-time Sufi master with a small following. In all probability, he was forced to migrate to Ili Valley for agrarian development during the Zunghar rule. One notable feature about him was his mobility. He moved around in Ili and Turfan with roughly five hundred followers. In other words, Niyas Sufi came from the same background as most of the oasis begs, who initially were leaders of mobile settler groups, moving around Central Asia to search for land to settle as well as a patron to provide for them. After all, Emin Khwāja and his moving band of people, migrating across Turfan and Gansu, were fundamentally the same kind of mobile oasis settlers.

In other words, Niyas Sufi was one of the people who could have become powerful and a wealthy beg under the Qing rule, but did not. He thought that the major reason he had become impoverished was that he had been unjustly deprived of the chance to establish political ties with the Qing administration. He believed that Emin Khwāja, his competitor for political privilege under Qing rule, had blocked him from establishing those precious ties. Therefore, Niyas Sufi harbored resentment and accused Emin's descendants.

It is debatable whether we can trust Niyas's claim of a meritorious act at the time of the Qing conquest, or that he was awarded the seal of Turfan governor by the Qing general. In most likelihood, the Sufi may have received some minor reward for some minor contribution. However, that is beside the point. What is important here is that a minor oasis notable like Niyas Sufi—a Sufi leader, with modest followers, who had some minor beg position in Turfan—thought that he had lost the chance to become rich and powerful because he had failed to establish political ties with the Qing state.

What it means then is that the begs considered close political ties with the Qing state as the prerequisite for their becoming wealthy and important. Niyas Sufi may have thought that the political patronage of the Qing could have provided him privileged access to the logistics trade with the Qing troops, and access to the coveted silver and Chinese goods. He may have thought that if he had a connection to the Qing administration, he could have obtained more landed property, such as the abandoned Qing military colonies, which would have made him prosperous. He may have thought that he could have received a preferential loan of seeds and tax exemption, which could have enabled him to weather one or two years of bad harvest. All of these preferential treatments, crucial to the accumulation of the wealth that Emin Khwāja had, could have been available if Niyas Sufi had had a similar political tie with the Qing administration. In that sense, his accusation against the Emin Khwāja family was an ironic but powerful testimony about the importance of Qing patronage for the Muslim begs' agrarian development and accumulation of wealth.

Conclusion

This chapter has explored how the begs' interests in securing resources, labor, and silver set them on the path of a profitable partnership with the Qing Empire. In turn, at the center of this story was the presence of the Sufi migrants and their families, the mainstay of the pro-Qing begs. This chapter argues that Sufi migrants' interests in developing commercial agriculture in the oasis under the changing environment of trade in Eurasia spurred their settlement into Eastern Turkestan and also into an alliance with the Qing. They had experienced a crisis in the local political economy in the seventeenth century caused by a sudden, if temporary, decline in the China trade. In their view, an alliance with the Qing, and, even better, one that provided a direct connection to the China market, would be a viable solution to mitigate that problem.[78]

Conceptualized in this way, the begs' alliance with the Qing can be considered a brave act, Central Asian landlords reaching out to initiate new connections to offset the precarious climate of the commercial environment in Eurasia. Within a broader framework at that time, the dual expansions of European maritime commerce in the Indian Ocean, on the one hand, and the Chinese trade and empire moving in from the east, on the other, changed the economic and political landscapes of Central Asia significantly. While the rerouting of the long-distance overland trade routes to the Indian Ocean promised to disturb the fortunes of Central Asian merchants, the appearance of a greater China trade offered enticing opportunity. What the Sufi settlements in Eastern Turkestan and their alliance with the Qing show is that Central Asian Muslims maneuvered within these two fronts, "as new markets and producers emerged" in Eurasia.[79]

The ventures taken by Emin Khwāja's family from mid-1500 to 1750 in the Sino-Central Asian borderland illustrates this point clearly. It was a constant trek to the east, starting in the 1550s, when Muhammad Sharīf, the supposed ancestor of Emin's family, lived in Samarqand in western Central Asia. When the journey ended, in the 1750s, Emin Khwāja resided in a Chinese frontier town in Guazhou. What motivated this easterly direction of the Sufi family was the lure of China trade—one that carried silver and silk expanding westerly with full force from 1500. When the tribute trade declined sharply in the early seventeenth century, the Sufi developers scrambled to find the best way to cope with the change. Emin Khwāja discovered a solution to the crisis in their economy caused by the reduction of the China trade by allying with the Qing Empire. Emin sought the "protection" "under the feet of the divine (Qing) Lord's horses"[80] to achieve the stability of the political economy of the oasis. And he found what he had wanted. The politics of the oasis became stable. Agriculture and commerce flourished again.

By no means, however, was their submission to the Qing the only political choice that the Muslim begs could have taken. They could have entered into alliance with the Zunghar and become a participant in their initiative. They could have participated as the facilitators and handlers of the Zunghar rulers' monopoly tribute trade with Qing China, and collaborated with the Zunghar agrarian development in the oases. Indeed, some prominent oasis begs chose to do so. However, Emin Khwāja made quite a different decision. Perhaps for a religious leader like him, the threat of the nomads represented by the Buddhist Zunghar Mongols was just too destructive to Islam and the Muslim community to consider.

The examination of the role of the begs in the agrarian development and Qing expansion offers intriguing insights into some broader issues of early modern Eurasian history. First, the landlocked part of Eurasia was well connected with the global trade expanding since the sixteenth century, along its overland routes as much, for example, as its own maritime activity in the Indian Ocean. Keenly aware of the rhythm and geography of the expanding China trade, the Sufis in Central Asia moved and settled in Eastern Turkestan in order to exploit the growing commercial opportunities created by it. Second, there was a clear relationship between the expansion of Chinese commerce and the expansion of the Qing Empire in Eastern Turkestan. It was almost as if the eighteenth-century Qing expansion followed the footsteps of the Ming tribute trade conducted in the previous two centuries. However, the agents of the expansion of both Chinese commerce and empire in eastern Eurasia during this period were not primarily Chinese. It was rather Muslim begs that responded to the China trade, and it was they who brought the Qing Empire into the region proactively.

2   Capitalist Imperatives and Imperial Connections, 1759–1825

A local tale has it that in 1776 a trader from Yarkand entered by mistake mountain territory where a refugee community composed of the former followers of Kashgar *khwaja*s and the Zunghar was ensconced. The leader of the refugees, an oasis Muslim from Yarkand, arrested the man and put him in prison immediately. Then, one day, after killing his own parents, wives, sons, and daughters, the refugee leader called the trader out of the prison to see what he had done. Sha-guan-ji asked him whether his patron, the governor of Yarkand District, could kill anyone in Yarkand. To this question the trader responded that the governor would not dare to kill anyone because of the Qing Empire. If the governor could not kill anyone, the refugee leader replied condescendingly, "How can he be called a man?" Then the chieftain released the trader to return to Yarkand to report to the governor what he had seen. However, it turned out that the governor of Yarkand would have the last word. One day he captured one of the refugees and put him in prison for sixty days. Afterward, the governor removed him from prison and let him see the walled city of Yarkand, with its plentiful population, animals, weapons, and instruments, as well as jewels, silks, and satin. Then the governor returned the man to the mountain so that he could tell his leader what the governor had done in Yarkand.[1]

The governor was Ūdui, one of the numerous pro-Qing begs, who emerged as one of the undisputed power holders in Eastern Turkestan during the Qing rule. He managed to hold his position in Yarkand (1760–78), arguably the wealthiest oasis district, until he died. Clearly written from the perspective of the pro-Qing notable, this tale does retain an underlying partisan quality to its message—claiming the superiority of the civilized and urbane rule of the beg under the Qing, while denigrating the authority of the anti-Qing refugee communities in the mountains. What is especially interesting is the argument that the tale came up with to legitimate the client rule. It certainly has a developmentalist tone to it: client rule could be justified because it brought prosperity to the oasis city over which Ūdui presided, Yarkand. This argument is striking because it departs from the early political tradition in the region. The khans and *amīr* who had dominated the region for several centuries before the coming of the Qing would certainly not have considered economic prosperity as the centerpiece of their political legitimacy, if they cared about such at all. They would probably have agreed with Sha-guan-ji that military strength and judicial independence ("the power to execute" at will) were the ultimate justifications of their rule.

What does the language of prosperity and economic development crediting the governor's rule in Yarkand tell us about the rule of the begs in Central Asia? While Qing sources seem to describe the Muslim governors as mere officials of the emperor, the local people saw them differently. Iskandar, the governor of Kashgar (1788) and governor of Yarkand (1789–1811), did not even bother to mention the Qing emperor in justifying his family's rule in the area. Instead, he praised God and a Muslim saint (named Alp Ata) for giving his family the domain.[2] No begs under the Qing rule, however, would have denied that they served the Qing court and were under its control. At times, they even boasted about their relations with the emperors, in political correspondence to their Central Asian neighbors, in order to promote their political positions in the regional political hierarchy.[3] Nevertheless, they still understood themselves to be sovereign in their own districts and in their own right, respectively. Modern scholarship has tended to agree with the begs, and characterizes the Qing rule in Eastern Turkestan as an indirect relationship.[4]

This chapter examines the inner workings of the beg client regime—that is, its agendas, structure, and the social tensions it created in the oasis society, and argues that the Muslim clients appropriated the political and commercial connections provided by the Qing Empire to promote the wholesale economic transformation of the oasis. The begs took advantage of the empire's utter dependence on their resource development and radically expanded the scope of their composite commercial enterprises based on capitalistic principles—namely, private domination of resources (land and water) and the use of purchased labor both wage laborer and slave, as well as that of *yanqis* on duty to serve the begs financially.

Their connections to the empire were crucial in their efforts to develop their enterprises of capitalistic agriculture. The begs needed to conduct large-scale agrarian and mining projects in the rural hinterlands, because the Qing state presence in Xinjiang brought in the newly invigorated local, regional, and international trade to the oases, particularly in jade, silk, grain, cotton, fruit, vegetables, horses, tea, rhubarb, and silver. At the same time, the begs needed the Qing military presence for the success of their agrarian development projects in the rural areas, to back the begs' encroachment of common resources there as well as to provide a security guarantor against the social unrest that attended the intense economic transformation. The logic of this double dependence of the beg on the Qing state—as market and protector of their interests as developers in their quest for wealth—was where the Qing Empire stood in the late eighteenth and early nineteenth centuries and beyond.

However, the beg-initiated agrarian development set the beg clients on a long-term collision course with the rural village communities, which had witnessed the erosion of their control over members and common property. The large number of "corruption" charges brought by them to the Qianlong court against the begs were good testimony to this tension and contention. While begs were triumphant in their efforts to expand the urban domination of the rural hinterland for the time being, the contradiction inherent in their projects eventually gave rise to the emergence of a backlash of resistance against such development: the marooned refugee communities in the mountains led by the Islamic Kashgar *khwajas* in the early nineteenth century, a story that will be explored in the next chapter.

The careers of Ūdui and his son Osman provide an excellent opportunity to examine this important transition. Their tenure as governors of the two major oasis districts of Yarkand and Kashgar, respectively, is especially interesting because their relations with their local societies highlight the changing relationship between the begs and the rural villages, and the contradiction inherent in that change. Their stories are relatively well documented, because both had to face serious "corruption" charges brought by the oasis populations. By analyzing these cases, one gains substantial insight into the content and depth of the begs' activities as client rulers—especially their involvement in the violent upheaval that accompanied the transformation of the oasis political economy.

Qing Military Building and the Local Oasis Economy

Ūdui's governorship in Yarkand (1760–78) was known for its prosperity. Qishiyi, who relayed the local tale about the Yarkand merchant with which this chapter opened, also provided an inside glimpse of its boomtown atmosphere: it retained a taxpaying adult male population estimated at seventy to eighty thousand. Merchants from various parts of China, as well as Andijan, Tibet, Khoqandian, and Kashmir, flocked to it in large numbers. Its *bazaar* quarter

Table 2.1. The Qing Military in Eastern Turkestan, Early Nineteenth Century

Location	1774 Soldiers	1774 Tuntian	1777	1821 Soldiers	1821 Tuntian	1826	1829	1831
			Northern circuit					
Ili	13,184	M; O		14,641	M, O			
Tarbagatai	0			2,346	M			
Subtotal	13,184			16,987				
			Eastern circuit					
Urumqi	7,376			12,065	M (21,000 *mu*)			
Barkul	0			4,278	M			
Gucheng	200			2,027	M (11,000 *mu*)			
Ku-er-ka-la-wu-su	370 (350)	M		615	C			
Jinghe	0			410	C			
Turfan	330			2,342	M (14,700 *mu*)			
Hami	800	M		854	M (11,300 *mu*)			
Subtotal	9,076 (9,056)			2,2591				
			Southern circuit					
Qarashar	745			615				
Kucha	220			320				
Aksu	100			782	M, O (125 *mu*)			
Sayram	40			N/A				
Bai	10			N/A				
Ush	1,050	M, O		697	M, O (5,000 *mu*)			
Kashgar	959		679	1,284	0	1,250	4,900	4,000
Yangi Hissar	280		280	286	0	280	480	1,000
Yarkand	891		890	912	0	880	1,400	5,000
Khotan	232		232	228	0	230	230	500
Barchuk								3,500
Subtotal: Western four cities	2,362		2,081	2,710	0	2,640	7,000	14,000
Subtotal: Southern circuit	4,527	N/A	N/A	4,882	N/A	N/A	N/A	N/A
Subtotal: Eastern Turkestan (Southern circuit + Turfan and Hami)	5,657			8,078				
Total	26,787	N/A	N/A	44,460	N/A	N/A	N/A	N/A

Sources: XYTZ, vols. 31–33; XJShL, vols. 5–6; XZSL, DG11/10/yichou; Pan Zhiping, *Zhongya Haohanguo Yu Qingdai Xinjiang*, pp. 134, 135, 148; Kataoka Kazutada, *Shinchō Shinkyō tōchi kenkyū*, pp. 62, 65.

Note: (1) M = military *tuntian*, C = Chinese civilian *tuntian*, O = oasis Muslim *tuntian*; (2) The number of the western four cities' military was later reduced to ten thousand in 1831.

was 10 *li* long, bustling with goods and people like "clouds and bees," when the market opened. "Strange things and jewels could often be found. And animals and fruits are extremely numerous."[5]

Fundamentally, Ūdui achieved this prosperity in Yarkand because the structure of the Qing Empire's oversight in Xinjiang made it possible. The dimension of the latter's rule in Central Asia that most set it apart from its Central Asian predecessor in the area was the physical presence of its substantial military force occupying local society. This contrasted sharply with the previous ruler, the Zunghar, who did not station their military in Eastern Turkestan at all. Comprising Manchu, Mongols, and Chinese soldiers, the number of Qing troops in the area from Kashgar to Turfan was estimated to be around six to eight thousand in the late eighteenth and early nineteenth centuries, although the exact number and their distribution among the oasis districts fluctuated constantly during the period. In particular, Qing troops were heavily concentrated in a few major cities, including Kashgar, Yarkand, and Ush (see Table 2.1).[6]

Placed under the control of the Qing military administration, the native administration of Muslim clients constituted a separate political domain. Physically, its buildings stood within a Muslim city close by but separate from the Manchu fortress there, housing the *cancan dachen* and *banshi dachan* and troops. The Qing military governor did not involve himself with the internal affairs of the Muslim cities and villages, unless they involved Manchu soldiers or Chinese residents, or if he deemed it necessary for some security reason. The main political obligation that the Muslim clients had with the Qing military was the provision of revenue to the Qing troops, both in the delivery of a predetermined sum of tax and tribute as well as logistical supplies to the Qing military camp on monthly and annual bases, both in kind and in cash.[7] As long as these terms were fulfilled, the Muslim clients were left largely to their own devices.

However, in spite of this political structure of indirect rule, so to speak, the Qing military affected the life of the oasis Muslim residents significantly. Most important, the troops stimulated the local economy. The soldiers needed to be fed and clothed; they also needed horses. The Qing military administration in the oases used the tax receipts to purchase logistics supplies; this circular arrangement—collection of the tax in local currency (*pul*) and acquiring purchases from the local market—ensured that logistical troop demands would promote local trade and agrarian production. The Qing administration also paid the soldiers' salaries in *pul* coins, and thus the soldiers would buy their personal necessities directly in the *bazaar*.

For instance, in 1761–62, the Qing administration in Yarkand and Kashgar used tax money, totaling 10,000 *liang* worth of *pul* coins, to purchase livestock and horses. Ūdui and Emin Khwāja handled these transactions on behalf of the Qing.[8] The Qing administration in Yarkand purchased 134 horses, 29 cattle, and 54 donkeys locally, all from Kirghiz tribesmen and Andijan merchants in 1762, from the beginning of the first month to the beginning of the third month of QL (Qianlong Period) 27 (1762); the expense amounted to 2,099 *liang*. In Kashgar, the administration bought 279 horses from the oasis, paying 2,763 *liang* from the eleventh month of QL 27 (1762) to the third month of QL 28 (1763).[9]

Adding to the demand of local agricultural products was the Qing administration in Ili, which secured high-quality horses for the Manchu military stationed in northern Xinjiang through trade with the Kazakhs. Having initially used silk and silver transported from China to pay for the horses, the Qing administration came also to rely heavily on cotton and cotton cloth trade produced in the Eastern Turkestani oases.[10] In 1762, for example, the Muslim governor of Yarkand was charged to make about fifty thousand bolts of cloth; the native client purchased the amount with the 66,000 *tangga* of *pul* coins provided by the Qing, and shipped it all to Ili for an exchange of horses from the Kazakh.[11] In 1779 and 1784, the Qing administration placed an order in Ili for 26,760 bolts of white cotton cloth and 10,000 *jin* of raw cotton at an expense of 15,315 *tangga* 10 *wen* of *pul* coins; it shipped all the goods to the north for an exchange of Kazakh horses. In 1795, the Qing administration in the oasis spent 16,763 *tangga* and 20 *wen* to buy 29,545 bolts of white cotton cloth and 10,000 *jin* of raw cotton from the oasis. This increasing demand for cotton and cotton cloth stimulated cotton farming and weaving.[12]

Oasis trade in cotton products with surrounding nomads (including Kazakh and Kirghiz) was not new. These goods were the staples of oasis-nomad trading. However, the added demand from the Qing military boosted local and regional trade substantially. Not only did this stimulus involve bulk goods but it also included high-end luxury goods. A British diplomat visiting the region in 1873 relates that during the Qing rule, many competitive handicraft productions of carpet, gold wire, silk, and wool thrived in Khotan District. Those industries declined precipitously after the fall of the Qing Empire in Central Asia in 1864, "for there is nobody left to buy them," he observed.[13]

At the same time, the Qing occupation also gave impetus to the long-distance trade conducted with China. The imperial court allowed the transport of substantial amounts of high-quality silk and satin produced in the Imperial Silk

Workshop in Jiangnan to Eastern Turkestan, to partially defray Qing administration costs.[14] Chinese merchants (usually Chinese Muslim merchants from northwestern China) followed the Qing military as soon as the Qing conquest was completed. They originally came to supply the military with tea, under the encouragement of the Qing. However, the Chinese merchants also soon participated in trade with the oasis Muslims, offering tea and rhubarb, an herb grown in northwestern China widely known for its medicinal qualities and often used as a laxative and purgative throughout Central Asia; Central Asian merchants often re-exported it to Russia as well.[15] It was through this link with the Chinese merchants that jade, the most coveted commercial item excavated out of the oasis, made its way to the affluent market in Jiangnan.

Still, the most important commodity that the new connections with China brought into Eastern Turkestan was the one that oasis Muslims hungered for—namely, silver. The Qing court shipped 60,000 *liang* of silver to southern Xinjiang annually to defray the cost of administration and salaries to the Qing soldiers in the late eighteenth century. Also, northern Xinjiang received 650,000–700,000 *liang* from China during the similar period. It is reasonable to expect that some portion of it entered southern oases through regional trade.[16] In addition, Chinese merchants brought a significant amount of silver to the oasis for their own trade and loan businesses. Although the exact size of the private silver import is hard to determine, it was substantial to say the least. A Chinese merchant named Zhang Luan reportedly had lent Governor Ūdui 7,000 *liang* of silver by the time of the latter's death in 1778.[17]

Collectively, this new demand and supply created in the oasis after the Qing conquest increasingly attracted Central Asian and Indian merchants to the region and thus contributed to its rising prominence in the overland trade route. The attraction of silver seems to have been most important in this development. In 1760, a Qing general sent to Eastern Turkestan expressed uneasiness as to how the merchants from outside came to oasis cities as far as Hami, and actively sought silver as the price for their goods such as livestock and hides. Another Qing general, in the early nineteenth century, also complained that silver coming from China never stayed within Eastern Turkestan.[18]

The result was the extreme international variety of goods to be found in the *bazaar*s of the oasis in the eighteenth century. Yonggui, who worked as the Qing military governor of Kashgar in the late eighteenth century, provided a list of the "local" tributes that he collected for the Qianlong emperor. They included various textiles, either silk or wool products; fruit and grain; perfume;

and an artisanal product, a knife. Interestingly, many of them were not strictly "local" products. The list included goods from a wide area, including nearby places such as Margillan ("Nu-he-le" [sticky sugar]), Khoqand ("Ku-tu-ke-shi-mi-shi" [a fruit resembling a grape with the medicinal quality of ginseng]), and Andijan ("Pi-si-te" [a sweet fruit looking like a pine cone]) in Fergana Valley; in Transoxiana such as Bukhara ("Bukhara cinnamon flower perfume"); and also from "Hindustan" ("satin woven with golden yarn," "five color fur rugs," "Hindustan white rice," "Kan-ti" [solid sugar], "Nu-he-le").[19]

Begs emerged as the major beneficiaries of the intensifying commercial boom that was stimulated by the new commercial connections under Qing rule. As the main organizers of agriculture and commerce in the oasis, they supplied grain, livestock, horses, and cotton clothes to the Qing administration for payment. In addition, the Qing authority also instituted a set of policies favorable toward them. Throughout its rule, it maintained a low rate of taxation on trade. The court did not collect any taxes at all from local commerce, nor on the trade conducted by the members of the tribute missions coming from neighboring Central Asian countries. It also lowered the rate of the customs duties from the level that had been administered under the Zunghar reign. Several months after the Qing conquest, upon receiving petitions from the beg officials of various "Muslim cities" that wanted to attract more merchant traffic, the Qing military governor of Kashgar District, Shuhede (Manchu. Šuhede), lowered the tax rate on the cattle that the local Muslims imported to Kashgar and Yarkand, from 1/10 to 1/20 part and on the cattle that the foreign merchants imported, from 1/20 to 1/30 part. This reduced rate in customs duties remained effective until the early nineteenth century, when the Qing decided to stop collecting the customs duties in effect because of political pressures coming from within and without the empire.[20] In addition, the court also systematically undertaxed the regions' China trade, especially tea, one of the major trades between China and Eastern Turkestan. The scale of the undertaxation of the tea was staggering. An early-nineteenth-century Qing military governor, who attempted to solve a black market problem, estimated that roughly a full half of the total amount of tea imported to Xinjiang—200,000 to 300,000 cases out of 400,000 to 500,000 cases (that is, 2 to 2.5 million *jin*) per year—was smuggled and thus not taxed at all at the time.[21]

The Qing maintained a low tax rate on agriculture as well. In 1759, when the imperial court determined the quota of the grain tax (*ezhengliang*), a combination of poll and land tax, in the major oasis, it lowered the tax quota from the level that had been imposed by the Zunghar. After an initial adjustment to it made in the 1760s, the Qing kept the rate constant at the level of 70,000

Table 2.2. Grain Tax Quota, Eastern Turkestan, 1750s–1864 (Unit: *shi*)

Tax Quota	Initial (Year)	1772	1776	1784	1821	1833	1862
Turfan	1,565 (1762)	4,229	3,423.2	3,423.2	3,423.2	4,565	4,565
Kurla	700 (1761)	1,400	925	982	982	982	982
Bugur	700 (1761)	N/A	N/A			N/A	
Kucha	3,170 (1759)	960	2,345.8	3,228.4	2,885.6	4,785.6	2,080
Shayar		560	872.6	N/A	N/A	N/A	800
Sayram	975 (1759)	750	782	1,146.4	N/A		946
Bai	550 (1759)	364.2	364	N/A	N/A	11,000	553.5
Aksu	6,835 (1759)	6,835.5	3,945.2	3,945.2	7,635.4		6,835.5
Ush	2,010 (1761)	2,250	2,010	2,010	N/A	1,000	N/A
Kashgar	21,200 (1759)	2,0924.4	25,193.5	25,193	10,466.6	38,300	21,200
Yarkand	19,402 (1759)	16,960	21,371	21,371.7	21,360	41,000	21,300
Khotan	14,013 (1759)	8,692	13,934.8	13,934.8	13,934.8	16,000	13,800
Total	71,120	63,925.1	75,167.1	75,234.7	60,687.6	116,300	73,062

Sources: XYTZ, vol. 34; HJZ, vol. 4; XJShL, vol. 9; XZSL, vol. 233, DG13/3/bingxu; *Qinding Da Qing huidian shili (Guangxu Chao)*, vol. 163; Saguchi Tōru, *Jūhachi-jūkyū-seiki Higashi Torukisutan shakaishi kenkyū*, pp. 205, 208, 235.
Note: 1 *batman* = 5.3 *shi*.

to 75,000 *shi* until the 1820s. The rate even decreased to 60,000 *shi* in the early nineteenth century.[22] Notably, until 1828 and 1829, the Qing did not make any serious attempt to conduct a new direct land survey, which would have put any newly reclaimed land into the tax register. Furthermore, the land survey did not continue after 1828 and 1829 (see Table 2.2).

In the earliest years, the Qing made this policy decision regarding taxation on agriculture and commerce from expediency; at least at first that was so because of the sharp decline in agrarian production caused by damage done by the war of the Qing conquest. However, the fact that it maintained this policy throughout its rule shows that it was a conscious political decision. Situated far from the Chinese metropole, the Qianlong emperor realized that the security of the Qing rule depended upon the support and alliance of the oasis begs of Eastern Turkestan. Sheer military presence would not have been enough to secure the area. The Qianlong court decided that the best way to do so was to convince the influential begs that they had embedded interests in the Qing Empire; for landed notables well connected with commerce such as the begs, the best way to convince them was to maintain the economic policies that openly favored their landed and commercial interests.[23]

Table 2.3. Local Administration of the Oasis under the Qing Rule: Kashgar District
(Unit of Land: *batman*; Unit of cash: *wen*)

Administrative Division	Position (beg)	Qing Rank			Number			Compensation				
								QL			Early JQ	
		QL	Early JQ	Late JQ	QL	Early JQ	Late JQ	Land	Yanqi	Cash	Land	Yanqi
Main city	Hākim	3	3	3	1	1	1	200	100	30,000	150	80
	Ishikagha	4	4	4	1	1	1	150	50	15,000	100	50
	Kazanachi	4	4	4	1	1	1	150	50	12,000	80	30
	Shang	4	4	4	2	1	2	150	50	12,000	80	30
	Qādī	5	5	5	1	1	1	100	30	x	60	15
	Nou-ke-pu	5	5	5	1	1	1	100	30	x	60	15
	Mo-ti-se-pu	5	5	5	1	1	1	100	30	7,500	40	15
	Mi-tu-wa-li	5	5	5	1	1	1	100	30			
	Duguan	6	6	6	1	1	1	50	15	5,000	30	4
	Ba-ji-ge-er	6	6	6	1	1	1	50	15	x	30	4
	Ba-ke-ma-ta-er	6	6	6	1	1	1	50	15	5,000	30	4
	A-er-ba-pu-er	6	6	6	1	1	1	50	15	5,000	30	4
	Pa-ti-sha-pu	6	6	6	1	1	1	50	15	5,000	30	4
	Mīrāb		6		[1]	1						
	Ming	6		6	1		1	50	15			
	Ming	7	7		1	1		30	8	x	10	2
	Ke-le-ke-ya-la-ke	6			1			50	15			
	Shi-huo-le	6		6	1		1	50	15			
	Ming			7			2					
Faizabad	Hākim	4	4	4	1	1	1			12,000	80	30
	Ming	4	7	7	1	2	1			x	10	2
Ta-si-hun+	Mīrāb		5	5		1	1			x	40	15
	Ming		7	7		2	2			x	10	2
Ti-si-gun+	Mīrāb	5			1			x	5			
Astin Artush	Hākim	5	5	5	1	1	1			7,500	40	15
	Qādī	6	6	6	1	1	1			x	30	4
	Ming	7	7	7	5	5	5			x	10	2
Beshkerim	Hākim	5	5	5	1	1	1			7,500	40	15
	Qādī	6	6	6	1	1	1			x	30	4
	Mīrāb	6	6	6	1	1	1	x	5	x	20	3
	Ming	6	6	6	1	1	1			x	10	2
A-la-gu	Hākim	6	6	6	1	1	1			5,000	30	4
	Qādī	6	6	6	1	1	1			x	30	4
Ta-shi-mi-li-ke*	Hākim		6	5		1	1			5,000	30	4
	Qādī		7			1				[?]		
	Ming			7			1					

Administrative Division	Position (beg)	Qing Rank QL	Qing Rank Early JQ	Qing Rank Late JQ	Number QL	Number Early JQ	Number Late JQ	Comp. QL Land	Comp. QL Yanqi	Comp. Cash	Comp. Early JQ Land	Comp. Early JQ Yanqi
Ta-shi-ba-li-ke*	Hākim	4			1							
Üstün Artush	Hākim	6	6	6	1	1	1			5,000	30	4
	Qādī	6	6	6	1	1	1			x	30	4
	Ming	7	7	7	1	1	1			x	10	2
Khan Ariq	Qādī	6	6	6	1	1	1			x	30	4
	Mīrāb	6	6	6	1	1	1	x	5	x	20	3
	Ming	7	7	7	1	1	1			x	10	2
Huo-er-han	Mīrāb	6	6	6	1	1	1	x	5	x	20	3
	Ming	6	7	6	1	1	1			x	10	2
Huo-se-er-bu-yi+	Mīrāb	6	6	6	1	1	1	x	5	x	20	3
	Ming		7	7		1	1			x	10	2
Sai-er-man	Mīrāb	6	6	6	1	1	1	x	5	x	20	3
	Ming		7	7		1	1			x	10	2
Tuo-gu-sa-ke	Mīrāb	6	6	6	1	1	1	x	5	x	20	3
	Ming		7	7		1	1			x	10	2
Tuo-pu-lu-ke	Ming	7			1							
Wu-pa-er	Hākim	6	6	6	1	1	1			5,000	30	4
	Ming	7	7	7	1	1	1			x	10	2
A-er-wa-te	Mīrāb		6	6		1	1	x	5	x	20	3
	Ming		7	7		1	1			x	10	2
Mu-shi-su-lu-ke	Ming		7	7		1	1			x	10	2
	Mīrāb		7	7		1	1	x	5	x	10	2
Yangi Hissar	Hākim	4	4	4	1	1	1			12,000	80	30
	Qādī	6	6	6	1	1	1			x	30	4
	Mīrāb	6		6	1		1					
	Ming		7	7		1	1			x	10	2
	Guantai Beg (Beg managing station)			7			1					
	The Begs managing five places of *karun*	N/A			1							

Sources: XYTZ, vol. 30; HJTZ; XJShL, vol. 3.

Note: (1) QL: Qianlong Period (1736–95); JQ: Jiaqing Period (1796–1820) (2) The two places marked with * could be the same place; the two places marked with + could be the same place.

In this regard, it is worthwhile to note that the Qing provided additional economic benefits to the begs working with them. As Qing "officials," the begs were exempted from the poll tax as well as the onerous duty of forced labor for the government, which was arguably more onerous than the payment of tax. And there was more. The Qing provided the beg clients the package of a land grant, comprising land, cash, and *yanqi*.[24] For instance, the governors of the major districts such as Kashgar, Yarkand, Khotan, and Aksu, received 200 *batman* of land, one hundred people to cultivate it, and 30,000 *wen* of *pul* coins (see Table 2.3).[25]

The practical purpose of this grant allowed the begs the right to mobilize certain numbers of oasis farmers to cultivate a certain amount of unused land under government control. In 1768, for instance, the Qing administration appointed three "beg headmen" (Manchu: *bek data*), one *hākim,* and two *ming* begs, in order to control a new rural settlement of two hundred households established in the district of Ush. The new *hākim,* a certain Mamadabula, received as his land grant a plot of wildland belonging to a tax-paying village that amounted to 30 *batman.* In order to help him to cultivate it, the Qing provided him as *yanqi*s the fifteen households that he had retained as *yanqi* in his previous post in nearby Aksu oasis. Two new *ming* begs received 15 *batman* of land each.[26] Since they did not have any prior *yanqi,* because these were their first appointments as beg officials, each of them received as *yanqi* five households, from "their older brother and inner people, relatives (clansmen)."

In this arrangement, the *yanqi* would cultivate the land granted to the beg to whom he was assigned, while maintaining his own farming operation. A Manchu language expression used by a beg client that referred to his *yanqi* as the "Muslim who cultivate[s] land for/to me" (Manchu: *minde usin tarire hoise*), supports this interpretation.[27] However, a *yanqi* did not suffer like a "serf" in this arrangement. There was no oasis Muslim born to that status. Any oasis farmer could be taken as a *yanqi* by the beg. In the arrangement of the above cases, the Qing even designated the begs' brothers and clansmen as *yanqi*s.

The most important benefit of this arrangement for begs constituted the tax-exempt status attached to the land grants. The begs did not pay tax on land they developed. Nor did the *yanqi*s who were mobilized in the development of wildland. They were exempted from the onerous burden of the payment of tax and corvée labor to the Qing administration. Therefore, the term reflected a privilege rather than a burden. This privileged status of the *yanqi* worked to the advantage of the begs. Since the beginning of Qing rule, many rich oasis

Muslims had enlisted into its service to secure the exemptions. Presumably, these rich *yanqi*s were able to develop the assigned wildland for the begs much better, using their own captial.[28]

Therefore, in a sense, the Qing land grant did not merely reflect a policy of appeasement toward the begs. It also formed a crucial part of the imperial government's deliberate scheme to develop local resources—in this case, government-controlled land that otherwise would remain unused.[29] From the beginning of Qing rule, Qing military governors showed serious interest in developing local agriculture in oasis. They had often proposed plans for irrigation and new farmland in the oasis from the beginning of the Qing conquest.[30] They also settled nomads (Dolan and Kirghiz) in wildlands within the oasis district and put it under cultivation.[31] Even if the increase of agricultural production did not lead to a corresponding increase in tax, the promotion of local agrarian production was nevertheless critical for securing an inexpensive and consistent supply base for the Qing military. After all, the Qing bought most of the military logistics sold in the local markets.

The Qing Empire also showed a keen, often blatant interest in the development of local mining resources. In fact, it unequivocally intended to exploit local resources to the maximum. Copper mining fell under its control. The Qing deployed the Muslim governors to conduct mining with forced Muslim laborers, and commandeered certain outputs annually as a part of its tax levy. It minted local copper coins, *pul,* out of the local production. In case of lead, the Qing contracted Chinese miners to develop the lead mines, and collected "tax silver" from the Chinese merchant developers. Its military governors even established guard posts (*karun*), staffed with Qing soldiers, along the major passes and roads leading into the mines, located in a mountain within Qarashar District, so that "the nation's (Manchu: *gurun* [Manchu nation]) tax is not to be neglected."[32]

Jade mining received special attention from the court. The Imperial Household Department, the agency that managed the Qing emperors' privy fund, monopolized the jade excavated from the two mining centers of Yarkand and Khotan. The department ordered that the entire volume of the stones, a huge amount, be sent to Beijing. In 1778, a high point in the jade tribute sent from Yarkand to the Qing, for instance, the amount equaled around 20 tons (31,000 *jin*).[33] This figure does not even include the jade tribute coming from Khotan, the larger center of the two. Once it arrived in Beijing, the Imperial Household would process the stone in the Imperial Handicraft Workshop for the emperor's consumption. However, the Imperial Household Department also made a substantial profit through the resale of second-hand jade pieces in the market.[34]

The Qing relied on the beg clients to handle the resource enterprises. This policy was set early in its rule in Central Asia. In spring 1760, a Qing commander proposed to do irrigation and land reclamation in the vicinity of the Yarkand and Aksu districts. He suggested to the court the idea of recruiting impoverished Muslims who could not support themselves to do the work. Seed could be lent for the reclamation and then collected back after the first harvest. Beijing approved this measure in principle. However, the court advised against the Qing local administration's getting directly involved in the land development, reasoning that it would become too costly. It also reasoned that any recruitment of poor people would also require food, and even the transportation of these supplies, in their behalf. The rulers instead suggested a charge that local people could make as a contribution on their own to conduct the land reclamation.[35] From the beginning of their rule, then, the Qing were set on relying upon the oasis network for capital and expertise to foster local resource development.

On their part, the begs also saw this partnership with the empire as desirable. As the commercial traffic grew in Eastern Turkestan, they realized the great need to produce more. Their partnership with the Qing came in handy, because the Qing emperor, as the ultimate sovereign of the oasis domain, maintained exclusive rights over the vast amount of undeveloped resources, all state properties by definition. By working for the Qing administration, the begs would have access to these holdings.

Therefore, in a most concrete sense, the beg-Qing alliance in Central Asia cemented the convergence of interests between the two in the rural hinterlands. Showing this mutual dependence most clearly was the policy of confiscating landed property. In the wake of its conquest, the Qing administration quickly identified "rebel properties," landholdings that had formerly belonged to the Kashgar *khwajas* and their associates, and turned them into government properties. Beg clients played a pivotal role in the transfer. Not only did they identify them in the first place, but the Qing administration also leased these properties to the governors to manage and develop.

For instance, in 1761, the Kashgar governor, Gadaimet, and his lieutenant governor (*ishikagha* beg), Abduriman, received 200 *batman* of "rebel properties," scattered across its rural subdistricts, such as Beshkerim, Faizabad, and

Üstün Artush. They set half of it to lie fallow, and put the other half under cultivation. They recruited three hundred Muslim households as well as one "wretched" (Manchu: *yadahūn*) Muslim to develop Beshkerim first. The begs provided twenty cattle purchased from their own funds to help the new settlers. At the same time, the begs also asked the Qing for a loan of 103 *batman* of seeds for the enterprise. After the first autumn harvest, the new rural settlement would pay half of the harvest as a tax every year.[36]

However, in developing the confiscated properties, the Kashgar governor and beg officials did not work solely for the Qing. They worked for their own benefit. In 1762 it was revealed that the governor had under-reported the inventory of the properties and had kept a substantial number of them; this had been done earlier in 1760, when the first inspections took place. That year he had reported thirteen fruit gardens (orchards), but, it turned out, had hidden twenty-nine of them from the count.[37] However, this exposure did not lead to any punishment. After scolding the governor mildly, the Qianlong court eventually decided nevertheless to distribute the orchards that the begs had hidden. Of the twenty-nine orchards, the Qing kept only two as government land and awarded nine outright to the beg as land grants: two went to Gadaimet; four to Abduriman (Ishikagha Beg), Taka (Kazanachi Beg), and Abul Asan and Mamademin (both of them Šang Begs); and three to Akima (a Kirghiz chief with the Qing title of Sula Amaban), Sultān Khwāja (the governor of Yangi Hissar), and Awan (a Kirghiz chief). The rest, eighteen in number, were rented out under the begs' management, as was usual. The parcels that did not have fruit or trees on the grounds but only grass and shrub were to be turned into ranches. The Qing even affixed their official seal on the begs' certificates of private ownership.

In other words, the Qing Empire in Xinjiang became developmentalist in orientation, to cover its financial need to support the Qing military and for the coffers of the Manchu court. However, because of its inability to directly develop the resources in the remote borderlands, the Qing administration utilized the begs, who had expertise and organizational capability, to run local agriculture, irrigation, and mining sites. That is to say, the developmentalist empire, which could not develop the resources on its own, used the Muslim governors and pro-Qing begs as codevelopers. The Qing provided the begs the legal right to develop the government resources, power to mobilize the oasis residents for such work in their name, political protection for such efforts, and occasional capital investment. The begs took advantage of the new empire's initiative to push for their own capitalist agendas.

The Rise of Mercantilist Beg Regime

The Muslim clients strategically shaped their native administration in each oasis to take advantage of this profitable nexus of empire-building in trade, both local and international, and agrarian production. A simple analysis of the spatial and institutional structures they devised illustrates that their system was decidedly city-centered, strategically located in the hubs where international, regional, and local trade mingled. That was where most of the official positions were located within the city. In contrast, the small towns contained only a rudimentary level of beg governmental administration. At this middle level of the hierarchy of beg administration, the only state functions that the Muslim clients assumed were tax collection (performed by *hākim* and *ming* begs) and the management of irrigation (performed by *mīrāb* begs). Further down, in village communities, the beg administration did not have any presence. These settlements were controlled by village headmen (*yüzbashi* and *mingbashi*), whose function was again defined as tax collection by order of the Qing regulation (see Table 2.3, above).

From the urban nodes figuring at the top of the geographical hierarchy within in the oasis districts, the Muslim clients engaged in three major sectors: revenue collection, managing and promoting merchant traffic, and the promotion of agrarian and mining production. For instance, the native administration in Kashgar under the Qing retained thirty-one posts. Among them, six beg positions (*kazanachi, shang* (Manchu *šang*), *ba-ji-ge-er, a-er-ba-bu, ming,* and *yu-zi*) specifically collected taxes from the oases and international traders. Four beg positions (*dugan, shi-lu-er, zhe-bo,* and *mi-er-zha-er*) mobilized supplies to the government offices and foreign envoys, an important part of revenue collection in the oases. Six beg positions (*nuo-ke-bu, ke-le-ke-ya-la-ke, se-yi-de-er, ba-zha-er, duo-bei,* and *da-lu-qian*) managed the market, trade, and international trader communities. Two beg positions (*yi-er-ha-qi* and *wei-tang*) opened and maintained the communication and transportation infrastructure, which had much to do with the trade flow. Three positions (*mīrāb, mi-tang-wa-li,* and *ba-ke-ma-ta-er*) handled agriculture, irrigation, and the trade of landed property. Three positions (*ha-shi, a-er-tun, and mi-si*) controlled and promoted the mining of gold, jade, and copper. This leaves only seven positions out of the total of thirty-one that were not specifically designated to revenue collection, trade, agriculture, and mining. Of course, among these seven positions, *hākim* and *ishikagha* were the final overseers of the three major sectors (see Table 2.4).

2.4. Muslim Begs of Kashgar and Their Duties: Comparison between the Zunghar and Qing Beg Systems

Zunghar Beg System	Duties	Qing Beg System	Duties
Hākim	Overseeing a city	1. Hākim	Overseeing affairs of a Muslim oasis
Ishikagha	Helping *hākim*'s duties	2. Ishikagha	Cohandling affairs of a Muslim oasis
		3. Khazanachi	Overseeing a tax [collection] of a place (*qianliang*)
Shang	Handling tax (*zhufu*)	4. Shang	Handling the collection of the tax of satellite cities and towns
Qādī	Handling punishment	5. Qādī	Handling punishment and handling of the rebels (those who flee and those who hide)
Mīrāb	Managing irrigation	6. Mīrāb	Handling adult labor, making a creek, irrigating farmland
Nuo-ke-bu	Managing (artisan and labors)	7. Mao-te-se-bu	Mediating (arbitrating) regulation, educating customs, and selecting [Muslim] script
Pa-cha-sha-bu	Catching thieves	8. Mi-tang-wa-li	Handling the sale of landed properties
Mao-te-se-bu	Handling religion (scripture and teaching)	9. Nuo-ke-bu	Handling construction and managing each guild (*hang*) of artisan (or artisan and labor)
Mu-te-gan-li	Managing farmland and houses	10. Ba-ji-ge-er	Collecting customs duties (*maoyi shuifu*)
Dugan	Managing motels and postal stations	11. Ke-le-ke-ya-la-ke	Watching over and managing outsider (*wailai*) traders and other various duties according to the direction of Governor Hākim*
Ba-ji-ge-er	Managing tax (*shuike*)	12. Dugan	Providing grain and horses to the envoys from foreign tribes, providing various supplies to the public offices
A-er-ba-bu	Mobilizing compulsory labor	13. Pa-cha-sha-bu	Managing prison
Shi-hun	Helping Dugan's duties	14. Zha-bu-ti-mo-ke-ta-bu	Managing education, managing administration of exams to educators, and administering exams to students
Ba-ke-mai-ta-er	Managing gardens and forest	15. A-er-ba-bu	Collection of overdue taxes and helping in the management of miscellaneous expenses
Ming Beg	Like "*qianzhong*"	16. Shi-hu-er	Helping with Dugan Beg's duties; being prepared to perform as acting Qādī, Pa-cha-sha-bu, A-er-ba-bu Beg
		17. Se-yi-de-er	Regulating the market, and mediating the guild's account book**
		18. Ba-zha-er	Supervising each guild (*hang*) of merchants

63

Zunghar Beg System	Duties	Qing Beg System	Duties
		19. Duo-bei	Managing weights and measures
		20. Da-lu-qian	Investigating the sojourners' thefts and watching over troublemaking
		21. Yi-er-ha-qi	Managing construction of a city, all roads, market, and the "opening of mountain and road"
		22. Zhe-bo	On behalf of Ka-la Dugan or Bang-la Duang, handling their duties
		23. Ming	Head of 1,000 people; handling his people's payment of tax
		24. Yu-zi	Behind the Ming Beg, handling duties, head of 100 people
		25. Ha-shi	Scouring jade
		26. A-er-tun	Scouring gold
		27. Wei-tang	Managing the Muslims who staffed Qing guardposts and postal stations
		28. Ba-ke-ma-ta-er	Watching over fruit gardens
		29. Mi-si	Managing the smelting of copper
		30. Ka-lu-er	Managing the Muslims who work in the guardpost "*kalun*"
		31. Mi-er-zha-er	Comanaging the duties of Dugan and Shi-hu-er Begs

Sources: (1) Beg system under Zunghar rule is based on Commander Zhaohui's report immediately after the conquest of Kashgar in 1759 (GZSL, vol. 593, QL24/7/gengwu); (2) Beg system under Qing rule is based on the description of Yonggui in HJZ. A few other Qing sources present the structure of the Beg system under Qing rule: *Xiyu Tongwen Zhi*; XYTZ; HJZL; and HJTZ. They provide a similar picture about it under the Qing, although slightly differing in their lists of beg officials and their job descriptions. For the difference among the works, see Saguchi Tōru, *Jūhachi-jūkyū-seiki Higashi Torukisutan shakaishi kenkyū*, pp. 109–10. The eight-volume version HJZ shows the most complete list of beg officials, encompassing thirty-one kinds of offices. Although published in the late nineteenth century, the materials included in the work reflected the situation of the earliest years of Qing rule during the 1760s and 1770s, when Yonggui worked in Muslim Xinjiang as resident general. In addition to the fact of his being an eyewitness to the earliest phase of Qing colonial rule, I also chose to utilize this list for my research because no scholarly work records this version. The above-mentioned Saguchi's list records the HJZ version of the beg list, but it was based on the latter's four-volume version, categorizing only twenty-seven kinds of beg officials.

*XYWJL provides an alternative job description, "levying commerce tax" (*shangshui*). *Xiyu Tongwen Zhi* provides another description: "managing tax collection from outer vassals." Outer vassals, in this case, in most likelihood means merchants from the outer vassals.

**The four-volume version of the HJZ provides an alternative explanation of the duty of the Se-yi-de-er Beg. It records it as "regulating market and mediating between peddlers." On the other hand, HJZL explains the job description of this beg as "regulating the market and managing peddlers."

In other words, the administration of the client regime was mercantilist, promoting and exploiting the local economy for the purpose of increasing revenues. And comparing the direction of their innovations under the Qing to the one under the Zunghar also confirms this observation. In the case of Kashgar District, the native administration system under the Qing represented significant growth from its Zunghar predecessor in terms of size. In Kashgar, under the latter, it held only sixteen beg posts. Notably, what induced the subsequent growth was exactly the rise of the beg positions in the three sectors. Most of the newly installed posts in the local beg administration were concerned with the maintenance of the market; maintenance of the merchant traffic through the city; management of foreign traders; development of the mining industry (gold, lead, and so forth) and cash cropping (fruit and the like); and finally, taxing the commercial wealth, all added after the Qing conquest.[38]

In addition, the native officials or functionaries exerted a presence in a few other strategic sectors outside of the urban centers, important for controlling and exploiting trade and mining. For instance, in Kashgar District, during the Qianlong Period (1736–95), twenty Muslims were deployed to military postal relay stations (*juntai*), located on major points of the transportation and communication route. Later during the Jiaqing Period (1796–1819), the Qing administration in Kashgar deployed fifteen Muslims in a saltpeter and sulphur mine; it deployed numbers of Muslims to work in frontier *karun*, presumably for the convenience of taxing transborder trade, and for taking care of floating bridges in the river that ran through the district (*chuanqiao*). It could be that the latter two categories of Muslims, who began to appear in the Qing record during the Jiaqing Period, had already worked in this capacity unofficially during the Qianlong Period, and the Jiaqing government institutionalized the practice. Needless to say, altogether, these three nodes—the urban centers of major oasis districts, important roads, and mining resources—constituted strategic locations for taxing, controlling, and promoting trade, both international and local, and mining.

Ūdui, the Imperial Revenue Contractor

Throughout his roughly twenty-year career as governor of Yarkand (1760–78), Ūdui ably took advantage of commercial and political connections to the Qing Empire to build a thriving commercial enterprise in the oasis. We would not have any detailed record of his involvement in the economic activities prevalent during his tenure as the Yarkand Hākim were it not for a major corruption scandal that broke out in 1778. In this case, billed as the biggest corruption exposé during the Qianlong Period if not the entire Qing era, the Manchu military governor of Yarkand District, Gao Pu, was accused of embezzling the profit derived from the jade mining operation in Yarkand, rightfully belonging to the Imperial Household Department. The investigation revealed Ūdui's heavy involvement. As a result of his participation, he was posthumously deprived of his imperial aristocrat rank ("*beile* rank"), which had been awarded by the Qianlong emperor. However, fortunately for us, the detailed investigation resulting from the case preserved information about the scope of Ūdui's economic activities, in which jade smuggling featured as only one part.[39]

Among the most important of his economic activities was his role as revenue contractor for the Qing. As governor, Ūdui performed the duties of chief tax farmer, government contractor, and developer of government-controlled resources, all in one. He delivered regular and irregular revenue levies on demand in response to the Qing military governor. For instance, in 1777, to fulfill a request for supplies to the local Qing administration, Ūdui collected 5,326 *tangga* of *pul* from oasis Muslims. Under his direction, the "begs and headmen" (Manchu: *data;* Chinese: *toumu*) of each city district and rural village personally collected the cash according to the level of wealth of the residents.[40] In addition, a certain Guo-pu-er, a sixth-rank Shi-hu-le beg of Yarkand District, collected money from the oasis residents to purchase firewood and grass for the Qing administration every month, in most likelihood under the direction of the governor.[41]

However, Ūdui was not merely the tax collector—an official who collected taxes from oasis households according to the rate set in Qing regulations—that the Qing record painted him to be. In the mid-nineteenth century, reform-minded Qing military governors called the begs' practice *baolan* (payment in a lump sum on behalf of others), and often condemned it as a "corruption" in their communications with Beijing. However, in practice, both the Muslim governors and the Qing military governors must have seen the collection as a set of de facto contractual relations, a mutually agreed upon list of the amount of goods that the Muslim governors regularly had to deliver to the Qing camp. This list included cash, grains, fodder, fruit, as well as firewood.[42]

Needless to say, their work as tax farmers provided the begs huge opportunities for enrichment. Another nineteenth-century Manchu official reported that a major beg post usually cost several thousand *yuanbao* in silver. The begs "thus appointed" utilized "the expense of the big and small *yamen* [administrative office] [as an excuse] to exploit the oasis Muslims." It was the governor and the Manchu clerk of the Office of the Seal and the Bureau of Muslim Affairs that benefited most from selling beg positions: they profited tenfold, while the military governors' cut was 2/10 or 3/10 of the entire amount. The reformer summarized: "The begs spend to the higher ups, and exploit from the low. . . . Gradually they all became big rich."[43]

In the meantime, as developer of government-controlled resources, Ūdui oversaw jade mining in Mount Mi-er-tai in Yarkand District to fulfill the obligation of tribute payment. For most of his tenure, Mount Mi-er-tai produced around 20 tons (31,000 *jin*) of jadestones annually. In 1777 he dispatched thirty-two hundred Muslims on government duty to the operation; among them, two hundred Muslims were tasked to divert some of the jade to Ūdui and Gao Pu, and other involved begs and Manchu officers.[44]

This domination over the jade resources of the oasis opened the way for Ūdui's domination of long-distance trade with China, arguably the most lucrative sector of commerce for the oases. Although the Qing government held the monopoly right over the entire excavation of jadestones mined in Yarkand, Ūdui, for twenty years until he died in 1778, operated a large-scale jade smuggling operation that diverted the precious commodity mined in Yarkand to the center of the jade processing industry in the affluent Lower Yangzi Delta area (*jiangnan*), in collusion with fellow begs, adventurous Chinese merchants, as well as the Manchu military governor of Yarkand, Gao Pu. The total scale of the illegal jade mining and trade operation was enormous. According to the Qing administration's investigation, for instance, the output of jade smuggled from Yarkand in 1778 was roughly 50 tons (76,000 *jin*); in the same year, the amount of tribute jade sent to the Imperial Household Workshop in Beijing was 20 tons (31,000 *jin*).[45]

The profit he gained was invested in the development of local agriculture and ranching in the rural oasis hinterland. These enterprises included livestock ranching, cereal farming, and fruit farming The properties confiscated from Ūdui's family after the investigation included two orchards; two plots of farmland (50 *batman* and 200 *tahar* each),[46] scattered in urban, suburban, and rural locations; one watermill; and livestock. The original number of the livestock could not be known, the Qing investigator noted, because Ūdui's wife moved the entire herd to her own land in Kashgar when the governor was implicated in the corruption charges (see Table 2.5).

All in all, Ūdui's economic portfolio included four major components—revenue farming, jade trade, ranching, and farming. Each sector functioned distinctively in his portfolio. The jade trade provided the biggest profit; ranching (livestock raising) and fruit and cereal farming gave him the most stable income. The latter sectors entailed local and regional trade, and the income de-

Table 2.5. Economic Portfolio of Oasis Begs

	Ūdui	Alima	Osman (Aksu Beg; Participant in the Jahangir War) (1828)	'Abd al-Rahīm (Ishikagha Beg of Kashgar District) (1764)	Suranchi (Kirghiz Chieftain)
1. House	1 (U)	1 (111 *jian*)	1 (440 *jian*)		1 (15 *jian*; S)
2. Fruit garden (orchard)	2 (R)	5 (U; R)	57		1 (government garden)
3. Farmland	50 *batman* (S)	Undisclosed	81 plots	20 *batman* 4 *galbir,* and 3 *charak*	6 *charak*
4. Building	1 (28 *jian*) (R)				
5. Watermill	1 (R)	1 (U; R)			
6. Tree	747 (R)				
7. Livestock	horse, camel, cows, lambs	348 horses, 132 cows, and 2,369 lambs			
8. Luxury goods	Pearl ornaments, blue jade small knife, white jade ornaments, etc.				
9. Cash	570 *liang* of silver (500 *liang* in silver; 70 *liang* in *pul*)				7 *chuan* 5,000 *wen* of *pul* (annual payment)
	Animal skins; Cloth made of satin				
10. Slaves		34 Bolor Galcha, including male and female			
Size/worth of property	325 *liang* 5 *qian* (silver) (Sale price of his farmland, building, and textile goods)			64 batman (amount of annual harvest)	

Sources: GPYSA, p. 846, doc. 370, QL43/12/20; HJFL, vol. 61, DG8/3/wuchen; Kun'gang, ed. *Qinding Da Qing Huidian Shili (Guangxu Chao),* vol. 163; XZSL, vol. 16, DG1/7.
   Note: U = urban; S = suburban; R = rural locations.

rived from them was less prone to fluctuating violently, unlike the long-distance trade. In the end, however, it was Ūdui's role as a revenue farmer that anchored his entire commercial enterprise. Particularly, his duty to purchase government logistics for the Qing wielded him the power to manipulate the local market. As a producer himself, he could set himself up as the preferred party to fulfill these requisition requests, better than any other landlord and merchant in the oasis. Indeed, widespread criticism was levied against the Muslim governors' practice of allowing themselves to trade grain (the grain produced by their own farms) in the local market first, before any other local producers.[47]

However, more important, revenue farming provided direct access to government resources, the jade mines particularly. The stone was designated as an exclusive tribute item, under Qing monopoly, and its full output in Yarkand was ordered to be sent to Beijing under guard. As the official government revenue contractor, Ūdui had singular permission to directly engage with the mines, to the exclusion of any other potential competitor in the oasis. In addition, his position as an imperial agent required him to mobilize and supply oasis workers to do the arduous extraction operations in place, in the name of the Qing. Thus, under the cover of invoking the authority of the emperor, Ūdui could pull in necessary quantities of oasis people from the rural villages to the mines as he saw fit, which he could not have done as easily otherwise.

The governor must have been mindful of the prospects this advantage could render to his personal fortunes. In fact, he was the one who had brought the existence of the local jade mine resources in Yarkand to the attention of the Qing in the first place. Originally, Khotan alone, among the Muslim oases, was designated to present jade as tribute. In 1760 Ūdui led local begs from Yarkand into the venture of mining jade from a mountain within Yarkand District and then presenting it to the imperial court. Subsequently, the latter approved the endeavor. From then on, he led thousands of local Muslims to mine the jade from the mountain twice a year in spring and fall expeditions.[48]

Ūdui's economic enterprise shows how the formation of a highly commercialized composite economy—mining, ranching, agriculture, trade, and revenue farming—interplayed with the pivotal role maintained by the Qing Empire in the oasis. The latter provided him handsome investment opportunities, power to manipulate the local market, connection to the China market, and, most important, access to untapped resources under Qing control. However, perhaps this aspect of Ūdui's portfolio unduly highlights the imperial side of the business conducted by the beg clients. After all, only Yarkand and Khotan had jade mines. Yet, overall, more wealth was still to be gained from other enterprise occurring in a broad sweep across the oasis region—in ranching and farming for the local market, which constituted a main staple of the begs' economy.

The private fortune amassed by Alima, governor of Yangi Hissar in the late eighteenth century, illustrates this point well. In a survey of properties confiscated from him in 1785, three major items (see Table 2.5) were cited.[49] The first, landed properties, included a house or shop, about the size of 111 *jian* (Manchu: *giyalan*); a watermill; and five "fruit gardens," scattered in six places, the central city of Kashgar and five rural villages (Sirama, Harhan, Hesen Bui, Yostu, and Artush). The second item was livestock, which included 348 horses, 132 cows, and 2,369 lambs. Alima also had an undisclosed amount of land, whose use was unspecified. In addition, he held thirty-four "Bolor Galcha," including both male and female. The Galcha constituted a branch of the Tajik people living in the mountainous area of eastern Central Asia, in vicinities close to Bukhara and Badakhshan.

Alima's portfolio reveals the predominance of investments he made in the local sectors of commercial and the rental business, livestock raising, cereal and fruit farming, and possibly cotton farming and weaving, scattered all over the oasis district of Kashgar. At the same time, the existence of the Bolor Galcha hints at the *capitalistic* nature of his agricultural endeavors—namely, production based on the employment of hired hands. In Central Asia, the Galcha usually worked in the oasis as hired ranchers, raising livestock.[50] In the case of eighteenth-century Eastern Turkestan, however, they were also trafficked commercially as slaves. Oasis merchants and the mountain Taijik rulers actively engaged in the Galcha slave trade.

In 1795, for instance, five Muslim merchants (Manchu: *hūdai hoise*) from Yangi Hissar, including a certain Abdurman, and four other Muslim merchants reportedly traveled to Sik-nan, a small Tajik polity in Pamir, and bought twenty Galcha (Manchu: *Galca*) from the ruler there, "Sultan Yaladin." However, on the way, four Galchas killed four of the merchants. Upon receiving the news, the sultan soon captured the four murderers. But he nevertheless tried to sell the rest of the Galchas (sixteen people) who were not directly involved in the murder to other merchants. However, the sixteen Galcha managed to escape. Fearful of Qing administration punishment, the sultan selected sixteen people from among his own tax-paying subjects (Manchu: *albantu*) and sent them, along with the four criminals, to Kashgar.[51]

Slaves were not the only employed labor available for ranching in the oasis. Farmers also hired out as wage laborers to work in the commercial farms and ranches. Certain documents relate many cases of homicide involving these people. In 1849, a seventeen-year-old Muslim boy, Qurbanmät, who was hired by a Chinese merchant to tend sheep, was murdered. The killer was a certain Iliyas, who was also hired by the same man.[52] Jade smugglers also hired Muslim wage laborers (*yonggong huizi*) to transport jade between the oases.[53] In 1784, a married Muslim woman living in an oasis village of Yarkand District accidently killed her younger brother who was heckling her. The brother had done so after she stopped helping him financially, when he had refused to work any longer as a *yonggong*.[54]

The increase of these wage laborers and their mobility worried the military governors of the oases, prompting the Qing local administration in 1827 to issue travel permissions ("road tickets") to travelers, including laborers, traders, as well as those Muslims who traveled to fulfill the work of forced labor for the government. If any trader or laborer did not come back immediately as anticipated, the Muslim governors of the districts would follow up in their reports the specific details of the completion of their travel journey at the end of the year collectively; the *hākim* were also ordered to inquire at the original place of registration of such laborers, to assess whether they were resisting the duty of forced labor and tax payment.[55]

In addition, impoverished Kirghiz tribesmen also went into the oasis as hired hands for the begs.[56] And substantial numbers of Andijan laborers worked on oasis farms. In fact, contrary to the impression offered by previous scholarship that the latter group lived as wealthy merchants in the oasis, large portions of them were farmers or laborers. Ūdui reported, in 1764, that Khotan's six towns had eighty-five "Andijan" sojourners. Among them, twenty-nine had been sent to Ili agrarian colonies to farm in previous years. The majority of them were not merchants but farmers and weavers.[57]

If the development explored above indicates an emergence of labor resources in the oasis markets, a crucial condition necessary for the emergence of its *capitalistic* agriculture, the region also witnessed the rise of a vibrant private land market, another important factor. After the Qing conquest, the begs and non-beg oasis Muslims actively expanded their private landholdings. These buy and sell transactions were certified by the local religious courts. One of the first of these documents records a certain Mīr A-di-li Sufi's sale of 50 *mu* of land and 10 *jian* house/building to 'Yakūb Bay in 1771 (see Appendix D-1, case no. 1). Given the fact that the currently published collection of these contract documents was not an exhaustive holding of all the oasis contract documents, we can draw only a limited conclusion from this observation.[58] While we cannot conclude that the private land market in the oasis emerged in the late eighteenth century for the first time, we may conclude, at the very least, that the private land market became more active after the late eighteenth and early nineteenth century. While we have some contract documents about land transactions dated even prior to the eighteenth century, they were all records of the khans' grants of land either to an individual or to a religious institution as a *waqf*.[59] Therefore, the appearance of the private land transaction documents in the collection since that time testifies at the very least to the increasing vitality of the private land market during the Qing rule.

The begs were big buyers in that market. In 1807, for instance, one individual purchased 16 *batman* of land from the family of Na-si-er-khwaja, 8 *batman* on each side of the Shao-er-xian-du-ke ditch; as well as a house of 28 *jian*; and garden, paying 16 *yuanbao* silver in price (see Appendix D-1, case no. 2).[60] He was none other than Emin Khwāja's grandson, Yūnus Wang Beg, who served as the governor of Kashgar (1812–15). In fact, the scale of his land purchase was the largest transaction recorded during the Qing rule, as far as the available documents are concerned.

In addition, Yūnus Wang also established a *madrasa*, dedicated to the family's supposed ancestor Muhammad Sharīf, sometime during his governorship, and accumulated land through this venue. In 1820, for instance, Yi-si-feng-de-ya-er Bay donated 1/2 *batman* of land located in a subdistrict called A-la-xia-er as *waqf* to this *madrasa* (see Appendix D-2, case no. 5). Later, Emin Khwāja's family collectively appointed one of its members as manager of the donated endowment. Its income seems to have been so substantial that serious fighting occurred among the involved *madrasa* functionaries and teachers over its distribution.[61]

The expansion of private landholdings was not a phenomenon limited to begs. Non-beg landlords also made private land purchases. Indeed, most of the private land transactions in the oasis in the eighteenth and nineteenth centuries were small-scale, including those by these latter individuals. Many religious leaders of the oasis—*mullās, akhūnds, khalīfas,* as well as people with Sufi and *khwaja* in their names—acted as major buyers and sellers of land (see Appendix D-1, cases 1, 3, 4, 5, 6, 9, 10, 11, 12, 13, 14, 15, 20, 22, 23, 24, 26, 27, 30, 31, 33, 34, 35, 36, 38, 39, 42, 43). Also, many ordinary oasis men and women participated in the land market. Simply called *bays* ("rich men"),[62] these individuals were simply rich landlords without religious and political distinctions, although *bays* were often identified as sons or fathers of *mullās* and *akhūnd*s. In addition, foreigners from Khoqand and Andijan in Fergana Valley also participated in the land market. Technically, the merchants were sojourners, and thus not lawful residents and eligible to buy land in the oasis, according to Qing legal precepts.[63] However, they did so anyway, but in relatively small parcels. Most of the private land sales were smaller than 1 *batman* and mostly measured in the scale of *charak* (one *charak* of land is 1/64 of 1 *batman,* roughly equivalent to 1 *mu*). These sizes were minuscule in contrast to Yūnus Wang's land purchase, at 16 *batman.* They were even smaller than the land grants that the begs received from the Qing government, which ranged from 50 to 200 *batman* during the Qianlong Period and from 10 to 150 *batman* during the Jiaqing Period.

Furthermore, capital, critically necessary for the development of large-scale commercial farms, was also available in the oasis. What is notable in this regard was the growing indebtedness of begs to Chinese merchants in the late eighteenth and nineteenth centuries.[64] As noted previously above, Ūdui borrowed 7,000 *liang* of silver that he never repaid from Zhang Luan, a leading Chinese merchant partner.[65] In most likelihood, this availability of Chinese credit helped the begs to expand their agricultural enterprise further. The late eighteenth and early nineteenth centuries in the oasis were remarkable in terms of the rapid expansion of irrigation facilities and their effectiveness, a key factor that improved agrarian productivity. During this period, irrigation facilities extended across the board in the entire area of Eastern Turkestan during the Qing rule. In places like Yarkand, canal and other irrigation facilities grew exponentially, thus contributing to the constant increase of arable land at the fringe of the oasis system.[66] In part, the begs funded this development out of their own pockets. However, loans provided by Chinese merchants also helped them to do so. Hori Sunao persuasively shows how key the Chinese investment was in the radical development of irrigation in Turfan and how its new irrigation facilities *(kariz)* made possible the unprecedented expansion of cotton farming in the area.[67] There is no reason to suspect that places like Yarkand were any exception to this investment.

All evidence points then to a rapid rise of capitalistic agriculture in the oasis, a commercialized operation conducted by the begs, for profit making in the context of the reinvigorated trade that ensued during the post-Qing conquest period. This development must have applied constant pressure on them to further their domination over the resources in the countryside. While the trade boom intensified, the begs had to develop their agrarian operations to meet market demand. In order to do so, they were compelled to expand their domination over the land, water, and finally labor. At this juncture, their political connections with the Qing ruler came in handy.

The Beg Development of the Wildlands and Rural Hinterlands

In 1790, the Muslim governor of Ush, Toktonidza, petitioned the Qianlong emperor to award him his father's "tomb" compounds and the land surrounding it in Toksun and Qara Khwaja. During the Zunghar rule, according to him, his family had held rights not only to the *mazār* but also to the houses and land attached to it. However, after the Zunghar moved the family to the Bai area in Aksu District, and scattered their entire "household" there, the family left their properties in the two tomb compounds abandoned.[68]

Toktonidza enumerated two purposes in his request. The first was to secure a permanent income from the land in order to make the ancestral offering in the *mazār*, as was to be properly expected. The second purpose was to secure a permanent source of income for his descendants. If the Qing were to award the land surrounding the *mazār*, which had also been originally theirs, they could secure permanent income from that land to pay for the cost of "chanting scripture" in the tomb. At the same time, the land would also provide an income with which "[their] descendants [will] manage to get by, and nourish themselves." After ordering the Qing military governor in the region to go to the location in person to investigate whether the award would cause any harm to the nearby village community, the Qianlong emperor decided to grant the petition, giving to Toktonidza 5 *tahar* of "idle" land in Toksun and 4 *tahar* in Qara Khwaja.

The Qing authority termed this kind of uncultivated land located at the center of the oasis district in close proximity to towns and villages, interspersed with their farmland, "government wildland" (*guan huangdi*). It may have once been cultivated but was now deserted and put under the government's control. The Qing administration used this term in order to distinguish it from "new wildland" (*xin huangdi*), the land bordering on the desert, situated far away from irrigation networks concentrated at the center of the oasis district, and never utilized by anyone. For the land-hungry beg developers, the *guan huangdi* parcels were the most attractive pieces of real estate by which they could extend their commercial farming and ranching endeavors. It lay in close vicinity to the oasis urban centers, where the demand for local agrarian products such as grain, meat, fur, and animal hides could be conveniently supplied. For the beg developers who had the ability to mobilize labor forces and capital to conduct irrigation and land development, *guan huangdi* was the best option.

However, there was one problem. By customary right, the rural village community actually controlled it as common land, even though all land may have belonged to the Qing sovereign, in theory. According to another contract precedent dated in 1817, a couple of brothers had to seek and then receive the village community's approval for taking over their father's position as *shaykh* of a *mazār* located on the village outskirts, after he had passed away (see Appendix D-2, case no. 4). As the case documents, at issue was whether the village community could give consent to the brothers' request. The religious endowment of the *mazār* was originally *guan huangdi* located in the vicinity of the village but rarely visited. However, the brothers' father had reclaimed it with his own labor, donated it to the *mazār*, and then become its *shaykh*. The fact that the brothers still had to seek the village's approval to continue the arrangement shows well how the community held customary rights over this kind of wildland as common property.[69] Generally then, if the begs wanted to expand their private land holdings by also reclaiming *guan huangdi*, they too would need to deal with the village community's claim over it—that is, if they could not co-opt the village elders in the first place.

In Toktonidza's request, we could thus interpret his petition to the imperial court as a scheme to bring in the Qing emperor to override village authority in this matter. Indeed, the conditions surrounding his request confirm this suspicion. What is important to note in the exchange is that the Qing administration did not have prior awareness of the existence of this land until the governor brought it to their attention, in the same way that the Qing local administration had little knowledge about Yarkand's mountain jade, until Ūdui mentioned it.

In other words, both cases show that the begs might intentionally involve the Qing authority to deliberately bypass both the authority of the village community and the religious establishment to secure rights to *guan huangdi*. It may well have been the truth that the governor's *mazār* in question was the abandoned property of his family, as Toktonidza argued. However, it was also possible that the wildland claimed was not originally theirs, if one reads his petition cynically.

Other instances arose when the begs made similar efforts to appropriate the common resources, under the strategy of using Qing authority. One Manchu military governor advised the imperial court that there was in fact precedent for this kind of case. Previously, the *hākim* of Oseolo Bugar, Mamadabula, and the *hākim* of Bi Hofon, Alahuli, made petition to the Qianlong emperor and also gained the right over the supposed "tomb compounds" of their fathers, as well as the land surrounding it.

Toktonidza's petition in 1790 was part of a broader beg movement underway to undertake cultivation of wildland in the late eighteenth and early nineteenth centuries. Qing records report several large-scale projects in Yangi Hissar, Yarkand, Khotan, and Kucha from the 1760s to 1820s. The size of each varied, ranging from 20,000 *mu* to 120,000 *mu*. A general pattern emerges from an examination of the primary sources. Once the begs obtained the right to develop the wildland from the Qing government, either as an outright land grant (like Toktonidza) or as a government patent, they recruited people and developed irrigation (see Table 2.6).

The best example of this was the land development of 20,640 *mu* (approximately 323 *batman*) in Yangi Hissar in 1767.[70] The beg developer in this case was Sultān Khwāja, a former Andijan, probably a merchant, who became the governor of Yangi Hissar District right after the Qing conquest. In 1767, he developed a waterway to pull the water of Yarkand River into the area of development. Reportedly, he donated a section of this land, or a certain amount of its harvest, as *waqf* to a *mazār*. The composition of the donated agrarian product shows that Sultān Khwāja conducted a highly commercialized agriculture there. He donated 9 *batman* of grain, three *glabir* of cotton, and alfalfa.[71]

Land development in neighboring Khotan also proceeded similarly. In 1799, the governor of Yarkand, Akbeg, hired seven hundred Muslim laborers (Manchu: *beyei hūsun i hoise*, "Muslim [living] with body's power") who "dug out the river and led the water to go through."[72] We do not know the progress of how the irrigation development led to the expansion of arable land in detail. However, the next governor of Yarkand, Muhammad Hasan (Ūdui's grandson), developed 1,290 *qing* (129,000 *mu*) of land in the district in 1815.[73] Plausibly, the irrigation river channel in 1799 began the large-scale land development project that was completed in 1815.

Muslims sometimes became much more proactive, and even hijacked the land development initiated by the Qing administration. There were 6,000 *mu* (Manchu: *imari*) of wildland located just outside the eastern gate of the city of Khotan in 1799. This land was originally taxable but was left uncultivated at that

Table 2.6. Land Reclamation in the Oasis, 1760s–1820s

Year	Place	Source of Labor	Size (mu)	Size (batman)	Tax Rate (shi; per year; per household)	Additional Explanation
1760	Barchuk	Muslims				
1760	Hang-e-li-ke (Aksu)	Poor Muslims				
1760	Beshkerim (Kashgar)	300 poor Muslims		2,400		500 *li* from Kashgar city; Difficulty to get water; established posts (*mīrāb, ming,* and *qādī*)
1765	Yangi Hissar	Kirghiz				
1766	Ush	Muslim; 600 households	47,400	740	3	79 *mu* were given to each household on the settlement; Provision of animals, tools, seeds
1767	Yangi Hissar	Poor Muslims	20,640	323		Establishing beg posts
1815	Yarkand		129,000	2,015		Done by Yarkand Hākim, Muhammad Hasan
1800	Khotan	752 households of landless Muslims				
1821	Bie-shi-tuo-gu-la-ke (Kucha)		53,000	828		Ishikagha, A-bu-du-la, and other begs managed the process of work; the Qing awarded fourth rank to Ishikagha, A-bu-la; fifth rank *shang* Beg, Si-di-ke; sixth rank Qādī, Ai-mo-te; seventh rank *mīrāb,* Tuo-hu-ta; sixth rank empty button, A-ke-bo-ke; each, one large bolt of satin
1821	Khan Ariq (Kashgar)	Rich Muslims		150		

Sources: GZSL, vol. 610, QL25/4/yichou, Edict; ibid., vol. 625, QL25/11/xinyou; ibid., vol. 798, QL31/11/bingshu, Edict; MW, vol. 54, p. 369; RZSL, vol. 71, JQ5/7/xinsi; ibid., vol. 311, JQ20/10/renzi, Yulian's memorial; XZSL, vol. 11, JQ25/12/yisi, Edict to Grand Secretariat; HJFL, p. 3688; ibid., vol. 3; ibid., vol.15, DG1/3/jisi, Qingxiang's memorial.

time.[74] The Qing administration decided to develop the parcel into a rice paddy, and to use Chinese convict labor to implement the task. A pilot cultivation was done in 57 *mu* and tested successfully. Hearing of those results, a group of Muslims approached the Qing administration to propose to develop an even larger rice paddy there, 4,200 *mu* altogether. The Qing administration allowed them to do so. The records do not name these Muslim developers. However, given the substantial capital outlay needed for the investment, they must have included the begs. Then, the Qing administration decided to involve other "large and small" begs in this project, in order to develop the rest of the land (1,800 *mu*) into rice paddy.[75]

Land development by the begs did not elicit peace in the oasis. Instead, irreconcilable tensions arose, particularly within an urban-rural divide. The essence of this tension erupted around the competition for the control of water, arguably the most vital factor underlying agrarian production in Eastern Turkestan, given its arid ecological conditions.

An interesting homicide occurred in the late eighteenth century, and its report provides an excellent entry point into understanding the dynamics accompanying the beg-initiated rural development. In 1788, a Kucha Muslim, Duo-la-te, a twenty-eight-year-old, was captured on the charge of killing a neighbor Muslim, A-er-zu-ke.[76] In the ensuing investigation, Duo-la-te admitted his guilt and explained his reason, a dispute over water distribution. According to Duo-la-te's deposition, the village had a public irrigation facility, a "big ditch" running in front of the settlement, from which the households of the village drew water in rotation. On the night he murdered A-er-zu-ke, Duo-la-te was supposed to draw water from the big ditch to water his family's land. However, he later found out that A-er-zu-ke had stolen it out of turn to water Beg Yi-si-la-mu's land. In the fight that ensued, enraged by a brazen response given by A-er-zu-ke, Duo-la-te killed him.

A-er-zu-ke was a *yanqi*, belonging to a beg, a certain Beg Yi-si-la-mu. The main issue driving the contention between a young villager, on the one hand, and a beg and his *yanqi*, on the other, was the use of water. The beg clients' unofficial, but undeniable, power to use water, whenever they wanted, greatly distressed the village communities. Sometimes the tension of the village did not merely result in a deadly fight between individuals but would often trigger the destruction or relocation of an entire rural settlement.

The *Xinjiang Shilue*, an early-nineteenth-century Qing publication (1821), mentions an interesting record in this regard about an underground river in Kashgar District: "This water enters into Ulan Usu (Wu-lan-wu-su) River; recently, because irrigation was built to water Muslim villages' farmland, there is no remaining water (in the river) to enter into the big river. This river just reaches the Yue-pu-er-hu village and stops."[77] The passage clearly shows the impact the begs' initiative to build man-made irrigation facilities had on the local distribution of water resources. The new irrigation developed by them would help agriculture in one place but harm it elsewhere. New rural settlements popped up in the sites of new constructions of canals and ditches; however, downstream the amount of water available to rural settlements would be reduced, resulting in their destruction, displacement, or relocation.

The Qing administration was well aware of this dynamic. Its court and military governors warned the begs not to develop irrigation upstream if it caused disruption to farming downstream; they warned: "If the big and small begs farm the land, and monopolize the irrigation, they will be accused, immediately investigated, and punished!"[78] However, it is doubtful whether the Qing could realistically take any serious measure against such actions; the Qing record does not contain any case of serious punishment of begs for their irrigation developments. Indeed, punishing these ventures would be detrimental to the Qing's overall goal to encourage land development by the begs.

In no small part, irrigation contributed to the reorganization of the geography of the rural settlements in the oasis in the late eighteenth and early nineteenth centuries. From the 1770s to 1810s, their numbers decreased from forty to thirty-six in Yarkand District. During the same period, twenty-eight of them disappeared, and nineteen new ones appeared. Also, the population of each village settlement fluctuated erratically during this period, even when the overall figures for the district generally reflected growth—for example, from around 14,738 in the 1770s to 61,444 in the 1850s. While the village of Posgam grew from 1,626 in the 1770s to 4,873 in the 1850s, Huo-mu-shi-gan, a big rural settlement that once boasted 2,513, disappeared altogether in the same time period. In the meantime, many rural settlements relocated (Appendix E-1). While most of them concentrated in the western part of the oasis district in 1776, villages mostly occupied the southern part in the 1810s. However, after that time, the numbers stabilized. Most of the settlements appearing then continued to exist until the 1850s (see Figure 2.1).[79]

Yarkand was not the only oasis district displaying this phenomenon. Indeed, all oasis districts experienced similar turnover. In Aksu, where we do not have population data per se but only information on the rural village settlements themselves, records show the latter's numbers decreased from thirty-eight to seventeen from the 1770s to 1821, while the population overall most likely had increased during the period. The majority of the rural settlements that spanned this time had disappeared in the latter years. Only seven rural settlements appearing in the 1770s continued to exist in 1821, about 19.4 percent of the prior total of rural settlements in the 1770s. The rural settlements also changed lo-

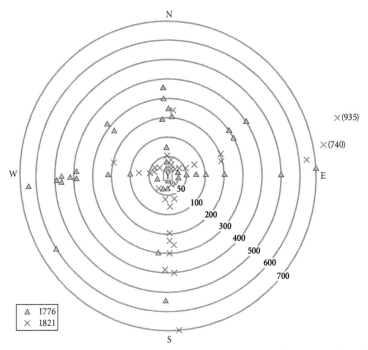

Fig. 2.1. Yarkand: Rural Villages, 1776 and 1821. Source: XYTZ, vol. 14–19; XJShL, vol. 3.

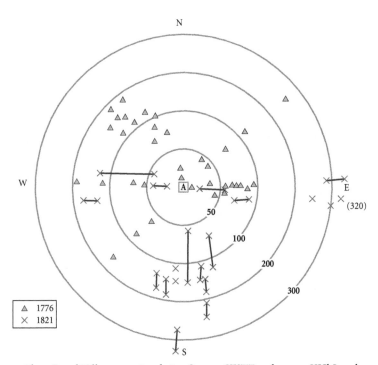

Fig. 2.2. Aksu: Rural Villages, 1776 and 1821. Source: XYTZ, vol. 14–19; XJShL, vol. 3.

cations: in 1776, more of them were located in the northwestern part of the district; in 1821, the southern part had emerged as a new concentration center (see Figure 2.2).

On the other hand, the number of rural settlements in Kucha District increased dramatically from 15 in 1776 to 98 in 1821. During this time, thirteen settlements disappeared and ninety-six settlements newly appeared (see Table 2.7).[80]

The impetus behind the extreme turnover of the oasis rural settlements reflected, in large part, both the lure and menace of the beg land development relating to its impact in the oasis. The rise in new rural settlements, composed primarily of new settlers the begs had brought in from within the oasis districts or mountains (as well as defectors from other villages), proceeded apace with the development of the wildland and the actual disintegration of the old rural settlements.

In the wake of this tumult fell large numbers of "poor or wretched Muslims" (Manchu: *yadahūn hoise*). Their mention frequently appeared in the Qing record in the late eighteenth and early nineteenth centuries, and the terms were used interchangeably with others—for example, "unemployed/property-less Muslims" (Chinese: *wuye huizi*; Manchu: *sula hoise*) or Muslims "who had the tax obligation but did not have land."[81] The last expression describes their plight most concretely. They may have had land originally but lost possession as a result of desolation caused by the lack of water. In other words, these Muslims were the very people who were hurt the most by the beg land development.

Table 2.7. Overview: Oasis Rural Settlements, 1776–1821

District	1776	1821	Net Gain/ Loss	Disappearing Settlements	Added Settlements	Constant Settlements	Settlements Changing Location
Aksu	38	21	−17	32	14	7	7
Sayram	11	9	−2	7	5	3	0
Bai	22	18	−4	19	15	3	3
Kucha	15	98	83	13	96	1	0
Shayar	10	33	23	7	29	5	3
Ush	23	0	−23	23	0	0	0
Yarkand	40	36	−4	28	19	13	11
Kashgar	20	25	5	4	9	16	15
Khotan	29	19	−10	25	15	4	3

Sources: XYTZ, vols. 14–19; XJShL, vol. 3.

Not unexpectedly, such impact incurred serious resistance from the rural oasis communities. In addition to the dynamic of the irrigation politics elucidated above, beg development also removed village community control over another valuable common resource, pasture for their livestock. This reuse also disrupted the small-scale livestock raising so essential to the livelihoods and economy of the dismayed villagers.

For the development, the begs also extracted additional manpower from the villages by taking village members into service as their illegal *yanqi*. As a basic administrative unit, the village community had to deliver a fixed amount of tax to the *hākim* of its district no matter what the fluctuation in its population numbers. Because the *yanqi* received a tax exemption by definition, one more oasis farmer turning *yanqi* meant one less taxpaying member for the village. More burden would thus fall on the remaining members of the community to meet that tax quota. This change wreaked havoc, driving the rural villages into serious financial distress, and increased the uneven distribution of wealth.

In the late eighteenth century, the villagers tried to fight back. They brought their cases to the Qing authority articulating their discontent over the begs' increasing land encroachments in the vague hope that the Qing emperor living far away in Beijing would be impartial and intervene with justice in their behalf against the beg developers. They would soon be hugely disappointed.

Oasis Capitalism, Challenged and Upheld

In 1786, the military governor of Yangi Hissar reported to his superior in Kashgar a piece of rather disturbing news.[82] Two recent Muslim governors of Kashgar District, Gadaimet and Osman, who were in office at the time of the accusation, had illegally occupied 560 *batman* of land and forced 176 households into work there as his *yanqi*, again illegally. The numbers exceeded by seven times the Qing quota of twenty-five households of *yanqi* allowed and eight times more than the Qing quota of 70 *batman* of tax-exempt land allowed to a Kashgar governor. The men taken illegally were Muslims of the six villages in Yangi Hissar, all formerly tax-paying subjects of the village communities.

However, the consequences resulting from the investigation of this case were not what the Yangi Hissar military governor, named Falingga, anticipated. The Qianlong emperor fired him in the end after months of letter exchanges with the Qing generals in Xinjiang and after long deliberations. The Qing court punished the Manchu governor for his mishandling of the affair, although its ruling did not find him guilty of reporting false information.

The information in Falingga's case shows the reality of the beg clients' development of the Qing land grants in detail. When Gadaimet became the governor of Kashgar in 1760, he reportedly claimed twenty-five households (119 people) of *yanqi* and 70 *batman* of land in the three rural villages in Yangi Hissar—Ingge Icikiye, Terima, and Karayar—as the Qing regulation stipulated. However, over the years, he had added more *yanqi* from the same villages, plus ten households from the village of Barin as well. By the end of his career, he retained eighty-four households of *yanqi*. This number represented an excess of fifty-nine households, a 330 percent increase above the original Qing quota. Although the primary material does not mention any change in the size of the land grant he held, it must have increased accordingly, much beyond its original Qing dimensions.

When Osman became the new governor of Yarkand in 1778, he acted likewise, adding new *yanqi*s from the villages of Ingge Icikiye (twenty-eight new households) and Karayar (forty-two households). In addition, he claimed *yanqi* from two more villages for the first time, the villages of Borya (eighteen households) and Arab (four households). By the time of Falingga's accusation in 1786, Osman held 176 households of *yanqi*s, and 560 *batman* of land in Yangi Hissar. This number represented an increase of 151 households of *yanqi* and 490 *batman* of land, a 704 percent increase of *yanqi* and 800 percent expansion of land from the original Qing grant.

A correlation exists between the number of the *yanqi* claimed in each village and the amount of land reclaimed there, respectively. For instance, Ingge Icikiye village, where Osman supposedly claimed sixty-three villagers as *yanqi* (Qing quota: eleven), also had the biggest land development of 250 *batman* (Qing quota: 30 *batman*). In a remote section, the village of Terima, where Osman claimed twenty-three *yanqi* (Qing quota: five), land development stood at 150 *batman* (Qing quota: twenty-five).

This illegal expansion of the land grants by the governors in the vicinities of the villages, using labor from there as well, caused the rural settlements many serious problems that have been explored above. Adding to the difficulties of the villagers, the begs' *yanqi*s also used their connections to the begs to conduct their own unauthorized expansions of farming operations. A corruption case levied against the governor of Yangi Hissar, Shah Mansur (Manchu: Šamangsur), in 1800 sheds light on this activity as well. One of the charges raised against

Shah Mansur was that a *yanqi* working for him encroached the farmland of his neighbors. The governor did not dispute it but admitted the guilt and replied, "Maihamet [name of Shah Mansur's *yanqi*], who has cultivated land for me, occupied by force the land that belonged to Abdurman [name of the accuser] and others. Maihamet gave me two *galbir* and five *charak* of grain from the encroached land. I mistakenly thought that the amount was harvest from my land, and received it without examining where it come from carefully."[83]

Notably, the ones who brought the charge against Osman to the military governor Falingga in the first place were the village headmen of Ingge Icikiye (*ming* begs [lowest-rank begs handling the tax payment of a higher-level rural district, literally, the beg of one thousand people] and *yüzbashi* [semiofficial headmen of a lower-level rural district, literally, the head of one hundred people]). In fact, in order to make sure that this charge made its way to the Qing military governor, the village headmen bypassed in the chain of report the Muslim governor of Yangi Hissar, who may have had close relations with Osman.

Predictably, the latter denied the allegation and came up with a self-defense, an explanation of a long-standing relationship between his family and the *yanqi* households who were serving him. The Osman family's history with these *yanqi* households started when his grandfather, Polit, claimed the ancestors of these *yanqi* for the first time while serving the Zunghar ruler (1680–1754) in Kashgar. With his family's absence from Kashgar, the *yanqi*s had served the governors of Kashgar, including Gadaimet. When Osman assumed the position of governor of Kashgar (1778–88), however, he regained control over the *yanqi*. He claimed, "The family of the current *yanqi* (Manchu: *yangci*) Muslims held by me have been [serving *hākims*] several generations. Now, there are many old people who are 70 or 80 years old among the *yanqi* Muslims living in the five villages of Ingge Icikiye. Not only will they confirm this fact for you, if once [you] ask these people, but also the old documents all recorded this fact. All the old Begs and Muslims know this."[84]

Indeed, the "old documents" confirmed Osman's claim. Falingga did not relent from accusing Osman of "corruption," in spite of the defense Osman brought forward as well as the Kashgar military governor Booceng's strong support of the latter's claim. The real issue of contention between Falingga and Osman, it turned out, was the current number of members per household that might have been added to the original membership of *yanqi* households, such as offspring or servants. Osman and Booceng seem to have considered them as natural additions to the original number of *yanqi* households too. According to this calculation, Osman did not occupy more than the stipulated Qing quota of *yanqi*: twenty-five households, altogether 119 people. However, Falingga and the village headmen did not agree and considered that Osman maintained an illegal addition of tax-exempt dependent households, which they calculated at 176 households or 176 people as *yanqi*.[85]

As a matter of fact, the Qing regulation set up at the time of the Qing conquest did not provide specific guidelines about how to define *yanqi*, or *yanqi* households. Perhaps the Qing did not want to stipulate the matter rigidly at an early stage of the occupation. While they knew of the begs' desire for adding on more *yanqi*s for agrarian development, the imperial court may not have anticipated the serious social consequences the increase might cause. Or perhaps they did realize but deliberately chose not to intervene, to keep the begs happy.

At any rate, because of this lack of specificity, even Booceng, who supported Osman's claim, at one point was at a loss as to what to do with the newly added members to the *yanqi* households. He asked the emperor for instruction on this issue. To him, there were two possible options. One was to pull out the original *yanqi*s' brothers, sons, and grandsons, and make them ordinary *alban* (head-tax) -paying members of the village community, leaving Osman with only twenty-five people among these *yanqi* Muslims; the second option was to manage the situation according to the old regulations, meaning acknowledging Osman's claim on the entire number of *yanqi* households, incorporating the increased household members.

In the meantime, Falingga had a different solution in mind, one that seems to be radical considering the conventional practice up until that point. He proposed to remove the original *yanqi* households altogether from service to Osman and make them tax-paying members of the village, and to provide Osman with twenty-five new Muslim households as *yanqi*. Clearly, he suggested these changes on two grounds. First, if the Muslim begs were officials of the Qing Empire, and the *yanqi* and lands were given to them as compensation for their service, and the begs were not the owners of *yanqi*, a periodic redistribution would indeed be advisable and necessary; second, if the Qing removed the old *yanqi* from Osman, the problem regarding the tax-paying status of the dependent people would be resolved.[86] But Booceng opposed this. If the Qing decided to redistribute the *yanqi* of Osman, then the Qing would have to do so systemwide. That would likely foment local disturbance in the oases, and contempt and grudges among the begs.[87] The Qianlong court in Beijing agreed with Booceng. In the end, however, a piece of information came to light, and made the discussion about the definition of the *yanqi* irrelevant. Booceng summoned the fifty-seven people that Falingga argued Osman unlawfully kept as *yanqi* for an interview in Kashgar. Twenty-three among them showed up. The interview reveals that they were not *yanqi* at all but wage laborers from Yarkand who had arrived in Yangi Hissar's villages to work for Osman's land development. "They were poor." "They are working as laborers in order to get by." Booceng even found among their number those who had come to work as laborers for *yanqi*s.[88] Booceng decided that the village headmen had accused Osman falsely, without sufficient evidence, and punished them.

However, the villagers seemed not to have agreed with the decision. According to Booceng, they refused to admit guilt of falsely accusing Osman, even though they indeed admitted that they had half-erroneously written the charge.[89] The villagers had their reasons for doing so. In fact, when they accused Osman of illegally occupying the *yanqi* beyond the Qing quota, what they tried to criticize was not the mere legality of the *yanqi* used by Osman in and of itself. Rather, they wanted to problematize the reality of the beg-initiated land development that happened rapidly in the government-controlled wildland near the villages, as well as the disastrous impact it caused on the livelihoods of the members of the village community.

In their view, it did not actually matter much whether the Qing government should classify as lawful the *yanqi* of Osman, for instance, whether they were the increasing sons and grandsons of the original *yanqi*; the increasing numbers of agrarian laborers migrating in from outside of Yangi Hissar; the Tajik slaves taken from the mountains; or the former tax-paying residents living within the village, who all went on to work for Osman and his large-scale agrarian project, either full or part time. What mattered were the economic problems that the increasing number of dependent households of Osman inflicted upon the village community. The begs' land development for private farming and ranching in the formerly unused land around the villages rapidly reduced the common resources that the villagers had relied upon for a long time. These common resources included the pasture that had been used for livestock raising collectively by the villagers but was now reserved for the begs' private livestock enterprise and cereal farming; it also included water resources that had previously been controlled by the villagers collectively but was now put under the begs' capricious control to benefit their enterprises.

The pain of the loss of the common resources was only exacerbated when paired with another problem that the beg development caused. Namely, the numerous wage laborers, illegally claimed *yanqis*, and slaves working for the begs' land development did not contribute to the tax obligation of the village community. These people did not pay tax to the Qing, because they did not own land in the villages and, more important, were under Osman's protection. As the oasis villagers saw it, the situation became untenable in that he did not contribute anything to the village community, while taking away precious common resources on whose use the villagers' livelihood greatly depended.

The Qianlong emperor knew exactly what was going on. However, he decided not to act on the villagers' accusation. As a result, this case ended only with the dismissal of Falingga from his position in Yangi Hissar. Certainly though, if this situation had occurred in a China metropole, Falingga would have won the debate. However, regarding the development in the Muslims' domain, the Qing rulers took a different approach.

In the end, the 1786 Osman case tested the very essence of the Qing protection of the Eastern Turkestani oases. As expressed by Emin Khwāja when he joined the Qing side in the late seventeenth century, its "protection" was provided to the oasis Muslims as a patronage of the loyal Muslim community as a whole—that is, against the destructive nomadic forces like the Zunghar. However, in the wake of the Qing conquest, when the Qing articulated the notion of protection into actual policies, it did so reflecting a profound bias of upholding one class orientation. In an effort to sustain the Qing Empire in its remotest region at the smallest cost possible, the imperial court decreed its patronage as protector of the Muslim clients' domination over the land, resources, and labor of the oases in its concrete regulations. But if it became clear that specific interests of the Muslim beg clients and Muslim community in general collided with each other, what would happen then? The Osman case posed this question. What it showed is that under the pro-beg policy of the Qing, the broad protection of the Muslim community as a whole was not possible.

Conclusion

This chapter has examined the formation of the beg client regimes in Eastern Turkestan, the agendas entailed and the consequences that ensued in the aftermath of the Qing conquest in 1759. The reality of the client rule in Eastern Turkestan emerging from the study of two dynamic Muslim clients, Ūdui and Osman, is a dramatic unfolding of capitalist transformation of local society in the oasis, one that engulfed its politics, economy, and society and swept it along, in one direction: to exploit the expanding avenues of global trade.

This capitalist transformation of the oasis political economy involved three variables. The first was the Muslim clients' building of mercantilist political institutions, which aimed to promote increased merchant traffic into their domains, and to better manage and exploit it. The second was the process of the expansion of the beg capitalists' rural production. In order to feed the growing local, regional, and international demand for its goods emanating from the urban centers, they expanded their commercially oriented capitalist agriculture and ranching endeavors, which employed large numbers of laborers. The third process involved the rapid expansion of the begs' domination of the common resources and villagers' labor to support even further agrarian expansion. The begs would encroach on the wildland that had been formerly managed by village communities as common property, and recruited large numbers of the villagers to work this land with the lure of tax exemption, by providing them with the status of dependent households, *yanqi*.

In this critical capitalist transformation of the local economy, the Qing Empire played an integral role. The begs capitalist transformation required the Qing state presence as a necessary condition to its structure, both as a market and a military umbrella. Furthermore, the Qing authority proved to be more than a mere structural benefit of support to the beg capitalist. Because of their security concerns, and the need for revenue extraction, the Qing Empire was willing to work as the guarantor and supporter of the begs' economic and social agendas: supporting them in their struggle to gain private domination of the wildlands against the common property interests of the village communities, and supporting the begs in the face of the growing social discontent that emanated from the now estranged and beleaguered village communities.

However, the structure of the beg client regime was always precarious at best, full of tensions and contentions. The large number of "corruption" charges brought by the rural villagers against the begs during the late eighteenth century testifies to this instability very well. For a brief moment in the late eighteenth and early nineteenth centuries, the oasis villagers hung on to their own slight hope of receiving protection from the Qing rulers, by bringing their petitions to its attention to remedy local conflicts and ultimately to request protection from the interests of the begs. However, the beg clients remained triumphant for the time being. In his astute political calculation that the best way to maintain the security of the remote Central Asian frontier was to convince the begs of their having embedded interests in the Qing Empire, the Qianlong emperor, so sensitive to the issue of "corruption" in the metropolitan context, generally dismissed the corruption cases brought forward relating to the begs. While he still retained the power to judiciously punish their "corruptions," he would have chosen to do so only when it was politically expedient. Meanwhile the contradictions and tensions that were articulated in these corruption cases continued to intensify in the oasis societies. Such discontent provided a backdrop against which the influence of the Kashgar *khwaja*s, who had been expelled from Kashgaria by the Qing, suddenly revived in full force in the early nineteenth century.

3

The "Holy Wars" of the Uprooted, 1826–30

Jahāngīr Khwāja (1790–1828), leader of the fiercest Muslim resistance against the Qing Empire in Central Asia, was a man without a home. A descendant of a famous *khwaja* who had also offered the Qing a failed resistance and died in 1759, Jahāngīr moved around Central Asia and northern India in a wide circuit, frequenting various locations during his short life. A band of mobile people followed him always, their numbers swelling and diminishing. Probably, Jahāngīr was born in a major oasis city such as Samarqand, and certainly he found his biggest political success in another oasis, Kashgar. However, the holy man was most comfortable when staying in the rugged mountains of Tianshan. From his mountain base, he frequently launched attacks and raids on the Qing border outposts and the oasis begs and, for a short period of time in 1826 and 1827, he found success in his efforts. When he was finally defeated by the formidable Qing troops, he retreated back to the mountains and continued to resist arrest by the Qing until he could no longer. He died in Beijing in 1828.[1]

In the wake of a long period of economic expansion and relative political stability in the late eighteenth and early nineteenth centuries, Eastern Turkestan witnessed a sudden upsurge of Muslim resistance against the Qing and beg regime. From 1826 to 1864, Jahāngīr Khwāja and his families led five wars against their opponents that severely threatened the security and wealth of the Qing-beg regime in Central Asia. Granted, the *khwaja* wars did not end the Qing rule in Central Asia in 1864. The combined development of the Chinese Muslim rebellion in the oases and the military expedition by a military commander, Ya'qūb Beg, from the neighboring country of Khoqand did. However, it is hard to deny that the *khwaja* wars created a crack in the Qing Empire's facade of invincibility, and thus would set the stage for its fall in 1864.[2]

Chapter 3 examines this crucial transition period in Qing rule of Central Asia in the nineteenth century. What the brief summary of the first and the most successful among the Sufi resisters, Jahāngīr, reveals is the importance of mobility as an analytical factor for examining the nature of the *khwaja* wars. The *khwaja*s and their followers, who contributed significantly to the fall of the Qing, were essentially floating migrants—transfrontier, transnational migrants at that. They slipped across the political borders between the Qing-beg regime and its neighbors, as well as across the landscape divide of mountain and oasis. To understand the nature of the *khwaja* wars is to understand the nature of mobility. Who were the mobile followers of the *khwaja*s, after all? Why did they begin to move around in Central Asia in the first place? How did they become the followers of the *khwaja*s?

The central argument of this chapter is that the *khwaja* coalition formed from a community of refugees, who were uprooted in the capitalist transformation of oasis society in the eighteenth and nineteenth centuries. Such communities, comprising displaced farmers, runaway slaves, as well as renegade merchants and disgruntled Kirghiz tribesmen, grew rapidly in the rugged mountain rang-es of the Pamir and Tianshan surrounding the oasis, rising in reaction not only to the early days of the Qing conquest but also the progress of the beg-initi-ated agrarian development. These communities of uprooted people provided the émigré *khwaja*s manpower to challenge the beg capitalists and their Qing patron. The *khwaja*s, with their religious charisma, organizational skills, and connection to a network of global Islamic communities, articulated the politi-cal vision of the uprooted oasis farmers. In this sense, the nineteenth-century *khwaja* wars constituted an integral part of the grand drama of the capitalist transformation and state-building occurring in the oasis under the beg and Qing rule. The *khwaja* war was a "holy war" of the uprooted.

This understanding challenges the previous scholarship's characterization of the *khwaja* wars—namely, as a local Eastern Turkestani struggle against outside conquerors, led by local religious leaders and supported by local populations. Most recently, Laura Newby characterizes the *khwaja* wars as the result of the emergence of a local Islamic alliance extending across Eastern Turkestan that transcended the previous sectarian difference between the factions of "White Mountaineers" (*Aq Taghliqs*) and "Black Mountaineers" (*Qara Taghliqs*) in op-position to the infidel Qing. What gave rise to this broader Eastern Turkestani solidarity in support of the *khwaja* wars, Newby argues, was the shared ex-perience of oppression by oasis Muslims under Qing rule. In a way, the Qing brought this disaster upon themselves by failing to articulate a credible and effective religious policy toward local Islam in the oasis.[3]

Instead of pursuing this religiously rooted local versus conqueror dichotomy, this chapter stresses the class-based dynamic of the *khwaja* wars. When the *khwaja* groups attacked the Qing-controlled oasis, their primary target was the oasis notables and their wealth. They attacked the Qing because they saw them as the patron of the beg-initiated agrarian development, by which they had been uprooted from their hometowns and villages. For a short period of time in the early nineteenth century, indeed, the *khwaja*-led refugee community successfully built a mirror image of the beg client state in the mountains. They achieved not only an alternative polity organized from the people marginalized from beg-initiated agrarian development but also one that stood upon an alternative economy, combining the robbery and looting of the begs' wealth with contraband trade and clandestine agriculture in the mountain enclaves. The khans and begs knew this well and saw the resisters as the archenemy of their property. The ruler of Khoqand at the time, Muhammad ʿAlī (Madalī) Khān (r. 1822–42), referred with disgust to these people as "a few hooligans" (*bir näččä lükčäk*).[4] And another khan nicknamed them "robber/beggar"*khwajas*.[5]

The *khwaja* wars quintessentially were a transnational and transfrontier development. The transnational character of the *khwaja* group was obvious. It included diverse groups of Kashgarians, Andijans, Khoqandians, and, most important, Kirghiz mountain nomads. The reason was that the intense agrarian development and state-building, which gave rise to the refugee community in Eastern Turkestan, was a global phenomenon occurring throughout Eurasia in the eighteenth and nineteenth centuries. Most significantly, across the Qing border from Eastern Turkestan, in places like Khoqand and Bukhara, Uzbek rulers initiated a dual military buildup and agrarian development also, in the context of resolving fierce military competition among themselves and in taking advantage of the new commercial opportunities offered by the Qing expansion. This development produced uprooted oasis farmers throughout the period, and they would feed the emerging streams of refugees into mountain communities at ever growing speed. The *khwaja* coalitions, in other words, were not only the product of specific Eastern Turkestani development but also of broader regional development in Central Asia. To that extent, they were the enemy not just of the Qing and beg state but of all organized states and development in Central Asia.

Thus, a characterization of the *khwaja* wars as a religiously motivated local resistance toward the Qing conqueror is largely misleading. To the extent that the capitalist agrarian development was the prime driving force of local politics in Eastern Turkestani oases after the Qing conquest, the forces of the *khwajas*, emerging as the major oppositional force in Eastern Turkestan in the early nineteenth century, were a transnational alliance poised against the equally transnational force of development. For this reason, the most important analytical factor in the realignment of local politics in the wake of the Qing conquest was not locality or religion but the positionality it took in regard to the beg-initiated agrarian development, and, to a lesser degree, state-building. Of course, there is no denying that Islam played a crucial role in this development. However, the social meaning of Islam and Islamic resistance in Eastern Turkestan was clearly reconstituted against the backdrop of the broader politics of the capitalist agrarian development in the oasis as well.

Sarimsaq Khwāja's Entreaty to the Kashgar People

In 1784, a Sufi named Sarimsaq sent four messengers to carry nine letters to various groups of oasis Muslims in Kashgar District, both rural and urban residents, some of whom were working as beg officials. This incident was first revealed when a head of a rural district reported to Osman, the governor of Kashgar at the time, that Sarimsaq's messengers had contacted its villagers. Osman sent trustworthy people to all the villages to appraise the situation, and captured the messengers. A month-long investigation ensued. As a result of the investigation, roughly sixty-seven local Muslims were punished, including Alima, the governor of the second largest town in the district. In the meantime, a younger brother of a powerful pro-Qing Kirghiz chieftain had to flee from his tribe, because it was revealed that he had helped Sarimsaq's efforts to communicate with the Muslim villagers.[6]

Sarimsaq's attempts instantly alarmed the Qing court. He was none other than the missing and supposedly only son of the Khwaja Burhān al-Dīn, the charismatic Naqshbandī Sufi leader who had offered a failed resistance to the Qing conquest and died in the mountains while being pursued by the Qing army. Fearing that the *khwaja*'s family could become the rallying point of potential resistance against the nascent Qing regime, they initiated an extensive search for this rumored only son. In hot pursuit, the Qing military governors sent spies to discover his whereabouts in various places in Central Asia and northern India. They even caught several alleged sons of Burhān al-Dīn. But the Qing eventually failed to secure the real son of the *khwaja*, Sarimsaq.[7]

The Qianlong court's fear about a subversive plot developed by Sarimsaq

Fig. 3.1. Qalandar (Wandering Sufi) (Chinese: Hai-lian-da). Source: HJZ (four-volume version), stored in Institute for Research in Humanities, Kyoto University.

proved unjustified, however. The *khwaja* had sent out the letters primarily to solicit donations from the faithful, probably from people who must have held a financial obligation to their Sufi shrine (Āfāq Khwaja's *mazār*) or who were former followers of his father. Even the Manchu generals who read Sarimsaq's letters all agreed that there was nothing subversive about them. Moreover, he was not successful even at this modest attempt at fundraising. Only a handful of people that the *khwaja*'s messenger contacted provided a donation, and then only halfheartedly.[8]

In the meantime, the investigation uncovered a tidbit of information that would prove dangerous to the security of the Qing-beg regime in the long run. Sarimsaq claimed that "2,000 households of people" had gathered around him, wandering with him to various places in Central Asia. In fact, his letters plainly mentioned that the need of support for these people was the reason why he had solicited donations from the Kashgarian villagers. The Qing investigators discounted the information, however, reporting that he had merely become a lone wandering Sufi (*qalandar*), with two to ten people following him; the *khwaja* had made up a lie about his followers in order to gain donations from the people of Kashgar (see Figure 3.1).

Given our hindsight that in the early nineteenth century Sarimsaq indeed did not act individually but with a substantial group of people following him, it may not have been wise for the Qing governors to dismiss the *khwaja*'s claim outright. It is highly plausible that his group, so to speak, began to form in 1784, although Sarimsaq may have exaggerated the number of his followers a little. Valikhanov confirms this suspicion. He mentioned that Sarimsaq relocated to Khoqand in order to be nearer to Kashgar, "whence he derived his revenue," at the end of his life. The partisans of Sarimsaq's family (White Mountaineers) began to migrate to Khoqand, located on the opposite side of the Tianshan Mountains. Central Asia was gradually overrun by Kashgarians as a result. "[The Kashgar people] gave exaggerated descriptions of the misfortunes of their country, and of the injustice and oppression of the Chinese, and complained that the infidels carried off their wives and daughters, and prohibited the free observance of their religious rites."[9]

In this account, Valikhanov puts foremost importance on the religious factor—for example, the migrants being White Mountaineers and that one of their complaints was about a "prohibition of the free observation of their religious rites." However, contrary to his assertion, evidence suggests that there was in fact no effort by the Qing to control, not to mention suppress, the religious life of the oasis Muslims. Read in conjunction with the growing toll imposed on the rural oasis population by the begs' agrarian expansion, it would be more plausible to see that the "injustice and oppression by the Chinese" that Valikhanov refers to was the marginalization and exploitation of the rural oasis villages, brought on by the beg agrarian expansion carried out under "Chinese" protection. The floating people produced in the wake of such exploits gathered around the *khwaja*.

What supports this interpretation is that, in 1784, a clear social and geographical division existed in the support of Sarimsaq's entreaty for donations. While he sent all of his letters to former followers and supporters of his father, curiously, only the rural population came out to donate either money or in-kind goods to him. His messengers met with no success in the urban areas. It was not because of a lack of effort on his part. Sarimsaq's messengers delivered the letters signed by him to former followers. But the beg elites in the cities did not cooperate. Even Alima, whom Sarimsaq identified as a former follower of his father, Burhān al-Dīn, did not help Sarimsaq. The Qing authority would go on to punish Alima eventually, but not because he helped the *khwaja*. Alima was punished because he had falsely accused Osman of helping Sarimsaq.

In other words, the *khwaja*'s appeal was exclusively a rural phenomenon, not a widespread "Muslim" response. This geographical dimension is intriguing in that it was the time of the beg elites' great expansion into the agrarian frontier by means of a growing exploitation of rural villages, and the rising difficulty they suffered in the progress of this development. Just two years after the 1784 Sarimsaq incident, Osman received an accusation by the leaders of a village community because of difficulty caused by his allegedly unrestricted expansion of *yanqi* and landed properties in the Yangi Hissar countryside, as the previous chapter shows. In other words, just as Sarimsaq was making an effort to gain an inroad into the rural villages of Kashgar, the oasis villagers' dissatisfaction with the begs and their capitalist transformation of rural society coincided with his attempt. The same frustration of the village community, which was easily felt in the Osman corruption case, drove some members of the village community to provide some modest donation to the *khwaja*.

In this regard, it is interesting that the native officials identified the oasis villagers, whom the *khwaja*'s messengers contacted, as "idle Muslims" (Manchu: *sula hoise;* Chinese: *xiansan huizi*) (oasis Muslims not employed in an official capacity in the native administration; however, the term has also been used to refer to Muslims who did not own landed property to cultivate within a village community in a rural context). In other words, the choice of the term to identify the supporter of the *khwaja* highlights the social nature of his support.[10] It was the property-less people in the rural hinterland that came out to support him most enthusiastically.

Then, the case of Sarimsaq's entreaty to the Kashgars in 1784 points to the convergence of the *khwaja*'s struggle with the rural communities' struggle against the beg agrarian development in the oases. He quietly reconstituted his base onto a new social foundation: the displaced farmers of the oases. With their religious charisma and genealogy as political exiles from their own "hometown," Sarimsaq and later his descendants would provide the leaders rallying points that would motivate the uprooted populations from the oases. And the uprooted would provide a political and military base for them generally, if the holy men chose to challenge the begs and the Qing Empire. Initially, this new coalition of the *khwaja* found a true home in an unexpected place: deep inside the rugged mountains of Tianshan and Pamir.

Muslim Resistance in the Oasis and the Formation
of the Mountain Enclaves of the Marooned

On a late summer day of 1760, roughly forty local Muslims raided a Qing military outpost in Kashgar District. These oasis Muslims came on foot, bearing wooden clubs in their hands. Rudimentary and even primitive though their weapons may have been, their raid was successful. The band of unnamed Muslim men stole cattle, clothing, and grain that belonged to the Qing soldiers guarding the *taizhan*. The bandits went on to attack another group of Qing soldiers, who were approaching from Yarkand at the time, and stole their horses and camels as well. Eventually the Qing troops regrouped and defeated the Muslims, as well as the one thousand local Muslims who later came to join them. However, their leader Mai-la-mu and numerous Muslims were able to flee to the Kirghiz territory within the mountain ranges of Tianshan.[11]

It is best to understand this incident, its anti-Qing nature, and its explosiveness—the local violence that began with the forty Muslims from Faizabad soon mushroomed into a small-scale riot of a thousand people—in the context of the beg clients' agrarian development under the Qing protection. The Qing military governor of Kashgar District, Shuhede, immediately stressed the social nature of the incident in his report to the Qing court. He characterized the attackers as "poor people without job and property" from Faizabad, a rural village in Kashgar District.[12] Local begs also noticed the social nature of this village disturbance. While the incident was still on going, three begs from Beshkerim, another rural village in Kashgar District, gathered their villagers and told them to mind their own business. In addition, they moved three hundred households of poor villagers from Beshkerim and settled them in a faraway place, located about 500 *li* from the main city of Kashgar.[13] In so doing, the begs must have tried to remove a potential source of future troublemakers from their home villages.

Breaking out almost immediately after the Qing conquest, this particular incident of 1760 was the first recorded incident of social unrest in the oases in the Qing records. Yet, it was certainly not the last. It is not easy to examine the overall scale and frequency of such events under the Qing rule with any certainty, given that small-scale social disturbances may have not been reported in the records. However, at least one of these developed into a major revolt. In 1765, the rural oasis population of Ush District, enduring the begs' excessive tax collection and mobilization of labor for transportation of oleaster trees, attacked the walled city of Ush where the Qing military governor, Sucheng, and the Muslim governor, 'Abd Allāh, resided. The revolt lasted approximately six months, fending off an offensive of Qing troops until the fall of 1765. The Qing commanders, who managed to suppress the revolt, put roughly twenty-three hundred oasis people to death.[14]

However, more participants of large and small disturbances ended up fleeing from their villages rather than being killed. What the story of the 1760 unrest shows is that these bands of Muslim rioters often ended up hiding out in mountain terrain, whose prohibitive landscape often limited the reaches of the Qing military power. Joining them there were the numerous other rural villagers who had left their homes searching for relief from the growing burdens of taxation and forced labor. Also heading into the mountains, if less willingly, were the oasis men and women who were captured by the Kirghiz mountain nomads. In response to the begs' insatiable need for labor in their farming, ranching, and mining projects, the Kirghiz took on the role of slave raiders. They attacked the oases, also, and seized hold of the oasis population, carrying them away into the mountain recesses, there to enslave and then sell them to different oases. Of course, these slaves in turn also escaped within the mountains from time to time.[15] On top of it, the economic adventurers and smugglers also converged on the various mining sites scattered in the terrain surrounding the Xinjiang oasis—the most important in this regard being the gold mine in the mountain south of the Khotan District. The Qing governors were well aware of this, sending in troops and begs to patrol those sites.[16] However, it was not certain how effective this patrol was.

In this way, the mountains became a volatile society, teeming with dangerous elements, displaced oasis farmers, slave traders, would-be slaves, runaway slaves, smugglers, and the like, a potentially menacing place that could cause serious threat to the beg clients and Qing governors. Surely, the Qing had allies in the mountains too. During its conquest, many Kirghiz headmen (*bī*) and the small Tajik rulers of small agrarian regimes that dotted the mountainsides joined the Qing side. They sent tribute to Beijing and received military rank and payments of silver, tea, and other Chinese goods from the Qing administration. However, these pro-Qing rulers were not able to exercise effective control over such a volatile mountain society. For every pro-Qing Kirghiz and Tajik headman, there were numerous rival headmen who fell out of the Qing's political favor and resented its influence in the mountains. Because of the shifting political alliances among the headmen and diverse political elements, the loyalty of even seemingly staunch pro-Qing *bī* would prove uncertain. As a result, the uprooted people could still find pockets of safe haven in the mountains and could always haunt the beg capitalists and the Qing Empire from there—if not out of preference, then from necessity.

Batur Sart, "The Courageous One," and the Transformation of the Mountain Society

In 1788, a band of Kirghiz tribesmen raided "Andijan" caravan merchants traveling into Kashgar District. The raiders stole the cargo carried by the merchants and killed two of them. After hearing news of it, the Qing governor dispatched Manchu commanders, begs, and pro-Qing Kirghiz headmen deep into the mountains. They eventually captured three people, including the band's leader, Batur Sart.[17] A Kirghiz raid on caravan merchants was nothing new, however. Even before 1788, the Qing military governors had to handle numerous Kirghiz raiders with unusual severity. What made the raid of 1788 distinctive is the identity of the leader of the raid.[18]

Batur Sart was one of tens of thousands, if not hundreds of thousands, of oasis villagers who disappeared into mountain enclaves under the Qing rule. In fact, his name, "Batur Sart" indicates that. The name features two components. The first, "Batur" (Courageous One) was a title widely used among many nomadic people, bestowed as a title of honor to an extraordinary warrior. In the Kirghiz society of the nineteenth century, this honorific referred to military leaders known for the success of their raiding expeditions on sedentary societies or caravan merchants, an activity holding enormous importance and prestige for the Kirghiz tribes.[19] The second part of his name, "Sart" (meaning, in the narrow sense, ethnic Turki people settled in the Central Asian oasis, or, in a broader sense, the whole of the settled population, including Tajiks),[20] indicates that he was originally from an oasis village, probably from a farming family. The two names together thus signify an improbable combination of roles: Kirghiz warrior raider and Turki oasis farmer. If we use a comparable twentieth-century ethnic term, he might be called a Uyghur-turned-Kirghiz. However, in the context of eighteenth-century Eastern Turkestan, in which ethnic consciousness had yet to be formulated, a more appropriate term might be oasis dweller–turned-mountaineer.

Batur Sart's personal history confirms this transformation. He was originally a Muslim from Suo-huo-lu-ke Village in the Kashgar District. However,

Fig. 3.2. Batur Sart's Transformation: From Muslim Child to Kirghiz Man. Source: HJZ (four-volume version), stored in Institute for Research in Humanities, Kyoto University.

he had been captured by a Kirghiz raider in 1751 and taken to the mountains at the age of seven. In most likelihood, then, Batur Sart was a victim of a Kirghiz slave raid. From then on, he would live among the Kirghiz tribesmen in the mountains, until he was able to escape to Khoqand seven years later. There he had traded ever since. However, for some reason, he reappeared in the mountains among another Kirghiz tribe in the late summer of 1787 (see Figure 3.2).

After six months of sojourn there, Batur Sart informed two acquaintances—a Kirghiz tribesman and a Kashgarian merchant trading among the Kirghiz—of his intention to commit a robbery. The Kashgarian merchant, named Ismail, proposed a potential site for the robbery, along a road crowded with the traffic of the Andijan merchant traders. Their raiding party became larger along the way, as more Kirghiz joined them when the three passed by the tribes. Eventually a party composed of twenty-six Kirghiz executed the plan. They captured a few bands of Andijan caravan merchants, killed a Chinese and two Eastern Turkestani Muslims in the process, and threw their bodies into the river. They stole thirty-one cargoes in total: fifteen cargoes of grain and sixteen cargoes comprising hides, cotton cloth, and carpets.

Batur Sart's remarkable career reveals the transformation of the mountain society caused by influx of the oasis refugees. It resulted in the formation of a rogue community within the mountains, a community that fed on the wealth created by the flourishing oasis trade. Nominally under the control of the pro-Qing Kirghiz *bī,* these enclaves were in effect independent political communities. The vast and rugged terrain of the mountains permitted the formation of these kinds of rogue assemblies. In this regard, it is notable that the Kirghiz *bī* of the unit controlling the territory of the Sayak branch, the unit to which Batur Sart and the other two coconspirators belonged, could not prevent his robbery, although the Kirghiz headman was eventually able to capture his raiding party for the Qing. The "*bī*" lived quite far way, four or five postal relay stations distant from the place where the leaders of the raiding party lived.

The composition of this new political community was unabashedly nontraditional. Although contemporaries called this community Kirghiz, the actual composition of the "Kirghiz" tribes was not Kirghiz at all. Their leaders were oasis refugees just like Batur Sart. Their members included an eclectic collection of oasis mountain traders and estranged Kirghiz tribesmen. What they shared in common seems to be their estrangement from the mechanics of the accumulation and distribution pattern of wealth secured by the *begs* as well as other associates of the new Qing regime. For instance, the mountain oasis trader who joined the 1787 raiders may have had to come to the mountains because he had lost his small stake and livelihood to the expanding influence of Chinese and Andijan traders. The Kirghiz headmen and tribesmen may have joined the raid because they felt estranged from the pro-Qing Kirghiz headmen who accumulated increasing wealth through the distribution of the material awards granted by the Qing.

The rogue economy revolved around the robbery of caravan merchants and the looting of the begs' wealth. Such acts of robbery acted as a profitable system of underground trade. The goods that Batur Sart's party divided up from the raid included valuable commodities: hides, cotton cloth, and especially carpets. What they did not divvy up was grain, which made up the bulk of the cargoes. In most likelihood, Batur Sart would have disposed of the stolen goods in other oasis markets located beyond Eastern Turkestan in other parts of Central Asia, if he had not been captured. In this sense, his seemingly contradictory existence as trader and robber is understandable. His fellow conspirator, the

Kashgarian merchant, Ismail, was also this kind of merchant-robber. The majority of the goods that Batur Sart traded in Khoqand back in the day must have been funded from the spoils of his robbery.

Indeed, there was a direct relationship between the mountaineer's robbery of the oasis farmers and the caravan traders, on the one hand, and the promotion of the political position of the nontraditional leadership in the mountains. Given that they did not belong to the lineage of hereditary notables among the Kirghiz tribes, the most effective way for the new leaders like Batur Sart to gain political influence among the mountaineers was through a profuse distribution of wealth among their followers.

A certain case of Bai Bursuk, an obscure Kirghiz chieftain living in the mid-nineteenth century, illuminates this point clearly. The reason why we have information about this figure is that the Russian officer Valikhanov met him on his way to Eastern Turkestan through Tianshan in 1856. While we do not have any detailed biographical information about Bai Bursuk, Valikhanov's account of him during their encounter shows that he may have been a part of the new leadership emerging in the Kirghiz Mountains. Although he may not have been an outsider like Batur Sart, he was a tribesman of nonnoble background. Bai Bursuk did not belong to the class of the Kirghiz aristocracy called *manap*:[21] he was not a participant in the council of the chiefs, and he was poor. For that reason, in order to obtain the position of hereditary chief, Bai Bursuk carried on constant "depredatory warfare" (*baranta*) "in order to enrich himself." This consumed him so much that even when other tribes were preparing a funeral for a famous deceased Kirghiz noble, the "High Manap Burambai," Bai Bursuk and his sons were off engaged in horse stealing in some remote place.[22]

Valikhanov viewed the nineteenth-century Kirghiz society as an open and democratic, or nonhierarchical, society.[23] What he described as a democratic society was the newly emerging mountain community in which the political influence of nontraditional elites was rapidly replacing traditional tribal leadership, which we examined earlier. In this "open" society, the nontraditional political aspirants in the mountains had to get rich in order to obtain political influence, even for the position of a hereditary chieftain. And, in order to get rich, they had to steal.

All in all, the preceding examination of the basic structure of the new mountain communities reveals the intricacy in the relations existing between the mountain society, on the one hand, and the oasis and its expanding commercial economy, on the other. Indeed, the mountain community was not an isolated entity. On the contrary, it was a fully active participant in the expanding world of commerce anchored at that time by the oasis economy, albeit via underground means. The wealth generated by the expanding commerce was crucial to the enrichment and promotion of the political influence of the leaders in the new mountain enclaves.

However, the mountain communities occupied a different position within the broader landscape of the commercialization and capitalist transformation of Central Asia. In fact, they formed a mirror image, the structural opposite, of the oasis society. Not only were the new enclaves constructed from the debris and fragments of humanity spewed out by the mechanism of the capitalist transformation of the oasis—the uprooted and displaced oasis farmers and laborers—but the structural principle of their economic organization was also opposite from that of the oasis society. While the latter's economy aimed at concentrating wealth in the hands of the begs, by appropriating oasis farmers' labor and common resources, the new mountain communities aimed at redistributing that wealth back to the uprooted farmers by directly stealing the concentrated wealth of the begs and traders in turn.

Batur Sart may have understood this point. The leader of the band admitted, "[I] would like to rob goods, because I was poor," when he proposed the idea of robbing the caravan merchants to his two coconspirators. It was as if he considered poverty in itself a justification to steal, regardless of any monetary gain it may or may not have provided. If the reason for his poverty—indeed, the very reason why he ended up in the mountains in the first place—was the capitalist transformation of the oasis, what Batur Sart implied by his remark may have been that he wanted to counter the capitalist transformation by acts of robbery. In other words, robbery was neither a simple crime nor a money maker necessarily for the leaders in the new mountain communities. It was rather a political act of resistance against the broader effect of the capitalist transformation of the oases.

Throughout the late eighteenth and early nineteenth centuries, the enclaves of the marooned refugees grew rapidly. As a matter of fact, Sha-guan-ji, mentioned at the beginning of Chapter 2, was a leader of such a refugee community. A former follower of Kashgar *Khwajas* who resisted the Qing conquest in 1759, Sha-guan-ji fled to a no-man's-land located west of Yarkand. It took about thirty days by horse from Yarkand. This land was separated from Yarkand by a vast desert, where no grass or fodder for the horses grew. This no-man's-land became the new home of Muslims who had fled from the oasis and Zunghar

Mongols. The refugees made Sha-guan-ji their ruler. They gradually grew into a community of five thousand, armed with three hundred iron-armor and five hundred rifles. They built houses and reclaimed farmland, and became rich. Always violent, they assailed the merchants traveling within and outside the Qing boundary. They became a perennial problem for the rich town of Yarkand. Whether Shah-guan-ji actually lived is a moot point. The very existence of such a tale, fiction or not, shows the prevalence of the refugee communities emerging at the mountain fringe of the Qing Empire. Condescending tone aside, what the tale describes about the Sha-guan-ji community—that is, arming themselves, the robbery of caravan merchants, and enrichment as a result of underground economic activities—could easily be applied to Batur Sart's community.

Indeed, from the Qing records in the early nineteenth century, one can also identify two names of Kirghiz leaders who may have had career paths similar to that of Batur Sart. One is Galcha, and the other is E-luo-si. Both were tribal leaders of the Kirghiz who lived within the frontier guard post of Ush in the 1820s. Galcha is the pejorative ethnic name for the sedentary mountain Tajik people living in the region; many Galchas worked as slaves within the oasis in Eastern Turkestan, as mentioned above. E-luo-si is the Chinese term for Russian. In other words, both Kirghiz chieftains featured names drawn from the name of a sedentary society that was in contact with the Kirghiz tribes in the region. In that sense, their names represented what the "Sart" part in the name of Batur Sart represented. These Kirghiz chieftains may have originally come from a sedentary society, probably captured in slave raids by the Kirghiz like Batur Sart, and later became leaders in the new mountain societies.[24]

Thus, the swelling number of mountain robbery cases that graced the Qing chronicles during the late eighteenth and nineteenth centuries are easy to understand. For instance, in 1761 a group of Kirghiz nomads stole the goods of the caravan of Andijan merchants traveling across the Qing border in the Pamir. The subsequent investigation found that these Kirghiz nomads belonged to a chieftain named A-wa-le-bi. The Qing prodded him to return the goods to the Andijan merchants. A-wa-le-bi's younger brother, Wu-mu-er-bi, who was responsible for assailing the merchants, was sent to Beijing. Immediately after Wu-mu-er-bi's robbery, another robbery occurred. Two Muslim merchants on their way to the Chong-ga-ba-shi Tribe of Kirghiz for trade were robbed by a gang of thirty people. Soon, the leader of the band, a Kirghiz chieftain named Ma-er-ka-bi, was captured. "The Muslims pleaded [to the Qing generals] to remove this bad 'rebel.'" The Qing generals immediately executed him and cut the hands off a participant in the robbery, according to "Muslim law" *(huifa)*. The Qing returned all the stolen commodities to the merchants.[25]

Perhaps, the Qing administration responded to the mountaineer robberies with unusual firmness in this case, because the Qing military governors and the *begs* knew what they were dealing with. They knew that these "Kirghiz" were the major threat to the security of the empire they were building in the lowland.

The Khoqand Khanate and the Dispossessed

For the time being, however, the Qing Empire was able to fend off the dangerous *khwaja*-refugee inroads into Kashgar because of its formation of an international, or interstate, coalition against the challengers. The first to join in were the caravan merchants, whose wealth depended upon the health of China trade going in and out of the Qing-controlled oasis. The caravan traders knew that such mountain upstarts as Batur Sart, with whom the *khwaja*s now mingled, targeted and would cause harm to their wealth and business. Also, many of the merchants owned land in the oases, if unofficially, in spite of the fact that the Qing regulations forbade it, as we have seen above. (This principle also applied to Chinese merchants.) Although the merchants had formerly been and probably still were adherent to Āfāq Khwāja (ancestor of the Kashgar *khwaja*), they decided to join the Qing side nevertheless. When governors like Emin Khwāja and Osman organized extensive espionage networks to track down the *khwaja*s' whereabouts and the status of their potential alliances, the Central Asian caravan merchants willingly worked for the begs and the Qing.[26]

The international coalition arrayed against the *khwaja*s contained another component to it as well: the Khoqand Khanate, an emerging regional power, across the Tianshan from Kashgar District. The Khoqand khans had kept watchful eyes over the *khwaja* movement. Sometimes they kept the *khwaja*s under custody within the confines of their palaces. Sometimes they tipped off the Qing about their whereabouts, especially when they traveled outside of Khoqand territory. According to various Central Asian sources, in order to make sure that the Khoqand rulers reined in the *khwaja*s, the Qing paid the Khoqand ruler 'Umar Khān (r. 1809–22) 2,250 to 3,000 pounds of silver annually, starting about 1813.[27] One cannot confirm whether such payoffs actually happened, since Qing sources do not mention it. However, the Khoqand rulers hardly needed Qing pensions or bribes. It was in the Khoqand rulers' deep interests to keep the *khwaja* under control.

First of all, the rulers did not want to disturb the Qing rule in Eastern Turkestan. The khans gained enormous political and economic benefit from their relations with the imperial court. Huge profits derived from sending out tribute trade missions directly to Beijing or by collecting fees from Central Asian merchants, either to be included in them or for the passage of their caravans traveling through Eastern Turkestani cities. The fact that the rise of the centralized power of the Khoqand Khanate coincided with its participation in the tribute trade with the Qing shows how much revenue the Khoqand rulers made from the China trade. Such participation in the lucrative exchange as a privileged party must have given them the ability to distinguish themselves financially from their domestic and foreign rivals to the extent of making them a rising regional power in the late eighteenth and early nineteenth centuries in Central Asia.[28]

Additionally, the khanate might need the military help of the Qing because of intensifying struggle with Central Asian regional rivals. The most prominent rivals included the Bukhara Khanate. Also, the khan needed to subdue domestic rivals such as the powerful Kirghiz nobles, who were not going away. In this situation, the prospect of military protection from the Qing military, located in neighboring Eastern Turkestan, or at least the illusion of it, came in handy for the Khoqand khans. The Qing military machine was one of the most feared military forces in that part of the world then, until at least the early nineteenth century.[29]

In addition, on a fundamental level, the *khwaja* coalitions were not a threat just to the Qing but to the Khoqand rulers as well. The formation of the refugee communities not only fed off the destruction and displacement caused by the capitalist transformation of the oasis in the Qing-controlled Eastern Turkestan but also fed off the state-building underway within the Khoqand domain. Menaced by the military threats all round and drawing upon the huge revenues accumulated by its strong China trade, the Uzbek rulers of Khoqand succeeded in establishing a centralized khanate a strong military force in the eighteenth century under the rule of 'Ālim Khān (r. 1799–1811) and 'Umar Khān.[30] In order to secure financial resources, the Khoqand rulers drew substantially on the huge profit of their tribute trade with Kashgar and China. Yet they also conducted energetic agrarian developments in Fergana Valley. In 1819, 'Umar Khān built a major ditch to draw water from Naryn River to Namangan, an oasis city in the valley. The khan ordered the people in the Namangan area to work on the project for twenty-five days without compensation. The mobilized people were ordered to come with their own equipment and food. Also, as early as in 1764, the Khoqand ruler expanded into the mountain; in that year, the Khoqand invaded the Kirghiz territory of Osh. The khan sent fifty households of oasis people from Fergana Valley to the territory and opened new irrigated farmlands there.[31]

Khoqand state-building also ended up producing large numbers of displaced people. This gave 'Ālim Khān the reputation of being a tyrant (*zalim*).[32] In a way, its toll had been more severe on them than on Eastern Turkestan. The Khoqand rulers had also imposed the burden of a military draft on their subjects, which was not the case in Eastern Turkestan because its defense fell under the arm of the Qing military umbrella. In the 1820s, Khoqand conquered the Edigene branch of the Kirghiz tribe, located in the aforementioned Osh area and numbering one thousand households/two thousand people. The Khoqand khan took their tribesmen as captives and used them as soldiers in his fight against his major regional rival, Uratube. Furthermore, the Khoqand also collected money, cows, and horses from them as tax. The tribesmen complained to the Qing spies that it was hard to live there because of such double exploitation.[33]

As a result, many Kirghiz tribesmen and oasis townsmen and farmers left their own places, fleeing from the increasingly heavy tax, forced labor, and military levy applied to them. Their destination as well was to head into the rugged mountains. Thus, the *khwaja*s and their activities in the mountain could always explosively impact domestic politics within the Khoqand domain at any time. Its rulers had sufficient motivation themselves to watch over the Sufi holy men if only to maintain the security of their own regimes.

In other words, to the extent that the *khwaja*s' new coalition constituted transnational refugees, the political coalition arrayed against them emerging during that time also had a transnational composition, a coalition of the elements of property and order. For the time being, this latter transnational coalition of the two regimes across the Pamir and Tianshan Mountains—the Khoqand and the Qing beg—and their merchant associates kept the *khwaja*s and the mountain communities from becoming a full-blown threat. But the *khwaja*s would get their chance soon. As long as the intense agrarian development and state-building continued without pause, the refugees and the desperate would gather, and it was they who provided the *khwaja* political power, with an increasing intensity. It was only a matter of time before the *khwaja*s would seize the advantage.

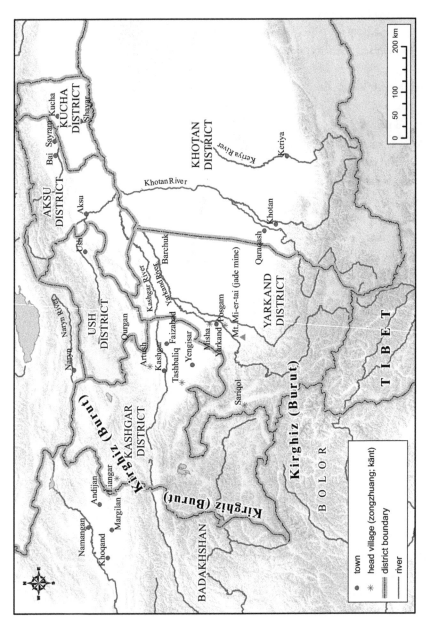

Map 3.1. Western Districts: Kashgar, Yarkand, Khotan, Ush, Aksu, Kucha.

The Jahāngīr Khwāja War and the Refugees Strike Back

Jahāngīr Khwāja was Sarimsaq's second son. Prior to his eventual, if short-lived, success in 1826, Jahāngīr Khwāja had—since the late years of the Jiaqing reign of the Qing dynasty (1796–1820), most notably in 1820—led a series of failed attempts to invade Kashgar. In that year, Jahāngīr entered the Kirghiz territory with "personally following Muslims." In the mountains, the *khwaja* eventually made a liaison with Suranchi, a Kirghiz headman of the Chong-ba-ga-shi tribes. Jahāngīr mobilized three hundred people, comprising Kirghiz, Andijan, and eastern Turkestani Muslims, to attack a Qing frontier guardpost, or *karun*. However, the Qing and local begs easily defeated Jahāngīr's contingent. The *khwaja* force was dispersed. Afterward, Jahāngīr was placed under the custody of the Khoqand ruler, 'Umar Khān (r. 1809–22). However, Jahāngīr's success waited just around the corner.

In 1822, 'Umar Khān passed away. The *khwaja* fled to the mountains at once, "together with several thousand Kashgarians and Koqandians."[34] He subsequently wandered around the Tianshan mountains, until he finally secured a solid base among the mountain Kirghiz located along the Naryn River within the Tianshan Mountains, among the Sayak branch of the Kirghiz, led by two powerful chiefs, Atantai and Taliak. The geography here is important, because the area was where the Khoqand were rapidly expanding to exploit the Kirghiz; finally, in 1827, the Khoqand Khanate built an earthen fortress at a place called Pishpek, located to the west of the Naryn River, and collected taxes and pressed the Kirghiz into military service (see Map 3.1).[35]

At the bank of the Naryn River, seething with uprooted and displaced people, Jahāngīr Khwāja finally found his political identity and put together the perfect political coalition that would enable him to challenge the Qing and beg domination of the oases for years to come. The *khwaja* gained popularity as an "inspired saint" and miracle worker among the mountain people and made followers among them.[36] We do not know exactly what kind of miracles Jahāngīr Khwāja performed in the early 1820s. Yet, the miracles must have had to do with the plight, needs, and anxieties inherent to all of the refugees-turned-mountaineers.

Evidence suggests that the *khwaja* aided the refugees' livelihood. He organized the refugee communities in the development of agriculture, to aid their subsistence.[37] For instance, in the summer of 1826, the Qing military governor of Kashgar reported that Jahāngīr had dispatched a major Kirghiz ally to cultivate mountain land to solve a grain shortage.[38] The *khwaja* was able to help the mountaineers with this effort because of his ability to collect religious donations from the Kashgarian countryside and also from the sympathetic Islamic population throughout Central Asia.[39] He may have even helped the mountaineers to develop clandestine, high-altitude highly profitable crops. Valikhanov reported in 1856, in his travel account of the Kirghiz in the mountains, his sighting of the farming of "red poppy."[40] Although the evidence is circumstantial, it is more than plausible that Jahāngīr Khwāja and his family were involved with growing opium, and even carrying out its transportation.

*Khwaja*s had long been operating a smuggling network that linked the oases and the mountain from their mountain residence.[41] They even had commercial agents in oases in Eastern Turkestan. For instance, in 1790 one such commercial agent was arrested by the Qing while purchasing Chinese stains in Aksu for the Jahāngīr's father, Sarimsaq Khwāja. At the time the agent, named Murmet, approached the "beg controlling the mountain path" in the district, who was about to leave for Beijing for an audience with the Qianlong emperor. Murmet asked the beg to buy Chinese stain for *khwaja*s. The merchant provided the beg four pieces of silver ingot for that purpose. The beg agreed to the deal, because of the profit that could be made, although he did not have any intention of helping Sarimsaq, as a Qing investigation later found out.[42] One can easily see that the *khwaja*'s smuggling network, which even coopted the pro-Qing beg gate guarding the mountain pass, was put to use to help the mountain community's underground trade with the oases, including opium.[43]

However, by far, the most important "miracle" that Jahāngīr Khwāja performed for the mountain refugees was political in nature. In the autumn of 1825, acquiring the information that he was roaming around the mountains gathering supporters, the Qing military governor in Kashgar District dispatched a small division of Qing troops to the area. When they visited the Kirghiz camp of the Sayak branch, where Jahāngīr was suspected of hiding, he happened to be absent. The troop commander rashly decided to massacre and loot the tribe. Learning of the news later, Jahāngīr and his Kirghiz decided to pursue the Qing troops and overtook them in a narrow defile. As a result of this surprise attack, only one among the entire contingent of Qing troops was able to escape and return to Kashgar.

Notably, the Kirghiz mountaineers saw this victory as a "miracle," probably the culmination of all the deeds they had seen from Jahāngīr. Although the mountaineers may have badly wanted to stage retaliation against the Qing Empire and beg clients whose agrarian development had driven many of them into the mountains in the first place, the prospect of the success of such actions had been slim: Qing troops were too many and too strong. Central Asians in the oasis even considered the Qing troops almost invincible.[44] In this sense, what Jahāngīr Khwāja achieved was nothing short of a miracle—what they had wanted so badly, but what had seemed so highly improbable, had come to pass.[45]

The "miracle" proved to be a new turning point for the growth of Jahāngīr's force, setting the stage later for the Jahāngīr War. After the miraculous victory, Jahāngīr Khwāja sent emissaries to spread the news to the Khoqand rulers, as well as to the different camping grounds of the Uzbek, Kazakh, and Kirghiz tribes. As a result, many people rallied from all different regions across Central Asia: "Kashgar emigrants, Khoqand 'Sepoys,' Uzbeks, Kipchaks, Turks, and other Mussulmen warriors, and mountain Tajiks in their picturesque black garbs" hastened to join his banner. Even many Khoqandian officials left their posts to take part in the *ghazat* (holy war).[46]

In other words, the *khwaja* did not necessarily gain his religious and political influence through his genealogical connection to his venerable ancestors, as previous scholars have assumed. Rather, Jahāngīr built his own religious base, as a charismatic Sufi leader, through miracle-making in the mountains. What it means is that he gained his popularity in his own right, by responding to the political, social, and religious transformation of the mountain communities prevalent at that time. This is important for understanding the nature of the Jahāngīr War: it was as much a struggle of the uprooted refugees against the beg clients of oasis capitalism as that of old Islamic forces seeking to regain their local domain against an infidel outside conqueror.

In order to build political rapport with the refugee communities, Jahāngīr Khwāja consciously portrayed himself as a refugee, one who had been expelled from his lawful home, or "ancestral land," by the Qing.[47] This claim was decidedly strategic, because his ancestral home could have been many places. His ancestors after all were wandering itinerant Sufis. He could have easily claimed Bukhara, from which his family migrated into Kashgar as a missionary of the Islamic faith, as his ancestral origin. However, he decided to call Kashgar home, a place he had never lived in up until the time of his successful occupation of the city in 1826. In so doing, Valikhanov noted, Jahāngīr tried to give his attack on the Kashgar "the lawful colouring of those of a Sovereign ruler endeavoring to regain his hereditary rights," and thus incur sympathy from both the religious establishment and secular elites from within wider Central Asia.[48] In addition, more importantly, such a claim would appeal to the many ranks of the displaced escaping dispossession and impoverishment in the oasis. That the holy man too was a refugee, uprooted from his home by the same Qing and begs, was a fact that would resonate deeply across the gorges and penetrate into many of the innumerable byways of the mountain passes.

On a July day in 1826, Jahāngīr came with five hundred followers and was able to break into the imperial military guard posts that marked the Qing border. For the next seven months, the Jahāngīr army and their local sympathizers crushed the four big cities of the area: Yarkand, Kashgar, Khotan, and Yangi Hissar; their occupation continued until the Qing reinforcement force from Ili arrived and reclaimed Kashgaria in March 1827.[49]

Typically, the Jahāngīr War was fought along a new sociopolitical fault line incurred by beg capitalism, a line dividing the urban centers of the oasis and its rural hinterland. Since the *khwaja's* entrance into Kashgar District, the rural villagers rallied in support for his warriors; they also besieged the city of Kashgar and the nearby Manchu fortress, where the beg residences, the international *bazaar*, and the Qing military were located. As some branches of the Jahāngīr force advanced to take other oasis districts, they could enlarge their size because of the large number of new recruits joining from the rural villages. The size of the Jahāngīr force mushroomed as they passed through each rural village on their way to other districts. Tens of thousands joined them.

With the help from the rural crowd, Jahāngīr was able to gain huge success in the early phase of the war. His troops were able to drive the Qing troops, and begs and merchants, into the small confines of a Manchu fortress. Here, the physical space of the client regime that had been rapidly intruding far into the rural countryside in the late eighteenth and early nineteenth centuries contracted into one place, and in a spot where its fundamental strength was defended: a Manchu military base.

No doubt, the White Mountaineers constituted the core group of the local supporters to Jahāngīr. However, if one focuses only on the religious characteristic of the Jahāngīr coalition, one may not be able to discern the crucial geographic disparity encompassing the levels of local support offered to the Jahāngīr force: the explosive response it received derived primarily from the rural hinterlands of the oasis, not from the urban centers, during the war. If local support had come only from his own White Mountaineer faction, this geographical disparity would then indeed be unexpected, because there is no evidence which shows that the White Mountaineers' affiliation had been exclusively a rural phenomenon prior to the nineteenth century. In other words, the local people who supported the Jahāngīr War represented a new *political* coalition, linked to, but still distinguished from, the old *religious* faction of White Mountaineers.

Meanwhile, the Jahāngīr War and the emergence of the new rural-based White Mountaineers coalition also prompted the emergence of a new Black Mountaineers association on the other end of the spectrum of the rural-urban division. In contrast to the rural coalition of the former, the new Black Mountaineers derived from the urban center and wealthy merchants and landlords. Granted, their adherents had certainly not been absent from the rural villages entirely. However, the latter's strongholds resided mainly in the urban centers of the oasis district. For instance, the prominent Black Mountaineer *akhūnd* Ni'mat, the leader of anti-Jahāngīr activities during the Jahāngīr War, lived in the city of Kashgar.[50]

Since this time, native oasis politics divided along this new fault line of an urban coalition of Black Mountaineers and a rural and mountain coalition of White Mountaineers—a split originally derived from the previous generation's sectarian divisions within the Naqshbandī Orders but largely reconstituted under the new social conditions of the capitalist transformation of the oasis. The old religious factional fights were given a new social and political meaning under the unprecedented initiatives of the beg client regime under the Qing. The oasis begs were a part of the urban coalition of the Black Mountaineers. From then on, the Qing administration consciously recruited the beg officials from the rank of this faction, realizing that most of the native officials had been coming from the group in any case, since the time of the Qing conquest.[51]

Muhammad 'Alī Khān of Khoqand was inevitably drawn into this conflict. When the khan heard the news of Jahāngīr's attack on Eastern Turkestan, he immediately became furious and showed his contempt and displeasure toward the *khwaja*. The khan gathered his confidants to discuss what to do. They advised him to go to Kashgar immediately. This advice was recorded both in the Eastern Turkestani source of the *Tārīkhi Hāmīdī* and the Khoqandian source of the *Tārīkhi Shahrukhī*. While a few differences between them exist in the details, both records relate essentially the same information.

According to the latter, the khan's advisors articulated two reasons for his intervention in the war. First, by participating in it, whatever the motivation was, the khan would be able to gain reputation and fame in fighting a "holy war" against the Chinese infidel. Second, more important, the khan should go into Kashgar in order to prevent the *khwaja*'s crowd from ruining the base of wealth in Kashgar on which the khan's finances largely depended. If Jahāngīr conquered the region, "the treasure of [the] infidel [collected during] many years [under their rule] would fall into the hands of these *unfit* and *useless* people and disappear." Furthermore, if or when the Chinese came to reclaim the area, the ensuing war between the troops and the Muslims would also destroy the wealth of the Kashgar completely. Therefore, they urged the khan, "with Padishah's generosity and nobleness," to enter Kashgar and save its wealth from ruin. In other words, the Khoqand khan and ruling elites conceived their participation against the Jahāngīr invasion as a damage control mission to restore the prospects of order and prosperity in Kashgar. The khan should protect the wealth accumulated under the beg and Qing regime from the *khwaja* and uprooted people.[52]

Qing Imperial Superintendent Nayancheng's Reform and Its Disastrous Consequences

In the aftermath of the Jahāngīr attack, the Qing court in Beijing dispatched Nayancheng, an energetic Manchu general, to Kashgar. He was to devise a comprehensive plan that would prevent the reoccurrence of another *khwaja* attack on Kashgar.[53] During his stay in Eastern Turkestan from 1828 to 1829, he implemented a wholesale reform of the Qing rule in the oases.

Three categories of measures constituted the kernel of his plan. The first was to reinforce the occupation of the Qing military in the oases. Nayancheng added eight thousand soldiers to the previously existing twenty-six hundred Qing troops in the "western four cities" (Kashgar, Yarkand, Khotan, and Ush), where Jahāngīr's forces had gained the most success. He also devised a variety of actions to increase revenue production from the oasis to support the increased Qing troop presence.

The second group of measures entailed a reform of the native administration. Here, the goal was to eliminate the de facto practice of revenue contracting by the begs, which had benefited them enormously. As soon as Nayancheng arrived in Kashgar, he identified the revenue contracting system as a "corruption"—that is, a practice of illegally selling offices to bidders who shamelessly exploited "the people below." In order to eliminate the practice, Nayancheng instituted various procedures that facilitated a tighter control over the appointments of the begs, and the application of the "rule of avoidance" in their approvals. The rule of avoidance was a principle that governed official appointments in the Chinese government. It prohibited locals from serving as the heads of their home administrative districts to prevent corruption, and had not been previously applied systematically to the appointments of beg officials in the oasis districts until then.

The third group of reforms taken was the punishment of the Khoqand Khanate, which Nayancheng believed (incorrectly, as it turned out) to lie behind the attacks of the *khwaja*'s war. Nayancheng embargoed the Khoqand trade in Xinjiang, prohibited merchants from its territory from entering Eastern Turkestan for trade, and furthermore, even eliminated for generations the Khoqand merchant communities existing in the oasis. He expelled the ones who had been living in Eastern Turkestan less than ten years; he turned the sojourning merchants who had been residing there more than ten years in Xinjiang into tax-paying farmers.

As Nayancheng saw it, the most pressing task for the future defense of the oasis region was to draw up military reinforcements that would prepare the Qing to respond effectively not only to the *khwaja*'s forces but also against the powerful Khoqand military. He perceptively noted that the root cause of the disturbance in the oasis was the beg clients' exploitation. "The disturbance of the Jahāngīr rebels in the western four cities last year was all due to the Muslims suffering from the hākim's exploitation."[54] However, the curtailment of that exploitation did not become his immediate priority at the time. As a general himself of the powerful Qing Empire, he could not rationalize the defeat of its mighty forces at the hands of such an unorganized, floating, uprooted people. He had to assume that these ragtag rebels had had the assistance of an organized state and its armed forces, such as the Khoqand Khanate.

As a result, the logic of supporting the buildup of military reinforcement took primacy in the implementation of Nayancheng's reform policies rather than the elimination of the beg exploitation. Even in the midst of the reforms, it continued on as before. For example, the governor of Kashgar, Ishāq, paid the total tax quota that was due, in the entirety of its sum, which had been sharply increased during the postwar period, by continuing the practice of de facto revenue farming.[55]

The irony is that Nayancheng's reforms, whose mandate intended to bolster the security of the oasis region, ended up undermining it greatly. The fundamental reason was predictably the financial burden that he added on to the oasis levies, to secure the additional military revenue. In addition to increasing the silver transfers from the metropole and opening state-run *tuntian,* Nayancheng made serious efforts to raise sources of revenue locally. He believed that the Qing could enhance its military presence in this region without difficulty, if only it could tax properly the fruit of all the economic development occurring in the oasis. After all, its agriculture and commerce, which had grown exponentially by any measure, had been in place under the begs' ambitious management for the past seventy years, since the Qing conquest.

For the first time during the Qing rule in the oasis, Nayancheng registered the private land reclamation, which as we saw above had been largely untaxed to that point. This initiative resulted in a spectacular doubling of the land tax (grain tax) revenue. In Kashgar, for instance, the total grain tax quota ran 20,924 *shi* in 1772 and increased to 38,300 *shi* in 1833, after the completion of his new land survey. The increase of the tax quota in Yarkand during the same period rose even more dramatically. The amount reported in 1772 was 16,960 *shi;* it became 41,000 *shi* in 1833. In Nayancheng's era, the tax quota equaled 24,040 *shi,* bigger than the amount in 1772. The total grain tax quota in the oasis from Turfan to Kashgar ran to 63,925 *shi* in 1772 and to 116,300 *shi* after the Nayancheng land survey (see Table 2.2).

In regard to trade, Nayancheng proposed measures that would increase the tax revenue on the tea trade, arguably the most important Chinese good exported to Xinjiang and one that had been hardly taxed until then. These measures included the establishment of new checkpoints—that is, tax stations—in various points in Xinjiang.[56] He also set up a new system of supervision of the region's trade with Central Asian neighbors, formerly controlled by the beg clients. The Qing taxation on the foreign trade had been low from the beginning, as mentioned in Chapter 2. By the Jiaqing Period, the customs duty became virtually exempt owing to lax control by the begs. Indeed, they worked together with the rulers of the neighboring countries to implement a virtual no-tax zone for the foreign traders. The *hākims* increasingly passed on to the Qing administration the requests for tax exemption made by the Khoqand rulers and sojourner merchants who came into Kashgar, Yarkand, and other Qing-controlled oases to trade. The Eastern Turkestani begs shared a strong interest in arranging these tax exemptions for the foreign merchants; this way, more merchants would be attracted to the oases, thus enhancing the begs' pursuit of building thriving international entrepôts in the urban centers of Kashgaria and elsewhere. The Muslim clients received gifts and payments from the foreign merchants for the service.[57]

Nayancheng also established new marketplaces under direct Qing military supervision, called trade pavilions (*maoyi ting*) and official shops (*guanpu*), in the vicinity of Kashgar and Yarkand in 1828; every foreign merchant coming to the oasis region, including the Kirghiz but excluding merchants from Khoqand Khan's domain, now conducted trade there. This was done with the Qing administration in official shops and with the foreign merchants with Chinese and local Muslim merchants in trade pavilions, both under the tight oversight of the Qing authority and also under the principle of barter.

In particular, the Qing administration invited Bukharan merchants, the main merchant group in Central Asia, to conduct their trade in this system. Once a Bukharan caravan approached a Qing border guard post, an officer noted the number of people accompanying it and the quantity of goods brought, and would then escort the caravan to the site of an official shop and trade pavilion. They would exchange 40 percent of the goods they brought in with tea and textiles stored in official shops; 30 percent of their goods, with merchants from China; and the remaining 30 percent, with oasis Muslims. On the completion of the barter transactions, the caravan would again be escorted beyond the Qing border.[58]

Previous scholars interpreted this reform measure as a part of the broader trade embargo issued on the Khoqand, and correctly emphasized particularly the political retaliation levied against them, whose merchants were excluded from this new system. The overall scheme of this reform, however, achieved, for the Qing, handsome financial gains. They emerged as the new dominant merchant in the foreign trade occurring in the oasis within this new system. For example, their local administration would inexpensively secure sheep and other livestock, an important part of the logistics for the Qing military, through this system.[59] At the same time, the fact that in this new system the foreign merchants had to pay customs duties, from which they had been virtually exempt in the early nineteenth century, also helped the Qing finances enormously.

The local oasis people complained about this financial side of the development, lamenting in Kashgar, "The Chinese scheme had the anticipated effect of increasing their trade and suppressing that of natives," referring to the effect of the Qing administration's official trade at the official shops.[60] Valikhanov, who reflected the local view, also took care to mention that the Qing erected customs house barriers at the villages of Tuguzak and Liangar, the sites of the trade pavilion and official market, where the Bukharan merchants were allowed to trade. If there had been a loss of revenue from the taxation of foreign trade before, this measure now prevented it from happening again at the source.[61]

Eventually, this system collapsed, ironically because it achieved one of its primary goals. The new market conditions that embargoed the Khoqand participation, a major force in the frontier trade, decreased the numbers of potential buyers in the Eastern Turkestani market and thus drove down the price of Chinese goods, especially tea. Continued efforts to smuggle tea by the locals and the Khoqand merchants also undermined the profitability of the new official trade system. While the Qing had to close down all the official shops as a result by 1829, however, Nayancheng did not give up hope of gaining new financial resources from the foreign trade. Subsequently, he urged Beijing to reinstitute and reinforce the 1/30 tax on the merchandise brought into Xinjiang by foreign merchants that year,[62] making sure that the foreign trade was properly taxed thereafter.

One can also understand his additional handling of the Andijan merchants, arguably the most controversial element of his reform, according to this logic. A local primary source and previous scholarship have focused on the expulsion of the sojourner merchants who lived in the oasis region less than ten years. This has essentially been understood as a retaliatory measure taken against the Khoqand ruler. However, there is another aspect to this reform. While Nayancheng expelled the Andijan merchants residing in Kashgar and other Eastern Turkestani cities who had lived there less than ten years, and confiscated their properties (tea, rhubarb, and land and buildings), he also registered Andijans living there more than ten years as civilian subjects who were now required to pay tax.[63]

The Andijan merchants belonged to the richest and most resourceful strata of the oasis society. They owned and operated a greater portion of Eastern Turkestan's commercial wealth, all at their disposal. They even held landed property in the oases, although illegally so, against Qing law. However, their wealth had hardly been taxed by the Qing administration: they were not subject to the poll tax, and their land was not taxed; nor were they subject to forced labor. The Andijan merchants comfortably stayed in a profitable tax limbo, so to speak. From a legal standpoint, their status of not being taxed was understandable. Andijans were not the formal subjects of the Qing; they were recognized as sojourners. What the Nayancheng reform achieved was to make the problematic status of the Andijans clear in regard to the tax payment: either they paid taxes and became the subjects of the Qing or they should leave Qing-controlled oasis territory altogether.

In other words, the intention of Nayancheng's reform was to tax the begs and their associated merchants, both local and foreign, from the newfound wealth made from agriculture and trade since the Qing conquest. If the reforms had gone as Nayancheng planned, the two groups should have shouldered the new revenue. However, in practice, that did not happen. The problem was that the Qing did not have enough of its own personnel to control their compliance. The Qing military governor's administration in each oasis (Manchu and Chinese clerks of the Bureau of Muslim Affairs) had to work through the same governor *hākim*s and beg elites, whose wealth Nayancheng targeted. In spite of his attempt to reform the practice of de facto tax farming at the time, the fact of the matter is that the *hākim*s of each oasis city continued to distribute the burden of the increased tax payments evenly among the oasis dwellers, rather than collecting it selectively from among the beg developers. What it meant was that the brunt of the revenue from the oasis for this purpose still came from the purse of the rural village communities. That exacted increasing hardship for them, and escalated the numbers of the floating people in the mountains. Thus, the structural problem that led to the exponential growth of Jahāngīr Khwāja's power—the continued growth of the uprooted oasis population and the mountain refugees, as a result of the hardship imposed by the beg-initiated rural development—was not solved. Rather, it was exacerbated throughout the Nayancheng reform period.

What made the situation worse is that his reforms also contributed, if indirectly, to the growth of the floating people from across the border, from Khoqand territory. He himself captured this dynamic brilliantly, predicting the following: "Khoqand's annual tax used to be 60,000, or 70,000 *liang* at most. Originally, this amount had not been enough for the expense of the khanate. By squeezing much from the region's trade with Kashgaria, it used to be possible for the khan to have enough income to pay for his spending. Recently [however], the trade was not allowed. Thus [the funding for] the expense of the khanate is not enough. There was no other way for the khan but to exploit the households that belong to the khanate at the level that is double of the earlier level. This, the people all resented. When the people of Khoqand heard that the Qing Empire prohibited bad practices in Eastern Turkestani oases and had lessened the burden of tax and forced labor, they adored Xinjiang. They all saw Xinjiang as a paradise."[64]

The usual hyperbole notwithstanding, Nayancheng had a point. The Qing embargo on Khoqand's trade had caused a serious internal political crisis in the khanate. Deprived of the important financial resources to be gained from the lucrative China trade, the Khoqand rulers had to make up for the lost revenue and did so by exploiting more from the oasis population. In so doing, the Khoqand khan had the effect of driving the oasis population out from the territory. Nayancheng predicted that these fleeing people would dream of resettling in the Qing-controlled Eastern Turkestan. What he did not anticipate was that the displaced people from the Khoqand territory heading to the mountains would instead join the *khwajas* and their struggle, before even reaching Eastern Turkestan. This development thus posed a serious threat to the latter's prevailing security, by greatly swelling the numbers of the *khwaja* forces.

At the same time, this development posed another danger to the Qing in the form of the growing belligerency and military adventurism of the Khoqand state itself across the mountain border from Kashgar. Having lost the precious financial resources of both the China trade and tax-paying oasis population, the Khoqand rulers took desperate efforts to find new financial resources. For instance, from the end of the Jahāngīr War in 1827, the Khoqand troops had expanded their presence in the Tianshan Mountains, deep into the Chu and Talas River basin areas, built a fortress, and taxed the Kirghiz and Kazakh.[65] However, as the Khoqand rulers saw it, the most tempting, and perhaps most fundamental, solution to their financial problem was to take military action against the Qing in Eastern Turkestan, thereby gaining a short-term windfall from looting and by forcing the Qing to reopen the China trade.

In that scenario, Nayancheng's strategic discontinuation of the Khoqand trade in Eastern Turkestan came at the worst possible time. Military competition among the Khoqand Khanate and its Central Asian neighbors was growing intense. The Khoqand ruler was thus engaged in multiple wars and conflicts with his neighbors—Bukhara and Uratube.[66] All these fronts forced the Khoqand khan to look ever more desperately for new revenue sources. If he had not been behind the Jahāngīr War in 1827 initially, he had sufficient reason to do so only a few years later, not only to support the *khwaja* war but also perhaps even to lead it. Nayancheng's miscalculation of identifying the Khoqand ruler as the backer of the *khwaja* war came to be a reality in the end. In no small part, it was of his own making.

The Yūsuf Khwāja War and the Devastation of the Oasis Economy

In September of 1830, a mere three years after the end of the Jahāngīr War, Jahāngīr's elder brother, Muhammad Yūsuf Khwāja, struck Kashgar again. Following him were forty thousand soldiers composed of various groups. They succeeded in occupying the Muslim city of Kashgar District and held on to it for about three months, while also constantly attacking other major Kashgarian cities; they were driven back out of the Qing border by Qing reinforcement forces arriving a few months later.[67]

A brief examination of the participants of the Yūsuf War reveals that it was primarily a continuation of the Jahāngīr War: a struggle of the uprooted people pitted against the oasis capitalists and state builders. The Yūsuf War drew three groups of people into its ranks: (1) the Khoqand or "Andijan" (35,000 people); (2) mountain Kirghiz led by two veterans of the Jahāngīr War, Atantai and Tailak (2,000 people); and (3) the floating migrants coming originally from Kashgar, led by a certain Imanchaq (estimated to be 3,000 people).[68]

Among the three components of the *khwaja* coalition, the latter two groups had been the mainstay of the Jahāngīr War. The numbers of their ranks had swelled exponentially in the wake of the Jahāngīr War, according to the dynamic explained in the previous section. In the meantime, what truly distinguished this war from the Jahāngīr War was the active participation from the beginning of the Khoqand. Two high-ranking officials or nobles of the Khoqand Khanate—Min-bashi Haqq Quli and Tashkent's Kush Begi, Miad-sharif Liashker—had commanded the *khwaja* army at the beginning of the invasion. The people from the Khoqand domain—twenty thousand Khoqand and fifteen thousand Tashkent—constituted the majority of the initial invading forces.

Thus the Khoqand source, *Tārīkhi Shahrukhī*, essentially described the Yūsuf Khwāja war as Muhammad 'Alī Khan's "holy war" against the Chinese, without even paying any serious attention to the role played by Yūsuf Khwāja. With a "countless army," the Khoqand khan descended upon the "Chinese fortress" (Gulbagh, Rose Garden) that had been restored by the Qing after the Jahāngīr War. After a serious fight that took a toll on both sides, the "Chinese" asked for a truce. The Chinese military commander offered the Khoqand commander many gifts, countless *yambu* (silver bullion), Chinese goods, porcelain vessels, and loads of tea; he also promised to give such gifts every year. The two armies came to an agreement that the Chinese would not prohibit the trade by Muslim merchants. After this, the Khoqand troops happily went back within their borders.[69] The Khoqand ruler thus solved the problem that Nayancheng's trade embargo had caused.

The difference between the descriptions of the Yūsuf and Jahāngīr wars in the *Tārīkhi Shahrukhī* is unmistakable. The source, which explains Muhammad ʻAlī Khan's participation in the Jahāngīr Khwāja's War three years prior as a damage control mission, put the Yūsuf War in a radically different light. It was a war waged by the Khoqand ruler first and foremost. Valikhanov agreed, and defined this war as a "holy war" against China, masterminded from beginning to end by the Khoqand ruler Muhammad ʻAlī Khan. As the most brilliant ruler in the history of the Khoqand, in Valikhanov's opinion, Muhammad ʻAlī Khan had been preparing for this holy war for a long time. He anticipated the opposition to his scheme from the neighboring Central Asian rulers, who were indisposed toward his plan because of their fear of the Qing forces, or the fear of a decline in the China trade. Muhammad ʻAlī Khan thus persuaded Yūsuf Khwāja, who was commanding universal sympathy among the Central Asians because of his family's suffering, to come to Khoqand and lead the attack on Kashgar, to elicit support for his plan among the Central Asian rulers.[70]

There is no doubt that the Khoqand Khan and his interest in reopening the China trade in Kashgar played a crucial role in the outbreak of the *khwaja* war. Yet, even in his "holy war," the Khoqand ruler acted from a position of weakness rather than strength, under the pressure of the armed migrant groups—the population that the Khoqand khan himself in part had helped to swell because of his efforts to apply more taxation and military mobilization. A major chronicle of the Khoqand, Vladimir Petrovič Nalivkin's narrative, related that it was Yūsuf Khwāja's party, or "crowd," that forced the Khoqand Khanate to permit the *khwaja*'s attack in the first place.[71] What this source suggests then is that the Khoqand ruler joined the *khwaja* war only reluctantly, forced into the situation from pressures incurred by the Khoqand Khanate's domestic politics.[72]

The *khwaja*'s "crowd" undoubtedly referred to the major contingents of the coalition, the Kirghiz mountaineers and Kashgarian migrants. Their number had grown exponentially since the early post–Jahāngīr War period, as shown above. Because of the geographical proximity to Kashgar, many of the migrants moved into the oases within the Khoqand's domain. On the one hand, the Khoqand ruler could see them opportunely, for his own cause. Muhammad ʻAlī Khan settled "several hundred families," about seventy thousand people,

Kashgar migrants, in the "suburb" of Khojend and Tashkent, giving them a ten-year immunity from all taxes, in order to spur on his own land development scheme in the wake of the Yūsuf War.[73] On the other, however, these migrants also caused serious problems in terms of collective social and political disorder within Khoqand. They constituted large numbers of floating people without means of sustenance. They formed either independent armed forces or gangs of robbers within the Khoqand territory. The distress they posed became even greater when the Khoqand's own oasis people, displaced by Khoqand state-building, joined their ranks. Thus, Muhammad 'Alī Khān may have seen the growth of this group with weary eyes.

His problem was that he could not get rid of them so easily. Even in the days of Jahāngīr Khwāja's father, Sarimsaq, in the 1820s, the Kashgarian migrants held the sympathy of the Central Asian Muslims. They became an object of "universal respect" among Central Asians, so much so that their emissaries were able to proceed from town to town to collect contributions for the planned "holy war." During and after the Jahāngīr War in the 1830s, the plight of the Kashgarian migrants became an important cause and rallying point for the so called fanatical Muslims of Central Asia, not only in Khoqand but also in places such as Bukhara.[74]

In this circumstance, the Khoqand ruler, being a Muslim ruler, could not eliminate the Kashgarian migrants and *khwaja*s without incurring the wrath of the religious establishment within and without Khoqand. At one point, he revealed his frustration with this group quite frankly, when he sent a messenger to negotiate the repatriation of these Kashgarian migrants with the Qing during postwar settlement negotiations after the end of the Yūsuf War. In his verbal report, the messenger mentioned that these people "resented" Muhammad 'Alī Khān. They claimed that they needed to leave Kashgar because of the trouble that Khoqand caused. Once they were in Khoqand, they all became beggars. The khan went on to mention that they needed to be pitied. Yet, by calling them "beggars," the derogatory term that the khan also applied to the *khwaja*s, the messenger indeed expressed fear and contempt toward them. He petitioned the Qing to take them back for his own sake.[75]

It is not clear whether he was directly challenged by the *khwaja* group or the local *'ulamā* sympathetic to their cause; nor is it known if he took the initiative to support the *khwaja* to placate this floating population by giving them the chance to loot Eastern Turkestan. However, at the very least, the Khoqand ruler may have seen a silver lining in his support of the Kashgarian migrants' war.

If he could not get rid of the Kashgarian "beggars" and "robbers," perhaps the war could.

What happened on the ground during the short Yūsuf War confirms the Khoqand ruler's weak position in the *khwaja* coalition. He did not have any effective control over the actions of the *khwaja* army, in spite of the fact that the Khoqand nobles held nominal command of the forces. What showed this most clearly was when two powerful Kirghiz chieftains, Atantai and Tailak, and the mountain Kirghiz they commanded, withdrew early from the coalition and returned to their territory, after spearheading the invasion and acquiring substantial loot in Kashgar.[76] This withdrawal contributed significantly to the early disintegration of the *khwaja* coalition.

The basic nature of the Yūsuf invasion then was the same as the Jahāngīr War: it was a war of the uprooted and refugees, who gathered around charismatic religious leaders, a war against the order of wealth in Eastern Turkestan. This view accounts for the predatory nature of the Yūsuf War. According to a Qing commander, Changde, of the ten thousand "rebels" who attacked Kashgar, half besieged the main city of Kashgar and half looted it. And they were not satisfied with simply looting goods. They were also interested in capturing people—the most important commodity at the time was slaves or laborers. They stole "sons, daughters, jade, and satin" from the Kashgar oases.[77] Valikhanov corroborated these facts by mentioning the seventy thousand Kashgarian outmigrants, five hundred Chinese captives, and large spoils of tea and silver.[78]

The Yūsuf War was not able to replicate the success of the Jahāngīr War. It succeeded in occupying only Kashgar District; it failed to gain any success in occupying other cities, despite the enthusiastic initial support aroused among the rural population. Perhaps the begs and the Qing commanders were better prepared this time; also, the destruction, looting, and violence of the war alienated many oasis Muslims from the *khwaja*s. Still, even the modest success of the Yūsuf War did enough to show to the Qing rulers that the program of Nayancheng's reforms would not work in Eastern Turkestan. After the end of the Yūsuf War, the Qing court sent Changling to Kashgar as an imperial superintendent to come up with another postwar settlement plan. Changling undid the reform measures that Nayancheng had put in place a few years prior. The embargo on the Khoqand trade in Kashgar was lifted. The reforms of the beg institution were nullified. And the increased tax quota in Kashgaria was reduced to levels instituted prior to the hike taken in the Nayancheng era.

Conclusion

The Jahāngīr War and its success definitely caught the Qing rulers off guard. Since the early period of the Qing conquest—with the single if notable exception of the outbreak of the Ush Rebellion, which occurred in 1765—anti-Qing violence on such a scale, not to mention success, had been rarely seen. For that reason, the Daoguang emperor wanted to make an example of the instigator of the war. The emperor had him publicly executed in Beijing. However, it turned out that the Jahāngīr War was only the beginning of the anti-Qing violence in Xinjiang. Five more *khwaja* wars followed within the short span of about fifty years, although the later *khwaja*-led rebellions never achieved the success and popularity of the Jahāngīr rebellion.

The continued *khwaja* wars were essentially of the Qing's own making. Under the patronage of its empire, the commercially oriented Eastern Turkestani begs conducted unprecedented levels of agrarian development in the oasis. While this agrarian development contributed to the rapid expansion of agrarian production and population growth, its consequence was to magnify the numbers of the uprooted, floating refugees escaping into the mountains, forming encampments that could potentially threaten the security of the regime of both the oasis capitalists and their "Chinese" protector.[79] The *khwaja*s were there to give leadership, organization, and religious sanction to this new political contingent of the uprooted.

The initial Qing response to it, the Nayancheng reform policies from 1828 to 1829, increased, rather than lessened, the power of the *khwaja* coalition. Military reinforcements and additional revenue extraction to support that military reinforcement inflicted more burdens of taxation and forced labor on the oasis villagers, if unintentionally, and thus contributed to an upsurge of impoverished people fleeing the oasis. Also, the Qing trade embargo on the Khoqand had the same effect on the uprooted people from the Khoqand side. In addition, it forced its ruler, who had until then been a reliable ally of the Qing in restraining the *khwaja* influence in the region, to instead join forces with them, if only to reopen the Khoqand China trade.

After two rounds of *khwaja* wars, the Qing rule in the oasis fell into total crisis. However, almost miraculously, the Muslim begs had something to gain from this development as well.

4 The "Just and Liberal Rule" of Zuhūr al-Dīn, 1831–46

Henry Walter Bellew, a British diplomat who traveled as a member of the Forsyth Mission to Kashgaria in 1873, left a short description of the reign of Zuhūr al-Dīn, Muslim governor of Kashgar District from 1831 to 1846. Bellew praised him, noting that the "country" of Eastern Turkestan "enjoyed peace under the just and liberal rule of Zuhuruddin [Zuhūr al-Dīn], the Governor on the part of the Chinese." Indeed, the scattered information, conveyed in the writing of Bellew and Valikhanov, regarding Zuhūr al-Dīn's rule is rather positive, as it reflected much of an upbeat picture of the economic prosperity and political stability of the local society, ranging from the rebuilding of the urban spaces in the district to the growth of the caravan merchant communities in Kashgar. The records provide an unmistakable impression that the locals, from whom the Europeans gathered their information, considered the reign of Zuhūr al-Dīn as *the* brightest spot in the history of Qing-beg rule in Eastern Turkestan.[1]

Read within the context of the actual historical developments occurring in Eastern Turkestan, this impression is truly ironic, however. When Zuhūr al-Dīn assumed the position of governor of Kashgar in 1831, the beg rule in the oasis had become almost defunct, as shown previously. However, suddenly and unexpectedly, the beg clients resuscitated the vitality of their rule in the 1830s. From 1831 to 1846, Kashgar enjoyed about sixteen years of stability under the rule of Zuhūr al-Dīn as the new governor. Not only did the *khwaja* attacks stop, but during that period the district reached new heights of prosperity. Large numbers of international caravan merchants—the key to building wealth in an oasis entrepôt in the overland trade system—flocked to Kashgar from as far away as Crimea, northern India, and its neighbor, Andijan. The agrarian development in the rural villages continued at an unprecedented scale.[2]

In this chapter, we shall see how the oasis capitalists achieved this extraordinary feat by proactively supporting the Qing military buildup in Eastern Turkestan. The number of imperial troops had radically increased in the aftermath of the Jahāngīr and Yūsuf wars in the 1830s. The beg clients increased their private donations and also developed *tuntian* on behalf of the local Qing administration, and thus virtually took over the military financing of its troops stationed in the region. The vastly expanded military presence in turn helped the begs to attract caravan merchants into Eastern Turkestani oases by providing them shelter from the attacks of the *khwaja*-led refugees and, more important, from the exploitation of Central Asian state builders.

Furthermore, the begs successfully turned the military buildup in the post–*khwaja* war period into a new investment opportunity. Especially crucial in this shift was the new Qing initiative to augment development of the *tuntian* in the oasis.[3] The agrarian colonies were state farms that the Qing local administration operated using the combined labor of Chinese soldiers, civilian migrants, as well as convicts. Since its conquest in the 1750s, the Qing state had been utilizing on a large scale the *tuntian* in the northern part of Xinjiang, such as Ili Valley and Urumqi, where the native population of the Zunghar had almost been wiped out by the Qing massacre, as a major means to finance its military. However, in the oasis, the Qing instituted its "agrarian colonies" only reluctantly, because of their fear of triggering potential strife between Chinese migrants and the local oasis population. Under pressure to financially support its increased troop presence after the two *khwaja* wars, however, the imperial court began developing the *tuntian* in the oasis from the 1830s onward.

While the agrarian colonies opened a new era of Qing-initiated agrarian development in the oasis, the beg clients took control over this newly designated land initiative as soon as it started. In collusion with the military governors, they managed the land, mobilized the oasis Muslim laborers, and turned the state-initiated agrarian development projects into new entrepreneurial opportunities. Zuhūr al-Dīn successfully took over the Qing military financing and appropriated the Qing state resources as new private investment opportunities; in this way, via control of the *tuntian,* his actions marked the conclusion of the logic first characterizing the government-protected beg capitalist development of the borderland oasis that had commenced since the 1759 Qing conquest. What began as the begs' capitalist transformation of the oasis under imperial protection in the beginning had come full circle by this point in the mid-nineteenth century: the Qing Empire itself became privatized and the target of beg capitalist investment.

One can understand then the two seemingly unrelated aspects of the "just" and "liberal" rule of Zuhūr al-Dīn—the begs' initiative both to expand commerce and to support the Qing military—coherently. The two facets were mutually necessary conditions. The presence of the Qing military, as provider of an enhanced local market, protector of their properties, as well as being a prospective investment opportunity, established the foundation for the expansion of commerce and agriculture in Eastern Turkestan. Conversely, the wealth that accrued to the begs also sustained the Qing military. And upon this circular logic of military buildup and new prosperity resulting from the ensuing trade and agriculture stood the new equilibrium of the beg client state in the wake of the Jahāngīr and Yūsuf wars. In this new balance, one can surely see the ever-growing structural dependence of the beg clients on the Qing imperial presence in Eastern Turkestan, not as an occupation force but as an integral part of local production relations.

Resurgence of the Kashgar Entrepôt

As soon as the Yūsuf War drew to an end in 1830, Muhammad ʿAlī Khān of Khoqand dispatched a messenger to the newly appointed governor of Kashgar, Zuhūr al-Dīn, requesting the resumption of trade between Khoqand and his city. Zuhūr al-Dīn duly reported the request to the Qing military authority. The imperial court initially rejected this overture, telling the Khoqand messenger that the khan should capture and turn over Yūsuf Khwāja to them and ask for forgiveness for his participation in the *khwaja*'s war first. However, it did not take long for the Qing to reopen the trade with the Khoqand. By the end of 1831, it allowed the Khoqand merchants to buy commodities of tea and rhubarb and other goods from Kashgar, and permitted them to settle in Kashgar once again.[4]

In fact, the Qing needed the Khoqand ruler and the caravan merchants as active participants in an international coalition standing against the hazards of the refugees and uprooted people of the oasis of the post-Nayancheng era, to ensure security in Eastern Turkestan. They were not to be alienated, if the Qing wanted to defend its interests in the area. By resuming trade in Kashgar, the Manchu court could strengthen all of their embedded interests in keeping the peace in Kashgar.

The reopening of the trade turned out to be a huge success. In its wake, Kashgar witnessed an unprecedented growth in the number of international merchants settling within its perimeter. According to an estimate, the number of Andijan merchants residing in Kashgar reached six to seven thousand in

1837, merely six years after the Qing reopened the Kashgar trade in 1831.[5] This figure represents a large increase over an earlier era in the number of Andijan merchants present. In preparation for purging the Andijans from Xinjiang, Nayancheng had conducted a survey and located 715 households of Andijans residing in Kashgar in 1827. This figure of 715 could be computed to 3,575, depending on whether the Andijan households constituted only a single male merchant household, or, more usual, an oasis family comprising five people.[6] The Andijan sojourners in Kashgar District had increased two- to tenfold from the levels of both the pre–Jahāngīr War period and within four or five years after the end of the Yūsuf War.

Previous scholarship rarely problematizes the success of the resumption of international trade in Kashgar. Because the commercially oriented Khoqand ruler wanted to reopen trade there, the merchants from his domain followed suit by coming to the city. The assumption is that the Khoqand ruler and the merchants held shared interests. However, as a matter of fact, the two parties rarely saw eye to eye. The conflict between them revolved around the Khoqand ruler's frequent appropriation and seizure of their wealth to bolster his war efforts. During the Yūsuf Khwāja War in 1830, for instance, many merchants had fled from the Khoqand-ruled oasis cities (Andijan, Margilan, Khojent, and Tashkent) in order to escape the khan's wartime mobilization.[7] What made the situation progressively worse was that the Khoqand Khanate was continually fighting ongoing battles not only with neighboring Central Asian rulers but also with the Russians throughout the nineteenth century.

The Eastern Turkestani oasis was able to attract merchants from the Khoqand domain precisely because the former could protect them from the exploitation of the Khoqand ruler. The beg clients in Eastern Turkestan did not have to appropriate merchants' wealth for a military buildup, because the Eastern Turkestani cities remained under the military umbrella of the Qing Empire. Also, the rate of the Qing taxation was lower in Eastern Turkestan generally, and particularly with regard to merchants. Except for paying custom duties at 1/30 or 1/40 parts of the goods they imported and exported, merchants were exempted from other tax burdens, such as poll and land taxes. The Qing Empire classified the nonlocal merchants, whether they were Chinese or Central Asian, as sojourners. Thus, they were exempt from local taxation by definition, although many of them owned a substantial amount of land in the oases.

What this means is that despite the potential for *khwaja* attacks in the future, the Qing-controlled Eastern Turkestani oases provided the safest haven for the merchants' security and property. The *khwaja* and refugee attacks posed sporadic threats of looting and robbery. However, the Central Asian state builder posed a permanent threat that systematically appropriated the merchants' wealth. On their part, the Eastern Turkestani begs, whose continued accumulation of wealth depended on the ample existence of caravan merchants in their oases, made pleas to the Qing government to bring back the Khoqand merchants. Even before the imperial court made the final decision to reopen Eastern Turkestan to Khoqand merchants, the Muslim governor of Aksu, for instance, appealed to the Manchu military governor there: "Andijans have not been different from the local Muslims, since they resided here during the Qianlong reign. The Andijans expelled during the era of Nayancheng reform accumulated teas and rhubarb, married with local women, and have households there. When they were expelled outside of Qing border, they wept while leading their sons, carried their daughters [out of the Qing border]. They could not bear it."[8]

However, the very success of Kashgar in attracting wealthy merchants created a new tension in its local politics. The revenue-hungry Khoqand khan saw in the growing international merchant community there a new financial opportunity. If he could tax the caravan merchants gathering in Kashgar, he could satisfy his ever-growing financial need for military mobilization. In part, he must have felt justified in formulating this idea, because many caravan merchants now settling in Kashgar originally hailed from the oasis of Fergana Valley, which was under Khoqand control.

In this context, in 1831, the Khoqand Khanate made a unique effort to extend its taxing power into the interiors of Qing-controlled Eastern Turkestan. It requested the Qing to acknowledge: (1) the Khoqand ruler's right to collect duties on all merchandise brought by Muslim traders to the towns of Aksu, Ush (Ush Turfan), Kashgar, Yangi Hissar, Yarkand, and Khutan according to Islamic law (*baj*); (2) the Khoqand ruler's authority to appoint in each of those towns a superintendent of trade (*acsaqal*) to collect these dues, under the purview of a Khoqand inspector to reside in Kashgar as a Khoqand political representative; and (3) the power of these Khoqand agents to be exercised over all foreign Muslims, including non-Khoqandians, residing in these towns in administrative and political matters.[9]

This petition was a dangerously bold move for the Khoqand ruler. After all, it was unprecedented, and encroached upon the fundamental expression of the sovereignty of the Qing in Eastern Turkestan—the exclusive right to levy tax. Such request to exercise extensive tax right in the Qing controlled territory could easily enrage the Qing ruler, and thus could prompt the court to cut off once again the Khoqand ruler's access to the lucrative trade conduits in Kashgar. However, if it was a dangerous move, it was also a desperate one. Growing military competition with neighbors and the swift desertion of its merchants from the Khoqand domain pressed the Khoqand khan to quickly find a new revenue source.

This request was critically important to the sojourning caravan merchants in Kashgar and their allies, the local beg elites. If accepted, the safety of merchant property and wealth in Eastern Turkestan—the very condition underlying the sudden success of the Kashgarian entrepôt—could have been seriously undermined. The rate of the customs duty according to the *baj* that the Khoqand ruler would apply was 2.5 percent for Muslims.[10] In theory, this rate was less than the 3.3 percent that the Central Asian merchants were supposed to pay to the Qing. However, given that the foreign merchants ceased to pay virtually any duties in the early nineteenth century, this imposition of the customs duty according to Islamic law represented a significant hike for them. Furthermore, under the new system, the merchants might also have been vulnerable to the Khoqand Khanate's arbitrary appropriations as well.

It is not clear whether the Khoqand ruler achieved the ambitious goal. The Qing source shows that the court satisfied the Khoqand requests only halfway. On the one hand, it offered a tax exemption for Andijans, as the Khoqand ruler requested, and in fact extended the tax exemption to all other sojourner merchants. On the other hand, the Qing court rejected his demand to establish its taxing authority over the Muslim sojourner merchants (including the Andijans) in Eastern Turkestan. Yet, curiously, the local and European sources claim that the Khoqand succeeded in establishing its tax jurisdiction in Kashgar.[11] Overall, the truth seems to lie somewhere in the middle. Even without Beijing's *official* approval, it stands to reason that the Khoqand gained some success in collecting taxes, especially from the Andijans, probably with the tacit consent of the beg clients and the Qing military governors in the area.

However, what is important to note here is that the Khoqand attempts were never entirely successful, even at the local level. The clearest evidence for its failure is that the Khoqand ruler continually made requests for the tax exemption of Central Asian merchants—in 1835, in one instance, for Badakhshan and Kashmir.[12] This is indeed a strange request in light of the fact that the Qing had already granted a tax exemption to all the Central Asian and South Asian and Middle Eastern traders from outside the Qing border. The best way to understand it is that the Central Asian merchants likely claimed that they continued to pay tax to the Qing. Thus, they were under Qing protection, and should not be subject to the new Khoqand taxation. Here, the merchants used the Qing protection to withstand the Khoqand demands that would tax and appropriate their wealth. The Khoqand could not ignore this claim. Otherwise, it would not even bother to make the request to ask for a tax exemption on the merchant communities. In other words, the Qing military still carried weight in Eastern Turkestan.

Here, we can see the growing importance that presence had for Eastern Turkestani cities and their commercially oriented begs. The cities' economic success depended upon their ability to protect the merchants, who settled in their cities fleeing from the growing squeeze by the regional state builders, and looting from the mountain refugees. The occupation of the Qing military was the reason why Eastern Turkestan was able to provide such protection, and unexpectedly attracted the record number of foreign merchants in the aftermath of the two *khwaja* wars. However, the very success of the city invited another threat—in the form of a Khoqand initiative to expand its taxing authority into Eastern Turkestan precincts. Thus, the begs and merchants had every reason to support the reinforcement of the Qing military presence at any cost.

Governor Zuhūr al-Dīn and Localization of Qing Military Financing

Zuhūr al-Dīn had a career that illuminates this intricate relationship between the beg initiative to develop commerce and Qing military buildup in Eastern Turkestan. He came from a distinguished pedigree, that of Emin Khwāja of Turfan. We do not know exactly when Zuhūr al-Dīn came to Kashgar. However, it is certain that he held the position there of shang beg (an important post that handled the collection of taxes from satellite cities, towns, and villages) sometime before the Jahāngīr War in 1826. Many of Emin Khwāja's descendants served as Muslim governors of Kashgar in the late eighteenth and early nineteenth centuries (see Appendix C-1). These Turfanese often brought their younger family members to Kashgar to serve in lower-rank positions. Most likely, when Mai-ma-sa-yi-te became the Kashgar governor, Zuhūr al-Dīn followed his uncle to Kashgar.

During the Jahāngīr War, Zuhūr al-Dīn migrated to Khoqand, either as a captive or a voluntary migrant. However, he successfully escaped from the Khoqand, traveled to Petropavlovsk (a Russian town located in current-day Kazakhstan, in Central Asia) and Kazan, and returned to Ili, where he presented himself to the Qing authority. At any rate, in 1827 the Qing court decided to send him back to Kashgar to await appointment to an official position. Subsequently, he became its lieutenant governor (*ishikaga*). By 1831 he had been referred to as a governor of Kashgar District in the Qing record.[13]

Viewing the Kashgar governor's career, and certainly drawing from local sources, both Valikhanov and Bellew commonly noted the expansion of the commercial activities and infrastructure of Kashgar as the governor's crowning achievement. They highlighted his reconstruction and expansion of the Muslim city in 1838, on a gate of which was placed a plate that inscribed the governor's name and title. The rebuilt city of Kashgar had seventeen *madrasa*s, seventy schools, two marketplaces, and most important, eight caravanserai for housing the caravan merchants. Foreign merchant communities, originating from various locations across Central Asia, occupied shops in the quarters. The more prominent among them were the Andijans, Margilans, and Afghans. Others included merchants from Bukhara, Yarkand, and Aksu, as well as the Tajiks and Jews.[14] Valikhanov even enumerated as one of Zuhūr al-Dīn's major achievements the attraction of Russian Tartar merchants into Kashgar, an achievement that the Qing source did not mention.

Given the unmistakably mercantilist nature of the Muslim client regime following the Qing conquest, Zuhūr al-Dīn's active promotion of trade in Kashgar is not surprising. What is, however, concerns another aspect of the Zuhūr al-Dīn rule—namely, his proactive support of the Qing military buildup. In an unspecified year, the governor reportedly built a new military base, called "Mangshin" (Manchu fortress) or "New City" in the local record, near the central Muslim city to replace the former Manchu military base, called Gulbagh, which had been destroyed in the *khwaja* wars.[15]

Unfortunately, the imperial court's record does not recognize the governor's major contribution to the rebuilding of the new military base that housed Qing troops in the wake of the Yūsuf War. However, it did recognize several Muslim begs' contribution to the rebuilding of the Qing military bases in various Eastern Turkestani oases, including timber, grain, and laborers.[16] In other words, the record about Zuhūr al-Dīn's private contribution to the rebuilding of the new Manchu fortress of Kashgar reflected the general change underway in the method of military financing of the Qing troops stationed in Eastern Turkestan after the Yūsuf Khwāja War.

Certainly, the European observers did not see any direct connection between Zuhūr al-Dīn's two major achievements. Valikhanov even portrays him as an anti-Chinese ruler who "protected the interests of the inhabitants of [Kashgar] against Chinese officials."[17] However, certainly that was a one-sided characterization of his career. Even based solely on the information provided by European observers, Zuhūr al-Dīn proactively supported the Qing military buildup. Careful examination of his career reveals that there was indeed a connection between the two achievements. The Qing military provided the material conditions that supported the "just" and "liberal" rule of Zuhūr al-Dīn. To the extent that this was the case, he had every reason to support the Qing military in Kashgar, even from his own pocket. He needed the Qing military to build up a new order of prosperity and wealth in Kashgar. This mutually reinforcing dynamic between the promotion of trade and agriculture and Qing military buildup defined Zuhūr al-Dīn's relations with the Qing empire during his entire reign.

The beginning of Zuhūr al-Dīn's rule in Kashgar coincided with the Qing reform policy applied in Eastern Turkestan under the seasoned hands of the Manchu general Changling. This veteran of the frontier administration had once worked with Nayancheng after the Jahāngīr War. In 1831, the Qing court sent Changling back to Kashgar to readjust Nayancheng's plan. During his short tenure as the prime imperial agent in the oasis, Changling rolled back many different aspects of Nayancheng's reforms. For instance, he reopened the trade with Khoqand and allowed the Andijans to settle in the oasis again. Also, in order not to alienate the Muslim begs, Changling abandoned Nayancheng's reforms of the beg administration, including the application of the rule of avoidance and the establishment of centralized control over beg appointments.

Most fundamentally, however, Changling shared with Nayancheng his strategic judgment regarding the defense of the oases. The most immediate and effective solution to the *khwaja* threat was the reinforcement of the Qing military within the territory. If anything, the need for a troop increase was even greater during the post–Yūsuf War period than at the time of the Nayancheng reform, because the Yūsuf War showed that the *khwaja* threat would not go away soon, and was there to stay. Meanwhile, what made Changling's job complicated was that the Yūsuf War clearly revealed the vicious circle in which the Qing's action of increasing revenue extraction from the oasis population would contribute to the enlargement also of the *khwaja* force, the very threat it wanted to eliminate.

Changling thus had to achieve a substantial level of troop increase in the oasis without overly burdening the oasis population. An important part of the conundrum was to find the minimum level of troop increase that could secure the oasis. The number Changling calculated was five thousand; this was a substantial reduction from the number originally floated by Nayancheng: seventy-five hundred to eight thousand.[18]

Yet, more imperative was Changling's need to devise financial measures that would support such an increased troop level without increasing the level of burden imposed on the oasis population, at least directly. He found the solution by increasing the development of a nontax, nontribute revenue. Changling and the Qing court identified four new revenue sources that could be described as a nontax resource. The first aspect of this plan was the increase of the silver transfer from China to Xinjiang. The post–Jahāngīr War era witnessed a threefold increase in the volume of silver transferred from China to Xinjiang by the Qing government. From 1759 to 1827, it transferred 60,000 *liang* per year from the imperial coffers; from 1828 to 1852, the imperial court transferred 200,000 *liang* annually to the oasis from the provincial government of Shaanxi and Gansu provinces.[19] Previous scholars have focused on this aspect, and tended to understand the Qing policy during the post–Yūsuf War period as a model of deficit financing of the Qing military enterprise. However, the Qing also made significant efforts to develop local nontax revenue sources, and gained success from the endeavor.

First, they solicited private donations (*sunna*) from the local Turkic oasis residents—a measure that the imperial court implemented throughout its empire on a wide scale in the early nineteenth century. Those who donated could expect to be awarded beg positions, the Qing official rank, or Qing military ornaments (button or feathers). These awards could be translated into palpable benefits—for example, receiving exemption from forced labor, local influence and honors, and tax farming opportunity.

This was a new turn of the wheel in Qing policy in effect in Eastern Turkestan. Even prior to this period, local begs had donated funds to the Qing military administration, from time to time. They donated food and clothing for the Qing army during major battles; they also built irrigation facilities with their own funds during times of peace. However, the Qing court rarely rewarded such financial contributions with awards of offices at government rank. Such a financial contributor then would receive only gifts of silver, tea, and other material items in return. Especially during the Qianlong Period, the only contribution that entitled the oasis population to a reward of government office and rank was military service in the battlefield. Only when the oasis elites fought alongside the Qing army for a major victory in the battlefield did they receive such official favor. For instance, if a beg official died while fighting against the Qing's enemies, his son would receive the prestigious reward of an inheritable beg post.[20] Thus, Changling's measure signaled a radical departure from previous policy.

The second measure that the Qing newly adopted during this period was the expansion of *tuntian* in Eastern Turkestan. Its local administration would directly operate the agrarian colonies, using Chinese migrants, Green Standard soldiers, as well as convicts and exiles. These people would eventually settle there on a permanent basis with their families, so that their sons and descendants could also serve the permanent or future base needs for military conscription duty in Xinjiang. In fact, this idea first came about right after the Jahāngīr War. However, it was only after the Yūsuf War in 1830 that Eastern Turkestan saw widespread *tuntian* expansion.

This initiative also represented a big departure from previous Qing policy. Previously, the Qing did not allow the establishment of agrarian colonies cultivated by either Chinese or Manchu soldiers in Eastern Turkestan, except for the two easternmost districts of Turfan and Hami. Scholars attributed this to the Qing authority's caution about arousing possible conflicts in the predominantly Muslim Turki area.[21] As a result of this concern, while the Qing may have established large-scale Chinese-operated *tuntian* in Zungharia in places like Ili Valley and Urumqi, a vast space without a substantial agrarian population, the Qing had refrained from establishing them in the Eastern Turkestani oasis. However, the Daoguang court also reversed an earlier policy on this front and began establishing the *tuntian* there on a large scale.

This scheme of raising finances from private donations and new land reclamation generally worked. As a result, the Kashgar Muslims saw a reduced tax burden levied during this period, in spite of the growing revenue needs to support the increase in the Qing troops. In 1827 and 1835, the Zuhūr al-Dīn successfully negotiated with the Qing administration the reduction of the tax and other miscellaneous revenue quota on behalf of the oasis community of Kashgar District; as a result, he was able to roll back all the increases of the tax quota that Nayancheng had instituted.[22]

Muslim Begs and Their Development of the Qing Military's *Tuntian*

Zuhūr al-Dīn and the Muslim notables responded to the new Qing measures enthusiastically. The begs proactively increased private donations to the Qing military and received awards and posts. However, the new financial scheme of the Qing that the begs responded to the most were not the donations and awards. Rather, it was the development of the *tuntian*. Ever since the beginning of that initiative in Eastern Turkestan, they had sought to take over their direct operations, a move that was not solicited by the Qing court in Beijing.

For instance, in 1831 the Muslim governor of Ush, Musa, requested taking over the agricultural colonies at Boxing, formerly cultivated by the Qing soldiers. The governor wanted to do this so that the Qing soldiers could return to the main city [of Ush] to practice military drills. Given the importance of the Qing military for the enrichment of the oases especially after the Yūsuf War, the begs' concern for the maintenance of the competencies of the Qing troops is easily understandable.[23] However, in taking up the operation of the Qing *tuntian*, they had one more motivation other than helping the Qing military.

The begs wanted to use the development of the government *tuntian* as a new entrepreneurial investment opportunity. Through participation in their development, the beg capitalists could obtain tracts of land and secure additional labor, which they could not have done under ordinary circumstances; now they could do so and incur the excellent condition of government support, not the least feature of which was a tax benefit—a point that will be explained below. This marked the beginning of a new era in the beg capitalists' relations with the Qing state. While the begs had received a measure of protection from the Qing for their agrarian developments up to this point, the Qing state and its expansion itself would become the target of the oasis capitalists' venture investments now.

Indeed, the specific economic environment prevalent since the 1830s had encouraged the begs to invest money in landed property rather than keeping it in currency, either in silver or *pul*. The sudden silver influx from China by the Qing government during the period devalued the currency from a rate of 1 *liang* of silver bullion (*yambu*) to 400 *wen* of local copper coins (*pul*) in the late eighteenth century, to the ratio of 1 *liang* to 80 or 100 *wen* in 1827.[24] In order to prevent further devaluation of the silver, and thus stem a disastrous decrease in purchasing power of the Qing administration in the oasis region, the imperial court increased the volume of the copper currency in circulation by issuing devalued *pul* ("worth five coins" and "worth ten coins").[25] In other words, the oasis region saw a huge increase in the amount of currency in circulation (both silver and *pul*) from the time of the Jahāngīr War, resulting in inflation in the local economy. In that situation, beg landlords and other members of the propertied class accumulated their wealth reluctantly in currency values and preferred instead to invest it in land.

In many cases, the Qing military governors became a partner in crime in this development. Many of them even preferred to use the begs in the operation of the *tuntian* in direct violation of the Qing court directive to use Chinese for the development. For instance, in 1844 the military governor of Aksu District, Jirui, gave Ahmad, the governor of Aksu District, the green light to begin land reclamation of the wildland (100,000 *mu*), even before reporting it to Beijing. In this project, Ahmad contributed grain and sheep. When chastised by Beijing for using local Muslims instead of Chinese migrants there, the military governor argued that, while previously Kashgar had used Chinese civilians in land reclamation, now there was simply no need for Aksu to do so. The Qing court, however, remained suspicious about his claim, thinking that Ahmad was the real driving force behind this land development project and that the Muslim governor had exploited the local Muslims in developing the land. The Qing court ordered a temporary halt to the reclamation until further investigation had been conducted.[26]

It is easy to interpret the Qing military governors' cooperation with the Muslim governors as corruption. While it is an important part of the story, however, the reason for the development of this cooperation was more structural. Chinese migrants were not forthcoming to such a remote frontier of the empire, as many Qing military governors freely admitted. And the oasis begs knew the native agrarian conditions there much better. To outsource the management of the agrarian colonies would be much easier for the military governors, rather than directly managing recalcitrant Chinese civilians, soldiers, or convicts. Most of all, the military governors were able to gain much more revenue from the Muslim begs than previously, precisely because of its illicit nature. And the military governors must have welcomed any extra revenue in the 1830s and 1840s to keep up with the intensifying threats of the *khwajas*, Khoqand, and Russia.

In the end, the convergence of the interests between the begs and the Qing military governors on the ground determined the actual course of the *tuntian* development. Except for the eastern sector of Eastern Turkestan (Turfan, Hami, and Qarashar), the majority of the *tuntian* developments were conducted by the Muslims (see Table 4.1). The period right after the two *khwaja* wars, from 1828 to 1857, was the highest point of this Muslim dominated *tuntian* development. Former frontiers of oasis agriculture came under cultivation under this initiative for the first time.

In Kashgar, these years of energetic tuntian development overlap almost

Table 4.1. Qing *Tuntian* Development in Eastern Turkestan

Year	Place (District)	Source of Labor (household number)	Size (mu)	Size (batman)	Tax Rate (Sheng; per mu)	Additional Explanation
1828	*Daheyan* (Kashgar)	Oasis Muslims	1,000,000			
1828	Yarkand	Poor, property-less Muslims	100 *li*			
1828	Ush	Soldiers	8,000	125		3,000 (currently under cultivation per fallow system)
1829	Tatar (Yarkand)	Oasis Muslims	160 *li*			A small settlement 50 *li* east of the city; Contribution to the irrigation by *shang* beg and *mīrāb* beg
1829	Khoshabād (Yarkand)	Oasis Muslims	150 *li*			A small settlement west of the city; Contribution to the irrigation by *shang* beg and *mīrāb* beg
1833	Shayar (Kucha)	Poor, property-less Muslims	50,000		Taxation after three years	
1834	Barchuq (Kasghar)	Chinese civilians (360)	24,000 (100,000 in 1836)	375 (1,562 in 1836)	3	*tuntian*
1833	Shayar (Kucha)	Poor, property-less Muslims	50,000	781	Tax after three years	
1843	Qarashar	Chinese civilians	100,000	1,562		
1844	Ilaliq (Turfan)	Chinese civilians	110,000	1,562		
1845	Lang-ha-li-ke (Aksu)		102,300,	1,598		
1844	Aksu	Oasis Muslims	100,000	1,562	5	
1844–45	Davak (Khotan)	Oasis Muslims	101,000	1,578		
	Kucha	Property-less Muslims				
1844	Kashgar	Oasis Muslims				
1845	A-qi-wu-su (Kucha)					Contribution to the land reclamation by Hākim Beg, Ha-lo-za-te, *shang* Beg Lai-li-zhu-pu, and Du-guan Beg Yi-si-ma-yi-er.

Year	Place (District)	Source of Labor (household number)	Size (mu)	Size (batman)	Tax Rate (Sheng; per mu)	Additional Explanation
1845	Qurghan (Yarkand)	Property-less Muslims (800)	98,000	1,531	5	Each household was allocated 120 *mu*
1845	East bank of river (Kashgar)	Oasis Muslims	67,200	1,050	5	
1845	West bank (Kashgar)	Chinese civilians	16,098	251		
1847	Kucha	Oasis Muslims	120,393	1,881		
1845	Hami	Chinese civilians	5,720	89		Donation by the Hami *junwang* to the Qing
1845	Hami	Chinese civilians	4,832	75		Same with above
1848	Davak (Khotan)	Oasis Muslims	28,100	439	5	Additional 4,100 *mu* allocated as *yanqi* land
1849	Atbash (Khotan)				5	
1857	Lotbash (Ush)				5	

Sources: MZSL, vol. 82; XZSL, vols. 160, 241, 249, 254, 398, 405, 409, 410, 412, 419, 425, 428, 441, 459, 464, 475; HJFL, p. 3688; Kun'gang, ed. *Qinding Da Qing huidian shili (Guangxu Chao)*, vol. 163; ibid., vol. 178; *Tongzhi hubu zeli*, vol. 6.

Note: Size: 1 *batman* = 64 *charak/mu* = 5 *shi* 3 *dou*. See Wang Shouli and Jinxin Li, *Xinjiang Weiwu'er Zu Qiyue Wenshu Ziliao Xuanbian*, p. 11. There are different opinions about this measurement: 1 *batman* = 100 *mu*. See Hori Sunao, "Jūhachi-nijū seiki Uiguru joku no doryōkō ni tsuite," p. 64. In this table's calculation, I followed the first, more widely used, rate of conversion.

identically with Zuhūr al-Dīn's tenure. Notably, the major sites in Kashgar were built up in 1828 (Daheyan), 1832 (Ka-la-he-yi), and 1844–45. Careful examination of these developments in Kashgar, which were unusually well documented, sheds light on the structure and dynamics of the begs' entrepreneurial development of the *tuntian*.

Governor Zuhūr al-Dīn's Entrepreneurial Developments at the Margins of Kashgar

The agrarian colony development in Kashgar began slightly before Zuhūr al-Dīn became the Governor of Kashgar. In 1828, right after the end of the Jahāngīr War, a Chinese court politician in Beijing, Qian Yiji, suggested that the Qing administration develop an agrarian colony in the Kashgar area, at a place called Daheyan, 100 *li*, or 10,000 *qing* of land, along the River Ulan Usu, which streamed eastward across the Kashgar oasis. This development would help to defray the costs of the Qing residential forces that would be increased in the area in the aftermath of the Jahāngīr War. For the purpose, Qian proposed to dispatch southward Green Standard soldiers who had previous experience with the *tuntian* in northern Xinjiang, specifically relating to the projects' development in the oasis.

However, the Qing military commanders on the ground in Xinjiang had a quite different idea. Changling, working as the supreme military commander of the Qing forces arrayed against the *khwaja* at the time, and other Qing military commanders such as Ili General Wulong'a, questioned the wisdom of using Chinese soldiers for *tuntian* development in the predominantly Muslim area of the oasis. They were worried primarily about potential conflicts that might arise between the two groups stemming from such an initiative. Yet, they did not reject outright the idea of *tuntian* development, Instead, the Manchu generals proposed to dispatch the local Muslim soldiers and "poor Muslims without property" from Kashgar District first to do irrigation work, a prerequisite for the successful development of agriculture in the area. If a year of an initial test cultivation by the Muslims succeeded, then the major effort of the *tuntian* development could be undertaken, this time using Chinese soldiers.[27]

However, the *tuntian* development in Kashgar took a new turn under the direction of Nayancheng in 1828.[28] Citing the concerns about the cost of the project, Nayancheng dispatched five hundred *bederege* who had wanted to fund their own reclamation project in the area, instead of "poor Muslims". The *bederege* would open irrigation ditches to reclaim the land at their own expense. It is not difficult to imagine that as chief developer of this pilot phase of test cultivation to recruit oasis labor and organize them for the task, on the call of the Qing military governors, the Muslim governors of Kashgar, first a man named Ishāq and later Zuhūr al-Dīn, would have had a significant say in the sudden change of Nayancheng's proposal.

In other words, from the beginning, the Manchu and Muslim governors of Kashgar conceived of the *tuntian* development projects as commercial land development endeavors sponsored by a consortium of commercial developers. The numbers of caravan merchants were increasing exponentially during the period, as has been shown above. These sojourner merchants always had an interest in acquiring land ownership in Kashgaria, at least during the Qing rule. Especially given the general circumstances of the devaluation of currency during this time, they saw the profitable opportunity available to them if they could participate in the Qing's land development. Certainly, not all five hundred *bederege* were wealthy caravan merchants. A majority of them were landless oasis farmers, sojourners as well, recruited by the merchants with promises that they could secure their own land.[29]

In so doing, the Kashgar governors expanded what the beg officials had already been doing, if illegally. In 1824 the military governor of Kashgar accused a fifth-rank beg, Yūnus, of privately purchasing government lands and selling them to Andijan merchants. This practice was against law and regulation in 1824. However, Nayancheng now legalized this practice. In relying on the caravan merchants in the *tuntian* development in Daheyan, Nayancheng saved the Qing the onerous costs of the construction of irrigation facilities, the most intrinsic component to any land enterprise in the oasis. The Qing governors were content to allow the merchants to develop ditches and waterways on their own,[30] although they provided other land development–related costs (that is, seeds, cattle, and farming equipment); they did it indirectly, by subtracting it from the first year's tax payment.[31] If the Qing administration were to have conducted the *tuntian* development directly using Chinese or Manchu labor, it would have had to cover this expense of irrigation. For one such direct development of *tuntian* in Ush (8,000 *mu*), which took place during this period, Nayancheng invested 3,000 *liang* of silver to build a canal, ditches, and other irrigation facilities.[32]

The initial result of the *tuntian* development in Daheyan was successful. According to Ishāq, the developers planted 500 *batman* of mixed grains, and they had all ripened one year later. Probably acknowledging the capital contributions of the merchant developers, the Qing set a light tax quota for the new oasis settlements: 2,000 *shi* (1,000 people [500 Muslim soldiers and 500 *bederege*]). Set at the rate of 2 *shi* per person, this amount was less than the usual tax rate of 2.4 to 3.5 *shi* levied per household in the newly reclaimed land.[33] Also, this payment of a fixed amount of tax per person was different from the sharecropping method that Wulong'a originally had proposed—the payment of one-half of the harvest.[34] This new agreement of payment at a fixed low rate undoubtedly extended much more profit to the entrepreneurial developers than did the sharecropping levy.

However, evidence suggests that Zuhūr al-Dīn's and the caravan merchants grew unsatisfied with the terms of their investment in the *tuntian* land development in Daheyan. Thus, the merchants consequently asked for a reduction in the tax payment quota that they had to pay, blaming the poor soil quality and irrigation problems of their *tuntian* settlement, now referred to as Cha-la-gen village. Of the total 300 *batman* constituting the land area, 150 *batman* were "salty" and sterile, they argued. Another 70 *batman* of land had water problems. "The land is located high and the water and river, low. The land could not be cultivated."[35] By 1835, only 80 *batman* lay under cultivation.

In order to meet the tax quota of 2,000 *shi,* Governor Zuhūr al-Dīn had to pay half of its total, 1,000 *shi,* to the government out of his own pocket on behalf of the settlers after 1829.[36] The Qing military governor decided to reduce by half the tax payment quota to 1,000 *shi.*[37] Yet, in the end even the newly renegotiated term did not satisfy Zuhūr al-Dīn and his associated merchants. In 1838, Zuhūr al-Dīn asked to relocate the one thousand Muslims who had worked in the village to another place.[38] Claiming now that the one thousand Muslim households had all abandoned their land there and dispersed because of the destruction caused by the Yūsuf War in 1830,[39] the governor requested giving them a new site that had been recently discovered. Named Song-gu-la-qi, it was virtually empty, although the land was fertile. If he received permission from the Qing, Zuhūr al-Dīn would work with the Muslim households to put the empty land under cultivation, and pay tax according to the old quota.

A newly appointed Qing military governor, Fuxing'a, became immediately suspicious about Zuhūr al-Dīn's claim—and rightly so. In fact, his excuse did not add up. First of all, when he had negotiated a reduction of the land tax quota three years earlier, in 1835, Zuhūr al-Dīn was citing low productivity of the *tuntian* to request a reduction in payment from the Qing administration. However, he did not mention any disturbance caused by the aftermath of the Yūsuf War in 1830, nor did he mention the dispersal of the people there as a result of the disturbance.[40]

In greatest likelihood, therefore, the 1838 request was less a petition brought forward by the poor oasis farmers who had directly suffered from the political disaster than a Muslim developer's calculated attempt to relocate their precious resources and labor assets to a more profitable spot for land development, one with better soil quality and water conditions. In response, Fuxing'a immediately dispatched a Qing official to the Cha-la-gen area, to investigate thoroughly whether the *tuntian* there had indeed become so desolate, or whether something else lay behind the request. He also sent Qing officials to examine the new land in the Song-gu-la-qi area to investigate whether the place was indeed largely empty, meaning whether Zuhūr al-Dīn's party would want to drive out the local residents already there to occupy the promising land.

Unfortunately, we do not know the specific conclusions of those reports. Yet the history that has been examined so far of Zuhūr al-Dīn's involvement with Cha-la-gen village makes this much clear: the mechanism that drove the begs' involvement in the Qing *tuntian* development featured entrepreneurial opportunity writ large. The governor orchestrated this activity by organizing a developer consortium with the sojourner merchants, who provided the capital and recruited the labor. In turn, the Muslim governors' further commercial development of *tuntian* made possible the enhanced expansion of the Qing state in the oasis desert. It enabled the Qing administration to broaden its revenue base to include the former wildland that had been outside the purview of Qing state appropriation for agrarian development. With the newly increased revenue, the Qing could also expand its military capacity in the oasis.

Under this scheme, the expansion of the Qing state during the period went hand in hand with the expansion of the influence of the oasis capitalists in its sphere as well. Once a new settlement was established in a *tuntian* site, the Qing administration installed new beg posts and provided a grant of land and *yanqi* and cash to each one accordingly. Given that the *tuntian* were developed by the begs and their developer associates, they could themselves claim larger numbers of new positions in order to manage them and increase the land grant packages attached to the positions, along with exercising revenue contracting rights associated with the posts. For instance, Zuhūr al-Dīn retained within the Cha-la-gen village a plot of "private" land cultivated by his own *yanqi*, with whose production the governor help the village community pay its tax to the Qing administration from 1829 to 1835. In another instance, in 1848 the Qing government established a new settlement in Khotan called Davak under the scheme of commercial development. Among the 28,100 *mu* of its total reclaimed land, 4,100 *mu*—that is, one-seventh of the total amount—was provided as "*yanqi* land" to the new begs established there.[41]

This indicates that the structural problem that had threatened the security of the Qing empire throughout the late eighteenth and early nineteenth centuries—the begs' capitalist exploitation of rural oasis society—had been transplanted whole into the new venture settlements, probably at an amplified level. Qing military governors' power of overseeing and intervening in the capitalist development occurring at these new sites was weak, even if they had wanted to intervene. The projects were virtually all begs' private commercial colonies, located at the margin of the oasis system far from the eyes of the Qing military authority in the urban centers. This predicament would eventually undermine the great success of Qing state building conducted during Governor Zuhūr al-Dīn's regime.

Some military governors felt uneasy about the political implications of the unchecked expansion of the begs' control over land situated on the outskirts of the oasis districts. These military governors drew up a new strategy, to provide the new begs established in the new settlements with cash payments of *pul* coin as compensation for their service, paid from local administration treasuries, rather than in options of tax-exempt land and *yanqi*. This measure would certainly curtail the expansion of the beg-dominated land grab and thus reduce a source of potential social conflict between the begs and their associated merchant developers, on the one hand, and the settlers-laborers recruited by the former to conduct the actual work in the new settlements, on the other. Also, this measure strengthened the Qing military governor's control over the begs in the new settlements by putting them directly on the military governor's cash payroll. Such arrangements took effect in the reclaimed land in Qurghan (Hou-er-han) and Yangi Hissar, both established in the 1840s.

However, the Muslim governors opposed this plan. Thus, in 1849, the governor of Yangi Hissar, A-bu-du-ha-li-ke, even proposed to offer his own private land, a plot of a "vegetable garden" (45 *mu*), to pay the cost of providing *yanqi* and tax-exempt land to two newly established begs in the new settlements in the reclaimed land area.[42] After all, what the oasis landlords and the sojourner merchants wanted from their participation in the land development was actual domination over the land, not cash payments. Without the promise of such dominion over the new settlements, the Muslim governors could not attract any investors to join in the consortium of developers.

The Daoguang court in Beijing was not entirely comfortable with the beg land initiatives either. In 1845, in the midst of the latter's land development frenzy, the emperor expressed a worry regarding it. In that year, the military governor of Kucha had reported his completion of a survey of "waste land" that the Qing could utilize for new *tuntian*. His intention was to use the impoverished oasis Muslims to develop the colonies. But the emperor responded negatively. While he preferred using Chinese migrants for the land reclamation, the emperor ordered that, if the military governors wanted to conduct land development with native Muslims, they should pay attention to the Muslim workers' reactions regarding it. At any sign of their exploitation, the military governor should not force the reclamation. What the emperor was concerned about was the reality of the land reclamation contracted to the beg developers.

The arrangement may have worked on the surface to help the Qing expand its revenue and help impoverished, property-less Muslims to gain a livelihood. However, the logic of the commercial development behind the great expansion of the new *tuntian* dictated that intensifying socioeconomic tensions simmered behind the state-initiated land projects; in turn, the ramifications that might ensue held dire consequences for the security of the Qing Empire.

As the Qing military governors on the ground saw it, however, while political logic dictated that the Qing move away from the beg-initiated resource developments, the daunting demographic and ecological realities in the oasis forced the imperial court to stay the course. Only three months after the Daoguang emperor's warning, the Ili General, Bu-yan-tai, reported another project in the vicinity of Khotan by the oasis Muslims. In defense of his recommendation to the skeptical emperor to allow this new project, the general again articulated the inevitable logic behind his prior initiative. He said, "Khotan is 800 li away, southeast from Yarkand, remote even within the Muslim domains. And the newly reclaimed land is more remote; not only is it difficult to recruit Chinese civilian households but also the Muslims who have property would not be easy to force to come."[43] Commercial land development by the merchants and their hired workers was the only way to develop valuable resources in the far-off oasis.

Yet, what this Manchu general did not mention or notice was that this potentially dangerous commercial development of the government-controlled land did not occur solely at the limited fringes of the oasis system. In fact, it was well under way even in the urban centers of the oasis during Zuhūr al-Dīn's reign. There at the center, however, the government land that the begs and their merchant associates developed did not involve *tuntian* per se. The Qing military base itself, the most unlikely candidate for commercial development, occupied the attention of the oasis capitalists.

The Price of Privatization of the Qing Military Financing

In those years, the Qing authority investigated a commander of the Chinese Green Standard Army (*zongbing*), Liu Yunzhong, in Kashgar District, in regard to a charge brought by a group of Chinese migrants working on the Qing *tuntian*. A piece of information had come up during their questioning and had caught the attention of the Qing authority: Oasis Muslims from rural villages had been occupying the interior of a small former Qing military fortress. Located to the south of the Manchu compound, it contained about fifty buildings. There, the

Table 4.2. Land Use of the Military Land in Kashgar District

Place	1828–30	1830–34	1835	1836	1837
(1) Ka-la-he-yi	Military base (1000 troops); *tuntian* (315 *batman*; cultivated by 506 Chinese households)	Military base (1800 troops); *tuntian* (315 *batman*; cultivated by 506 Chinese households)	Military base (1800 troops); *tuntian* (315 *batman*; cultivated by property-less Muslims)		
(2) Qilihe	Military base (600 troops)	Empty	Private use by the Muslims on duty (*tongshi*)		
(3) Gulbagh	Military base (200 troops)	Empty	Pasture to be used by the foreign tribute envoys' sheep, cattle, etc.		
(4) Unnamed, 3 *li* south of the Muslim city	Military base		Private use by Muslims on duty (2–3 *mu* per person); 50 earthen buildings rented out to local Muslims and traders		

Sources: XJZDHB DG, pp. 187–90, docs. 104 and 105, DG17; XZSL, vols. 129, 260, 269;
Note: 1 *batman* = 64 *charak*/*mu* = 5 *shi* 3 *dou*.

Muslims sold cotton cloth. The information triggered an investigation, which found that in 1835, Zuhūr al-Dīn had gained permission from the military governor of Kashgar District to develop the land there. Additionally, three other tracts had been granted by the local military governor to him for that purpose.[44] Table 4.2 shows a schematic review of the change in land use on the site.

The four tracts all constituted formal government landholdings belonging to the Qing military. The first place in question was Ka-la-ha-yi, where the Qing military built a new Manchu fortress in 1828 (site one in Table 4.2). This was also the site of a Qing government-run *tuntian*.[45] The second place was Qilihe (Seven Li River), located between the new Manchu fortress and the Muslim city, approximately 20 *li* away from the Muslim city (site two in Table 4.2). It was also the site of another former military base, where the Qing military had stationed six hundred troops. The third place, called Gulbagh, featured the site of an original Manchu fortress used since the Qing conquest, which once had stationed two hundred soldiers (site three in Table 4.2). This land had also been the camp of the Kashgar *khwaja*s when they held power in the city prior to the Qing conquest. The fourth place was an unnamed site located 3 *li* south of the Muslim city (site four in Table 4.2). It had a small round fortress, where a small number of Qing forces had been stationed.

Except for the new Manchu fortress in Ka-la-he-yi, other military land had fallen into disuse by the Qing military after the Yūsuf War in 1830. During the war, the Qing military commanders had recalled the Qing soldiers who had been formerly stationed at three other sites to consolidate them into the new Manchu fortress, so that they could mount an effective defense against the *khwaja* warriors. These recalled Qing soldiers did not go back to their original stations of duty, even after the end of the war.

Even if the Qing military governors had wanted to send the soldiers back, they would not have been able to. After gaining permission from the Qing military governor in 1835, Zuhūr al-Dīn had turned this land to commercial use. He lent site two to the Muslim *tongshi* (interpreters) for cultivation and turned site three into grassland, supposedly in preparation for the tribute envoys, who would come with flocks of sheep. He used site four in two ways. One part was again given to the Muslim *tongshi*. On the other portion, he constructed buildings and rented them out to rural villagers and merchants selling cotton. Every month, Zuhūr al-Dīn collected several hundred *wen* of rent from them; this complemented other funds he needed to pay wages and food costs for the oasis Muslims he had mobilized elsewhere, for mining saltpeter for the Qing administration.

This investigation reveals the intricacy of how the Qing government lands were actually utilized in the Eastern Turkestani oasis in practice after the *khwaja* wars ended in the early nineteenth century. Without the accidental revelation uncovered during the investigation of a charge brought forward by migrant Chinese agrarian colonialists, we might only have known the land use of these plots generically, simply as government land. However, such sites were all contracted to the Muslim governors for development, if unofficially. First and foremost, the Qing military governor and Zuhūr al-Dīn used income from these landholdings to defray the costs of local administration. Supporting interpreters working in local government and the miners working on government duty, as well as receiving the tribute missions, were all important government functions.

Still, Zuhūr al-Dīn took in much more revenue than he actually paid to the Qing administration in his commercial use of these former military land sites. Location mattered in this regard. These tracts all existed within a short distance of a Muslim city and the new Manchu fortress. The value of suburban land in the Eastern Turkestani oasis system was highest when the lots were situated nearest to the major consumption centers of the central Muslim cities and Qing fortresses.[46] Thousands of Qing soldiers needed vegetables, grain, and meat, and likewise, thousands of local and sojourning Muslim populations needed the same. That proximity to the marketplace skyrocketed the value of land in the prime area of the suburbs.[47]

That Zuhūr al-Dīn was able to rent out one section of the military land to local village traders testifies to the commercial value of the former military lands. It may even be that the local village traders were not village traders at all. Wealthy oasis traders were present who used such suburban sites as collection points to buy cotton cloth from the surrounding villages to sell to growing numbers of international wholesale merchants, who also would come, in the nineteenth century, to the urban centers of the oasis to buy cotton.[48]

Thus, one should take the claims of the Qing military governor and Zuhūr al-Dīn, that they did this merely to support the functions of government, with a grain of salt. Truly this development, which privileged Zuhūr al-Dīn, should be understood as his gaining the right to develop commercially viable plots of land on behalf of a consortium of affluent local begs and merchants. Indeed, the *tongshi* interpreters were not the poor government functionaries that they were painted out to be. They were affluent landlords and merchants in their own right. As the story of the Guo-pu-er, a *tongshi*-turned-beg, in Chapter 2 shows, they developed personal relationships with the Qing generals and Muslim client rulers, who in turn could provide them privileged positions in government trade as well as opportunities to participate in government land and mining development. Thus, as commercialized oasis landlords who wanted to use government service as a crucial means to promote their economic agendas, indeed, the *tongshi* were social peers of the begs. Many later became beg officials.[49]

In this regard it is notable that it was the Chinese agrarian colonists who in the first place had brought forward to the Qing authority the information about its military governor's contracting out government land to the begs. As the colonizers, the Chinese agrarian colonists may well have seen the privilege to own and occupy this kind of coveted land as rightfully theirs. In other words, the Chinese colonists who leaked the information about these transactions were the kinds of merchants and adventurers who were interested in these tracts themselves. Their fury most likely derived from the fact that they had been cut out of the action; such coveted land deals would likely have fallen into their hands if not for the collusion of the local Qing military governors and Zuhūr al-Dīn.

This state of affairs had dangerous implications for the security of the Qing Empire. By subjecting the centrally located land of the occupying military bases to beg commercial development ventures, the local Qing military governors brought a volatile element of social crisis right into its midst, into the actual heart of Qing power in the borderland oases: on the premises of the Qing military base itself. To implement the many schemes of land development, the governors and their associates permitted many landless poor oasis farmers, locals and foreigners, on-site, and seriously exploited their labor. Now, at the center of the power of the Qing-beg regime, a cauldron simmered.

Clearly, the local Qing military authority in Xinjiang sensed the inherent dangers in such "liberal" development policies. In the follow-up to the 1837 investigation of the use of the military lands, examined above, the Qing military governors debated what to do next.[50] Two camps came up with two different ways to ensure peace and security in the new context of the diverse, vibrant international entrepôt that was Kashgar. One side advocated adapting to the new situation of the expanding presence of the Muslim space of commercial land use and capitalist agriculture. They argued: "[T]he affairs of [the] frontier should be managed on the basis of the consideration of [the] situation in the area." If the Qing considered a strategic response only, it would need to send troops back in, to recover the two abandoned military bases and restation soldiers in all three places. However, if the Qing administration took into consideration the local condition in the Muslim domain, such an operation would not be appropriate; in taking away the land from the Muslims, thus depriving oasis Muslims of their livelihood, social unrest would be stirred up.

In spite of two rounds of the devastating *khwaja* wars, Kashgar had become a bustling international entrepôt; the state space—that is, the military bases of the Qing—had contracted, and, in its place, the local Muslim space had expanded. However, ironically this change now also provided the Qing military sufficient finances, and peace, or the semblance of it, at the very least. This camp's point of view concluded that it would not be advisable to reverse course.

The other camp eyed the same development—the bustling commercial and agrarian developments in Xinjiang—warily. One Qing commander argued the following: "In 1828, Imperial agent Nayancheng stationed soldiers in the Qilihe and Old Manchu fortress in addition to the New Manchu fortress, and had the three places communicate with one another. At the time, the Qing expelled Andijans outside of the Qing border, and prohibited their trade of the tea and rhubarb in the oasis. The Muslims became pacified and respectful. Thus, there had been no trouble inside the Qing border. Now, the Qing allows the oasis to trade with Andijan again." "The Andijan Muslim traders residing in the old city are 6,000, or 7,000. If there is trouble, we cannot be sure whether the Andijan would not have the same intention [as] the Khoqand." In contrast, "Now, the number of Manchu soldiers from Ili stationed in Kashgar city is 500, and the number of the Green Standard soldiers is 3,500. They are total 4,000 in number. For several years, they are all stationed within the [new] Manchu fortress." Their point was not so subtle. The Qing troops were outnumbered by foreign residents in their own stronghold.[51]

This camp's exclusive fixation on the Andijans as the foremost threat to the security of the Qing Empire in Xinjiang had it wrong. However, nonetheless, those worried Qing commanders had a point. Interpreted broadly, what these military commanders pointed out was the political danger inherent in the expansion of the commercial and capitalist space within the oasis of Kashgar. Once set in motion, its logic would bring dangerous elements—especially Andijans, in the eyes of some concerned Qing military commanders—into the very citadel of strength of the Qing state in Kashgar—namely, the military base occupying the center of its district. Not only would this pose a threat to the security of the empire from within, but it also represented an irony. What these military commanders did not know, or simply did not mention, was that this quandary was of the Qing's own doing. The benefit of Qing military protection was what in the first place had brought so many wealthy sojourner merchants into Eastern Turkestan in the early nineteenth century. And it was the Qing administration that had permitted the overtaking of its now shrinking military space by allowing the expansion of capitalist development. This had been done when local military governors had contracted out the *tuntian* development to beg capitalists for the convenience of raising increased revenue for the benefit of Qing power.

The Seven Khwaja War and the End of Zuhūr al-Dīn's Regime

As the potential for social unrest in the oasis actually materialized into frequent local violence in the 1840s,[52] a new *khwaja* war broke out after long years of hiatus. In the summer of 1847, while the Khoqand ruler was away fighting against Tashkent and Bukhara, the Walī Khān Khwāja, a nephew of Jahāngīr Khwāja, led a group comprising Andijan "bandits" and Kirghiz to break into the Qing border outside of Kashgar District. This was the first *khwaja* attack on the city in sixteen years. With supporters also joining from the rural villages of

Kashgar District, the *khwaja* put its main city under siege. Soon, Named Khan, a Tashkent merchant living within the city, opened the city gates from inside and helped them to occupy it.[53]

This *khwaja* attack was known as the "Seven Khwaja War," for it was led by the seven sons and younger relatives of Jahāngīr Khwāja. This time, unlike the earlier two events, the fighting gained only a limited success. The Muslim city of Kashgar did fall to the *khwaja* side. However, their success stopped there. The Qing troops and pro-Qing begs retreated into the new Manchu fortress and made a firm defense against the *khwaja* forces, anticipating reinforcements of Qing troops from the east and north. Although the *khwaja* troops sent their forces into Yarkand, they were routed by Chinese convicts stationed in the city. Soon, as the Qing reinforcement forces arrived, the *khwaja* forces were quickly defeated and they dispersed, some running away to Khoqand.[54]

With the *khwaja* attack in 1847, the surprisingly prosperous regime of Zuhūr al-Dīn ended abruptly. In spite of its being short-lived and unsuccessful, the Seven Khwaja War left the rural oasis villages totally devastated. The depopulation of Kashgar caused by the war was extensive. In fact, it was much greater than the depopulation caused by any of the previous rebellions. A pro-Qing beg individual, who had hidden in the mountains within the territory of a like-minded Kirghiz headman during the war, witnessed a march of some twelve or thirteen thousand "male, female, big, and small" Muslims from Kashgar and Yangi Hissar, who joined retreating pro-*khwaja* Kirghiz; they moved through the mountain passes to a destination located beyond the Qing realm, in a procession lasting for four days.[55] Many died en route, the bones of the dead still visible where they had fallen even thirty years after the event.[56] Certainly, many of these oasis residents (pro-Qing in their loyalties) had left the oasis involuntarily, carried by pro-*khwaja* Kirghiz chieftains as "captives." But chances are, some of the farmers may have voluntarily followed the pro-*khwaja* force and left Kashgar, fleeing from the entrenched beg exploitation, especially in the new settlement.

Their numbers—twelve or thirteen thousand people—may seem unrealistically high. However, some evidence supports this begs' estimation. By 1847, immediately after the Seven Khwaja War, Qing commander Yishan reported, from the rural village of Artush, that some 3,160 households of former tax-paying oasis Muslims on the register were still missing. Of the "households without property"—that is, those who were not on the tax register—the Qing commander did not know how many were missing. If we assume that a household consists of five people, then fifteen thousand people from the tax register went missing after the war. After a month's persuasion, a later report shows, twelve hundred households came back. By the beginning of 1848, however, nineteen hundred or so households, or ninety-five hundred people, were still missing.[57]

What makes this number astounding is that it derives from a single village, Artush. Even considering that the settlement was a hotbed of *khwaja* agitation, having the shrine of Afāq Khwāja there, this is an impressive loss. One must conclude then that the actual figure of outmigration from Eastern Turkestan as a whole exceeded the level of twelve or thirteen thousand people, considering the possibility that many more oasis people went into the mountains, and across, even without accompanying the *khwajas*. What must have worried the begs and the Qing military governor even more than the sheer numbers was the upward trend of the outmigration. The Qing commander, Yishan, reported that the missing people from Artush were more numerous this time than after the previous *khwaja* war, the Yūsuf War in 1830, noting: "In 1830, when the Great Army arrived, the Muslims who remained [in Kashgar] were many, although there were also Muslims who fled." This time, it was different. Also, in spite of his effort at containing the migration—for instance, sending Qing officers to Muslim cities and villages to call the fleeing Muslims back—they returned only slowly.[58]

The fact of the matter is that these migrants fleeing out of Eastern Turkestan dragged the new regime of prosperity that took root in Kashgar during the Zuhūr al-Dīn' rule into the ruin in their wake. Without a supply of sufficient labor, the new *tuntian* development projects, on which the begs' enrichment as well as the financing of the Qing military largely depended, would have been impossible. Therefore, the begs and Qing military governors were greatly worried, and correctly so.

Conclusion

The beg capitalists unexpectedly built an order of wealth in the Eastern Turkestani oasis in the aftermath of the Jahāngīr War (1826) and Yūsuf War (1830). The increased Qing military presence there in the wake of the two *khwaja* wars had the effect of sheltering the begs and their merchant associates from the double threats troubling their trade and production—namely, the neighboring Central Asian state builders and the refugees. Not only providing a security umbrella, the Qing military presence also invited a new investment opportunity, official and illicit, by granting permissions for the development of its government land in the oasis. Thus the begs effectively hijacked the Qing *tuntian* development that the imperial court had originally designed, envisioning that it would be operated by Chinese migrant farmers, merchants, and soldiers. The begs turned the *tuntian* into an investment opportunity instead, in collaboration with the Qing military governors who became ever conscious about shortages in the military finances supporting their occupation in the oasis. Through this engagement, the begs achieved access to a new resource for agrarian development that had not been available to them previously—namely, choice pieces of landed property at the center of the oasis system and newly irrigated wildland tracts located at its outermost fringe.

In other words, the Qing military took on a new significance for the begs and their developmental agenda in the aftermath of the two *khwaja* wars. If the Qing military had been a protector of the begs' developmental interests prior to these events, it would now become an interested direct participant in local production after the *khwaja* wars. The local Qing military governors developed a collaborative relationship with the beg clients, often in conflict with directives from the Qing court in Beijing. And this new arrangement worked out well for the former. If there is any doubt of the effectiveness of the new military-developer regime, we have the "just and liberal rule" of Zuhūr al-Dīn to demonstrate it.

However, the beg development of the *tuntian* at that time created its own problems, reproducing into its midst the most politically dangerous elements of its society, the displaced oasis population, local and foreign—both at the expanding margins of the oasis agrarian frontier and at the center of the oasis where the Qing military was located. In other words, the expanding space of the beg-initiated agrarian development could rapidly become the expanding space of social resistance against the development as well. The Qing government responded to this latent potential for local unrest by dispatching the beg officials, who had primarily been concentrated in the urban area, into the rural hinterland for the first time. For instance, in 1829 the Qing court ordered the begs within the Yarkand city (regardless of their stated duty) transferred to the new settlements in the district, in order to manage the newly increased rural settlements.[59]

However, the newly established begs faced steep resistance to their survival in the hinterland. In 1837, the Qing military governor of Kashgar had Zuhūr al-Dīn issue an order, that the begs assigned to the rural villages stay in their assigned places and not come back to the main city, unless they had official duty–related work to attend to there.[60] What this order reveals was the tremendous reluctance, or uneasiness, that the local begs felt about their relocation to the rural villages. Obviously, a reluctance to leave the conveniences of urban life played a part. However, seen in combination with the growing social and economic tensions seething within the Muslim villages, this reluctance must also have reflected the animosity the rural villages held toward the relocated urban begs.[61]

In the end, a much more powerful display of control would be needed to reestablish stability to the rural hinterland. The begs needed the Qing military there. If the main reason for the collapse of security in the villages was a lack of the Qing state and military presence in the expanding rural frontier—in other words, the lag between the speed of the agrarian expansion and a lack of state capacity that could safeguard it—then the answer to the problem would be to expand the Qing state and military presence in the oasis. However, it turns out that an unexpected military development taking place at that time along the southeastern coast of China, some 2,500 miles away from the oasis, would make that solution impossible.

5   Global Crises of
Oasis Capitalism, 1847–64

Looking back from the first decade of the twentieth century, Mullā Mūsa Sayrāmī started his narrative of the fall of the Qing Empire in Eastern Turkestan in 1864 with an unusual event.[1] "At this time, the territory of the Chinese emperor was invaded by English Christians; its 72 towns were occupied and destroyed." Amid political turmoil ensuing in China including rebellions of Chinese (Khitay; "kara khitay" in the original text), the Chinese emperor decided to cut the provisions that would sustain the Qing soldiers in the "Seven Cities." In response, the Qing military governors and the pro-Qing begs, headed by a certain "Ahmad Wang Beg," conducted mining developments, instituted a new tax, and sold beg positions to the greedy oasis nouveaux riches, who used to be the servants of the begs and *tongshi*. Together, these measures applied an unbearable burden on the "people," he said, which made them cry out to God in prayer. God replied to the people's prayer, it seemed. The Qing-beg regime fell in 1864.

Moving skillfully across three spatial scales of narrative—global, regional, and local— Mullā Mūsa Sayrāmī presented an unexpectedly broad interpretation of the fall of the Qing-beg regime in the oasis in the late nineteenth century. Its fundamental cause was the growing difficulty and insecurity of livelihood of the oasis "people," a development that made the "people" cry out desperately. This difficulty was in large part caused by exploitation of beg clients and local Qing military governors; however, at the same time, what was responsible for the intensification of the exploitation was a globally rooted event: the crisis of the Qing military financing in the oasis frontier caused by the Opium War (1839–42) between the Qing and British empires in the South China Sea.

Following Mullā Mūsa Sayrāmī's insight, this chapter examines the interplay between the global and local politics that contributed to the fall of the Qing, and explores how the Sino-British war and the subsequent discontinuation of the silver transfer from China to the oasis created crisis in both the Qing military and oasis capitalism in Central Asia. The oasis capitalists adopted monetary solutions to solve the crisis of the military financing primarily. They developed copper mining and minted local copper currency to compensate for the loss of the silver provision. Its inflationary affect, however, aggravated the economic stratification and social tension underway in the oasis since the Qing conquest; it privileged the wealthy merchants and landlords (local begs, Chinese, and Andijan merchants), who owned land and silver, and prompted them to invest more in landed property in order to weather the inflationary storm. However, this same development worsened the livelihood of the wage earners of the local oasis. In combination with the increasing burden of the labor mobilization of the oasis farmers to work the copper mines, this growing economic stratification and social tension resulted in two developments that proved dangerous to the vitality of the oasis economy: increasing rates of local violence and the outmigration of the people in the 1850s. In the end, the local Muslim and Manchu governors abandoned their policy of currency manipulation; they made last-ditch efforts to save the Qing regime by imposing new taxes on propertied elites. However, that effort came too late. The beg and Qing regime fell in 1864, amid a new round of *khwaja* attacks.

With the fall of the beg client regime, development of the oasis capitalism under the Chinese influence came full circle. In the sixteenth century, the lure of the trade with China that had brought the New World silver into the midst of the Central Asian borderland drew the oasis begs (coming from the background of Sufi migrants and nomadic tribal leaders) into the political orbit of China. In the eighteenth and nineteenth centuries, they conducted an unprecedented development of capitalist enterprise in the oasis under the protection of the Qing military, which also brought diverse goods and silver. More than ever, the collapse, even if temporary, of this oasis capitalism in the 1850s and 1860s also came abruptly from transnational connections.

The Opium War and the Begs' Monetary Solution to the Depleted Military Financing in the Oasis

Arguably, the most important consequence of the Opium War on Muslim Xinjiang was the discontinuation of the silver import from China to the region. Under the severe financial aftermath of the war, the imperial court found it necessary to cut its transfer of silver to southern Xinjiang, which had constituted a substantial portion of its overall military financing. At first, the Qing had been able to maintain their previous level of silver transfer, roughly 200,000 *liang* per year—or even initially increase it during the Seven Khwaja War, following the Opium War.[2] However, other local rebellions erupted, most notably the Taiping Rebellion (1851–64), and added to the burden of the already financially stretched empire. By 1853, Eastern Turkestan was receiving virtually no silver from China; by the beginning of the Tongzhi Period (1861–75), the bullion had all but stopped.[3]

Its discontinuation spelled out a significant crisis not only for the local Qing military but also for the oasis capitalists, for success of the latter's commercial enterprises required the robust purchasing power of the Qing military and its military protection. The discontinuation seriously undermined both of the conditions. What made the situation worse is that the stoppage came at the worst possible time—exactly when the Seven Khwaja War reminded the court that the *khwaja* threat to the oasis was not going to disappear, and highlighted the need for further military reinforcements in the area.

In order to cope with this crisis of military financing, the Qing administration opted for a monetary solution.[4] The Qing issued a new volume of *pul* coins in the local society to compensate for the loss of the silver imports and to artificially sustain the government's purchasing power. In order to do so, it conducted large-scale copper mining developments all over Eastern Turkestan. When the new excavations were not enough, the Qing-beg regime issued even more devalued coins, which circulated at artificial rates fixed at ten, or one hundred, times the actual value of the copper in them, respectively.[5]

This monetary solution represented quite an innovation in the Qing policy regarding its military financing in Xinjiang. While the Qing artificially increased the volume of the *pul* currency in order to stabilize the value of the increasing volume of silver bullion coming into Xinjiang in the 1830s, that had never been the mainstay of the Qing government's solution to its military financing needs. In addition, this time, the local *pul* currency was increased without a matching increase of an influx of silver bullion from China. It was as if the Qing government, to maintain the military's purchasing power in a stopgap measure, had issued a local currency not backed by any reserve currency.

The local begs enthusiastically participated in this process. According to the *Tārīkhi äminiyä*, the Muslim as well as the Qing military governors were the ones who first came up with the idea, upon hearing the emperor's decision to stop sending provisions to the Muslim domain because of the court's financial difficulty in China. They then proposed their idea to the emperor, that they would mine gold, silver, and copper and nourish the soldiers. Soon "the officials in the towns" conscripted the oasis Muslims for mining duty. Dispatched to the mountains, desolate lands, and foothills, the workers "dug many holes like rats."[6] Meanwhile, the oasis begs laid plans to gain something additional from all this enterprise. Like Ūdui's involvement in the jade mining and smuggling business in the late eighteenth century, the local Muslim governors plotted to mine—for themselves—more than the stipulated official quotas, so they could privately mint coins, quite profitably, all the while enhancing their relationship with the imperial court.

However, this monetary scheme backfired in no time. Severe inflation caused by the sudden and great increase of local *pul* currency acutely disadvantaged those people who derived their subsistence from it—for example, wage earners, including the local and sojourner laborers from Fergana Valley and from China, small-scale local shop keepers, and Qing soldiers; it simultaneously encouraged the landlords and merchants, including both local and sojourners, to increase their investments in land development. As a matter of fact, this problem had begun in the 1830s, when the Qing issued devalued *pul* currency to match the increasing influx of silver, as discussed earlier. Now, the discontinuation of the silver transfer ironically exacerbated the problem. The value of the *pul* coins, not underwritten by silver, had fallen as never before. This problem certainly intensified the social tensions that had been simmering between the property-less population in the oasis, on the one hand, and the propertied people who had silver and land in their possession, on the other, and would threaten the security of the Qing-beg regime significantly. If one also considers that the local Muslims were being pressed to develop new copper mines, an arduous undertaking in that era, the difficulty that the new monetary policy imposed on the local society could not be emphasized more.

Adding difficulty to the oasis economy was the damage done to Eastern Turkestan's trading relations within the region and with the outside world. The inflation of the local *pul* exchange rate between the international currency in silver and the coin became damaged beyond repair. It discouraged Chinese merchants, a potential alternative source of silver to the oasis, and also other Central Asian foreign merchants, from coming into the oases. This led to a collapse of international trade in the borderland economy, which had flourished during the Qing rule from the 1750s to the 1850s.

Such a scenario provided the backdrop for the sharp increase that arose in episodes of local violence and riots across Eastern Turkestan. The oases and foothills of Kashgar and Yarkand in the 1840s and 1850s witnessed a sweep of violence not only at the hands of Kirghiz raiders but also village revolts led by local artisans, farmers, and laborers—as well as small-time Muslim holy men not related with the Kashgar *khwaja*s. In 1855, for example, a Muslim from Kho-qand, Yusan Khwāja Īshān, collected a crowd and went into Kashgar to make trouble. However, Artush settlement's Muslims captured him and his thirteen followers, and turned them in to the Qing administration. According to the en-suing investigation, Yusan Khwāja Īshān had heard from an Andijan sojourner in Kashgar that copper mining was going on in Artush, and that the local Mus-lims resented it. Thus, realizing how easily he could lure them into his scheme, Yusan organized a crowd and headed into Artush.[7]

Even places not known for anti-Qing local violence showed similar distur-bance. For instance, in the summer of 1857, a rural village in Kucha District (Hu-na-si), which had never before participated in the *khwaja* wars, suddenly rose up in riot. The Qing-beg regime suspected that the villagers' protest was an action against paying the current grain tax. Instead, the riot was actually trig-gered by the excessive mobilization of corvée labor then underway. The Qing source did not mention the specific work project that the oasis Muslims had been called upon to do. Yet, given that Kucha was one of the two major cen-ters of copper mining in Eastern Turkestan, perhaps that excessive corvée labor involved work in the copper mines. In this regard, it is notable that about the same time as the outbreak of the riot, there was also a report noting that the Qing military governor of the Kucha District had opened a new copper smelt-ing factory, with his own private donation.[8]

Interestingly, the Fergana Valley across the Pamir also witnessed the same trajectory of an increase in local violence during the same time. After the death of Muhammad 'Alī Khān in 1842, the Khoqand Khanate virtually collapsed, leaving the valley in a state of near anarchy in which the Kirghiz and Kipchak tribal leaders as well as small-time Sufi leaders (*īshan*s and *khwāja*s) vied for political authority and power. Within this vortex, the oasis residents and the mountain nomads struggled increasingly. Previous scholarship has focused on the impact of the Russian expansion and the preexisting decentralized political structure of the Khoqand politics.[9] However, the timing of the development of this decentralization of the Khoqand Khanate, which overlapped with the period of sharp declines in silver exports to Kashgar from China, also shows a connection to the discontinuation of silver transfers after the Opium War. If the rise and sustenance of the power of the Khoqand khans in the late eighteenth century owed much to the availability of the China trade and silver in the first place, the loss of the silver supply was as devastating for the Khoqand and Fergana Valley as it was for Eastern Turkestan under the Qing.

Indeed, the local oasis population knew exactly whom to blame and where to go. In the many local disturbances and *khwaja* attacks occurring from that time, the first target to be hit was the Qing administration's local treasury, as well as silver hoards hidden in the begs' personal homes. According to the testimony of a sixth-rank *hākim* beg of A-er-hu-ke village of Kashgar District, in 1847, when the district had fallen during the Seven Khwaja War, some warriors of the *khwaja* war captured the *hākim* and presented him to an Andijan representative, Nai-ma-te, who had joined the *khwaja* force. Nai-ma-te told the *hākim,* "You bring 'silver coins' (*yinqian*) to redeem your life." He replied, "I am poor. I do not have 'silver coins.' I only have some food." Nai-ma-te then threatened, "I will give you five days. If you have silver coins, I will show you mercy. If you do not, I will kill you."[10]

Ahmad Wang Beg and the Politics of Local Copper Mining Development

In the context of the intense Qing drive for copper mining development, Ahmad, the great grandson of Ūdui, emerged as a pivotal figure in the larger story of the decline and fall of the Qing in Eastern Turkestan. A typical beg, Ahmad was an agrarian developer in the mold of his great grandfather, as well as Zuhūr al-Dīn.[11] Especially after the Qing adopted its policy of accelerated copper mining, Ahmad involved himself in the enterprise deeply. In 1856, he developed a new copper smelting factory (*tongchang*) in Aksu, and was recommended for a reward for that contribution.[12]

Ahmad's involvement in copper mining during the post–Opium War era was not incidental. His family had had a long-standing history in the copper mining industry in Aksu. Aksu, Kucha, and the outlying subregions constituted the major production center for excavating copper in Eastern Turkestan. For this reason, except for a brief period in the late eighteenth century, the Qing mint of the *pul* coins was located in the city of Aksu. In order to provide material for minting *pul* coins, the Muslim governors begs of the seven subdistricts of Aksu District sent teams of oasis Muslims to work the mines on rotation; in return, the oasis cities would get 60 percent of the coins minted at the Aksu mint.[13] Needless to say, producing numerous Kucha and Aksu governors, Ahmad's family extracted significant profits from this arrangement.

This previous experience led to Ahmad's appointment as the Muslim governor of Kashgar in 1856. In that year, the Manchu military governor there, Wenyuan, summoned Ahmad to operate a new copper mine and smelting factory that the Manchu governor had newly opened in the area of Mount Baer-chang, located near the rural village of Artush. Right after that, Wenyuan appointed Ahmad as governor of Kashgar District. By 1857 Ahmad was able to dispatch seven hundred unemployed Muslims to mine copper. Each worker was required to hand in 10 *jin* of copper annually, in total 7,000 *jin,* to support the minting of new coins.[14]

The mobilization of local labor for mining development increased social tension in Kashgar area, eventually becoming a direct trigger for the outbreak of another *khwaja* attack there in 1857. The Qing investigation into the cause of the 1857 Khwaja War found that many local villagers of Artush mobilized for copper mining felt discontent over their hardship, when Ahmad operated it there. They stormed his *yamen* to complain, only to be suppressed by Ahmad. A certain Mīr Ahmad, manager of a local shrine dedicated to the legendary Turkic ruler, Satūq Bughrā Khān—a *mazār* that had belonged to the Kashgar *khwaja* family for generations—seized the opportunity provided by this unrest. Having acquired support from a powerful villager, Mīr Ahmad decided to invite a *khwaja* to Kashgar. In preparation for the coming of the *khwaja*, Mīr Ahmad recruited four hundred people and drilled them in the handling of rifles every day. He paid all the expenses needed during this training, including food. When Walī Khān Khwaja, a nephew of Jahāngīr Khwaja, finally came in June 1857, disguised as an Andijan merchant, Mīr Ahmad joined the *khwaja* to attack Ahmad's seat in the city of Kashgar.[15]

Therefore, the 1857 Khwaja War was essentially similar to widespread local riots that swept Eastern Turkestan, caused by the labor mobilization for the copper mining development. Yet, the active involvement of individuals like Mīr Ahmad shows that there was another dimension to the local violence in Artush other than labor issues. Needless to say, as the local instigator and organizer of this *khwaja* war in Artush, Mīr Ahmad was hardly a poor, unemployed Muslim laborer. After all, the man was wealthy enough to provide all the expenses for training and arming four hundred men with firearms. This wealth had been gained, because Mīr Ahmad was the manager of the property and wealth of Satūq Bughrā Khān's shrine.[16]

For people like Mīr Ahmad, religious devotion to a venerated *khwaja* and personal economic interests closely intertwined. If he wanted to support the Kashgar *khwaja* financially in the long term—to fulfill his religious duties as the manager of important financial resources for the holy men—he needed to continue to find new financial resources from which to accumulate wealth. In the context of the new boom in copper mining, Mīr Ahmad may have identified a new source of income presenting itself locally and invested in copper mining.

This led Mīr Ahmad into a direct collision course with Kashgar's governor Ahmad, who had controlled copper resources on behalf of the Qing administration. Mīr Ahmad may have resented Governor Ahmad's development of copper mining, perhaps because Mīr Ahmad had formerly dominated its excavation in the area, before the governor took it over, or the latter blocked his new entry into the lucrative business. In other words, a competition between the local developers for domination of the newly emerging lucrative sector of the oasis economy during the post–Opium War period became another source of the local violence.

In this regard, the Ili military governor at the time made an interesting suggestion in 1858 after the suppression of the *khwaja* war. He proposed to close outright the copper mine in the Artush area immediately. He correctly diagnosed that its development had been one of the instigating causes behind the outbreak of the *khwaja* attack. Yet he also expressed a concern that the developers' competition to control the significant mining resource there would continue to fuel local violence in the oases, if the Qing did not close it off. Thus, he suggested that, after the closing of the copper mine, the Qing military should watch the mining site, to ensure that the Muslims did not collude with "bandits" to illegally mine the copper privately.[17]

The Walī Khān Khwāja War and the Emergence of a New Khwaja Coalition

Whereas Walī Khān Khwāja broke into the Qing border with only thirty followers initially, the number of his followers grew substantially as he descended from the mountains and approached the center of the oasis valley. When the *khwaja* marched into the city of Kashgar, the rebels' strength grew to the extent that two thousand Qing soldiers had to lock themselves in the Manchu fortress. When he launched an attack on the city of Yarkand a month later, the *khwaja* forces stood at four to five thousand. After establishing a short-lived government in Kashgar, he then commanded seventy thousand mounted horsemen and four thousand foot soldiers.[18] The *khwaja* forces were even able to march into the districts of Khotan and Aksu, an area rebel forces had rarely reached since the Jahāngīr Rebellion in 1826. In terms of the number of people mobilized from the local society, the Walī Khān Khwāja's action was one of the most successful *khwaja* wars. The figures compared only to those of the Jahāngīr War.

An anonymous poem (*qasida*), written by a local Muslim, described the *khwaja* invasion in terms of class struggle, an attack perpetrated by the property-less on the propertied people in the city. Written from the perspective of the pro-Qing begs, the poet labeled the attack as a rebellion of "bandits," railing against wealthy property owners and social order. The Islamic clerics, who allied themselves with the pro-Qing begs, issued a *fatwa* (a legal opinion issued by Islamic jurists) urging the local Muslims to fight against the *khwaja*. Circulated in the towns and countryside in Yarkand District, it read: "All men, great and small, having heard the commands of the Shari'a, or Holy Law, strike and kill the bandits wherever they appear—such is your religious duty—for you must save your lives. If opportunity offers, take them prisoners—but do not associate with them for if any one joins them, it will be an act of infidelity, and Faith will depart."[19]

Given the social nature of the earlier *khwaja* attacks, it is not surprising that popular frustration with the begs and their development projects provided the original impetus for the sudden upsurge of support on this occasion. What is surprising, though, is that a new ally joined the cause, and it came from the community of sojourner merchants from the Fergana Valley ("Andijan").[20] They had first joined the *khwaja* during the previous Seven Khwaja War ten years prior, while under duress, surrounded by forces in their small city quarter, and only after much deliberation. They were severely chastised for their act by the reigning Khoqand khan, who despised the *khwaja* as nothing more than beggar and robber.[21]

Yet, in many ways, this new alliance was a logical progression for the sojourner merchants. They saw benefit in supporting the *khwajas*, once they had displayed their ability to occupy the oasis. By aligning with them, the merchants could fend off the increasingly desperate attempts by the Khoqand rulers to exploit their wealth, as well as the potential moves by the Qing administration to do likewise. Of course, the sojourner merchant community had to negotiate carefully among these three contenders of political power in the oasis—the Khoqand, Qing, and *khwajas*—to achieve its goals. For their part, the *khwajas* had no reason to reject offers of support from the wealthy and powerful members of the sojourner merchant community. Such aid would give them the means to strengthen their own military capacity.

In the end, the sojourner merchants' participation in the *khwaja* war transformed the nature of the *khwaja* coalition in its wake. Prior to the merchants' participation, the *khwaja* military had derived its support from the mountain refugees, perhaps best represented by the coalition led by Jahāngīr Khwaja. Joined with an "Andijan" merchant contingent, however, the *khwaja*s could now transform themselves into state builders, building an independent regime supported by transnational refugees in terms of manpower, and funded by the wealth of the sojourner merchants.

Indeed, this design to give the independent sojourners in Kashgar the protection of the *khwaja*s was not that much out of line with the historical pattern of local state building occurring in Central Asia around Eastern Turkestan. In fact, there had been a precedent for it. The Kashgar Khwaja's own ancestor, Āfāq Khwāja, maintained such a regime in Eastern Turkestan in the late seventeenth century, although it was under the overlordship of the Zunghar Mongols. Āfāq Khwāja was a sojourner himself. His ancestors had hailed from Bukhara, and they too had experienced an extended period of exile in northwestern China. It was well known that they were supported by caravan merchants.

Walī Khān Khwāja and his followers wasted no time in making it clear that they were no longer the defenders solely of the uprooted oasis people's voice; rather, they were now also representatives of another, propertied class. The composition of the government that Walī Khān Khwāja formed after his occupation of Kashgar District reflected this changing nature of *khwaja* rule in the oasis. While the two former factions of its original coalition—namely, the refugee immigrants from Kashgar and the mountain Kipchak-Kirghiz—continued to be dominant in the inner circle of his regime, the Andijan sojourner merchants were also newly added to it. In the meantime, local Kashgarians were totally excluded from access. The only Kashgarian allowed to approach Walī Khān Khwāja was the aforementioned Mīr Ahmad of Artush, who later managed to get his daughter married to the *khwaja*.[22]

This composition was also reflected within the military ranks. During Walī Khān Khwāja's occupation of Kashgar, many local Kashgarians and Chalgurts (people born with an Andijan father and a Kashgarian mother) served in his army, holding the rank of colonel (*pansad*). However, none of these individuals possessed the confidence of the *khwaja* or had access to him. According to Valikhanov, the *khwaja*'s clear preference for "Andijans," who were originally common soldiers employed by the *acsaqal* in Kashgar, excited the "jealousy" of the local Kashgarians.[22]

In their eyes, this new regime acted just like the other regional state builders in the oases, such as the Khoqand Khanate, which they had fought. Walī Khān Khwāja impressed people for military service and into other forced labor venues, and exploited revenue from the locals with an intensity that far exceeded that of the Qing and begs. As a result, the *khwaja* was able to organize a standing army of seventy thousand mounted horsemen and four thousand foot soldiers, and a large force of "volunteer" troops, mustered up from the surrounding towns and villages. In order to equip the troops, the *khwaja* employed all the artisans of Kashgar in manufacturing arms and commandeered horses from the local residents. Fresh taxes were imposed daily. The *khwaja* also compelled foreign merchants to serve in person as well as to furnish requisitions for the army. When a battery of artillery with eighteen guns was formed, the guns were cast under the supervision of an Afghan. According to eyewitness testimony, the troops of Walī Khān Khwāja were much better armed and organized than those of the Emir of Bukhara, whose army served as a model for the whole of Central Asia.[24] Such a buildup of military organization soon exhausted the resources of the Kashgar oasis, and the cessation of trade as well as every branch of industry became felt painfully. "The horses and donkeys were impressed for the army; copper kettles, dishes, and other utensils were seized for casting cannon. During one hundred days (of the *khwaja* rule), the whole population was occupied in siege works."[25]

Certainly, the scope of this military organization and economic extraction increased the Kashgarians' disillusionment with the *khwaja*. The spiritual leader of the marooned refugees, who had fought against the exploitative state builders on the side of the displaced, proved an exploitative state builder himself. In addition, his reliance on the "Andijan" merchants as a political base further disillusioned the locals. According to one anecdote, the aforementioned Mīr Ahmad led his militia from Artush, and approached the *khwaja*'s palace in Kashgar to greet him. The Andijans, who were guarding the palace, refused to let them meet him. The Kashgarians militia raised a loud murmur of discontent. "If we may not call upon the *khwaja* after sacrificing our lives and property in his cause, what claims have the Andijans to his favor?" To this, the head of the *khwaja*'s bodyguard unit responded: "If your heads are not too heavy for your shoulders, then in the name of Allah himself hold your peace." After this, the Kashgarians dispersed, silent and thoroughly disenchanted.[26]

Yet, the relations between the *khwaja* and the Andijan merchant community did not remain stable, either. Soon after his occupation of Kashgar, Walī Khān Khwāja displayed a high degree of seemingly capricious cruelty, including numerous occasions of outright killing. Valikhanov considered such excesses as the prime reason for the failure of his regime. However, his cruelty was a problem neither of personal disposition nor of drug use (hashish), as Valikhanov proposed. The behavior, rather, represented a structural political disposition of the new "absolutist" state builder, who was intent upon exploiting the growing commercial merchant wealth, best epitomized by the *khwaja*'s constant disregard for the security of their persons and property. For instance, "Named-Khan," the Andijan *aqcasal* in Kashgar, the wealthy political representative of the sojourner merchant group there, was seized and executed while he was superintending the siege works during an early phase of the *khwaja* war. The civil and military officers serving in the *khwaja* government were continually fined. A high-ranking official (*mingbashi*) in his government, another merchant that had formerly served as *acsaqal* in Kashgar, was imprisoned by him several times. The merchant had to pay heavy sums to save his life. Such "absolutist" political authority maximized the *khwaja*'s ability to extract revenue and build a strong military. The irony of this whole situation is that the sojourner merchants faced under the *khwaja* rule the very conditions they had wanted to avoid by allying with him against the Khoqand ruler in the first place—namely, the insecurity of their persons and properties. "The lives of all were in constant peril."[27]

Exhausted, the oasis people welcomed the return of the Qing army in late 1857. They rejoiced upon its arrival. Nonetheless, the destruction inflicted by another round of *khwaja* war proved costly for the Qing and begs to bear. The oasis people moved out of Kashgar and other Eastern Turkestani districts to an ever larger degree. According to Valikhanov, during this period fifteen thousand individuals voluntarily migrated from Kashgar to Khoqand, roughly the same number in the outmigration that had occurred during the Seven Khwaja War ten years prior.[28]

The Yarkand Tax Register and the Structure of Oasis Agriculture

In 1858, Valikhanov visited the oasis region right after the Walī Khān Khwāja War and left a revealing account of the state of oasis agriculture. Despite the war devastation from the year before, he depicted a surprisingly vibrant landscape of commercial agriculture, the result of roughly a century of capitalist development. "Owing to careful irrigation and the long cultivation which the soil has undergone, the agricultural productions of Little Bukhara are sufficiently diversified. The outskirts of the towns and villages are surrounded with shady gardens, producing figs and pomegranates. Plantations of cotton and artificial meadows cover extensive areas of land, and the moist parts are sown with rice." He listed the production of various cereals (wheat, barley, rice, javary, red and black lentil, and, to a small extent, millet); "plants for dyeing and manufacturing purposes" (cotton, hempseed, sesame, madder, and tobacco); "fruit and vegetables" (several varieties of melons and watermelons, of "exquisite flavour," also carrots, radishes, beet root, onions, mint, peas, and saffron). He also mentioned cucumber, a "Chinese" variety, and did not neglect to mention poppies. The trees planted in the gardens included willow, poplar, pyramidal silver-leaved poplar, mulberry, wild olive tree, and chiliäni (a tree that yields fruit tasting like dates). The fruit trees were apple, pear, bergamot, peach, apricot, quince, pomegranate, and fig, as well as two sorts of grapes.[29]

Commercial agriculture also specialized, by locality, in terms of vegetation grown. For instance, the towns of Bai and Sayram (in Aksu District) had successfully cultivated grapes and cotton, while pomegranates and figs were absent in the region. In the meantime, Yarkand had specialized in producing prunes, cherries, and walnuts. The inhabitants of the rural settlements of Kargalyk, in the district, occupied themselves exclusively with growing nuts, which formed the staple of the trade of that place. Admittedly, vegetation in "Little Bukhara" was less diverse than other places in Central Asia, as a result of unfavorable climate conditions, most notably a lack of suitable rain. Still, as Valikhanov emphasized elsewhere, this was a surprising landscape of ample agrarian development.

The diversity of farming endeavors also reflected differing levels of economic stratification and a variety of social tensions accompanying each as well. The Yarkand District tax register, compiled around the 1850s, shows this point clearly. The only available tax record from the oasis at this time, it provided concrete data revealing details of what was happening on the ground in the mid- to late-nineteenth century. The records enumerate figures for population, cultivated land, and tax quotas by subdistrict. For example, the central city of Yarkand District had forty-three zones (*xiang*) within it; surrounding it were thirty-one large rural settlements (*zongzhuang*), scattered across the oasis district. These in turn were subdivided into 416 basic village units (*xiaozhuang*). In addition, the Qing administration operated seven places featuring government-owned watermills and vegetable gardens. The size of the rural settlements varied significantly. The largest (the aforementioned Kargalyk) had 6,122 residents; the smallest (Teräk Länggar) had seventy-six (see Appendix F-1).

At first glance, what stands out is the continuity of the names of the village communities appearing in the tax register and those appearing in early-nineteenth-century documents such as the XJShL. This contrasted with earlier development, when, as mentioned in Chapter 2, virtually no continuity existed in the place names in the records between the rural settlements of the late eighteenth century and those in the early nineteenth century. The rural settlements at the time of the Qing conquest in the mid-eighteenth century disappeared almost completely, and new ones emerged. This indicates the replacement and displacement of the preexisting rural settlements by new ones established by ambitious begs and other emerging oasis landlords under the Qing. However, what the Yarkand District tax register shows is that the rural settlements appearing by the early nineteenth century survived into the late nineteenth century. In other words, the volatility of the rural oasis caused by the beg land initiatives had consolidated or settled in the nineteenth century.

The registry also permits an analytical look at the structure of oasis rural settlements in the aftermath of the land development frenzy undertaken during the Zuhūr al-Dīn era in the 1830s and 1840s. The first and most salient feature of the village community was its demography, the high rate of the property-less people. Each village delineated the number of its population ("male and female; big and small") and the number of the people belonging to regular tax-paying households (*zhenghu huizi*). The unit of enumeration for both categories was "person." For instance, in the Rawatchi settlement located 40 *li* east of the city of Yarkand, there were 145 residents in total, among them 36 people belonging to regular households. From this record, we can deduce that this rural settlement had 109 non–tax paying residents out of a total of 145. The record about Köna Tatar "*zhuang*" reads: "This *zhuang* does not have any 'regular household Muslims', who cultivate land." "'Idle Muslims' (*xiansan huizi*) from other rural settlements came to this village to pay tax grains" [according to the size of the land they cultivated on a temporary basis].[30] Regular households in this context were the households that owned and cultivated land and thus by definition held a tax obligation to the Qing government. "Idle Muslims" did not have an obligation to pay regular tax to the Qing administration other than the fee they paid on a temporary basis for the government land they cultivated.

On average, roughly 80 to 90 percent of the total residents living in the rural settlements in Yarkand District constituted "idle Muslims." In the case of Qu-long (a basic village unit), for instance, the rate of the regular households/non-regular households was 8:103. For Ji-ge-da-ai-li-ke (a basic village unit), the rate was 7:111. In the case of Su-pu-la-ha-lang-tuo-hu-li-ke (a basic village unit), the rate ran 31:342. Extreme examples can be found in the compositions of the rural village established within *tuntian*. The settlement of Qurghan (a basic village unit), located 50 *li* north of the city (see Appendix E-1), included eight *tuntians*; its population was reportedly nineteen hundred Muslim people (at eight hundred households). However, there was no regular tax-paying household in the settlement. Presumably, they were all property-less oasis farmers who had been recruited by the merchant land developers to work in the *tuntian*.

How do we explain this extremely high rate of property-less households in the village communities in Yarkand District? On the one hand, a simple un-der-reporting of the number of the landed Muslims could be at fault.[31] The oasis Muslim communities, the ultimate base unit responsible for tax surveys and tax collections, may have deliberately reported some regular tax-paying households as "idle" Muslim households, thus distorting the ratio between the two. Under-reporting the tax-paying household was in their interest, for a re-duction in the number of the former in the village community meant a reduc-tion in the land tax payment due from the village as a whole. However, in all likelihood, such a high rate of property-less residents in the village community, hovering on average around 80 percent of its total population, might be better interpreted as a phenomenon reflecting the actual reality of demography and land distribution in place in the Yarkand oasis, more or less. That is to say, the number of property-less oasis Muslims in the rural settlements did indeed in-crease rapidly in the late eighteenth and early nineteenth centuries—probably directly resulting from the begs' land encroachments.

For this reason, there emerged the curious disparity between rural and ur-ban areas in terms of the rate of property-less people in the community. The urban centers held a much higher percentage of regular households than the rural settlements. "City district three" in the Yarkand District tax register, for instance, showed the highest rate of regular household population, at 48 percent (see Appendix F-1). Other city districts also reflected rates of regular households above 30 percent, except for "city district five," which had 26 per-cent (Appendix F-1). It is counterintuitive that the rural regions would hold the higher concentration of nonregular households versus the urban cities, given that the entrepôts entertained numerous transient populations in their midst, who should be identified as nonregular households by definition. What this rather surprising observation suggests is that the high rate of property-less people in the rural sectors likely resulted from the specifics of the rural development occurring there—namely, severe economic stratification, caused by the concentration of the begs' agrarian initiatives on site.

Contributing to the increase of the property-less Muslims was the accumulation of landed properties by the merchants and landlords. Evidence from contract documents available in the late nineteenth century shows that many merchants and begs came in from outside the village community to buy up land from the impoverished villagers, all now living under increasing economic pressure because of the inflationary trend of the local currency, particularly after the Opium War.[32] Also, some rich oasis farmers within the village communities did the same. What was also at fault was the expansion of the developers' private appropriation of the desolate land around the villages. In this process, oasis villagers, who had utilized the wild land as a common resource (for small-scale livestock raising or seasonal subsistence farming), fell into trouble.[33] This was the plight especially of those oasis farmers who held on to the lower rung of the economic ladder. When they lost their livelihoods and fell into debt to merchants or wealthy landlord neighbors, they would have to sell their land, become wage laborers, and thus end up property-less. In this way, the oasis landlords' and merchants' land development contributed directly to the increase of the property-less people within the rural villages.

The second salient feature of the oasis villages shown in the Yarkand District tax register is the low rate of the land tax imposed on the village community as a whole. Both the amount of the tax quota for each village and the size of its land, measured by the amount of seed that could be planted there, are listed. In 1759, a Qing commander general stationed in the oasis related that the harvest rate in the oasis was two to three times the amount of planted seed in bad years, and seven to eight times of the planted seed in good years.[34] We can calculate the average amount of harvest per year then at five times the planted seed (see Appendix F-1, "Average Harvest" Column). If we divide the amount of the annual payment of grain tax ("Grain Tax" Column) by this average potential harvest, we can estimate the rate of the land tax that each village paid ("Average Grain Tax Rate" Column). The result shows that each oasis village paid four percent of its harvest; this was much less than the 10 percent of the harvest due in the official rate of grain tax from private land collected under the Qing. In reality, however, each rural settlement paid much more than its official quota. The Qing government collected additional irregular taxes. As tax farmers, beg governors also collected additional amounts on top of their official quotas, as shown in Chapter 2. Still, a more important question to ask at this juncture is how the rural settlements on the ground in the 1850s were assessed land tax at a rate much lower than the original rate levied in the 1750s. Because the official 10 percent tax rate policy had not changed during this time, the only logical explanation is that substantial amounts of untaxed or undertaxed land occurred in the rural settlements. These untaxed land allotments were none other than the parcels of newly reclaimed land that had become available after the last land survey in the 1830s. Private land development continued strong in the oasis even during the chaotic years of the late nineteenth century, while the tax quota did not increase to keep up with the increase in the actual arable land (see Table 2.2).

The Yarkand tax register thus reveals a stunning capitalistic structure of agriculture in the oasis at that time. In this society, oasis landlords (both the beg and non-beg landlords) expanded their landholdings greatly through the new land development initiatives. They used "idle Muslims" as the manpower to accomplish the capitalist projects. Consequently, increasing numbers of oasis villagers became landless and wage laborers. This interplay of oasis begs and landlords and wage laborers made possible the landscape of highly commercialized agriculture that Valikhanov saw when he visited the oasis region in 1858.

The Politics of Taxing the Propertied Class

The post–Walī Khān Khwāja War period, from 1858 to 1864, signaled a new phase of the Qing state building then occurring in the oasis. During that time, the Qing-beg regime turned back to direct state building efforts, a program that had long been abandoned since the era of the Nayancheng reform policies in 1830. The Qing military governors and the Muslim clients—at least some of them—concluded that they had no other choice but to increase revenues by direct taxation of the oasis agriculture and commerce developed by the propertied class—for example, the begs, non-beg landlords, and merchants, who had been systematically undertaxed up to that point, in order to solve the crisis in the Qing military financing.

The Qing-beg regime may well have anticipated that this measure would certainly incite resistance from some propertied people. But then, it had no other alternative. Silver would certainly not be forthcoming. Their initial copper monetary manipulation to buttress local military financing had failed miserably, and the destruction in the aftermath of the Walī Khān Khwāja War showed it unambiguously. Collecting the revenue through the mechanism of revenue farming continuously, and thus inflicting a further intense squeeze on the oasis people, would certainly spell disaster for the future of the Qing Empire and beg capitalism in the oasis. The further squeeze would be bound to result in the population's mass outmigration, as the previous history of the *khwaja* wars had demonstrated. Without sufficient laborers in the oasis, there would be no agriculture, no enrichment, no revenue, and finally no Qing military—the ultimate buttress of the Qing imperial rule and the protector of oasis capitalism.

The first target were oasis merchants and their local commerce. After the war's end, the Qing administration immediately began to impose a new tax on local commerce (*shangshui*), in order to compensate for the revenue lost with the end of the issuance of devalued *pul* coins and new copper production. Reminiscent of Nayancheng's initiative twenty-eight years earlier, the imperial court in 1858 also began raising revenue by collecting a tax on tea.[35] By 1861, the Qing administration had even floated a plan to establish a transit tax on roads in Eastern Turkestan—including strategically important but remote locations such as Barchuk. Still, most important, the Qing administration began to levy a tax on cotton textiles from Kashgar in 1858, collecting 2 *wen* of "worth 5" *pul* coins (a new stable version of *pul* coin valued at five times the face value of the copper) on every bolt of "big cotton cloth" transported for sale out of Kashgar District,[36] and 1 *wen* on every small bolt of cotton cloth. It was the first attempt by the Qing to tax the cotton trade, arguably the most important local trade item in oasis Xinjiang. The military governor argued that because the Qing would collect this tax from the traders, no burden would be applied on the Muslim households doing the weaving, as if he wanted to assure the imperial court that such new measures would not inflame the resistance of the oasis people. If successfully implemented, the revenue from this tax would almost match the amount that had been generated from copper mining. Later that year, every city in oasis Xinjiang began collecting a cotton tax.[37] By 1859 Turfan had also begun collecting tax on the trade of raw cotton from the area, this time referred to as the *lijin* tax (an internal tariff instituted in China during the Taiping Rebellion in 1853).[38]

This new policy radically changed the terms of the relationship between the Qing-beg regime, on the one hand, and the propertied elites in the oasis, on the other, since in the new plan merchants were supposed to bear the burden of significant tax payment directly. Then, the Qing military governors and beg governors moved on to a much tougher task—namely, taxing the landed wealth of the begs and non-beg landlords. Ahmad spearheaded the effort. In 1860, he visited the rural oasis settlements in Yarkand District personally, at the request of the Ili General, the highest-ranking Qing military governor in all of Xinjiang. There, Ahmad conducted a thorough audit of oasis villages and their properties (*huichan*) on behalf of the Qing government.[39]

However, this plan did not proceed as planned. Ahmad discovered that a Manchu clerk, working as a staff member for the military governor of Yarkand at the time, had exploited the oasis villagers, and reported his finding to the Qing court in Beijing. Feeling vulnerable, the military governor, named Yingwen, soon counteraccused Ahmad, claiming that the latter and his seventy staff members had frightened the villagers, and that they had all fled in advance of the new property inventory. Yingwen added that Ahmad was not a good person to lead the audit, because he had lost the "mind [confidence and loyalty] of the local Muslims" during his stint as Muslim governor of Yarkand and Kashgar. As a result of the counteraccusation, Ahmad was relieved of his duty, and the Qing court instead dispatched the Muslim lieutenant governor of Kashgar District to continue the audit.[40]

Back in his home district of Aksu in 1860, he continued to make serious efforts to devise plans for raising revenue from the propertied class in collaboration with Mianxing, a reform-minded Qing military governor of the district. Now reinstated as governor of Aksu, Ahmad proposed eliminating the customary "taxes" collected by the Muslim governor from the oasis Muslim community on top of the official tax quota, which amounted to two or three "strings" (2,000 to 3,000 *wen* of *pul* coins) for a Muslim household annually. Half of the amount (1,000 to 1,500 *wen*) would be eliminated outright. The other half would be converted and added to the quota of the official taxes. In this way, the imperial court could raise additional tax revenue while reducing the tax burden on oasis residents.

Ahmad and Mianxing envisioned the eliminated amount to come from the tax farmer's portion that the begs kept as profit. However, in order to succeed in this reform, the Muslim governor actually had to intervene in the very process of tax collection within the oasis society. Without such intervention, as the Qing court correctly pointed out in response to this proposal, such a measure might only be able to increase the government tax coffers generally. But it would not be able to lessen the actual oasis population's tax burden. In this view, tax farmers in the Xinjiang oasis, from the district governor on top to the village headman at the bottom, could simply collect more from the oasis residents to pay more to the Qing government, without giving up their own share.[41]

But intervene Ahmad did, locally. He personally visited each rural settlement in the district to conduct a new audit of oasis households and properties. In the process, he discovered and punished two low-rank begs (seventh-rank begs), who had collected more than the expected quota the Qing allowed from the rural settlements.[42] Furthermore, in this expedition, Ahmad tackled two most fundamental problems of the Qing tax system in oasis—namely undertaxation of the begs' landed wealth and the unfair distribution of the tax burden within the village community. In the villages, he made sure that there would be no omission of any taxable people or landed properties from the district tax register, to prevent local begs from under-reporting their own landed properties and falsely claiming any oasis Muslims as tax exempt *yanqi*—schemes reminiscent of Ahmad's grandfather Osman.

Ahmad and Mianxing did not stop there. In 1861, they established a new "salt tax" that would be collected from every oasis resident in the district of Aksu.[43] This new tax was again a radical departure from earlier Qing tax regulation in the oasis. Not only was the concept of imposing a consumption tax on salt itself novel in the oasis, but it also was imposed more heavily on the begs. The Qing administration collected 50 *wen* to 30 *wen* from the third-rank to seventh-rank begs according to their rank, whereas it collected 2 *wen* of *pul* from every ordinary oasis resident every month. Still more important, this tax was also imposed on "Andijan" sojourner merchants—the wealthiest sector in the oasis, which had paid virtually no tax to the Qing-beg regime until then.

The Andijan merchants did not like the idea, however. They fed information about this new salt tax to Yingwen, the aforementioned personal rival of Ahmad, to be brought forward to the Qing court. Yingwen claimed the measure to be corrupt, an illegal addition of tax burden on local Muslims. Mianxing soon responded to this accusation with a counteraccusation of "corruptions" committed by Yingwen. However, the Qing court's own suspicion about the political wisdom of the new tax measure led the court to fire Mianxing and Ahmad from their positions, ending their experiment with the new tax collection system.[44]

As it turned out, however, Ahmad was not the only Muslim governor who attempted to tax the sojourner merchants during this time. Afridun Wang Beg, a descendant of Emin Khwāja, made a similar effort in Yarkand District. As the governor of the district at that time, he reportedly killed a Khoqand khan's tax agent and his thirty staff members when they arrived in Yarkand. He did this in the anticipation that he could seize taxing power over the sojourner merchants. However, this measure backfired. Fearful of the resistance of the powerful sojourner groups, or provided with ample bribes by them, the Manchu military governor of the district fired Afridun from his position as governor.[45]

Although their attempts ultimately failed, the overall importance of these pilot tax measures can not be overemphasized. If successful, the reform of exacting revenue from the landlords; local merchants; and Andijans, the wealthy tax-exempt sojourners, could have solved the fiscal woes of the begs and the Qing. It would have made it possible for the beg clients to provide the necessary military protection to the oasis notables, without burdening the ordinary oasis population, and thus increasing the political risk of instability in the oasis. However, the efforts came too late.

In 1864, the local Muslims rose in *jihad* against the Qing-beg regime, and the rebellion prompted the Kashgar *khwaja*s to invade the oasis one last time. Amid the political chaos created by local Muslim revolts and the *khwaja* attacks, Ya'qūb Beg, a military adventurer from Khoqand territory, emerged as the final victor. He succeeded in occupying the Eastern Turkestani oases from Kashgar to Turfan. The Qing Empire in the region fell, about a century after its establishment in 1759.

The Depression and Reformulation of Oasis Capitalism after the Fall of the Qing Empire

The fall of the Qing Empire in 1864 plummeted the oasis into ruin. The essential conditions for the success of oasis capitalism all but disappeared in its wake. What was lost first was the crucial connection with China commerce that had made the oasis economy flourish in the previous century. Silver ceased to flow into the oasis, a development that began in the 1840s and 1850s but became complete with the fall of Qing rule in the oasis in 1864.[46] Jade, the most important and lucrative commodity coming out of Eastern Turkestan, had a hard time finding buyers once access to the lucrative China market had been lost. The Qing soldiers were gone, and Chinese merchants stopped coming in. Tens of thousands of people who had once formed the backbone of demand for local goods (not only staples such as grain but also luxury goods such as carpets) were nowhere to be found.

The loss of access to the China market wielded a tremendous blow to the oasis economy. One report of a British diplomatic mission, which visited the region in 1873 to explore potential opportunities for establishing trading relations between British India and Eastern Turkestan under the rule of Ya'qūb Beg, vividly described a local economy plunged into depression and utter ruin. Money, in silver as well as the local *pul,* had disappeared altogether from economic transactions. For a while, the oasis economy devolved into a pervasive system of barter exchange. Even on busy market days, little coin was current. "[A]ll exchanges are by barter," noted the members of the Forsyth Mission.[47] Observing the formerly bustling market district of the city of Yarkand, arguably the most affluent city of Eastern Turkestan, for instance, the British reported: "In the time of the Chinese it is said to have been a lively scene of activity and trade, but, as we found it, full three-fourths of the space were in ruins, and the rest a miserable collection of cook shops and grocers' stalls almost as dilapidated as the ruins themselves."[48]

Especially hard hit was the trade and production of luxury goods, which used to be either exported to China or purchased by affluent Chinese residents in the oasis. Thus, in the district of Khotan, "[T]he jade trade, which formerly supported several thousand families in its collection and manufacture, had now entirely disappeared. So, the gold mines, which under the Chinese employed whole settlements, are now deserted. ... The carpet trade has similarly declined, and the rare productions of gold wire, silk, and wool combined, which under the Chinese found eager competitors, are now never seen, for there is nobody left to buy them."[49] Indeed, all major production and trade activities (especially in silk, carpets, gold, jade, raw silk, and the like, as the most valuable export goods) in Khotan languished severely.[50]

Oasis agriculture fared no better. The impression conveyed by the Forsyth Mission in regard to its current status then was certainly one of a deep depression. Its report mentioned a few pockets of well-irrigated and well-maintained farmland, especially around the urban centers of various oasis districts, but they were scattered within a vast sea of uncultivated, and even unsettled, land in the countryside.[51] The report expressed the perception that this underdeveloped state of oasis agriculture was in fact its natural state, "considering the limited water supply and the barren nature of the soil."[52] The British did not know that oasis agriculture could fluctuate considerably, vitally dependent as it was on the input of labor and capital. Nor did they realize that the barren nature of the farmland was in fact the result of a severe and direct decline of the population caused by a series of events occurring during the late nineteenth century.

Indeed, the depopulation, or rather sparseness, of the inhabitants struck the British observers, most noticeably in terms of oasis ecology and economy. After reporting that the total population of the Eastern Turkestan oases during the years of the "Chinese" rule was estimated to be 145,000 households/1,015,000 people, the Forsyth Report emphatically pointed out on numerous occasions that the actual population figures during that year (1873) was in no way close to that number. Travelers would encounter only a small number of houses, widely scattered as single homesteads, or in clusters of two or three (fifty tenements within a radius of a couple of miles), even in seemingly flourishing settlements extending over a good distance, along a river course and thickly planted with trees for all its extent. On market day a town might bustle, but the next day only a scant number of people could be found on "lonesome streets, with long rows of silent forges, empty cook shops, deserted grocers' stalls, and the tenantless sheds of the shoe-maker, hatter, and draper," until the next week's market day.[53]

Khotan District provides one of the most stunning cases featuring the depopulation of the Xinjiang oasis. Its namesake central city had six thousand households during Qing rule. However, from its fall in 1864 to the establishment of the Ya'qūb Beg regime in 1867, the district had lost nearly half of its male population. The British observer primarily attributed this decline to death incurred in the wars and violence during the strife of the 1860s. However, not all the loss was due to death. The people voluntarily dispersed and relocated from the district, once the disconnection from China and global markets had become pervasive. As, during the Qing Period, the growing economic opportunities and Qing military protection had once pulled people into the Qing-controlled oasis, the people now left the oasis once the jobs in gold and jade mining, silk weaving, and fruit farms disappeared. As is indicated earlier, Khotan lost several thousand families as a result of the decline of the jade industry, for instance.

It would be misleading nonetheless to say that the pulse of the oasis capitalism was completely lost during this time. While its overall economy went into a general depression, its severity was unevenly applied across the various sectors of agriculture and industry. Indeed, particular sectors even experienced growth. Even while it painted a portrait of an across-the-board collapse of the economy in the oasis, the Forsyth Mission did not fail to note the vibrant circumstances of the cotton industry. Men and women from rural villages still attended rural and suburban *bazaars* on a weekly basis to sell raw cotton and homespun cotton cloth. Local merchants in turn bought up the products in the markets and resold them in the *bazaar,* located at the urban central cities. The latter functioned as clearinghouses for the export of local cotton products to neighboring countries. The wholesale caravan merchants bought the cotton products there to sell in the markets of the Fergana Valley, the Russian cities of Almaty (Vernoe) and Tashkent, and among the mountain nomads.[54]

A few statistics may offer a more concrete sense of the vitality and significance of the cotton trade in the oasis economy. In 1873, for instance, ninety permanent shops specialized in trade in cotton cloth in the principal *bazaar* in the city of Yarkand. This represents 43 percent of the entire number of permanent shops (190). In addition to this regular *bazaar,* which opened every day, the city also hosted weekly evening market opening on every Thursday. About one hundred sellers of cotton attended this evening session regularly, far exceeding the number of sellers of any other items.[55] The situation was similar in other major oasis districts. In the city of Kashgar, there were 114 cotton textiles shops. This number accounted for roughly 20 percent of 573 shops in total, and constituted the majority of the shops operating there.[56]

This growth in cotton farming and cotton textile industries signaled an important change from the previous century in the composition of the portfolios of the oasis capitalists. To be sure, as Chapter 2 has shown, the cotton farming industry was an important part of the begs' commercial portfolio even under Qing rule. Indeed, the Qing government provided significant simulation to the growth of the local cotton industry, by placing large volumes of orders for raw cotton and cotton textiles to be made in the oases of Yarkand, Khotan, and elsewhere, to be used in the horse trade with Kazakh. However, even then, the importance of the cotton industry paled in comparison with the China-oriented luxury industry revolving around jade mining and carving, as far as the magnitude of profit it secured for the oasis capitalists was concerned. Most important, the jade trade had brought in coveted Chinese goods such as Chinese-made silk and satin, porcelain, tea, and silver, all in huge demand in Central Asia. That situation changed after the fall of the Qing Empire. While the China-oriented luxury trades declined, the cotton industry expanded swiftly.

This signaled the restructuring of oasis capitalism into a new, bulk product-based, low-profit-margin commercial enterprise. Yet one aspect of oasis capitalism did not change, even amid this general retooling under the Ya'qūb Beg rule: it still strove to connect its goods with international markets. Commenting on the general situation of the economy of Eastern Turkestan during that time, the Forsyth Mission noted decisively that "the impetus of the trade which finds a centre in Kashgar is, however, from without," and singled out "Andijanis" who had settled in Kashgar, and the "agents of merchants living beyond the border," probably Russians or Bukharans, as the major facilitators of the international trades of the region.[57]

These sojourner merchants and foreign traders vitally linked the region with the regions in the west, even at this period of severe contraction of the local economy and population in Eastern Turkestan. The Kashgar-Khoqand passage transported five to six thousand cargo loads of goods in both directions between Kashgar and Fergana Valley annually. Another route linked Kashgar to Almaty. The size of the trade conducted along this corridor was reportedly greater than that of Khoqand-Kashgar, and was increasing at the time of the Forsyth Mission's visit to Eastern Turkestan. In fact, the very reason why the cotton industry experienced an upsurge in spite of the general decline in population and other local trade within the Eastern Turkestan oasis—a seemingly contradictory set of circumstances—was the stimulus coming from this western direction. Cotton products emerged as the dominant items of international trade conducted on these two trade corridors. For instance, a caravan that left Kashgar in February 1874 to Khoqand carried a total of 871 loads of cargo; among them, 220 loads were cotton textiles woven locally in Kashgar. The total value of this export of cotton textiles was 132,000 *tangga*—roughly 32 percent of the value of the total exports carried by this caravan (413,890 *tangga*).[58]

This again shows the importance of global connections to the oasis economy, the most fundamental structural factor underpinning the capitalist development there. As the initial stimulus for oasis capitalism came from outside, from the direction of the east, China, since 1500 the impetus for its continued development derived also from the outside—but this time from the west, Central Asia and Russia. The small size of the local market within Eastern Turkestan may have accounted for the region's heavy reliance on global trade. At the same time, the area's geographical location, straddling the borders of two massive markets, located in China and Russia, made the region a great potential production base for the merchants and capitalists targeting these two lucrative constituencies. At any rate, even when the region had lost its crucial China connection, if temporarily in the aftermath of the fall of the Qing Empire, the pulse of oasis capitalism did not stop. It found another global connection and marched forward.

Conclusion

The Opium War spelled the end of the oasis capitalism that had developed under Qing protection since the eighteenth century. What was responsible for its demise was the crisis of the Qing Empire, which had until then anchored trade and agrarian development. Most important, the imperial government no longer was able to transfer silver into Xinjiang. In this radical context, the begs made their first earnest effort to initiate local state building—for example, raising new revenue to sustain the Qing military locally. In this sense, the fall of the Qing Empire–beg client regime in the oasis was indeed a globally conditioned development, a local crisis spurred by changes in the environment of global politics.

However, the initial measure that the Muslim clients had taken to save the Qing military had a serious negative consequence on the vitality of oasis capitalism. The begs' initiative to raise military financing by developing copper mining and manipulating the copper currency intensified the social stratification that accompanied their agrarian development in the oasis, prompting the success of another round of *khwaja* attacks. The begs revised their stance again after the 1857 *khwaja* war, and decided to raise military financing by taxing the wealth of the propertied class (begs, non-beg landlords, and sojourner merchants). However, that change in stance came a little too late. In the midst of the ensuing local Muslim revolt and Khoqandian invasion, in 1864 the Qing Empire fell.

Oasis capitalism lost its impetus after the fall of the Qing, showing how important the imperial presence in Xinjiang was for its success in the eighteenth and nineteenth centuries. However, this did not mean that oasis capitalism became totally defunct; instead, it forged a new connection to global trade, this time in a westerly direction (toward Russian cities and Khoqand territory, and also toward British India to a lesser degree), and reconstructed its base on the expansion of the cotton industry.

As for Ahmad, whose career this chapter has closely followed, he never wavered from his commitment to the Qing throughout this entire period of turmoil. In 1863, from his retirement home in Kucha, Ahmad donated logistics to the Qing armies stationed in Yarkand District and received a commutation of punishment for the numerous charges of corruption and wrongdoing he had accumulated.[59] Finally, when a group of the Muslim rebels of the Kucha area, who had brought down the Qing empire in 1864, asked him to be their leader, he refused to cooperate and was killed.

Yet, ironically, Ahmad's career and reputation were posthumously resurrected among the local Muslims not long after his death. When Mullā Sayrāmī wrote the first history of late-nineteenth-century Eastern Turkestan in the first decade of the twentieth century, he portrayed Ahmad in a surprisingly positive light, as a devout Muslim ruling the oasis according to Muslim customs and regulations. Perhaps, Ahmad's refusal to further exploit the oasis population through the revenue farming mechanism, because of his concern about its negative impact, and his efforts instead to tax the propertied class, contributed to a positive portrayal of his legacy. However, what was really at stake in a positive evaluation of Ahmad's career was the oasis Muslim's re-evaluation of the legacy of the begs and their strategy of capitalist development under Qing protection.

Mullā Sayrāmī stunningly defended Ahmad's collaboration with the Qing by putting the following words in his mouth, when he refused to cooperate with Muslim rebels: "As for me, my grandfather and father continuously worked for the Great Khan [Qing emperor], and received high offices. I also personally received land, water, and servants through the emperor's grace. . . . Surely, he is a non-believer, who does not have faith. However, continuing from my grandfather and father, I am bathed in his glory and continued to eat his salt. Under any circumstances, I will not betray my lord who has given me salt."[60]

In his depiction, Mullā Sayrāmī amply highlights the material foundation of Ahmad's collaboration with the Qing Empire. He paid loyalty to the infidel "Chinese ruler," because the latter provided salary, the "salt." This notion of paying loyalty to his political masters who provided salaries was a legitimate Central Asian (Turkic), if not Islamic, justification. Thus, in this way Sayrāmī was able to describe Ahmad's death as a martyrdom.[61] However, what is more important for the purpose of this chapter is the specific content of the "salary" given to Ahmad's family—that is, "land," "water," and "servants." If one agrees that "servants" here most likely mean *yanqi*, this statement summarizes the three core elements constituting the success of commercial, agrarian enterprises in the oases, which ensured Ahmad's and the begs' unprecedented wealth, all brought to them by Qing protection.

Then, Mullā Sayrāmī's surprisingly positive description of Ahmad's death indicates that, by the turn of the twentieth century, the local oasis people had come around to accepting the begs' agenda to secure the wealth and peace in the oasis under Qing rule. The oasis Muslims realized in retrospect that the beg alliance with the Qing Empire, the power that provided them a connection to the China market and strong military protection, was the fundamental condition for the economic prosperity and security of life that they had experienced for about a century. In the exciting but perilous new world spun into being by the expansion of global trade and destructive military competitions since the sixteenth century, that was all they could ask for, even though such an alliance accelerated local social tensions and humiliating political subordination to infidels. Having experienced the precariousness of life under the Islamic rule of Ya'qūb Beg, when the region's China connections had been completely lost, the oasis Muslims finally came to terms with Qing rule, if reluctantly and belatedly.[62]

Conclusion

In his report written for the Forsyth Mission on the current conditions of commerce in Eastern Turkestan under Yaʻqūb Begʼs rule,[1] Captain E. F. Chapman provided a generally upbeat, cautiously hopeful picture of prospects for future growth. Especially, the regimeʼs new commercial treaties underway with Great Britain and Russia would initiate a more "enlightened policy" regarding commerce by the Muslim regime. In particular, the treaties would put an end to the unfortunate habit the traders living in the oasis had of spending their accumulated wealth outside the country. Previously, owners of wealth in the oasis were afraid to acknowledge their good fortune, especially if capital was accumulated in Kashgar. Once the enlightened commercial policies came into effect, Captain Chapman predicted, the conditions, position, and privileges of traders in Yaʻqūb Begʼs dominions "will bear favorable comparison with what is met with in any other Mahomedan country in Asia."[2] In fact, the diplomatic achievement was already showing results: treatment by the governor of Yarkand, Mahomed Yunus Jan, toward traders journeying from India, Badakhshan, and elsewhere had been quite exceptional. The captain was confident that this change in policy would help liberate the accumulation of wealth and the growth of commerce in the region.[3]

In his rather low-key elaboration of the economic situation in the oasis border region in the late nineteenth century, Captain Chapman in fact raised a fundamental question implicit in his report to his superiors. Was capitalism, as a thriving profit-making modus operandi for commercial enterprise, possible in diverse places around the world aside from Europe—or England particularly, which had been under the control of an "enlightened" ruler? His answer appeared to be negative: the oasis rulerʼs oppressive policy regarding the merchants stifled the possibility of wealth accumulation in the region. Only the introduction of an enlightened commercial policy under the influence of the

British and Russian empires would change that situation. What the captain did not know, however, was that the oasis society had indeed already experienced intense capitalist development for a long time—since the year 1500—and especially so under the rule of the Qing Empire from 1759 to 1864, a period that he would also have been reluctant to describe as "enlightened."

This book has examined the surprising story of the rise of commercial landlords, begs, in the Xinjiang oasis from 1500 to 1864, and has shown how the oasis begs reorganized the political economy of the Qing frontier toward a capitalist path in order to take advantage of the emerging opportunities in local, regional, and global trade. In telling this story, this book has offered a new perspective on Qing imperial history, and also contributed to a revised narrative on the history of global capitalism and imperialism on a truly global scale, and in an interconnected fashion. This narrative takes into consideration the agency not only of the metropolitan state but also of the local society, one that would participate in the capitalist world order and, by so doing, shape its own place within it on its own terms.

An Overview of Oasis Capitalism, 1500 to 1900

Coming from various social backgrounds—former nomadic nobles, caravan merchants, and migrant Sufi holy men—the begs shared keen interests in expanding oasis commerce and agriculture. Sufi migrants, for instance, who constituted the majority of the beg contingents, relocated to this region in the first place in order to secure livelihoods and exploit advantages from the newly emerging Chinese tribute trade, and, in the second, upon their arrival to conduct energetic land reclamation and mining development.

From the sixteenth to the nineteenth centuries, begs shrewdly utilized their political connections, manipulating local, regional, and imperial politics to promote capitalistic transformation of the region. Through land grants, in the sixteenth century they used their political connections with the local Yarkand Khanate (1514–1680) to obtain access to precious resources such as jade mines and well-irrigated land estates. They also managed the Khanate's lucrative tribute trade with Ming China (1368–1644). In the seventeenth century, as the Yarkand Khanate collapsed under the dual pressures of a decline in the China trade and a growing military threat from a new Mongol power—the Zunghar Khanate (1634–1758)—the begs chose to ally themselves with the Qing Empire, undergoing an expansion into the region.

Under the mantle of Qing imperial military protection, the begs over-saw a radical development of the oasis economy. They placed unprecedented amounts of underutilized common land and wild-land under intensive cultivation, for commercial farms and ranches, and also conducted substantial mining development—especially in jade, gold, and copper. Increasing numbers of oasis people were mobilized and recruited to work for these new commercial enterprises, as nominal "*yanqi,*" wage laborers, and slaves. Even nomads and mountain people living on the outskirts of the major oasis systems were also settled in large number in the oasis for the first time to fulfill the same purpose.

The course of capitalist transformation produced unequal rewards for its participants, with great wealth accruing to the beg developers, and deprivation and onerous burdens to the oasis farmers and laborers. From the latter's ranks, resistance grew in the form of bandits and refugees fleeing into the mountains that surrounded the oases. There, these people would amass to form outsider, refugee communities. Eventually, led by Sufi holy men in the early 1800s into more overt political actions, they resorted to warfare. While these forces of resistance threatened the security of the regime of commercial wealth and prosperity in the oasis, the beg developers shrewdly turned this political crisis into another new opportunity for enrichment. The Qing reinforced its troop presence in the oasis in order to defend its imperial outposts in the remote frontier in 1830s, and to established new government-run agrarian colonies (*tuntian*) to defray the incurred military costs. The begs effectively turned the new ventures of *tuntian* into private investment opportunities by conducting their development on behalf of the Qing administration. They did so in cooperation with the wealthy local non-beg landlords, as well as caravan merchants sojourning in the local oasis. The latter hailed primarily from the neighboring region of the Fergana Valley.

This thriving enterprise unexpectedly descended into crisis when the Qing state, the protector of oasis capitalism, fell into trouble in the mid-nineteenth century. After the Opium War (1839–42) and amid the subsequent anti-Qing rebellions occurring all over China, the Qing government put on a fiscal strait-jacket and ceased to transfer New World silver to the oasis. The oasis capitalists made failing attempts to solve the Qing Empire's crisis of military finance by artificially inflating the amount and value of local currency—a policy that impacted the local economy disastrously in the 1850s. In the end, the begs made a last-ditch effort to save the Qing Empire, by raising tax collection revenues from local commerce and agriculture controlled by the elites and by imposing a regular tax for the first time on the wealthy sojourner caravan merchants. However, these efforts arrived a little too late. The Qing Empire fell in 1864, plunging the local economy into a deep depression. Even under those circumstances, the pulse of oasis capitalism never quite stopped. Instead, it found new global market connections with Russia, Central Asia, and, to a lesser degree, British India, and marched on.

Borderland Capitalism and the Chinese Imperial Expansion

The picture of the Qing Empire in the Xinjiang oasis emerging from this book is one of a dynamic and strategic political alliance, voluntarily initiated by a borderland commercial class intent upon taking advantage of expanding global trade. The begs *chose* to ally with the Qing Empire after the Yarkand Khanate fell in 1680, although they could have elected to ally with the Zunghar Mongols, the archrival of the Qing. They made this decision strategically, attracted primarily by the favorable prospect of stable access to the China market and the Qing Empire's development of economic policies favorable to the begs' economic interests. In this sense, the Qing imperial expansion into Central Asia was indeed a collaborative process of local negotiation that happened in the frontier, anchored by the begs' commercial interests.

This portrayal of the relationship between the Qing Empire and oasis capitalism sheds a new light on the underexplored social and economic dimensions of its imperial expansion. Previous scholarship, pioneered by Joseph Fletcher and developed by the New Qing History scholars, focuses primarily on the political, cultural, and ideological foundation of the Qing imperial expansion, and sees the eighteenth-century Qing Empire as a loosely connected political alliance between the Manchu emperor and culturally diverse Eurasian elites such as Mongol khans and Tibetan lama. This was an alliance glued together by the Manchu imperial court's multicultural political and moral persuasions, yet ultimately undergirded by the military superiority of the Manchu Qing in the fashion of the universal emperorship of Mongol grand khan centuries ago.[4] Therefore, its empire was not designed to disturb the status quo of the local society over which the borderland elites presided. At best, the Qing Empire was a detached political entity, cautiously refraining from intervening in the social and economic events of the borderland society in any meaningful way. At worst, it was a conservative force that helped to preserve the status quo of the already existing political, social, and economic institutions in place in the oasis.

However, the picture of the Qing Empire, as observed from the bottom up in the Central Asian hinterlands, leads us to a different conclusion. At least in the eighteenth and nineteenth centuries in Eastern Turkestan, the Qing were not indifferent bystanders in regard to the region's economic and social transformation. They protected and promoted the interests of an emerging new commercial class from the oasis, a class intent upon radically reorganizing its local economy; the Manchu court would actively protect the beg regime from the backlash of village communities that tried to preserve their "traditional" rights while being engulfed, detrimentally, in the change. On their part, these new commercial elites provided unwavering, continued political collaboration for the Qing Empire locally.

In itself, this portrayal is not necessarily out of line with the previous scholarship's depiction of the Qing as the patron of the Eurasian ruling elites' interests. However, this book's findings show that the borderland begs, which the Qing Empire endeavored to protect, were not necessarily "traditional" or "backward." If the Qing court were to support traditional ruling elites, they should have reinstated the members of the Yarkand khan family, who were still alive and eager to regain their lost domain at the time of the Qing conquest. But it did not. Instead, it supported the new landholding oasis elites, who were intent upon the radical reorganization of their society and its economic system in the oasis. By supporting the begs' interests, then, the Qing Empire helped facilitate the progress of this radical reorganization, rather than preserving traditional structural elements in place.

As a matter of fact, the imperial court's support of the beg commercial developers derived from proactive, consciously strategic decisions. The Qing badly needed the partnership of such resourceful commercial developers for the purposes of managing the efficient development of local resources in order to increase local revenues, ultimately to be extracted into the imperial coffer. By outsourcing the revenue collection and development to the frontier begs, the Qing ran their empire inexpensively. Furthermore, the imperial court profited commercially in a most cost efficient way from various commodity endeavors undertaken in the oasis, the most important being the jade trade. In turn, the Qing reciprocated in its political support to the begs local economy, with policies that were intended to protect and promote the interests of the commercial elites, helping the frontier landlords and merchants to accumulate greater surpluses. The borderland capitalists in turn reinvested their returns in further expansion of local agriculture, mining, and commerce.

If the Qing's role in the economic and social development explains the success of its empire in the oasis Xinjiang in the eighteenth and nineteenth centuries, it also explains the cause of the political crisis it experienced there by the late nineteenth century. The fiercest challenge to the Qing-beg regime during the late nineteenth century came from none other than the oasis farmer refugees. They had been uprooted in the process of the capitalistic transformation of the economy, the very process set in motion by the beg developers under Qing protection. In other words, the nineteenth-century crisis in the borderlands was of the Qing's own making, rather than a development caused by the disappearance of Qing multiculturalism.

This story offers broad insight into the history of the Qing Empire in Eurasia in the eighteenth and nineteenth centuries in general: the Eurasian borderland societies under the intense commercialization of the period were the locus of the Qing imperial history, in which the political fortune of its empire was fundamentally decided. That is to say, the rapid commercialization created both a group of local collaborators ready for the Qing conquest, people who were, on account of their own economic interests, willing to ally themselves with the Qing Empire, and also a force of resistance to the new imperial order. The latter's challenge would plunge the Qing authority into sudden political crisis in the frontiers later.

Perhaps, the best parallel to the Central Asian story was provided by the southwestern region of the Qing Empire, in Yunnan. Like Xinjiang, western Yunnan also saw an upsurge of commercial activity resulting from its growing commercial connection with China during the period from 1500 to 1850. There were two especially high points in its long-term commercial expansion. The first was reached in the sixteenth century with the coming of the Ming Empire. After a temporary dip in trade in the seventeenth century, the second high point came during the eighteenth century as a result of Qing military expansion and an upsurge in Chinese migration. The timeframe for the commercialization of the two different borderlands, Eastern Turkestan and Yunnan, was essentially the same—a period punctuated by two peaks in the sixteenth century, a long eighteenth century, with a brief low point in between. Xinjiang and Yunnan, two borderlands separated by considerable distance, were thus linked by the same rhythm of commercialization, emanating largely from China.

There, native society was an important agent in the commercial and agrarian expansion occurring in Yunnan. The landed native aristocrats of Tai origin in Yunnan, who worked as clients for the Qing under its policy of "indirect" rule, developed commercial agriculture in rice and tea for export to a receptive market in China. In addition, the native Chinese (the local Chinese who claimed their origin in Yunnan to the early Ming Period in the fourteenth century) emerged as dominant transnational merchants who linked the region with Burma and China in the eighteenth century. In the nineteenth century, they went on to build thriving capitalistic business firms that had shareholding structures and new accounting practices.[5]

This is not to say that the natives were the only force for the development of commerce and agriculture in western Yunnan. As a matter of fact, Chinese migrants constituted an even greater force in the agrarian development there. Three million new Chinese migrants settled in Yunnan between 1700 and 1850. The Chinese merchants and frontier farmers with political connections and capital accumulated ever-growing amounts of farmland in the valleys and expanded tea plantations in the mountains at the expense of the native people.[6] In fact, the dominance of Chinese migrants in the agricultural development of Yunnan reflected the general trends in the Qing frontiers generally. Along the vast steppe land from Inner Mongolia to Zungharia (northern Xinjiang), Chinese migrants settled in massive numbers and developed agriculture despite the Qing ban on such a practice. For instance, especially in the area surrounding Urumqi in Zungharia, Chinese migrants contributed to a spectacular expansion of agriculture there following the Qing conquest. By 1857 the number of Chinese civilian migrants in Urumqi and Barkul was reportedly 310,000.[7]

Also, numerous Chinese farmers migrated from Fujian to Taiwan from the time when the Dutch took control of the island in 1624, and particularly after the Qing colonization in 1673. There they developed rice and sugar plantations. By 1824 the Han Chinese had increased to 1.2 million. Such an onslaught of Chinese migration often put the economy of the natives of borderlands in difficulty. Chinese farmers in Taiwan had even encroached upon native hunting grounds, which had dominated native land use and had secured the supply of deer exported to Japan. In response, the Qing had to protect the native chieftains, instituting a system of "aboriginal land rights" that allowed the native chieftains to collect rent from Chinese farmers and land developers.[8] The native chieftains adapted to this system and became rice farmers themselves, taking Chinese surnames and adopting Chinese rituals.

However, at the most fundamental level, the dividing line in the social politics in Qing borderlands in general and in Yunnan in particular was more economic rather than purely ethnic. Often the native landed aristocrats allied

with the wealthy Chinese merchants and Qing officials, who provided market connections, capital, and political access needed for the development of
their land projects (the ultimate source of wealth and power in society). Thus,
one Tai ruler, who had political ties with Qing military officials in Yunnan, was
even able to pressure Chinese tenants to pay higher rent. Eventually, he drove
them out from his land with force, when the Chinese tenants did not com-
ply.[9] In other words, at the time of the unique commercialization and agrarian
development underway in the borderlands in the eighteenth and nineteenth
centuries, it would be much more reasonable to anticipate that such economic
development would engender major social and political divisions. The politics
animated by such economic tensions was as important as, if not more than, the
politics of ethnic conflict in formulating the political dynamics present in the
borderlands.

Yet, in the end, the different demographic compositions of each frontier significantly influenced the specific political details of the frontier crisis engen-
dered by commercialization in oasis Xinjiang and western Yunnan. That is to
say, the major political tension that constituted the crisis of the Qing Empire
in the Central Asian oases in the nineteenth century manifested in the form
of an intra-Muslim tension (between the *khwaja* and the begs), while the conflicts between the Chinese migrants and the oasis Muslims were largely, if not
entirely, muted. That was in considerable contrast to the situation in Yunnan,
where political strife caused by borderland commercial development erupted
into overt ethnic conflict—the Panthay Rebellion (1856–73), which engulfed the
Muslim and ethnic population against the Chinese migrants. Meanwhile, the
political tension caused by the native officials' agrarian development did not
figure much in the overall crisis of the Qing Empire in Yunnan's borderland.
The reason for this was the different demographic conditions existing between
the two regions: in starkest terms, about 310,000 Chinese migrants resided in
Xinjiang, including both northern steppe and southern oases, versus the mil-
lions who settled in Yunnan.[10]

In any case, this view from borderlands urges one to understand the Qing
imperial expansion as a part of the long-term trajectory of early modern Chinese history from the sixteenth to the nineteenth century. A curious gap between the Ming and Qing historiographies in the Chinese history field had
developed since the rise of the New Qing History. This revisionist scholarship
successfully challenged the long-standing assumption that perceived the Qing
as merely a Chinese empire, and recast it in a new light, as a multicultural Eur-

asian empire.[11] Yet, this revisionist scholarship also unintentionally detaches the latter from the long-term trajectory of early modern Chinese history. The logic contributing to the discontinuation between the two historiographies is rather easily understood, however. If the Qing state was quintessentially an Inner Asian state, and its empire essentially Eurasian, no need then exists for scholars to consider seriously the long-term historical development in China under the Ming when they explore Qing history.

This book's findings offer a different view. Without doubt, the Qing Empire in Central Asia can be characterized as Eurasian: in its formation, multiple Eurasian actors such as the Muslim begs played a decisive role. Nonetheless, when Eurasian actors joined the Qing Empire, they were primarily attracted to the prospect of enhancing their commercial connection with China upon which their economic success became increasingly dependent from the time of the Ming period. In other words, what joined the Eurasian components into the fold of Qing multiethnic empire was early modern China's long-term commercial engagement with its borderlands. Seen in this light, the Qing's Eurasian empire was an early modern Chinese empire as well. Therefore, this book illuminates the continuity of the Ming-Qing history and thus places it within a coherent historical trajectory of early modern China from the fourteenth to the nineteenth centuries, rather than fragmenting the long-term trajectory into two disconnected narratives, splitting into Ming China and the Manchu Qing.

Empire and Capitalism, a View from Eurasian Borderlands

In addition, this understanding of oasis capitalism and the Qing Empire sheds new light on the shared pattern of the interrelated expansion of capitalism and empire in Eurasia at this time. This book demonstrates that, lacking substantial local demands and having a relatively small agrarian base, the oasis begs needed constant access to the market in a nearby metropole to jumpstart economic expansion. Furthermore, they needed a state power, favorable to their cause of agrarian development, in order to expand their private claim over rural resources against resistances from the rural communities. The imperial Qing state was able to deliver both conditions. In this way, the empire became the integral, indispensible condition for the capitalist transformation of the oasis society at the heart of Eurasia.

Notably, the military financing and system of revenue contracting in the eighteenth century also played a critical role in the expansion of the British

Empire and the power and wealth of the "native" capitalists in northern India, some 1,300 miles south of Kashgar. During the chaotic period of decline in the Mughal Empire and within the context of the expansion of European commerce in the subcontinent in the late seventeenth and early eighteenth centuries, various people of different origins in northern India, including relatives of the nobility, merchants, and landholders of the villages (*zamindars*), began to emerge as commercial "class." Variously called "magnates," and "great households," these people increased their wealth and political influence in regional politics. The source of their power was their control over local commerce and agriculture.

Yet, by far the most important source of the wealth accumulation was revenue farming. The smaller regional states in India and the English East India Company that emerged during this time began to extract more revenue from local commerce and agriculture, in order to fund their European-style military reform. However, because of the lack of any realistic ability to implement their goal, they had to rely upon the commercial elites.[12] These new elites, as low- and high-level functionaries and revenue farmers, hijacked the state function to advance their "capitalist" agenda. They used revenue farming as a secure, stable investment opportunity, and did so most importantly, by working under the name of state prerogative. In so doing, these commercialized landlords were able to break down the village community's strong customary grip on resources and expand their private domination of them, thus clearing the biggest obstacle to the expansion of capitalistic production relations in rural hinterlands. These efforts were often resisted by the rural communities. However, the commercial *zamindar* successfully stemmed any challenge from the community by depending upon the protection provided by the regional state, and especially the British.[13]

For the new commercial landed elites or the indigenous protocapitalists, it did not matter whether they allied or worked for indigenous regional rulers or the English East India Company. Both kinds of regional states held the same economic and fiscal agendas—a mercantilist monopoly of resources and labor—for raising maximum revenue, traits that the new protocapitalists could exploit just as revenue farmers in their fight against village communities. However, the East India Company had a few characteristics that made it more attractive to the new commercial elites. The company also provided an outlet for their commodities to reach the global and European networks of commerce, which were rapidly rising as major markets for Indian goods such as cotton.

Also, the British legal system strongly supported the notion of alienable private property, which could come in handy in their efforts to expand private land-holdings and negate the village communities' rights to resources.[14]

Certain significant differences in details existed between the Indian and Eastern Turkestani scenarios. For one thing, in oasis Xinjiang, the local population had to raise significant military financial revenue, but not, however, because the Qing needed to adopt high-cost European military technology, as was the case in India. Rather, the oasis population of Eastern Turkestan had to do so because the Qing state decided to station a large number of military in Xinjiang permanently. But in terms of the general function of the revenue contracting and military financing for the commercial landlords' capital accumulation, the commonality between the two cases is hard to deny. And where there was a difference, if anything, the Qing version of military fiscal policy was much more beneficial for the native capitalists and their capitalist accumulation. The imperial court extended to the oasis begs the mandate of revenue farming but took a lesser portion from the total revenue they raised from the oasis society. The begs then could accumulate more wealth from the mechanism of revenue contracting.

Then, fundamentally, the imperial state and its mandate to develop local commercial and agrarian resource to generate revenue for empire building tremendously helped the native capitalists in both cases. Fortunately for the native capitalists, both sets of rulers, converging on the Eurasian frontier at the same time in the eighteenth century, had a long history of mobilizing the commercial networks already in place in their state-building efforts. Even in its oversight of the Chinese metropole and in the eighteenth-century episode of expansion into Gansu, the Qing Empire shrewdly and actively utilized Chinese merchants' commercial networks in place for performing various governmental and social functions. Especially in Gansu and other northwestern provinces, Chinese merchants were tapped to develop agrarian colonies, donate funds to local administration, and relieve the local society of food shortages. They were also asked to deliver goods to be used in the state trade with Central Asian nomads.[15]

From the vantage points of the borderlands, Central Asia and India, respectively, the British and the Qing empires look remarkably similar. What this parallel illuminates is the synchronically articulated, interrelated dynamic of the imperial expansion and capitalism occurring in Eurasia. At least in northern India and oasis Xinjiang, while uncoordinated, this movement resulted in no small part from the work of commercial elites who needed the presence of a strong imperial state to reorganize the borderland economy, politics, and environment in response to the imperatives of global commerce. In other words, in the transformation of an obscure Eastern Turkestani society from the sixteenth to the nineteenth century, one can feel the relentless pulse of global trade transforming local societies worldwide, and see as well the violent human and social consequences that the transformation caused.

This book then problematizes the tenacious geographical bias evident in the current understanding of the origin of modernity by world historians—that is, Western Europe. In this view, Europe and the coastal littoral around the Indian and Atlantic oceans that formed the "European world economy"—where the European empires, in general, and the British Empire, in particular, took hold eventually —became the original repository of modernity, and from where the development of an interconnected modern world history could only be properly narrated. If scholars no longer believe that European imperialists brought capitalism and attendant modern economic "development" outright into the backward hinterlands of Asia and America, a position now widely discredited, they still believe that European commerce triggered modern development in oceanic societies in parts of Asia and America interconnected with European trade.

Because of the presence of European traders there, the oceanic worlds— coastal South Asia, North America, and Southeast Asia—experienced an increasing integration into the circuits of global trade, as well as the rise of new commercial elites and protocapitalists.[16] Here, what we see is the curious teleology of European trade or commercial expansion in the explanation of the origin of modernity. On the other hand, the inland part of the world, the sphere of influence of the powerful Eurasian empires such as the Ottoman, the Mughal, and the Qing, did not formulate a part of the interconnected history of modernity. Disconnected from European trade, it was considered disconnected from the rhythm of world history marching toward the modern world; it remained backward until the arrival of European imperialists in the region in the late nineteenth century.[17]

This book challenges such long-standing presumptions favoring a geographical hierarchy of world history, by providing evidence for the interconnected developments of imperial expansion, world trade, and capitalist agriculture in the landlocked oasis territory of Eurasia, occurring simultaneously with similar developments in the Indian Ocean. Importantly, these developments happened in spite of the ostensible absence of the major European traders. The region's ever intensifying connection to Chinese commerce and empire was able to provide the same commercial stimulus and political protection to the oasis commercial elites. In light of that, a truly multifocal history of imperialism and capitalism on a global scale, one that does not privilege the European vector of expansion but highlights instead the convergence of political and economic transformations of the world from the sixteenth century onward may be not only possible but also necessary for a complete understanding of the expansion of global capitalism.

The Resuscitation of Oasis Capitalism and Renewed Resistance, 1870s

As it happened, the capitalist transformation that the Qing and begs set in motion in the oasis borderlands did not stop when the Manchu Qing Empire fell in the region in 1864. It continued on, albeit in different forms and with significantly weakened strength. After the Qing reconquest of the region in 1877, however, oasis capitalism roared back to full strength. The begs and non-beg landlords seized an ever growing portion of agrarian resources; their commercial enterprises flourished.[18]

So, however, did the local resistance to oasis capitalism. As long as this dynamic continued to spew out uprooted, desperate people, there was no reason for it to subside. Indeed, the rebels also came back in the late nineteenth century after the Qing reconquest of Xinjiang in 1878, but in a more diffused manner. Oasis districts that had formerly been immune to the nineteenth-century *khwaja* wars would now witness outbreaks of local violence. In other words, the oasis population's sporadic efforts to rise against oasis capitalism grew to become a broad-based movement, although each individual act of violence was decidedly smaller in scale. Curiously, when the dissidents struck back, they brought with them Islamic holy men, albeit mostly obscure figures.

That winter, for instance, the Muslim governor of Aksu—a city in the middle of Eastern Turkestan that had remained mostly outside of the action of the nineteenth-century *khwaja* wars—reported one such episode. In a rural village located 200 *li* southwest of the city of Aksu, a local mob of three hundred people from the rural villages attacked the Qing administration, killing a total of nine clerks and others. The uprising, however, was essentially a nonevent because the Qing military and the villages' *akhunds* put down the attackers quickly, killing about twenty. What makes this incident of local violence significant is its location, in a rural village called Yin-a-wa-ti that had been at the forefront of the agrarian expansion of the oasis system earlier in the nineteenth century. Originally a land first reclaimed during the Jiaqing reign (1796–1820), its development received zealous attention. The one thousand households that had first settled in the village multiplied several times, and the original village divided into ten large settlements (*da zongzhuang*).

That is to say, this small uprising happened in a hotbed of agrarian development, which had given rise elsewhere to the *khwaja* wars in the nineteenth century. The local mob attacking the Qing administration also comprised uprooted people who had suffered the most from the burdens imposed by the state, not unlike the original *khwaja* sympathizers. In order to make sure that others clearly knew the nature of their grievance, the rebels attacked the Qing Tax Bureau.[19] The similarity with the nineteenth-century *khwaja* wars does not end there. In the course of the uprising, the attackers threatened a random, itinerant Muslim holy man from Andijan, Yi-shan Khwaja (Ishan Khwaja), seizing him and forcing him to accompany their protest as a figurehead. There was an almost comical quality to the holy man's involvement. The Qing officials released him immediately after their investigation, since his involvement had been so nominal.

In a multiple of such small incidents, then, the *khwaja* wars of the early nineteenth century, with anti-"development" resistance at its heart, continued in the late nineteenth century, even without the leadership of the specific Kashgar *khwaja* family engaged. The wars would finally even encompass places like Aksu District, which had been totally immune to the previous *khwaja* violence. However, even here, the absence of *khwaja* leadership, however nominal, was felt. What compelled the local mob to set up Ishan Khwaja as its figurehead in almost a parody of earlier social and political dynamics must have been the memory, persistent and vestigial as it may have been, of the *khwaja*s who had for decades, once before, led the holy war of the uprooted.

Indeed, other than uniting behind his name, the local rebels did not know how either to frame or to justify their struggle. They were not fighting for their hometown or villages, for they must have been recent settlers in the villages, deployed for the agrarian development of the place; they were not fighting for their nation, if such a concept had existed at all at the time, for many of them came from outside of Eastern Turkestan, as Ishan Khwaja's foreign background testified. The only cause they shared among them was distress at the uprooting and resettlement caused by the development of capitalist agrarian enterprises in the oasis—the very frustration and anxious experience that Jahāngīr Khwaja, an uprooted refugee himself, first had given voice to deep in the Pamir Mountains in the 1830s.

In the complexity of such local acts of resistance raised against the capitalist appropriation of labor and common resources for "development," we see anonymous global dynamics of marketplace imperatives at play as much as we see personal instances of grief and hardship. Such global dynamics permeated down to the individual, to the extent that they compelled action and reaction, resistance against resistance, operating in a continuum on both sides of the coin, so to speak. As global capitalism takes hold in new models of modern venture capitalism and transcorporate investment beyond the ken of citizen/ nation state constructs in the twenty-first century, we see how the seeds of its genesis, and vision of development and profit, began in the sixteenth century, in the outposts and colonies of Western Europe no less than in the Chinese Central Asian oasis borderlands.

Appendixes

A-1. Population in Eastern Turkestan, 1759–1950

	1772	1776	1818*	1850s–70s	1909	1954
Total	198,140	261,078	271,627	1,015,000&	1,867,000	3,737,000
Kashgar!	60,799	66,413	61,230	168,000	595,000	N/A
Yarkand	56,347	65,495	71,530	224,000	500,000	N/A
Khotan	43,580	44,603	62,131	129,500	375,000	N/A
Aksu#	21,216	27,969	39,273	84,000	182,000	N/A
Kucha+	3,987	6,158	5,534	42,000	125,000	N/A
Ush	2,167	3,158	3,159	14,000	47,000	N/A
Qarashar@	5,501	5,390	5,388	70,000	43,000	N/A
Others	9,212	22,536	N/A	283,500	N/A	N/A

Sources: HJZ (4 vol. version); Xinjiang *tuzhi*, vols. 43–44; Hori Sunao, "Jūhachi-nijū seiki Uiguru joku jinko shiron"; Saguchi Tōru, *Jūhachi-jūkyū-seiki Higashi Torukisutan shakaishi kenkyū*, p. 198; Forsyth, *Report of a Mission to Yarkund in 1873*, p. 62.

*The 1818 population is an estimate calculated from the number of households reported in *Jiaqing Shili*, based on the assumption that one household has 3.9 members, which was an average size of a household in 1776, calculated from the record in XYTZ.

!The population number of Kashgar includes that of Yangi Hissar, a neighboring oasis, counted as a subadministrative unit of Kashgar District.

#The population number of Aksu includes that of Sayram and Bai, two neighboring oases that were counted as subadministrative units of Kucha District.

+The population number of Kucha includes that of Shayar, a neighboring oasis that was counted as a subadministrative unit of Kucha District under the Qing rule.

&This number was calculated on the assumption that one household was composed of seven people on average. The total household number at the time was reported as 145,000. This assumption of seven people per household needs further explanation, since one oasis household in 1772 (calculated from the record in HJZ) was 3.38 people on average, and in 1776, it was 3.9 people. It is possible that whereas the earlier Qing records only reported the adult population, which was the target of its tax collection, the 1850s–70s record also included non-taxable household members, such as servants, slaves, and children. At any rate, therefore, one can get an alternative number of the population in the oases for these years, if one follows the earlier calculation of the size of an oasis household. If one assumes that one household comprised 3.9 people on average, the total population in 1850s–70s stood at 565,500.

@Often, the population of Turfan and Hami, the two easternmost oasis districts, was not reported in the Qing record. The reason is that those two oasis districts did not pay tax, because their rulers contributed to the Qing conquest of the oasis region in the eighteenth century, and thus gained the right not to do so. Since the Qing collected the information about the local population for the purpose of tax collection, the two oases' population numbers often did not appear in the books compiled by the Qing government.

Appendix A

A-2. Arable land in Eastern Turkestan, 1759–1950 (Unit: *mu*)

Location	1772	1833	1850s–60s	1887	1909	1943	1954
Total*	3,400,000 –3,500,000	6,000,000	6,800,000	9,100,000	9,380,000	12,040,000	14,000,000
Kashgar	N/A	N/A	N/A	1,984,000	1,980,000	1,560,000	N/A
Yarkand	N/A	N/A	N/A	2,415,000	2,420000	3,510,000	N/A
Khotan	N/A	N/A	N/A	1,604,000	1,600,000	2,300,000	N/A
Aksu	N/A	N/A	N/A	1,405,000	3,100,000	3,990,000	N/A
Kucha	N/A	N/A	N/A	1,125,000	N/A	N/A	N/A
Ush	N/A	N/A	N/A	567,000	N/A	N/A	N/A
Qarashar	N/A	N/A	N/A	N/A	280,000	680,000	N/A

Sources: Hori Sunao, "Shindai Kaikyō no kochimenseki," pp. 17–19, 26–27; HJZ; XZSL; Xuanzong [Daoguang] chao (XZSL).
*The number for arable land here does not include the *waqf* land and land grants to beg officials.

B-1. Muslim Notables Submitting to the Qing, 1697–1760

Political Affiliation (Headman)	Place of Affiliation	Name	Local Position	Social Background	Year of Submission	Career under the Qing Empire
'Ubayd Allāh	Hami	'Ubayd Allāh	Darugha (governor) under Zunghar	Sufi	1697	
Emin Khwāja	Turfan	Emin Khwāja	Grand Akhūnd	Sufi	1732	
		Sha-pei (Sufi?)	Emin Khwāja's underling	Sufi?	1732	
		Lai-zi	Emin Khwāja's underling		1732	
		Hu-dai-ba-er-di	Emin Khwāja's underling		1732	
		Ma-men-ke-le-mu	Emin Khwāja's underling		1732	
		Aman Mīrāb	Emin Khwāja's underling		1732	
Manggaliq	Turfan	Manggaliq			1756	Rebelled
		Bai Khwāja	Manggaliq's son		1756	Settled in Beijing
Yi-bi-li-ye-mu		Yi-bi-li-ye-mu			1755	
Beg Toqto	Qarashar (Kurla)	Beg Toqto	Beg		1756	
		Sadiq	Beg Toqto's son		1756	
		'Abd Allāh	Beg Toqto's younger brother		1756	Governor of Dolan tribe settled in Qarashar; sent to be settled in Beijing (1761)
Wu-su-bu A-bu]du-la-yi-mu	Ili	Wu-su-bu A-bu-du-la-yi-mu			1755	
A-ke-zhu-er	Ili	A-ke-zhu-er	*Zaisan* (headman) of Puchin (Muslim artillerymen)		1755	
		Tai-la-ke	A-ke-zhu-er's son		1755	
		Huo-mu-hu-li			1755	
		Yan-da-shi	A-ke-zu-er's underling		1755	
Tong-ma-mu-te	Ili	Tong-ma-mu-te	Puchin (Muslim artillerymen) who formerly served Zunghar; headmen?		1755	

Political Affiliation (Headman)	Place of Affiliation	Name	Local Position	Social Background	Year of Submission	Career under th Qing Empire
Ma-mu-te	Ili	Ma-mu-te	*Headman of Bederege* tribe (*otok*)	Caravan merchants	1755	
	Ili	Azziz	Ma-mu-te's underling	Caravan merchants	1755	
Ūdui	Kucha		Beg of Kucha	Settled nomadic noble	1757	Governor of Aksu [1758–59]; Governor of Yarkand [1760–
		Osman	Ūdui's son		1757	Governor of Kucha [1758–74
		A-bu-du-er-man	Ūdui's nephew		1757	Ishikagha of Yarkand [1765]
Gadaimet	Ush/Bai		Beg of Ush/Bai		1757	Governor of Ba [1759]; Governo of Kashgar [1760–77]
		A-bu-du-er-man				Governor of Ba [1760–76]
Setib Aldi	Ush	Setib Aldi	Beg of Ush		1757	Governor of Ya Hissar [1759];
Governor of Aksu [1760–75]						
		A-ke Beg	Setib Aldi's younger brother		1757?	Governor of Qarashar (Bugu [1761]
A-gua-si-bai-kai	Sayram				1759	Governor of Sayram
		Bei-ge-ji	A-gua-si-bai-kai's younger brother		1759	5R Kazanchi Be of Sayram
		Mi-er-bo-luo-te			1759	4R Ishikagha of Sayram
		Mo-man			1759	7R Ming Beg of Sayram
Ma-ha-mo-di	Shayar	Ma-ha-mo-di				
		A-san Khwāja	Ma-ha-mo-di's son			
Xi-li-bu-a-san	Shayar	Xi-li-bu-a-san	Originally [Shayar] Governor			4R Ishikagha of Sha- ya-er [1761
Khwāja Si Beg	Turfan/ Ush	Khwāja Si Beg	Sufi?	Sufi	1758	Governor of Khotan [1760–6 settled in Beijin [1765]

Political Affiliation (Headman)	Place of Affiliation	Name	Local Position	Social Background	Year of Submission	Career under the Qing Empire
		Sali	Khwāja Si Beg's underling; originally Hākim	Sufi	1758	4R Khazanachi Beg of Yarkand [1759–62]; Ishikagha Beg of Aksu [1762–?]
		A-li-mu	Khwāja Si Beg's underling		1758	
		E-se-mu-tu-la	Beg of Lu-ke-cha-ke settlement		1758	
		La-mu-tu-la	E-se-mu-tu-la's son; Khwāja Si Beg's underling; "guide" Muslim		1758	
		E-shuo-er-duo-er-wa	Khwāja Si Beg's underling		1758	
		Mullā Khwāja	Khwāja Si Beg's underling*		1768	4R Ishikagha of Ush
	Ush (Khwja Si Bek's domain)	Sha-zi-ya-dong	Tuo-ke-tuo Beg of Ush		1759	
		A-bu-du-ji-mo-er	*Darugha*) Beg of Ush under Zunghar rule		1759	
		Mo-te*	Ush Ishikagha beg		1759	
		Huo-pu-er	Qādī Beg of the Ya-er settlements		1759	A leader of the Ush rebellion (1765)
		E-shuo-er	Mi-la-bu (Mīrāb) of the Ya-er "village"*; later a leader of the Ush rebel (1765)		1759	
	Aksu (Khwāja Si Beg's Domain)	Ba-ba-ke	Mullā*		1758	
		Po-la-te	Mullā*		1758	
		Ti-ni	Po-la-te's son		1758	
		Ni-ya-si	"A-ke-ya-er" Beg, Khazanachi Beg of Aksu		1758	

Political Affiliation (Headman)	Place of Affiliation	Name	Local Position	Social Background	Year of Submission	Career under the Qing Empire
		Ba-ba-ke	Ni-ya-si's younger brother		1758	
		A-bu-du-ga-po-er	Akhūnd		1758	
		A-er-za-mo-te			1758	
		A-ben-a-san			1758	
		A-li-mu Khwāja			1758	
	Khotan (Khwāja Si Beg's Domain)	A-shi-mo-te	Khwāja Si Beg's underling; Beg of E-li-ji of Khotan		1759	
		A-bu-du-ha-li-ke	Beg		1759	
		Te-mu-er	Beg, who took charge of the "golden vessels" before the Qing conquest		1759	5R Qādī Beg of Khotan
		A-lai-mo-te; Ta-la-*khwāja*	Muslims of Qarakash [Khotan]		1759	
		A-li-mu-sha	Beg of the Keriya [Khotan]		1759	4R Governor of Keriya [Khotan]
Kush Kipak	Kashgar		Governor of Kashgar under Zunghar rule		1760	Settled in Beijing
A-bu-du-la-yi-mu	Kashgar		Kashgar "big" Beg under Khwāja brothers		1760	
Sultān Khwāja	Yarkand		Yarkand Beg	Andijan	1759	
Sulaiman	Yarkand		Khushi Kipak's uncle; Shang Beg of Yarkand under Zunghar rule		1759?	
Mai-mai-za-er khwāja	Yarkand		Shang Beg of Yarkand, Tuo-ke-tuo Khwāja's son		1759?	
A-bu-du-ni-za-er	Yarkand		Shang Beg of Yarkand, Tuo-ke-tuo Khwāja's son*		1759?	
Hakim	Kirghiz (Burut)				1759	6R Governor of A-la-gu
Wu-mo-er	Kirghiz				1758	

Political Affiliation (Headman)	Place of Affiliation	Name	Local Position	Social Background	Year of Submission	Career under the Qing Empire
Mo-men	?		"Guide Muslim" for the Qing troops		1759	
Ka-la Khwāja	A-la-gu		A-la-gu's Hākim, Cha-la-ma's first son		1760	
A-bu-du-se-li-mu			A Muslim from the Wu-mo-er "village"		1760	
Ma-luo-mo-er-zan			Muslim		1760	
Ma-er-ga-lang			Muslim		1760	
Ke-li-da-ma-te	Dolan tribe		Small Beg		1760	
Mi-la-san	Dolan tribe		Small Beg		1760	
Hai-li-le	Dolan tribe		Small Beg		1760	
Shu-ku-er	Dolan tribe		Small Beg		1760	
E-mo	Dolan tribe		Small Beg		1760	
Qāsim			Moghul khan family		1759	Settled in Beijing
Hussein			Kashgar khwājas' family	Sufi	1759	Settled in Beijing
Tu-yi-du			Kashgar khwājas' family	Sufi	1759	Settled in Beijing
Ma-mu-te			Kashgar khwājas' family	Sufi	1759	Settled in Beijing
A-bu-du-er-man			Kashgar khwājas' family	Sufi	1760	Settled in Beijing
Pa-er-sa			Kashgar khwājas' family	Sufi	1760	Settled in Beijing

Source: GZSL; WGBZ; ZGEFL.
Note: 1. Numbers (1 through 9) indicate the official ranks of the Qing, given to the Muslims.

Appendix C

C-1. Muslim Aristocrats

a. *Muslim Aristocrats in Hami and Turfan*

Political Unit	Name	Aristocratic Title	Beg Post/Qing Generalship	Imperial Bodyguardship*	Year They Were given the Privilege of Inheritance without Demotion+	Termination of Aristocrat Title
Hami	ʿUbayd Allāh	First-grade Darugha (1697–1707)				
	Guo-mo Beg	I (1): First-grade Darugha (1707–11)				
	Emin	I (2): First-grade Da-er-han (1711–27); Zhenguo gong (1727–29); Beizi (1729–40)				
	Yūsuf	I (3): Zhenguog gong (1740–45); Beizi (1745–58); Beile pinji (1758–59); Beile (1759); Junwang pinji (1759–67)	Grand Minister Superintendent of Yarkand (1760–67)			
	Ishāq	I (4): Second-grade Taiji (1766–67); Juwang pinji (1767–80)				
	E-er-de-xi-er	I (5): Junwang pinji (1780–1813)			1788	
	Bo-shi-er	I (6) Junwang pinji (1813–40); Junwang (1840–?)				
Turfan	Emin Khwāja	Fuguo gong (1732–55), Zhenguo gong (1755–56); Bezi (1756–57); Beile pinji (1757–58); Beile (1758); Junwang pinji (1758–59); Junwang (1759–77)	Grand Minister Superintendent of Yarkand and Kashgar (1760–71)			

Political Unit	Name	Aristocratic Title	Beg Post/Qing Generalship	Imperial Body-guardship*	Year They Were given the Privilege of Inheritance without Demotion+	Termination of Aristocrat Title
	Sulaiman	I (1): Gong pinji (1756); First-grade Taiji (1762); Junwang (1777–79); First grade Shiwei (1779)				
	Iskandar	I (2): Junwang (1779–1811)	Kashgar Governor (1788); Yarkand Governor (1789–1811)	before 1788	1783	
	Yūnus	I (3): Junwang (1811–15)	Kashgar Governor (1812–15)			
	Pi-er-dun	I (4): Junwang (1815–16)				
	Mai-ma-sa-yi-te	I (5): Junwang (1816–27)	Kashgar Beg (1809?); Kashgar Governor (1821?–27?)			
	A-ke-la-yi-du (original name:					
A-pu-li-dun)	I (6): First-grade Taiji (1825); Junwang (1827–64)	Yarkand Governor				
	Mai-ma-te Yi-bu-la-yi-mu	First-grade Taiji (1811–12)				
	Mai-ma-te Ma-ha-su-te	I (1): First-grade Taiji (1812–14); Third-grade Taiji (1826–? / awarded for his father's Yūnus's death in the battlefield)	Yangi Hissar 4R Beg (1827)			
	Ma-ha-su-te	Third-rank Taiji (1827–?)				

Political Unit	Name	Aristocratic Title	Beg Post/Qing Generalship	Imperial Bodyguardship*	Year They Were given the Privilege of Inheritance without Demotion+	Termination of Aristocrat Title
	E-luo-mu-za-bu	First-grade Taiji (1766–88), Gong pinji (1788–1805)	Governor of Ili Muslim community (1766–1805)		1788	
	Mi-li-ke-za-te	I (1): First-grade Taiji (1805–11)				
	He-shi-na-zha-te	I (2): First-grade Taiji (1811–32)				
	He-li-za-te	I (3?): First-grade Taiji (1832–40); Sanzhi dachen (1840–?)				
	Pi-er-dun	Second-grade Taiji (1771–1816)			1788	
	A-mi-te-ba-ha-yi	I (1): Second-grade Taiji (1816–25)				
	E-luo-mu-za-bu	I (2): Second-grade Taiji (1825–28)				
	Zuhūr al-Dīn	I (3): Second-grade Taiji (1828–38); Sanzhi Dachen (1838–?)				

Sources: MLZZ; HJTZ; WGBZ; WGBZXZ.

Note: I (Roman numeral number) = the inheritance (the number of inheritance): for instance, I (2) means the second time the inheritance of the aristocrat title was designated.

b. Muslim Aristocrats: Muslims Settled in Beijing—Emin Khwāja, Kashgar Khwāja Family, Descendants of Chaghatai Khans, Khush Kipak

Political Unit	Name	Aristocratic Title	Beg Post	Privilege of Inheritance without Demotion +	Termination of Aristocrat Title
Beijing Hui	Khwāja Si Beg	Gong pinji (1758); Beizi pinji (1758), Beizi (1758); Beile pinji (1758); Beile (1759); Junwang pinji (1759–81)			
	Ha-di-er	I (1): Junwang pinji (1781–1830)		1787	
	Ke-ke-se-bu-ku	I (2): Junwang pinji (1830–31)			
	A-bu-du-er-man	I (3): First-grade Shiwei (1826–27); Sanzhi dachen (1827–31); Junwang pinji (1831–33)	Acting Yarkand Governor (1827); Yarkand Governor (1828–33?)		
	Mai-ma-te Ai-zi-si	I (4): Second-grade Shiwei (1828–33); Junwang pinji (1833–41)	Khotan Governor (1834?–41?)		
	Mai-ma-di-min	I (5): Junwang pinji (1842–?)			
	A-bu-du-sa-ta-er	First-grade Taiji (1796–1809), Gong pinji (1809–23)			
	Kushi Kipak	Fuguo gong (1760–81)			
	Yi-ba-la-yi-mu	I (1): Fuguo gong (1781–1805)		1788	
	A-bu-du-mo-min	I (2): Fuguo gong (1805–28)	Khotan 6R Beg (1821?–28)		
	Mai-ma-te re-yi-mu-sha	I (3): Fuguo gong (1828–?)			
	Hussein	Fuguo gong (1759–84?)		1787	
	Ka-shen Khwāja	I (1): Fuguo gong (1784?); Zhengguo gong (?–1797)			
	Ba-ba-ke Khwāja*	I (2): Fuguo gong/ third-grade Taiji (Pa-er-sa's) (1797–1842)			1842
	Tu-yi-du	First-grade Taiji (1759–62), Fuguo gong (1762–79)			

Political Unit	Name	Aristocratic Title	Beg Post	Privilege of Inheritance without Demotion +	Termination of Aristocrat Title
	Tuo-ke-tuo	I (1): Fuguo gong (1779–?)		1787	At the death of Tuo-ke-tuo
	Ma-mu-te	First-grade Taiji (1759–79)			
	Ba-ba	I (1): Second-grade Taiji (1779–1801)		1788	
	Sha-yin Khwāja	I (2): Second-grade Taiji (1801–13)			
	A-mu-er Khwāja	I (3): Second-grade Taiji (1813–18)			
	Bu-za-lu Khwāja	I (4): Second-grade Taiji (1818–28)			1828
	Qāsim	First grade Taiji (1760–65)			
	A-bu-le	I (1): Second-grade Taiji (1765–1803)		1788	
	A-ke-ba-shi	I (2): Second-grade Taiji (1803–5)			1805
	A-bu-du-er-man	Second-grade Taiji (1760–72)			
	A-bu-du-ni-za-er	I (1): Third-grade Taiji (1772–96)		1788	
	Sulaiman	I (2): Third-grade Taiji (1796–1811)			1811
	Pa-er-sa	Third-grade Taiji (1760–97)			
	Bābak Khwāja				
Bābak Khwāja *	I (1): Third-grade Taiji/Fuguo gong Ka-shen Khwāja's title (1797–1842)			1788	1842

Sources: See Appendix C-1-a.
*Same person.

c. Muslim Aristocrats: Muslims Residing in Xinjiang

Political Unit	Name	Aristocratic Title	Beg Post	Imperial Bodyguardship	Privilege of Inheritance without Demotion	Termination of Aristocrat Title
Xinjiang Hui	Ūdui	Sanzhi Dachen (1758); Nei Dachen (1758); Gong pinji (1759); Beizi (1759); Beile pinji (1759–78)	Aksu Governor (1759–60); Yarkand Governor (1760–78)			
	Osman	I (1): Third-rank (1759–69) Second-grade Taiji (1769–78); Beile pinji (1778); Sanzhi dachen (1778–84); Beizi (1784–88)	Khotan Beg (1760–70) Kucha Governor (1770–76); Aksu Governor (1776); Kashgar Governor (1778–88)		1783	
	Mai-ha-mo-te E-san	I (2): Sanzhi dachen/ Beizi (1788–1824)	Kucha Ishikagha (1788); Kashgar Governor (1788–1811) Yarkand Governor (1811–24)			
	Mai-ha-mo-te E-dui	I (3): Second-grade Taiji (1821); Sanzhi dachen/ beizi (1824–26)	Yarkand Shang Beg (1816–?); Yarkand Beg (?–1824); Yarkand Ishikagha (1824–25); Acting Yarkand Governor (1824); Aksu Governor (1825–26)			
	Ishāq	I (4): Sanzhi dachen/ beizi (1826–28); Junwang (1828–42)	Ili Governor (1812); Aksu Governor (1814); Kashgar Governor (1815–?); Aksu Governor (?–1826); Kashgar Governor (1828–31)	1827		
	Ahmad	I (5): Second-grade Taiji (1827); Third-rank Shiwei (1827); First-grade Shiwei (1827); Junwang (1842–64)	[Aksu] 6R beg; (1827); Acting Aksu Beg (1827); Shayar Governor (1837); Aksu Governor (1844); Yarkand Governor (1845–52); Aksu Governor (1852–56); Kashgar Governor (1856–58)	1829		

213

Political Unit	Name	Aristocratic Title	Beg Post	Imperial Bodyguardship	Privilege of Inheritance without Demotion	Termination of Aristocrat Title
	Setib Aldi	Fourth rank (1757); Third-rank Zongguan (1758–60); Sanzhi dachen (1760–63); Gong pinji (1763); Fuguo gong (1764–78); Beizi pinji (1778–88)	Aksu Governor (1760–78); Yarkand Governor (1778–88)			
	Mai-mo-te					
A-bu-du-la	I (1): Beizi pinji (1788–1805)	Kashgar Governor (?–1788); Aksu Governor (1789–?) Yarkand Governor (?–1805)			1788	
	Mai-ma-te A-san	I (2): Beizi pinji (1805–20)	Yarkand 6R Beg (1805–?)			
	Mai-ma-te Ai-ma-te	I (3): Beizi pinji (1820–43)	Yarkand 5R Beg (1825)			
	Mai-ma-te Ai-san	I (4): Beizi pinji (1843–?)				
	Gadaimet	Third rank (1758); Gong pinji (1759–75)	Kashgar Governor (1760–75)			
	A-bu-du-la-man	I (1): Second-grade Taiji (1769–75); Gong pinji (1775–76)	Bai Governor (1760–76)			
	Mai-ma-di-min	I (2): Second-grade Taiji (1776); Gong pinji (1776–96)	Bai Ishikagha (1780–?); Khotan Governor (?–1788); Kucha Governor (1789–96)		1783	
	Mai-mo-te					
Yi-ba-la-yi-mu	I (3): Taiji (1780) Gong pinji (1797–1828)	Yarkand 5R Beg (?–1828)				
	Musa	I (4): Fuguo gong (1828–37)	Ush Governor (1823)			
	Mai-ma-ta-li-pu	I (5): Third-rank Shiwei (1828); Fuguo gong (1837–?)				
	Sali	Fifth rank (1759–62); Third-rank Qingju duwei (1762–75)				
	Hai-se-mu	I (1): Third-rank Qingju duwei (1775–1815)			1783	

Political Unit	Name	Aristocratic Title	Beg Post	Imperial Bodyguardship	Privilege of Inheritance without Demotion	Termination of Aristocrat Title
	Ai-li-mu	I (2): Third-rank Qingju duwei (1815 –40)				
	A-bu-du-wa-yi-te	I (3): Third-rank Qingju duwei (1840–?)				

Sources: See Sources, Appendix C-1-b.

*"Qianqing men xingzhou" Imperial Bodyguard is a privileged position, given to the Qing imperial aristocrats and their family members to serve the emperor as the latter's bodyguard in close vicinity for a period of time.

+ Qing imperial aristocrat positions were not permanent. Once the person who received the original position died, the inheritor would receive a position that had been demoted from the original rank. The aristocrat positions would be demoted repeatedly. The Qianlong emperor, however, granted the "Privilege of Inheritance without Demotion (Shixi wangti)" to imperial aristocrats beginning in the 1780s. Some of the pro-Qing begs also received the privilege.

D-1. Private Land Transactions in the Oasis, 1750–1911

Case No.	Year	Seller	Buyer	Size of Land Transaction	Properties Attached to the Land	Location of the Land	Price	Origin of the Land
1	1771	Mīr A-di-li Sufi	ʿYakūb Bay	50 m	1 house (10 *jian*)		100	
2	1807	Na-si-er Khwāja's inheritors	Yūnus Wang	8 b	1 house (28 jian); tree; 1 garden		16	
3	1813	Ai-er-ken Beg	Mullā Tursun	Size unknown	None	Village	20	
4	1823	Tursun Khwāja	A-bu-du-re-yi-mu Akhūnd	2 c	Fruit tree		12	
5	1832	Du-lai-ti-jiang Bay (Khoqandian); Kurban Bay	Mullā Mu-ba-re-ke Khalīfa; Mullā Xi-ya-er Khalīfa	2 b (dry land)	House, tree; garden	Village*	450	
6	1833	Samsak Sufi	Mullā A-bu-la Khalīfa	12 c (dry land)	None	Village*	10	Inheritance
7	1833	Niyas Khwāja	Tuo-hu-ti Khwāja		1 house (5 *jian*); tree; garden; 1 big door	City (roadside)	45	Reselling
8	1834	Qiao-er-pang pi-pi	Tu-er-di Khwāja	20 c (dry land)		Village*	12	
9	1834	Mullā Nuruz	Ha-ji-er Khwāja			Village	4	Inheritance
10	1835	Kan-lan-mu Bay	Mullā Hai-da-er	3 c	Tree	Village*	200	Inheritance
11	1837	Lady Hai-mi-tan; her inheritors	Mullā Kan-ji	3 y			23	
12	1839	Mullā Nuruz		200 *jin*		Village*	10	Inheritance
13	1839	Mullā Nuruz	Ha-fa-er-a Bay	10 c			10	
14	1840	Tu-er-di ni-ya-zi's son	Re-he-mai-ti Akhūnd	1 1/2 m	Tree		3,500 qian	Inheritance
15	1841	Ai-ni-fa-a-yi-la; Huo-ti-ke Khwāja	Ai-he-lai-ti Sufi	2 c (irrigated)	1 house (4 *jian*); garden; furniture in the house/ building		72	
16	1843	Mullā Ta-li; representing the inheritor of Mai-si-tuo-re Khwāja and As-la Khwāja's inheritors	Islam Khwāja	1 b		Village*	20	
17	1843	Mai-si-tuo-re Khwāja's and Jia-huo-sa-la Khwāja's inheritor	Islam Khwāja	1 b		Village*	20	Inheritance

Case No.	Year	Seller	Buyer	Size of Land Transaction	Properties Attached to the Land	Location of the Land	Price	Origin of the Land
18	1843	Mai-si-tu-le Khwā-ja's children; Sa-la Khwāja's daughter; A-yi-xia Khwāja's relatives	Islam Khwāja	½ b		Village*	20	
19	1850	Na-xi-fa-ti Khwāja	Ke-zi-mu-la-ti-pai (order)		2/3 of 1 house building; furniture	City (cross-road)	48	
20	1850	Yūsuf Khwāja	Mullā xia Khwāja	1 c (irrigated)			30	
21	1856	Na-xi-fa-ti Khwāja	Wu-su-er Khwāja et al.	2 c	Tree		32	Inheritance
22	1856	Mullā Mi-xi-ken and Mullā A-bu-du-ha-mi-di	Ta-yi-Bay, Wu-su-er Khwāja, and Tu-he-ti Sufi	3 c	Tree	Village	44	
23	1858	Rustam Khwāja; A-ke Beg (Osman Mīrāb's inheritor)	Mullā Yūsuf		Watermill		325	Inheritance
24	1867	Mullā Si-ma-yi	A-bu-du Su-bu-er	3 c (irrigated land)	Unspecified "property"	Village	33	
25	1868	Ai-sha-mu Khwāja	Mu-han-mo-te-ya-er Khwāja	2 hu-la-qi			62	Reselling
26	1871	Tursun Khwāja (Mullā Yi-ke-mu's son)	Zi-bi-tan Mullā (Re-ha-mai-ti's daughter)	3 1/2 c	Tree	Village	70	
27	1872	A-bu-du-la Khwāja (Bay Khwāja's child)	A-bu-du-re-yi-mu Akhūnd (Ai-li khwāja's son)		House; 4 trees; furniture	Outside of a city gate	3,500	
28	1873	Tursun (Mullā Mu-ha-mai-ti's son)	Tursun (Ai-sa Mullā's son)	3 1/2 c	1 house; tree; furniture		17	
29	1874	Re-yi-tan pi-pi (Mullā Si-ma-yi's daughter)	Ha-li-ma pi-pi (Re-yi-tan pi-pi's mother)	1 1/2 c	Tree		40	
30	1876	Siddīq Khwāja (A-bu-du-la-li-ni-bu Khwāja's child)	Mullā Ai-he-mai-ti (Siddīq Khwāja's child)	2 hu-la-qi		Village	140	
31	1877	Mu-ba-la-ke Akhūnd (Mullā Yi-bu-la-yin Akhūnd's son)	Yi-bu-la-yin Akhūnd (Mu-ba-la-ke Akhūnd's brother)	2 1/2 c (irri-gated land)			18	

Case No.	Year	Seller	Buyer	Size of Land Transaction	Properties Attached to the Land	Location of the Land	Price	Origin of the Land
32	1883	Ka-zi-a-bu-du-sai-mai-ti	'Yakūb khwāja	3 m (the village's desolate land)		Village	Maize (50 c)	
33	1885	Tu-er-di-han's (Sa-li-he-ka-re's child) representative; Zuhūr al-Dīn Akhūnd (Zunun Akhūnd's son)	Ai-min Akhūnd (Mullā He-ya-si-ding's child)	10 c	Certificate (of the land)	Village	100	
34	1889	Mullā Yi-si-ma-yi-le-zong-hu-zi (Mullā A-la-yi-ding's child) et al.	Tuo-hu-ti Akhūnd (Qia-lu-ke Bay's son)	7 c		Village	100 copper coins	Inheritance
35	1889	Yi-bu-la-yin Akhūnd (Zunun Akhūnd's son)	Qia-lu-ke Bay (Mullā Ge-ya-si's son)	6 c		Village	85	
36	1896	Ismail Akhūnd (Ai-shan Khwāja's son)	Bahā' al-Dīn Akhūnd (Mullā Islam's son)	Empty land	1 house (2 jian); furniture; small alley	Outside of a city gate	1,100 copper coins	Inheritance
37	1898	Yūsuf Akhūnd's inheritors et. al	Bay	3 m (irrigated)	Tree		15 liang	
38	1899	Yi-ming Akhūnd (Yi-bu-la-yin Akhūnd's child) (an artisan making silver ornament)	Mīrzā Khān (Mu-han-mo-de Yi-ming Bay's child)		1 house (2 jian); furniture	City (road)	110 copper coins	
39	1899	Mullā Hu-da-bai-er-di (Mullā Khwāja Niyas Bay's son)	Bahā' al-Dīn Akhūnd (Mullā Islam's son)		Tree;1 yi-xie-ke of garden; small road; water ditch	City (road district)	90	
40	1900	Hu-sai-yi-ding Akhūnd (Samsak Bay's child)	Mīrzā Khān (Mu-han-mo-de Yi-ming bay's son)	2 c	Tree; furniture; small road	City (road side)?	615	
41	1900	A-yi pi-pi (Yi-da-bai-er-di Bay's daughter); Ai-san Akhūnd (Se-di-ke ba-yi's son) representing his wife et al.	Bahā' al-Dīn Akhūnd (Islam Khwāja's son)		Garden; furniture; small road	City (road-side)	90	

Case No.	Year	Seller	Buyer	Size of Land Transaction	Properties Attached to the Land	Location of the Land	Price	Origin of the Land
42	1908	Mai-mai-ti-ya-zi Akhūnd (La-zi-a-ji's son)	Yahyā Khwāja (Mai-mai-ti-ya-zi Akhūnd's brother)	3 1/2 m (irrigated by a-la-er's ao-ke-a-la-er-ju [ditch]'s water)	Tree		50 *liang* "white silver"	
43	1908	A-xi-mu Akhūnd (Ai-min Akhūnd's son)	Ai-min Akhūnd (Musa Bay's son)		1 house (6 *jian*); tree; furniture; small road	City (road-side)?	2,500	

Sources: Wang and Li, *Xinjiang Weiwu'er zu qiyue wenshu ziliao xuanbian,* pp. 1–45; Luo Xiaorui, "Qingdai Nanjiang Cha-he-tai wen qiyue wenshu yanjiu," p. 19.
Note: (1) b = *batman;* c = *charak;* m = *mu;* y = *yi-xie-ke;* t = *tangga;* (2) 1 *charak* = roughly 1 *mu;* 1 *batman* = 64 *mu;* 1 *yi-xie-ke* = 1/4 *charak* (Wang and Li, *Xinjiang Weiwu'er Zu Qiyue Wenshu Ziliao Xuanbian.,* pp. 11, 20); (3) land sales of property were conducted mostly in silver bullion (*yambu*). The unit of silver currency is the *tangga* (t); any units of measurement not listed here are as indicated in the table above; (4) village* indicates Khwāja Ariq (Huo-jia-ai-li-ke) village, which belonged to Re-wa-qi subdistrict, Yarkand District.

D-2. Waqf Donations in the Oasis, 1750–1911

Case No.	Year	Donor	Donation Recipient	Donation (Land)	Property Attached to the Donated Land	Origin of the Donated Land	Location
1	1773	A-li-hu-zi Beg	Local mosque	15 b	House; watermill; furniture in the house		Bai-shi settlement
2	1800	Si-la-mu Bay	Local mosque	20 c		Originally dry land; developed by Si-la-mu Bay	
3	1815	Mullā Niyaz Huo-tu-he-ti Sufi	Khanqa mosque	1 b		Inheritance from his father	Re-wa-qi settlement, Yarkand
4	1817	Shaykh Ai-fu-li	Local *mazār* (where he became *shaykh*)	Size unknown		Land he reclaimed	Fifth ditch, Yarkand
5	1820	Yi-si-feng-de-ya-er Bay	Khanqa *madrasa* established by *Yunus* Wang Beg	1/2 b			A-la-xia-er settlement
6	1828	Teacher tu-er-di	The place's main mosque	100 *jin*	House; tree		Rural settlement*
7	1837	Lai-li pi-pi	Local *madrasa*	10 c			"Five villages"
8	1837	Mullā Kan-ji ai-wu-xi-mu	Mosque established by Mu-er-ai-lai-mu Beg	3 y	House; garden; lumber; roof tile stones		
9	1838	A-bu-du Sufi (Ta-li pi-pi's son) et al.	Local mosque	1 and 1/2 m		Inheritance from their mother	
10	1844	Ku-er-ban Mai-mai-ti	Mosque (within the city?)		2 houses (located within the city)		
11	1850	Mullā A-bu-du-la Khalifa; his inheritors	Local mosque	9 c			Re-wa-qi settlement, Yarkand
12	1851	Bu-wei Xi-ke	*Madrasa* located in Ku-er-ma village	2 c (reconfirming the donation made 30 years earlier)			
13	1858	Hei-yi-ti Khwāja	*Madrasa* established by Ta-le-ke Khwāja Beg	19 c(reconfirming the *waqf* donation (made 22 years earlier)		Land he purchased with gold	
14	1885	Cha-pai-er Bay		2 Ai-er-ya-er* (reconfirming *waqf* donation)			settlement

Sources: See Sources, Appendix D-1.
Note: Ibid.; *ai-er-ya-er* = one-third of 1 *batman* (Wang and Li, *Xinjiang Weiwu'er Zu Qiyue Wenshu Ziliao Xuanbian*, p. 11).

E-1. Oasis Rural Settlements in Yarkand, 1770s–1870s

Subdistrict	1776[Location (Population)]	1821	1850s
Ya-ba-ke		E 25 (N/A)	
Pa-si-qian		E 30 (N/A)	E 30 (4,038)
Ta-ta-li		E 50 (N/A)	E 40 (595)
Bo-shi-qi-te	E 50 (N/A)		
Ai-ji-te-hu		E 70 (N/A)	E 80 (2,220)
Teräk Länggar			E 90 (76)
Yi-qi-su-ning-a-la-si	E 100 (N/A)		
Mo-ke-te-li		E 200 (N/A)	E 60 (753)
Ha-la-gu-zhe-shi		E 200 (N/A)	
Kosharab	E 200 (1,106)	W 200 (N/A)	W 180 (1,709)
Maralbash		E 600 (N/A)	
Barchuk	Location unknown (127)	E 740 (N/A)	E 7 stations (1,572)
Se-le-ke-guo-le	E 700 (N/A)		
Cha-te-xi-lin		E 935 (N/A)	
Kokyar	NE 300 (103)	S 300 (N/A)	S 380 (2,401)
Yu-la-li-ke	Yu-le-a-li-ke: NE 300 (311)	S 270 (N/A)	
Ta-ke-bu-yi	NE 300 (1,301)		
Ying-ge-qi-pan	NE 400 (298)		
Sai-er-le-ke	E (N/A)		
Ka-er-chong	E 500 (605)		
Orda Ustäng	W 20 (2,652)	W 5 (N/A)	
Khan Ariq	S 40 (N/A)	W 10 (N/A)	W 4 (283)
Kamra	E 20 (731)	W 20 (N/A)	W 15 (648)
Rawatchi	E 70 (1,124)	W 50 (N/A)	W 40 (1,101)
Sariqol		W 80 *li* (N/A)	Outside of *karun* (472 households)
Shu-ke-shu			W 300 (2,060)
Bai-lin	W 100 (N/A)		
Sha-tu	W 220 (N/A)		
Chu-lu-ke	NW 290 (N/A)		
Pi-shi-nan	NW 310 (N/A)		
Guma	W 380 (N/A)		
Zhang-gu-ya	W 390 (N/A)		
Sanju	W 400 (N/A)	S 400 (N/A)	S 400 (1,298)
Mu-ji	W 460 (N/A)		
Gun-de-li-ke	W 480 (N/A)		
Du-wa	W 500 (N/A)		
Pi-ya-le-a-la-ma	W 660 (N/A)		
A-ke-a-li-ke	SW 600 (N/A)		
Wo-du-si-tang			S 2 (413)
Aral	E 20 (1,421)	S 20 (N/A)	S 5 (930)

Subdistrict	1776[Location (Population)]	1821	1850s
Tagarchi*	S 20		
Otunchilik	S 40 (2,341)	S 30 (N/A)	SE 20 (1,627)
A-bu-pu-er		SW 30 (N/A)	
Posgam	N 70 (1,626)	S 60 (N/A)	S 60 (4,873)
Hei-se-er-mi-qi-te		S 60 (N/A)	S 40 (1,769)
Yi-qi-su-a-la-le		S 80 (N/A)	S 70 (2,291)
Köna Tatar			S 80 (0)
Zong-long			S 250 (209)
Qi-pan		S 280 (N/A)	W 250 *li* from Chinese city (600)
Tuo-gu-si-gan	Location unknown (2,812)	S 500 (N/A)	S 400 (7,049)
Ta-er-ta-ke		S 700 (N/A)	
Mishar	N 15 (2,831)	N 10 (N/A)	N 1 (1,612)
Yarbagh			N 20 (1,650)
Tagarchi*	Location unknown (2,813)	N 30 (N/A)	N 40 (1,621)
Opur	Location unknown (7,714)	N 40 (N/A)	N 30 (3,668)
Yakka Ariq	N 40 (N/A)		
Qurghan			N 50 (1,900)
Khoshabād			N 70 (317)
Kökrawat Länggar		N 100 (N/A)	W 90 (113)
Shu-tie	N 200 (2,128)		
Hu-mu-shi-qia-te	N 200		
Bei-la	N 220		
Kargalyk	N 220 (2,511)	S 200	S 150 (6,122)
Ku-er-ta-li-mu	S 300 (2,712)	N 230	N 250 (1,075)
Besh Ariq	N 300 (1,074)		
Tuo-gu-si-qia-te	N 350 (N/A)		
Cha-te-ji-lin	Location unknown (75)		
Bo-shi-gan	Location unknown (1,658)		
Da-ha-sha	Location unknown (390)		
Wo-tun-su	Location unknown (505)		
Huo-mu-shi-gan	Location unknown (2,513)		
Ba-ha-qi		Location unknown (N/A)	
A-ya-ke-qi		Location unknown (N/A)	
Shao-da-ga-er		Location unknown (N/A)	

Sources: HJZ; XYTZ, vol. 18; XJShL, vol. 3; Forsyth, *Report of a Mission to Yarkund in 1873*, p. 62.

Note: (1) the convention for identifying location is by direction from the main city (N = north, S = south, E = east, W = west), followed by the distance from the main city (as a number). For example, in the first entry in the 1821 column of Ya-ba-ke rural settlement, E 25 means that it was located 25 *li* east of the main city of Yarkand at the time. The unit of the measurement of distance is *li*. (2) the population number = the number of regular tax-paying households (*zhenghu*) belonging to each rural settlement.

* These two settlements could be the same rural settlement.

F-1. Yarkand Tax Register: Population and Land

Unit	Location	No. of Subunits	Total Popu- lation (people)	Regular House- hold (people)	Regular House- hold (%)	Culti vated Land	Average Harvest	Grain Tax	Average Grain Tax Rate (%)
City district 1	Within city	11	951	354	37	N/A	N/A	N/A	0
City district 2	Within city	8	679	250	37	N/A	N/A	N/A	0
City district 3	Within city	11	609	295	48	N/A	N/A	N/A	0
City district 4	Within city	11	832	272	33	N/A	N/A	N/A	0
City district 5	Within city	2	517	137	26	N/A	N/A	N/A	0
City Subtotal	N/A	43	3,588	1,308	36	N/A	N/A	N/A	0
Opur	N 30	64	3,668	960	26	1,498	7,490	685	9
Rawatchi	W 40	16	1,101	341	31	806	40,30	137	3
Mishar	N 1	21	1,612	476	30	216	1,080	104	10
Kamra	W 15	9	648	68	10	248	1,240	62	5
Pai-si-qian	E 30	7	4,038	501	12	592	2,960	278	9
Otunchilik	SE 20	12	1,627	262	16	538	2,690	112	4
Wo-du-si-tang	S 2	5	413	58	14	124	620	51	8
Aral	S 5	11	930	154	17	369	1,845	104	6
Mo-ke-te-li	E 160	3	752	144	19	84	420	62	15
Khan Ariq	W 4	2	283	73	26	92	460	24	5
Tatar	E 40	2	595	110	18	55	275	52	19
Yi-ken-su-a-la-si	S 70	19	2,291	718	31	11,77	5,885	300	5
Tagarchi	N 40	10	1,621	373	23	207	1,035	102	10
Ai-ji-te-hu	E 80	8	2,220	545	25	537	2,685	138	5
Yarbagh	N 20	12	1,650	234	14	567	2,835	144	5
Hei-zi-er-mi-qi-te	S 40	12	1,769	530	30	583	2,915	179	6
Gui-li-tie-li-mu	N 250	2	1,075	267	25	350	1,750	68	4
Tuo-guo-si-qian	S 400	30	7,049	1,606	23	1,767	8,835	451	5
Posgam	S 60	46	4,873	1,596	33	1,734	8,670	502	6
Kargalyk	S 150	60	6,122	1,343	22	2,415	12,075	768	6
Zong-long	S 250	N/A	290	93	32	N/A	0	17	N/A
Sanju	S 400	5	1,298	426	33	121	605	89	15
Kokyar; Yu-la-li-ke	S 380	9	2,401	442	18	542	2,710	239	9
Qi-pan	W 250	5	600	253	42	198	990	72	7
Kosharab	W 180	8	1,709	773	45	413	2,065	150	7

Appendix F

Unit	Location	No. of Subunits	Total Population (people)	Regular Household (people)	Regular Household (%)	Cultivated Land	Average Harvest	Grain Tax	Average Grain Tax Rate (%)
Shu-ke-shu	W 300	13	2,060	984	48	38	190		0
Qurghan	N 50	8 @	1,900 ^	0	0	800	N/A	4,900 shi	N/A
Khoshabād	N 70	1	317	114	18	120	600	27.7.4	N/A
Köna Tatar	S 80	1		0	0		0	25.7*	N/A
Sariqol	W	15	432	N/A	0	N/A	0	N/A	N/A
Barchuk	E	1 &	1,572	722+	0	53	265	0	0
Teräk Länggar	E 90	1	76	21	18	N/A	0	N/A	N/A
Kökrawat Länggar	W 90	1	113	42	18	14	70	7	10
Rural area subtotal	N/A	407	61,444	15,537	25	2,1820	109,100	5,170	4

Source: Ye-er-qiang chengzhuang lishu huihu zhengfu gexiang ce [Register of city, villages, distances, Muslim households, regular tax of Yarkand District], c. 1850s.

Note: (1) Location of the unit was calculated as the distance from the city of Yarkand. Unit of distance in the "location" section is li. (2) unit of measurement for land and grain is batman, unless otherwise as noted in the table.

*This amount was paid by the "Muslims without property," who came to the village and temporarily cultivated the land; each of them paid according to the amount of the land cultivated.

+These Muslims were stationed on duty in the eleven military stations, on rotation.

This place had ten government-owned watermills.

@ The eight settlements were all agrarian colonies (tuntian).

& The place also had eleven military stations.

^ The population of the 800 households was 1,900 people.

Notes

Introduction

1. Laura Newby, "The Begs of Xinjiang: Between Two Worlds," *Bulletin of the School of Oriental and African Studies* 61:1 (1998), p. 284. For a detailed examination of the Qing conquest of Xinjiang, see Jifa Zhuang, *Qing Gaozong shiquan wugong yanjiu* [Study on the Ten Military Accomplishments of the Qing Gaozong, Qianlong Emperor] (Taipei: Guoli gugong bowuyuan, 1982); Peter C. Perdue, *China Marches West: The Qing Conquest of Central Eurasia* (Cambridge, MA: Belknap Press of Harvard University Press, 2005). For the Seven Years' War, see Fred Anderson, *Crucible of War: The Seven Years' War and the Fate of Empire in British North America, 1754-1766* (New York: Alfred A. Knopf, 2000); P. J. Marshall, *The Making and Unmaking of Empires: Britain, India, and America, c. 1750-1783* (New York: Oxford University Press, 2005).

2. Sanada Yasushi, "Toshi, noson yuboku [City, Rural Villages, and Pastoral Nomadism]," in *Kōza Isuramu* [Lectures on Islam], vol. 3 (Tokyo: Chikuma Shobō, 1986), pp. 108-48; idem, "Oashisu ba-za-ru no seitaienkyū—jūkyū seiki gohan Kashugariano ba'ai [Static Study of the Oasis Bazaar: The Case of Kashgaria in the Late Nineteenth Century]," *Chūō daigaku daigakuin kenkyū nenpō* 6 (1977), pp. 207-20; Owen Lattimore, *Pivot of Asia: Sinkiang and the Inner Asian Frontiers of China and Russia* (Boston: Little, Brown, 1950), pp. 152; 165-70.

3. Hori Sunao, "Shindai Kaikyō no suiri kangai: 19-20 seiki no Yaarukanto wo chūshin to shite [Irrigation in the Muslim Domain during the Qing Period: Case of Yarkand in the Nineteenth and the Twentieth Centuries]," *Journal of Otemae College* 14 (1980), p. 73; Lattimore, *Pivot of Asia*, p. 152.

4. Sanada Yasushi, "Oashisu ba-za-ru no seitaienkyū," pp. 208-9; idem, "Toshi, noson yuboku," 3:116-17, 120-21. See also Hori Sunao, "Shindai Yarukando no noson to suiro [Rural Villages and Waterways in Yarkand during the Qing Rule]," *Kōnan daigaku kiyō: bungakuhen* 139 (2004): 153-91; idem, "Shindai Kaikyō no suiri kangai: 19-20 seiki no Yaarukanto wo chūshin to shite," pp. 72-99. The Qing Empire also built their local administration around this hierarchy of oasis settlements. The Qing used the *känt* as the basic unit of rural administrative unit, naming it rural subdistrict (*zongzhuang* ["con-

trolling village"]) and appointing the native officials (*hākim beg* or *ming beg*) there. The native officials were required to collect taxes from the headmen of the *mahalla* (*ming bash; yuz bash*) and transmit them to the Qing administration located in the central city. In the meantime, city districts (called *halla* or *mahalla*) formed the basic unit of the political, spiritual, and social life in the main city. These were formed around guild organizations. They were the basic unit of the Qing administration in the city. See Sanada, "Toshi, noson yuboku" p. 119.

5. This book's examination challenges the previous scholarship's understanding of the social and economic development of Eastern Turkestan under Qing rule. Dominated by the Marxist historians of Russia and Japan, previous scholars have generally agreed that the political economy in Eastern Turkestan under the Qing was stagnant and feudal. Those scholars understood the begs to be nomadic "feudal lords," who drew revenue from the land, while not being involved in the agrarian process at all. The begs received from the Qing emperor land grants as well as the *yanqi* (conceptualized by these historians as "serfs"), who tilled the land; the begs collected dues from the *yanqi,* as previous generations of nomadic nobles in the region had done. Therefore, the basic farming unit remained small scale, conducted by the yanqi households, also as it had been under the previous nomadic regime in the area. In so doing, the Qing sustained and even expanded the oppressively "backward" agrarian system and production relations that had existed for so long in the Muslim society of Xinjiang. For a thesis of feudal society, see L. I. Duman, *Agrarnaia Politika Tsinskogo (Manchzhurskogo) Pravitel'stva v Sin'tsziane v Kontse XVIII Veka* [Qing Government's Agrarian Policy in Xinjiang in the Early Eighteenth Century] (Moskva: Izd-vo Akademii nauk SSSR, 1936); idem, "Feodal'nyj Institut Jan'ci v Vostočnom Turkestane v XVIII Veke [Feudal Institution of Yanci, in Eastern Turkestan in the Eighteenth Century]," *Zapiski Instituta Institut vostokovedeniia Akademii nauk SSSR* 3, pp. 87–100; idem, "The Qing Conquest of Junggariye and Eastern Turkestan," in *Manzhou Rule in China* (Moscow: Progress Publishers, 1983), pp. 235–56; Saguchi Tōru, "Higashi Torukisutan hōken shakai josetsu: Hoja jidai no ichi kōsatsu [Introduction to the History of the Feudal Society in Eastern Turkestan: An Examination of the Khoja Period]," *Rekishigaku kenkyū* [Research on History] 134 (1948); Kubota Bunji, "Shindai Higashi Torukisutan nogyo mondai ni kansuru ichi kokoromi [Agriculture in Eastern Turkestan during the Qing Period]," *Shichō* 71 (1960), pp. 36–48. For a most recent articulation of this thesis of "feudal society," see Zhang Shicai, "Qingdai Tianshan nanbu weiwuer shehui de 'yanqi dimu' [The "Yanqi Land" of the Uyghur Society in the Southern Xinjiang during the Qing Period]," *Xinjiang daxue xuebao* (Zhexue shehui kexue ban) 4 (2006); idem, "Qingdai Xinjiang Tianshan nanlu Wei-wu-er shehui jiegou yu bianqian [The Social Structure of Uyghurs in Tianshan Nanlu in Xinjiang (Eastern Turkestan) and Its Transformation during the Qing Period]," *Xiyu yanjiu* [Research on Western Regions] 3 (2012).

6. This acreage is calculated by the conversion rate of 1 *mu* = 0.6609 acre; 1 *batman* = 64 *mu* = 42.2936 acres.

7. Zhongguo di 1 lishi dang'an guan (hereafter GPYSA), *Ye-er-qiang banshi dachen Gao Pu simai yushi an* [(Corruption) Case of the Grand Minister Superintendent Gao Pu], in *Qianlong chao chengban tanwu dang'an xuanbian* (Beijing Shi: Zhonghua shuju, 1994), doc. 301, QL43/11/21, Edict.

8. Su Beihai and Jianhua Huang, *Hami Tulufan Weiwu'er wang lishi: Qingchao zhi Minguo* [History of Uyghur Kings of Hami and Turfan: From the Qing Period to the Republican Period] (Wulumuqi: Xinjiang daxue chubanshe, 1993), pp. 57–59. It is difficult to compare the size of the pro-Qing begs' landholdings and those of prominent Sufis of the pre-Qing Period, because data for the latter are largely unavailable. To give some sense of the scale, the land confiscated by the Qing from Khwaja Jahan (youngest of the Kashgar *khwaja* brothers who offered a stiff resistance against the Qing conquest in 1759) was 900 to 1,000 *batman* (38,000 to 43,000 acres), depending on the records—a level that probably was not replicated by any beg official or Sufi leader during the Qing rule (HJZ) [8 vol. version], vol. 4; Kun'gang, ed., *Qinding Da Qing huidian shili (Guangxu chao)* (Shanghai: Shangwu yinshu guan, 1908), vol. 163. A one-time *waqf* land donation by a nomadic khan to a prominent Sufi's *khanqa* was 60 *batman*, approximately 2,538 acres. See Zhongguo Xinjiang diqu Yisilanjiao shi bianxiezu, ed., *Zhongguo Xinjiang diqu Yisilan jiao shi* [History of Islam in Xinjiang, China] (Wulumuqi Shi: Xinjiang renmin chubanshe, 2000), p. 274.

9. In terms of original definition, *khwaja* refers to Sufi holy men, the descendants of Ali through his wives other than Prophet Muhammad's daughter, Fatima, whose descendants were referred to as *sayyid*. However, in a Central Asian context, this distinction between *khwaja* and *sayyid* was not rigid, and the word *khwaja* refers to anyone who claimed descent from the Prophet Muhammad. Various prominent Sufi leaders claimed this title.

10. For examples of the studies of capitalistic developments in Asia, see Anthony Reid, *Southeast Asia in the Age of Commerce, 1450–1680* (New Haven: Yale University Press, 1988), pp. 267–68; Kenneth Pomeranz, *The Great Divergence: Europe, China, and the Making of the Modern World Economy.* Princeton: Princeton University Press, 2000; Rosenthal, Jean-Laurent, and Roy Bin Wong. *Before and beyond Divergence: The Politics of Economic Change in China and Europe.* (Cambridge, MA: Harvard University Press, 2011).

11. Fernand Braudel, *The Wheels of Commerce*, trans. Siân Reynold (Berkeley: University of California Press, 1992); idem, *The Perspective of the World: Civilization and Capitalism, 15th–18th Century*, vol. 3, trans. Siân Reynold (Berkeley: University of California Press, 1992), p. 65.

12. For a foundational study of the tribute system that emphasizes the system's focus on the security function, see John King Fairbank, *Trade and Diplomacy on the China*

Coast: The Opening of the Treaty Ports, 1842–1854 (Stanford: Stanford University Press, 1969). For an excellent recent rearticulation on Fairbank's view on the security-driven nature of the tribute system, see Peter C. Perdue, "A Frontier View of Chineseness," in *The Resurgence of East Asia: 500, 150, and 50 Year Perspectives,* ed. by Giovanni Arrighi, Hamashita Takeshi, and Mark Selden (New York: Routledge, 2003). For an excellent study on the reality of the working of the tribute system in an East Asian context, see John King Fairbank and Ta-tuan Chen, *The Chinese World Order: Traditional China's Foreign Relations* (Cambridge, MA: Harvard University Press, 1968). For classic studies highlighting the economic function of the tribute system, see Frederic Wakeman, Jr., "The Canton Trade and the Opium War," in *The Cambridge History of China,* vol. 10, pt. 1, ed. by Denis Twitchett and John K. Fairbank (Cambridge, MA: Cambridge University Press, 1978), pp. 163–212; Morris Rossabi, "Ming China's Relations with Hami and Central Asia, 1404–1513: A Reexamination of Traditional Chinese Foreign Policy" (diss., Columbia University, 1970). For recent studies highlighting the economic function of the tribute system, see Hamashita Takeshi, *Kindai Chūgoku no kokusaiteki keiki: Chōkō bōeki shisutemu to kindai Ajia* [Transnational Moments of the Modern China: Tribute Trade System and the Modern Asia] (Tokyo: Tokyo daigaku shuppankai, 1990); idem, *Chōkō shisutemu to kindai Ajia* [Tribute Trade System and the Modern Asia] (Tokyo: Iwanami shoten, 1997); Kishimoto Mio, "Higashi Ajia Tōnan Ajia dentō shakai no keisei [Formation of the Traditional Societies of East Asia and Southeast Asia]," in *Iwanami kōza sekai rekishi* [Iwanami Lecture Series on World History], rev. ed., vol. 13 (Tokyo: Iwanami shoten, 1998), pp. 3–73; idem, "Shinchō to Yūrashia [Qing Dynasty and Eurasia]," in *Koza sekaishi* [Lectures on World History], vol. 2, ed. by Rekishigaku kenkyuōkai (Japan) (Tokyo: Tokyo daigaku shuppankai, 1995); idem, *Higashi Ajia no "kinsei"* [Early Modernity of East Asia] (Tokyo: Yamakawa shuppansha, 1998). For Central Asian merchants' obsession with silver payment in the tribute trade with the Qing, see Perdue, *China Marches West,* pp. 263, 265. For a recent Chinese study on the tribute system, see Li Yunquan, *Chaogong zhidu shilun* [History of Tribute System] (Beijing: Xinhua chubanshe, 2004).

13. Isenbike Togan, "Inner Asian Muslim Merchants at the Closure of the Silk Routes in the Seventeenth Century," In *The Silk Roads: Highways of Culture and Commerce* (New York: Berghahn Books, 2000), p. 248.

14. The numbers regarding the Qing Period should not be considered as precise. In addition to the fact that they are compiled by the Qing administration for tax collection purposes, the records often do not provide direct numbers for population or farmland. Thus, the figures presented were calculated indirectly from the number of households and the amount of land tax quota for a given time. Nevertheless, the figures are good enough to provide a general sense of the overall scale of the oasis economy and the trajectory of its change from the mid-eighteenth to the mid-twentieth century.

15. In other words, the period of Qing-beg rule initiated a long-term phase of over-

all economic expansion from at least 1750 to 1950. This realization sheds new light on the importance of the Qing era (1759–1864) within the long-term transformation of the oasis borderland. Contrary to our assumption that the rapid expansion of the oasis economy was the function of the Chinese migrations that began in earnest in the late nineteenth century, the Qing rule marked the beginning of the new expansive phase in oasis economy that continued even after the initial fall of its empire in the region in 1864. There was a Muslim vector in the long expansive conjuncture of the oasis economy.

16. For a detailed explanation of the pivotal role of China in anchoring the early modern global trade, see Andre Gunder Frank, *Reorient: Global Economy in the Asian Age* (Berkeley: University of California Press, 1998). For a detailed explanation of the transformation of the economy of Muslim Eurasia, see Christopher Alan Bayly, *Imperial Meridian: The British Empire and the World*, 1780–1830 (New York: Longman, 1989.)

17. Christopher Alan Bayly, *Rulers, Townsmen, and Bazaars: North Indian Society in the Age of British Expansion*, 1770–1870 (Cambridge, MA: Cambridge University Press, 1983); Frank Perlin, "Of White Whales and Countrymen in the Eighteenth-Century Maratha Deccan: Extended Class Relations, Rights, and the Problem of Rural Autonomy under the Old Regime," *Journal of Peasant Studies* 5:2 (1978), pp. 172–237; David Washbrook, "Progress and Problems: South Asian Economic and Social History, c. 1720–1860," *Modern Asian Studies* 22:1 (1988), pp. 57–96.

18. Pomeranz, *The Great Divergence*, p. 24.

19. For foundational works in the field providing the narrative framework of the history of Qing Central Asia, see Saguchi Tōru, *Jūhachi-jūkyū-seiki Higashi Torukisutan shakaishi kenkyū* [Study on the Eastern Turkestan Society during the Eighteenth and Nineteenth Centuries] (Tokyo: Yoshikawa Kobunkan, 1963); Joseph Fletcher, "Ch'ing Inner Asia, c. 1800," in *The Cambridge History of China*, vol. 10, pt. 1 (Cambridge, MA: Cambridge University Press, 1978); idem, "The Heyday of the Ch'ing Order in Mongolia, Sinkiang, and Tibet." For a collection of the works by these foundational scholars, see Joseph Fletcher and Beatrice Forbes Manz, *Studies on Chinese and Islamic Inner Asia* (Brookfield, VT: Variorum, 1995); Saguchi Tōru, *Shinkyō minzokushi kenkyū* [Study on the Ethnic History of Xinjiang] (Tokyo: Yoshikawa kobunkan, 1986); idem, *Shinkyō Musurimu Kenkyū* [Study on the Xinjiang Muslims] (Tokyo: Yoshikawa kobunkan, 1995).

20. For recent studies on the dynamics of the Qing military and the state-building process, see Perdue, *China Marches West*; James A. Millward, *Beyond the Pass: Economy, Ethnicity, and Empire in Qing Central Asia*, 1759–1864 (Stanford: Stanford University Press, 1998).

21. For studies of the Qing ruler's multicultural representation of rulership, see Pamela Kyle Crossley, *A Translucent Mirror: History and Identity in Qing Imperial Ideology* (Berkeley: University of California Press, 2002); E. S. Rawski, *The Last Emperors: A Social History of Qing Imperial Institutions* (Berkeley: University of California Press, 1998).

For a discussion of Qing multiculturalism in the specific context of Qing expansion in Xinjiang, see Perdue, *China Marches West*. For a Japanese study on the multicultural articulation of Qing emperorship in the Muslim oasis, see Hamada Masami, "'Shio no gimu' to 'seisen' no aidade [Between the 'Duty of Salt' and 'Holy War']," *Tōyōshi kenkyū* [Research on Oriental History] 52:2 (1993). For a study of Qing multiculturalism from the perspective of legal history, see Wang Dongping, "Bo-ke ji qi xiangguan falü zhidu [Beg System and the Laws Concerned with It]," in *Qingdai Huijiang falü zhidu yanjiu, 1759–1884 nian* [Study on the Legal System of the Muslim Domain, 1759–1884] (Ha'erbin: Heilongjiang jiaoyu chubanshe, 2003).

22. George Macartney, "Eastern Turkestan: The Chinese as Rulers over an Alien Race" (London: Central Asian Society, 1909), pp. 15–16; Lin Enxian, *Qingchao zai Xinjiang di Han Hui geli zhengce* [The Qing Dynasty's Han-Muslim Separation Policy in Xinjiang] (Taibei Shi: Taiwan shangwuyin shuguan, 1988), pp. 71, 93–94.

23. For a discussion of Qing administrative reliance on Chinese merchants in military financing in Xinjiang, see Millward, *Beyond the Pass*. For a study of the Qing administration's use of Chinese migrant farmers in developing agriculture in Xinjiang, see Hua Li, *Qingdai Xinjiang nongye kaifa shi* [History of the Development of Agriculture in Xinjiang during the Qing Period] (Ha'erbin: Heilongjiang jiaoyu chubanshe, 1995). For a recent study on Chinese migration into Xinjiang in the late eighteenth and early nineteenth centuries, see Jia Jianfei, *Qing Qian Jia Dao shiqi Xinjiang de neidi yimin shehui* [Immigrant Society in Xinjiang: Centered on People from China Proper during Qianlong, Jiaqing, and Daoguang Reigns of the Qing Dynasty] (Beijing: Shehui kexue wenxian chubanshe, 2012).

24. For studies on Qing-Khoqand relations in the eighteenth and nineteenth centuries, see Laura Newby, *The Empire and the Khanate: A Political History of Qing Relations with Khoqand, c. 1760–1860* (Boston: Brill, 2005); Pan Zhiping, *Zhongya Haohanguo yu Qingdai Xinjiang* [Khoqand in Central Asia and Xinjiang during the Qing Period] (Beijing: Zhongguo shehui kexue chubanshe, 1991).

25. For a discussion of the failure of the Qing's Islam policy and its consequences, see Newby, *The Empire and the Khanate*, pp. 73–123. For a recent Chinese study on the *khwaja* revolts, see Pan Xiangming, *Qingdai Xinjiang hezhuo panluan yanjiu* [Study on the Khwaja Rebellion during the Qing Period] (Beijing: Zhongguo renmin daxue chubanshe, 2011).

26. Fletcher, "The Heyday of the Ch'ing Order in Mongolia, Sinkiang, and Tibet," p. 407.

27. For a recent study of the Ya'qūb Beg regime, see Kim Hodong, *Holy War in China: The Muslim Rebellion and State in Chinese Central Asia, 1864–1877* (Stanford: Stanford University Press, 2004). For a study of Qing rule in Xinjiang after the fall of the Ya'qūb Beg regime, see Kataoka Kazutada, *Shinchō Shinkyō tōchi kenkyū* [Study on the Qing Rule of Xinjiang] (Tokyo: Yuzankaku, 1991).

28. Fletcher, "Ch'ing Inner Asia, c. 1800"; idem, "The Heyday of the Ch'ing Order in Mongolia, Sinkiang, and Tibet"; Hamada Masami, "'Shio no gimu' to 'Seisen' no aidade." 29. Recently, the First Historical Archive published these sources in a 283-volume collection. See Zhongguo di 1 lishi danganguan, and Zhongguo bianjiang shidi yanjiu zhongxin, *Qingdai Xinjiang Manwen dangan huibian* [Collections of the Manchu Language Archival Materials on the Qing Xinjiang] (hereafter MW) (Guilin Shi: Guangxi shifan daxue chubanshe, 2012).

Chapter 1

1. ZGEFL, pt. 1. vol. 23, YZ9/6/Jiawu, Edict.

2. WGBZ, vol. 111, "Zha-sa-ke duoluo junwang Emin Huozhuo liezhuan [Biography of Jasak Duoluo junwang Khoja Emin]."

3. For previous studies on Emin Khwāja, see Onuma Takahiro, "Promoting Power: The Rise of Emin Khwaja on the Eve of the Qing Conquest of Kashgaria," in *Yūbokusekai to nōkōsekai no setten–Ajiashi kenkyū no atarashitana shiryō to shiten* [Interface between the Nomadic World and Agricultural World—New Primary Source and Perspective for Research on Asian History] (Tokyo: Gagushūin daigaku Tōyōbunka kenkyūjo. 2012), pp. 31–59; Kwangmin Kim, "Profit and Protection: Emin Khwaja and the Qing Conquest of Central Asia, 1759–1777," *Journal of Asian Studies* 71:3 (August 2012); David Brophy, "King of Xinjiang: Muslims Elites and the Qing Empire," *Etudes Orientales* 25 (2008).

4. Suraiya Faroqhi et al., *An Economic and Social History of the Ottoman Empire, Vol. 2: 1600–1914* (New York: Cambridge University Press, 1997); Bayly, *Imperial Meridian.*

5. For detailed accounts of the process of the Qing-Zunghar War (1697–1754), see Zhuang Jifa, *Qing Gaozong Shiquan Wugong Yanjiu* [Studies on Qing Gaozong (Qianlong Emperor's) Ten Military Achievements] (Taipei: Guoli gugong bowuyuan, 1982); Perdue, *China Marches West;* Saguchi Tōru, *Jūhachi-jūkyū-seiki Higashi Torukisutan shakaishi kenkyū.*

6. Their emergence to prominence was not totally due to Qing design. The Qing relied on other Muslim chiefs, such as Manggaliq and Khwāja Si Beg, during the war and early years of conquest. However, Manggaliq turned against the Qing under unknown circumstances; the Qing feared the Khwaja Beg's powerful political influence in the oasis and settled him in Beijing after the conquest in 1759.

7. MLZZ, 2917–2918, QL25/5, quotation taken from Onuma Takahiro, "Zaikyo Uiguru jin no kyojutsu kara mita 18 seiki chuo Kashugaria shakai no seiji teki hendo [Political Transformation of Kashgarian Society during the Mid-eighteenth Century Seen from the Depositions of a Uyghur Living in Beijing]," *Manzokushi kenkyu* 1 (2002), p. 61; for the original meaning of "beg," see Kim Hodong, Holy War in China (Stanford: Stanford University Press, 2004), p. 217, endnote 50 to Chapter 1.

8. Kim Hodong, *Holy War in China,* p. 37.

9. "Hami huiwang shiliao," quoted in Su Beihai and Jianhua Huang, *Hami Tulufan*

Weiwuèr wang lishi, pp. 3–4; Hamada Masami, "Satoku Bogura Han no bomyo o me-gutte [Mausoleum of Satuq Bughra Khan]," *Seinan Ajia kenkyū* [Bulletin of the Society for Western and Southern Asiatic Studies] (Kyoto University) 34 (1991), pp. 97–98; idem, "Supplement: Islamic Saints and Their Mausoleums," *Acta Asiatica* 34 (1987), p. 92.

10. Mullā Mūsa Sayrāmī, *Tārīkhi äminiyä* [History of Peace], trans. Muhämmät Zu-nun (Ürümchi: Shinjang khälq näshriyati, 1989), pp. 28–29.

11. Fletcher, "Ch'ing Inner Asia, c. 1800"; Hamada Masami, "Moguru urusu kara shinkyō e [From Moghulistan to Xinjiang]," in *Iwanami Kōza Sekai Rekishi* [Iwanami Lecture on World History] 13 (new ed.) (Tokyo: Iwanami shoten, 1998); Kim Hodong, *Holy War in China;* James Millward and Laura Newby, "The Qing and Islam on the Western Frontier," in *Empire at the Margins: Culture, Ethnicity, and Frontier in Early Modern China,* ed. by Pamela Kyle Crossley, Helen F. Siu, and Donald S. Sutton (Berkeley: University of California Press, 2006); Newby, "The Begs of Xinjiang"; Saguchi Tōru, "Torukisutan no sho han koku [Khanates of Turkestan]," in *Iwanami kōza sekai rekishi* 13 (Tokyo: Iwanami shoten, 1971), p. 69; Shimada Jōhei, "Hōja jidai no Beku dachi [The Begs during the Period of the Khoja (Rule)]," *Toho gaku* 3 (1952); Isenbike Togan, "Islam in a Chinese Society: The Khojas of Eastern Turkestan," in *Muslims in Central Asia: Expressions of Identity and Change,* ed. by Jo-Ann Gross (Durham, NC: Duke University Press, 1992).

12. Maria Subtelny, *Timurids in Transition* (Leiden: Brill, 2007), pp. 198–200, 220.

13. MLZZ QL23/2/21, 1685-31; re-quotation from Onuma Takahiro, "Zaikyo Uiguru jin no kyojutsu kara mita 18 seiki chuo Kashugaria shakai no seiji teki hendo [Political Transformation of Kashgarian Society during the Mid-eighteenth Century]," p. 58. From Ush, Ashūji's family expanded their power base to Aksu, Kucha, and Kashgaria and emerged as a major Muslim ally for the Zunghar rulers, before he joined the Qing side when the Zunghar regime collapsed.

14. Jo-Ann Gross, "The Economic Status of a Timurid Sufi Shaykh: A Matter of Conflict or Perception?" *Iranian Studies* 21:1 (1988), pp. 84–104; Jurgen Paul, "Forming a Faction: The Himayat System of Khwaja Ahrar," *International Journal of Middle East Studies* 23:4 (1991), pp. 533–48.

15. "Hami huiwang shiliao." There is other evidence for the existence of the former nomad converts traveling with Sufi masters. The *Tazkira i khwājagān* (a hagiography of the Black Mountaineer faction of the Naqshbandi *khwaja*s written in the late eighteenth century) called these followers of the rival White Mountaineer *khwaja*s (such as Āfāq Khwāja) "fanatics" or "fanatical devotees" (*diwana*). In many places, their numbers ran in the hundreds or thousands. The work noted that these groups were responsible for the political violence committed by Āfāq Khwāja. They killed a Black Mountaineer *khwaja* who was coming back to Kashgaria, upon the invitation of Āfāq. They were also identified as the people who killed the latter's wife. It also was recorded that "a thousand

fanatics killed the Akbash Khan [a Monghul khan]." In greatest likelihood, these were the people who provided the Khwaja a source of soldiers, when the *khwajas* went to battle. In all probability they came originally from nomadic peoples (Kirghiz, Qalmaq, Mongols) who were converted by the Sufis. The fact that they were mobile, that they represented a military capacity, and that the urban author of the hagiography put them in a negative light supports this suspicion.

16. WGBZ, vol. 118, "Yuanfeng beile pinji gushan beizi E-dui liezhuan [Biography of Ūdui Who Was Originally Appointed as *Belie*-Rank/*gushan beizi*]"; GZSL, vol. 517, QL21/7/guisi; ibid., vol. 519, QL21/8/wuwu, Cancan dachen Ya-er-ha-shan's memorial.

17. Onuma Takahiro, "The Development of the Junghars and the Role of Bukharan Merchants," *Journal of Central Eurasian Studies* 2 (May 2011), p. 91; Li Baowen, "'Bo-de-er-ge' Kaoshi," *Xiyu yanjiu* 4 (2009), p. 113.

18. For general descriptions of the works of the agricultural colonies of Turfan and Hami during the Yongzheng Period, see Wang Xilong, *Qingdai xibei tuntian yanjiu* [Study on the Northwestern Agricultural Colonies during the Qing Period] (Lanzhou: Lanzhou daxue chubanshe, 1990), pp. 197–208.

19. ZGEFL, pt. 2, vol. 65, QL23/12/yimao, Shuhede's memorial; ibid., vol. 66, QL23/12/wuyin, Shuhede's memorial.

20. There is debate about whether a beg during the Qing Period was an "aristocrat/noble" or an "official." Many scholars argue that the beg as aristocrat disappeared, if gradually, during that time, since the Qing attached "beg" as a suffix to a title within the native administration (such as "*hākim*-beg," "*ishikagha*-beg"); the oasis people then ceased to use the term "beg" as an honorific to denote the status of a "notable" or aristocrat. Begs as aristocrats with an independent power base disappeared. Certainly, the begs in the original, nomadic notables, disappeared. However, there is some strong evidence that "beg" was still used as a status signifier during the Qing. For instance, Ahmad, a prominent pro-Qing beg in the late nineteenth century (see Chapter 5), was usually referred to in the local historical record as "Ahmad Wang Beg," rather than by the title of his official post, such as the "Hākim Beg of Kashgar District." The class of the beg was reconstituted to include the leaders of all kinds of oasis communities of various origins, including sedentarized nomadic nobles. Therefore, the beg were both officials and notables, or notables during the Qing rule. Indeed, my argument is that the reason the begs were effective as native "officials" under Qing rule was that they had their own local power and economic base as "notables." The two were not mutually exclusive but rather mutually reinforcing in the context of the eighteenth- and nineteenth-century Eastern Turkestan.

21. SZSL, vol. 53, YZ5/2/bingyin.

22. ZGEFL, pt. 2, vol. 65, QL23/12/yimao, Xu-he-de's memorial; ibid., vol. 66, QL23/12/wuyin, Xu-he-de's memorial.

23. Hamada Masami, "Satoku Bogura Han no bomyo o megutte," pp. 97–98.

24. Wang Shouli and Jinxin Li, *Xinjiang Weiwu'er zu qiyue wenshu ziliao xuanbian* [Selected Editions of the Contract Documents of Xinjiang Uyghurs], doc. 51, January 31, 1902 (Xinjiang: Shehui kexueyuan zongjiao suo, 1990), p. 38.

25. Hori Sunao, "Jūhachi-nijū seiki Uiguru joku no doryōkō ni tsuite [The Measurement Used by Uyghur People from the Eighteenth to the Twentieth Century]," *Journal of Otemae College* 12 (1978), p. 60.

26. *Tazkira-i Khwāja Muhammad Sharīf* [Hagiography of Khwaja Muhammad Sharif], anonymous, in G. Jarring Collection: Prov. 73, 115b–16; Hamada Masami, *Higashi Torukisutan Chagataigo seijaden no kenkyū* [Chagatai Language Hagiography of the Muslim Saints of Eastern Turkestan] (Kyōto: Kyōto daigaku daigakuin bungaku kenkyūka, 2006), pp. 158–59.

27. *Tazkira-yi Mawalana Arsiddin Wali: uzun nusxasi* [Hagiography of *Mawalana Arsiddin Wali*], anonymous, in the Saint Petersburg Branch of the Institute of Oriental Studies of the Russian Academy of Sciences: C556, 58b–59; Hamada Masami, *Higashi Torukisutan Chagataigo seijaden no kenkyū*, pp. 97–98.

28. For detailed accounts of the Yarkand Khanate, see Hamada Masami, "Moguru urusu kara shinkyō e"; Saguchi Tōru, "Torukisutan no sho han koku"; Wei Liangtao, *Ye-er-qiang hanguo shigang* [Outline History of the Yarkand Khanate] (Ha'erbin: Heilongjiang jiaoyu chubanshe, 1994). For an account of Islam during the Yarkand Khanate period, see Zhongguo Xinjiang diqu Yisilanjiao shi bianxiezu, ed., *Zhongguo Xinjiang diqu Yisilanjiao shi*.

29. Shāh Maḥmūd Churās, *Khronika* (Moskva: Nauka, 1976), pp. 301–2.

30. Ibid., p. 178, fns. 100, 104.

31. For the "decline thesis," see Owen Lattimore, *Inner Asian Frontiers of China* (New York: American Geographical Society, 1940), pp. 4–5. For criticism on the decline thesis, see Morris Rossabi, "The 'Decline' of the Central Asian Caravan Trade,'" in *The Rise of the Merchant Empires: Long-distance Trade in the Early Modern World*, ed. by James D. Tracy (New York: Cambridge University Press, 1990), pp. 351–70; R. D. McChesney, *Central Asia: Foundations of Change* (Princeton, NJ: Darwin Press), 1996; Scott C. Levi, "Early Modern Central Asia in World History," *History Compass* 10:11 (November 2012), pp. 866–78; idem, *India and Central Asia Commerce and Culture, 1500–1800* (New Delhi: Oxford University Press, 2007).

32. Togan, "Inner Asian Muslim Merchants at the Closure of the Silk Routes in the Seventeenth Century," pp. 249–50, 258–59.

33. GZSL, vol. 594, QL24/8/jimao, Edict.

34. For a similar case of Central Asian Sufi migration induced by the expansion of trade and agriculture in Bengal in the sixteenth and seventeenth centuries, see Richard Maxwell Eaton, *The Rise of Islam and the Bengal Frontier, 1204–1760* (Berkeley: University of California Press, 1993), pp. 71–94, 194–227.

35. Zhang Wende, *Ming yu Ti-mu-er wangchao guanxi shi yanjiu* [The Relations be-

tween the Ming and the Timurid Dynasty] (Beijing: Zhonghua shuju, 2006), pp. 48–49, 106, 119–21.

36. Kwangmin Kim, "Saintly Brokers: Uyghur Muslims, Trade, and the Making of Qing Central Asia, 1696–1814" (diss., University of California, Berkeley, 2008), pp. 74–75, 118. It was also known that many tribute envoys from Tumurid were *dervish* (mendicant Sufi); Zhang Wende, *Ming yu Ti-mu-er wangchao guanxi shi yanjiu*, p. 97.

37. Mirza Haydar, Ney Elias, and E. Denison Ross, *The Tarikh-I Rashidi of Mirza Muhammad Haidar, Dughlat: A History of the Moghuls of Central Asia. An English Version Edited, with Commentary, Notes, and Map* (London: S. Low Marston and Company, Ltd., 1895), p. 127.

38. Regarding the Central Asian Sufi involvement in long-distance trade, see Togan, "Inner Asian Muslim Merchants at the Closure of the Silk Routes in the Seventeenth Century," pp. 247–63.

39. Henry Yule, "The Journey of Benedict Goës from Agra to Cathay," in *Cathay and the Way Thither*, vol. 4 (London: Asian Educational Services, 1916), pp. 218–19. For a detailed study of the Ming-Central Asian jade trade, see Zhang Wende, "Ming yu Xiyu de yushi maoyi [Jade Trade between the Ming China and Western Regions]," *Xiyu yanjiu* [Research on Western Regions] 3 (2007); idem, *Ming yu Ti-mu-er wangchao guanxi shi yanjiu*, pp. 124–27.

40. For a more detailed explanation about the Sufi orders during the reign of the Yarkand Khanate, see Hamada Masami, "Satoku Bogura Han no bomyo o megutte"; idem, "Moguru urusu kara shinkyō e"; Saguchi Tōru, "Torukisutan no sho han koku"; Zhongguo Xinjiang diqu Yisilanjiao shi bianxiezu, ed., *Zhongguo Xinjiang diqu Yisilanjiao shi*; Liu Zhengyin and Liangtao Wei, *Xiyu Huozhou jiazhou yanjiu* [Study on the Khwaja Families of the Western Regions] (Beijing: Zhongguo shehui kexue chubanshe, 1998).

41. Kim, "Saintly Brokers," pp. 80–90.

42. WGBZ, vol. 109.

43. Fighting with Zheng Chenggong in Taiwan (1661–83), for instance, cost the Qing government 4 million *liang* (150 tons) of silver, and the war with the Three Feudatories (1673–81) cost 100 million to 150 million *liang* (3,750 to 5,625 tons). Chen Feng, *Qingdai junfei yanjiu* [Study on the Military Expenses of the Qing Period] (Wuchang: Wuhan daxue chubanshe, 1992), pp. 244, 248.

44. Kishimoto Mio, *Higashi Ajia No "kinsei,"* pp. 13–18, 21–22. On the silver influx into China during the Ming-Qing Period, see also Dennis O. Flynn and Arturo Giráldez, "Cycles of Silver: Global Economic Unity through the Mid-eighteenth Century," *Journal of World History* 13:2 (2002), pp. 391–427; Richard Von Glahn, *Fountain of Fortune: Money and Monetary Policy in China, 1000–1700* (Berkeley: University of California Press, 1996).

45. Morris Rossabi, "Muslim and Central Asian Revolts," in *From Ming to Ching:*

Conquest, Region, and Continuity in Seventeenth-century China, ed. by Jonathan D. Spence and John E. Wills, Jr. (New Haven: Yale University Press, 1979).

46. Liang Fen, *Qinbian jilue* [Record of the Northwestern "Qin" Frontier], Kangxi Period (1662–1722) (Xining: Qinghai renmin chubanshe, reprint ed., 1987), vol. 1, "Quan qinbian wei [(Introduction to) All Garrisons of the Northwestern 'Qin' Frontier]," pp. 21–23, 63–64; Haneda Akira, "Hsi-ning to Tuo-pa [Hsi-ning and Tuo-pa]," *Tōyōshi kenkyū* 10:5, pp. 358–64.

47. Liang Fen, *Qinbian jilue*, pp. 78–79.

48. Ma Tong, *Zhongguo Yisilan jiaopai menhuan suyuan* [Origin of the Sects and Sufi Orders of Islam in China] (Yinchuan Shi: Ningxia renmin chubanshe, 1986), pp. 49–80. Ma's account of Āfāq Khwāja's three trips to northwestern China is based on the tradition of the Mufti Menhuan and his hagiography. For another account of Āfāq Khwāja's activities in Xining, see Alexandre Papas, *Soufisme et Politique Entre Chine, Tibet et Turkestan: Étude Sur Les Khwajas Naqshbandis Du Turkestan Oriental* [Sufism and the Politics between China, Tibet, and Turkestan: Study of Nashbandi Khwajas in Eastern Turkestan] (Paris: Librarie d'Amérique et d'Orient, Jean Maisonneuve successeur, 2005), pp. 112–14.

49. Ma Tong, *Zhongguo Yisilan jiaopai menhuan suyuan*, pp. 49–80.

50. I thus disagree with the hagiographic account's explanation that the Dalai Lama played the role of mediator for the formation of the alliance between the Khwaja and the Zunghar ruler. For Āfāq Khwāja's sojourn in the eastern part of the oasis region, Xining and Tibet, see Papas, *Soufisme et Politique Entre Chine, Tibet et Turkestan,* pp. 92–93; 97–100; 112–13; Ma Tong, *Zhongguo Yisilan jiaopai menhuan suyuan,* pp. 49–80; David Brophy, "The Oirat in Eastern Turkestan and the Rise of Afaq Khwaja," *Archivum Eurasiae Medii Aevi* 16 (2008/9).

51. Liang Fen, *Qinbian jilue*, vol. 1, "Xining wei," p. 74.

52. Perdue, *China Marches West,* p. 306; Cai Jiayi, *Qingdai Xinjiang shehui jingji shi gang* [Outline Socio-economic History of Xinjiang during the Qing Period] (Beijing: Renmin chubanshe, 2006), pp. 44–61; Onuma Takahiro, "The Development of the Junghars and the Role of Bukharan Merchants," pp. 83–100; Saguchi Tōru, *Shinkyō Musurimu Kenkyū,* pp. 236–306.

53. Togan, "Islam in a Chinese Society"; idem, "Inner Asian Muslim Merchants at the Closure of the Silk Routes in the Seventeenth Century," pp. 247–63.

54. Cai Jiayi, *Qingdai Xinjiang Shehui Jingji Shi Gang*; Perdue, *China Marches West.*

55. Muhammad Sadiq Kashgari, Robert Shaw, and Ney Elias, *The History of the Khojas of Eastern-Turkistan Summarised from the Tazkira-i-Khwajagan of Muhammad Sadiq Kashghari* (Calcutta: Asiatic Society, 1897), p. 37. A *tangga* is a small coin worth usually about one-sixth part of an Indian rupee. Ibid., p. 20, fn. 3.

56. Ibid., pp. 41–42; Onuma Takahiro, "The Development of the Junghars and the Role of Bukharan Merchants," pp. 89–90. For more studies on these forced migrants

called *tranchi* (*taranči*), see Saguchi Tōru, "Iri no taranchi shakai [Taranchi Society of Ili]," *Shinkyō minzokushi kenkyū* [A Study on the Ethnic History of Xinjiang]" (Tokyo: Yoshikawa kobunkan, 1986); David Brophy, "Taranchis, Kashgaris, and the 'Uyghur Question' in Soviet Central Asia," *Inner Asia* 7:2 (January 2005).

57. ZGEFL, pt. 1, vol. 7; SZSL, vol. 289, KX59/9/renwu, Fu'ning'an's memorial.

58. Kashgari et al., *The History of the Khojas of Eastern-Turkistan Summarised from the Tazkira-i-Khwajagan of Muhammad Sadiq Kashghari*, p. 42.

59. Ahmet Temir, "Ein Osttürkisches Dokument von 1722–1741 aus Turfan," *Ural-Altaische Jahrbucher* 33:1–2 (1961), pp. 194–97.

60. For a detailed explanation of the Islamic notion of protection (*himayat*), see Jurgen Paul, "Forming a Faction: The Himayat System of Khwaja Ahrar," *International Journal of Middle East Studies* 23:4 (1991), pp. 538, 541–42; Maria Eva Subtelny, "Centralizing Reform and Its Opponents in the Late Timurid Period," *International Journal of Iranian Studies* 21:1/2 (1988), p. 126.

61. Chen Feng, *Qingdai junfei yanjiu*, pp. 252, 254, 258, 261.

62. SZSL, vol. 53, YZ5/2/bingyin; ZGEFL, pt. 1, vol. 20, YZ8/10/xinchou.

63. Perdue, *China Marches West*, pp. 323–57.

64. 1 *dou* = 1/10 *shi* = 10.35 liters, 0.29 bushels, or 17.5–19.5 pounds in the case of milled rice.

65. Huang Wenwei, *Chongxiu Suzhou xin zhi* [Revised New Gazetteer of Suzhou], 1737, Qing Daoguang Period (1820–50) edition, vol. "Anxi xiace" [The latter volume on Anxi], Acting Shaaxi Governor-General Liu Yuyi's memorial (Taibei: Taiwan xuesheng shuju, reprint ed., 1967). As a result of this measure, Emin Khwāja and the Turfan refugees borrowed 17,000 *shi* of seeds and 2,271 *liang* of silver for transportation costs from the Qing court. They were supposed to repay it in six installments beginning in 1736. But Emin Khwāja requested a one-year postponement, to begin the repayment schedule in 1737, with the excuse of needing additional time for making clothing and for the purchase of mules. His request was granted. (See GZSL, vol. 31, QL1/11/jiwei, Acting Chuanshaan Governor Liu Yuyi's memorial.)

66. Huang Wenwei, *Chongxiu Suzhou xin zhi*.

67. Changjun, *Dunhuang suibi* [An Essay on Dunhuang] (2 juan, vol. xia) (Beijing: Yugong xuehui, reprint ed., 1937). For a more detailed explanation of the Qing agricultural colonies in Gansu, see Wang Xilong, *Qingdai xibei tuntian yanjiu*, pp. 152–230.

68. GZSL, vol. 524, QL21/10/yihai, Edict.

69. Ibid., vol. 31, QL1/11/jiwei.

70. Ibid., vol. 115, YZ10/2/yimao, Edict.

71. Ibid., vol. 127, YZ11/1/dingwei.

72. Ibid., vol. 153, QL6/10/renzi, Grand Secretariats' memorial.

73. For Central Asian demand for silver from trade with China before the Qing conquest, see ibid., pp. 263, 265.

74. Ibid., vol. 519, QL21/8/wuwu.

75. Ibid., vol. 634, QL26/4/xinsi, Edict.

76. ZGEFL, pt. 3, vol. 14, QL26/10/dingmao; ibid., vol. 16, QL27/3/jiawu.

77. MLZZ, QL46/3/12.

78. For previous studies on Emin Khwāja, see Onuma Takahiro, "Promoting Power," pp. 31–59; Kim, "Profit and Protection"; Brophy, "King of Xinjiang."

79. McChesney, *Central Asia*, p. 42.

80. MLZZ, YZ11/7/20, Emin Khwāja's memorial.

Chapter 2

1. XYWJL, vol. 3, "Sha-guan-ji."

2. Kim Hodong, "Chung'ang Asia ui Musulim sŏngja sungbae-Turupan ui Alpŭ Ata sungbae rŭl chungsim ŭro [Muslim Saint Worship in Central Asia: Case of Alp Ata Worship in Turfan]," *Chindan hakpo* 74 (1992), pp. 147–77. In general, one is hard pressed to find any reference to the governor's relations with the Qing at all in numerous descriptions of his rule in the local materials. See Rian Thum, *The Sacred Routes of Uyghur History* (Cambridge, MA: Harvard University Press, 2014).

3. Kwangmin Kim, "Profit and Protection," pp. 603–26.

4. The first to come up with the idea of indirect rule was the British diplomat George Macartney, who stayed in Xinjiang as British consul in the early twentieth century. Macartney, "Eastern Turkestan."

5. XYWJL, vol. 2, "Yarkand." In 1761, only a year after Ūdui's assumption of the governorship in Yarkand, the district's Manchu military governor confirmed this impression by describing Yarkand as a big town, where numerous diplomatic missions as well as Tibetan and Andijan merchants converged (GZSL, vol. 632, 4/8/1761).

6. In fact, the new population added to the oasis as a result of the Qing military occupation was much greater than six to eight thousand, considering that it also stationed various civilian officials and clerks to support the Qing troops. For instance, in 1761, the total number of the entire Qing military establishment in Kashgar and Yangi Hissar including the Muslim translators and the oasis Muslims manning the Qing military postal stations was reported to be twenty-two hundred people, double the number of the actual Qing troops stationed there (1,171) (GZSL, vol. 630, Haiming's memorial). If we add in personal servants and staff who followed their Qing military commanders into the oasis, the number of people sustained by the oasis economy became larger still.

7. For a list of the predetermined sum of the tax and tribute payments from Kashgar District in 1835, see Wu Fengpei, *Qingdai Xinjiang xijian zoudu huibian: Daoguang chao juan* (hereafter XJZDHB: DG) [Collection of the Rarely Seen Memorials and Letters on Xinjiang during the Qing Period: Daoguang Period] (Wulumuqi Shi: Xinjiang renmin chubanshe, 1996) pp. 163–64, doc. 79, DG15/r6/6 (1835); ibid., p. 173, doc. 87, Fu-xing-a, Fuxing'a gongdu, DG17/10/20 (1837) (originally from *Xilang'a Zougao*).

8. ZGEFL, pt. 3, vol. 10, QL26/2/yiyou; ibid., vol. 16, QL27/3/gengwu.

9. MLZZ, QL27/3/18 (MW, vol. 55, pp. 288–92), Sinju and Emin Khwāja's memorial; ibid., QL28/4/5 (MW, vol. 62, pp. 42–44), Yunggui's memorial.

10. Wang Xi, "Lun Qianlong shiqi Yili Hasake maoyi majia, sichoujia yu maoyi bizhi wenti [The Price of Horse and Silk at the Yili's Trade with Kazakh and the Rate of Exchange]," *Minzu yanjiu* 4 (1992), pp. 48–58; idem, "Qianlong shiqi Ka-shi-ga-er de guanfang sichou maoyi [Official Silk Trade in Kashgar during the Qianlong Period]," in *Qingdai quyu shehui jingji yanjiu* [Studies on Regional Society and Economy during the Qing Period], ed. by Ye Xian'en (Beijing: Zhonghua shuju, 1992); Millward, *Beyond the Pass*, pp. 45–46.

11. GZSL, vol. 18, QL27/5/jihai.

12. MLZZ, QL60/9/15.

13. Thomas Douglas Forsyth, *Report of a Mission to Yarkund in 1873, under Command of Sir T. D. Forsyth, with Historical and Geographical Information Regarding the Possessions of the Ameer of Yarkund* (Calcutta: Foreign Dept. Press, 1875), p. 33.

14. Wang Xi, "Qianlong shiqi Ka-shi-ga-er de guanfang sichou maoyi."

15. Audrey Burton, *Bukharan Trade, 1558–1718* (Bloomington: Indiana University, Research Institute for Inner Asian Studies, 1993), pp. 13, 39; Saguchi Tōru, *Jūhachi-jūkyū-seiki Higashi Torukisutan shakaishi kenkyū*, pp. 370–71.

16. For the silver transfer numbers to southern Xinjiang, see Hori Sunao, "Shindai Shinkyō no kahei seido—Furu (pul) chūzōsei [The Currency System of Xinjiang during the Qing Period—System of Minting *Pul* Currency]," *Nakashima Satoshi Sensei koki kinen ronshū*, vol. 1 (1980), pp. 581–602; For the silver transfer numbers to northern Xinjiang, see Millward, *Beyond the Pass*, p. 60.

17. GPYSA, pp. 466–47, doc. 88 (originally from Junjihu jixindang, QL43/10/6).

18. ZGEFL, pt. 3, QL25/7/yihai, Edict; Nayancheng, *Na Wenyigong Zouyi* [Memorials of Na Wenyigong, Nayancheng] (80 Juan), edited by hangjia Rong'an (Taibei: Wenhai chubanshe, 1968), vol. 77, DG8/8/3. Livestock was the most important good the Central Asian merchants brought to the oasis, a commodity with which it was historically undersupplied. For instance, in the budget year ending in QL 31/9/13 (1766), the Qing local administration in Kashgar collected twenty-five kinds of commodities as customs duties. Important among them were livestock: 86 horses, 25 cows, and 1,032 lambs. It also included animal products such as 32 perfumed cow skins, 129 fox pelts, and 1,648 *jin* of tobacco. Lin Yongkuang and Wang Xi, *Qingdai xibei minzu maoyi shi* [History of the Trade of Northwestern Peoples] (Beijing: Zhongyan minzu xueyuan chubanshe, 1991), p. 520. Valikhanov, a Russian-educated Kazakh prince, mentioned the lack of cattle in the region as one of the reasons why the Qing had to open Eastern Turkestan to Central Asian foreign traders. Chokan Valikhanov, "O sostoianii Altyshara ili shesti vostochnykh grodov Kitaĭskoĭ provintsii Nan-lu (Maloĭ Bukharii), v. 1858–59 godakh [Condition of the Altishar or the Six Eastern Cities of Chinese Province, Nanlu (Small

Bukhara), 1858–1859]," in *Izbrannye Proizvedeniia*.[Selected Works] (Moskva: Izd-vo "Nauka," Glav. red. vostochnoĭ lit-ry, 1986), p. 148.

19. HJZ, "Tuchan shigong [Local Products and Tributes]." Another equally important structural benefit that the Qing military presence provided for the local economy was military protection. Its military umbrella protected the oasis community and its agriculture and trade from potential threats, such as the aggressive Central Asian state builders in the mold of the Zunghar Mongols, as well as less organized bandits and raiders such as the Kirghiz. We have already seen how important this protection was for the security and prosperity of the oasis community in the examination of Emin Khwāja's story in Chapter 1, above. It seems that the Qing military protection remained effective for the most part in the late eighteenth and early nineteenth centuries. The oasis Muslims were able to rely upon the Qing troops to effectively suppress Kirghiz robberies of the caravan traders almost immediately after the Qing conquest of Eastern Turkestan in 1759. Also, the area was largely saved from outsider invasion while under Qing protection in the nineteenth century, when interstate warfare swept across the entire span of Central Asia until 1864, when the Khoqand invasion ended Qing rule.

20. GZSL, vol. 605, QL25/l/xinwei, Grand Minister Councilor Shuhede's memorial. For a discussion on the Qing court's intentions in approving this measure, see Fletcher, "Ch'ing Inner Asia, c. 1800"; Kim, "Saintly Brokers," pp. 181–87.

21. Millward, *Beyond the Pass*, pp. 106–7.

22. Kim, "Saintly Brokers," pp. 175–81.

23. For the Qing practice of not awarding the beg officials land and *yanqi*, if they had already owned landed properties such as farmland, shops and buildings, and watermills, from which they could make substantial income, see Saguchi Tōru, *Jūhachi-jūkyū-seiki Higashi Torukisutan shakaishi kenkyū*, pp. 132–34.

24. The Jiaqing (1796–1820) and Daoguang (1821–50) imperial courts tried to eliminate the grant of the land and *yanqi*, and granted only cash silver/annual cash payments.

25. MLZZ, QL26/4/21, Suhede's memorial (MW, vol. 51).

26. Ibid., QL33/11/6, Yunggui, Šuhede, and Yungkiang's memorial (MW, vol. 90, pp. 304–8).

27. Ibid., JQ5/2/7, Fugiyūn and Iskandar's memorial (MW, vol. 210, pp. 88–96). This kind of land grant was different from the Yarkand khan's land grant, which gave the right to collect dues from farming households within certain areas.

28. The grant of people was considered the most crucial part among the three components. In the environmental condition of dry farming in the oasis (like any agriculture in a "land-rich situation" in which the land itself is plentiful but labor for farming and ranching is scarce), the most important component of the land grants was the input of labor, and the input of capital to a lesser degree. The reason is that in conditions of dry farming, what determined the productivity of certain pieces of land was the availability of irrigation, assuming that the land in question was located within a reasonable dis-

tance from water. What made irrigation available was the input of labor first and foremost, and the input of capital to a lesser degree. Therefore, when seven Mirab begs of Aksu District were found to have owned land beyond the Qing quota, the imperial court decided not to provide the begs land and cash, but only *yanqi* as oasis landed elites (see HJZ, vol. 3). With the input of more labor, the Mirab begs could increase the production of the land.

29. According to Saguchi Tōru's estimation, the official land grants to the 257 beg officials working for the Qing administration in the oasis region amounted to 7,924 *batman* of land (419,970 *mu*) in total. This size of the Qing land grant to the begs was roughly 70 percent of the private landed property held by Muslims that Saguchi estimated at 600,000 *mu*. Saguchi Tōru, *Jūhachi-jūkyū-seiki Higashi Torukisutan shakaishi kenkyū*, p. 131.

30. GZSL, vol. 610, QL25/4/yichou, 5/29/1760, Grand Councilors' memorial; MLZZ, QL28/4/5, Kashgar Cancan dachen Yonggui's memorial (MW, vol. 62, p. 45–51).

31. MLZZ, QL27/1/11 (MW, vol. 54, pp. 369–70).

32. Ibid., QL49/4/12, Fulu's report on lead mining in Qarashar.

33. GPYSA, pp. 746–47, doc. 301, QL43/11/21, Edict to Grand Minister Superintendent of Ush, Yonggui.

34. Chang Te-Chang, "The Economic Role of the Imperial Household in the Ch'ing Dynasty," *Journal of Asian Studies* 31:2 (1972), pp. 254–56; Millward, *Beyond the Pass*, p. 300.

35. GZSL, vol. 610, QL25/4/yichou, 5/29/1760, Grand Councilors' memorial.

36. MLZZ, QL26/2/25, Haiming's memorial (MW, vol. 50, pp. 370–71).

37. Ibid., QL27/4/28, Yonggui's memorial (MW, vol. 56, pp. 121–23).

38. According to one study, the Persian and Turkic titles of beg posts used under the Qing had been known to the oasis Muslims before the establishment of the Qing Empire. But it did not necessarily mean that those posts were all in fact in place in the Muslim oases during the time of the rule of the Moghuls, Zunghars, and Kashgar *khwaja*. The Qing may have recycled the titles, which were known only on paper. See Miao Pusheng, *Bo-ke Zhidu* [Beg System] (Wulumuqi: Xinjiang renmin chuban she, 1995). This means that the Qing beg system was an active new re-creation rather than a passive adoption of a local Muslim institution. Also, each Muslim oasis had a different set of beg posts even under the Qing. Actually, some were a totally new invention of the Qing, and others did not have Persian or Turkic names but rather a Chinese name, which crudely described their duties, such as "the Beg taking charge of the mining of copper" (*juetong boke*) of Ku'erle (HJTZ).

39. For a collection of both Chinese and Manchu archival sources regarding the Gao Pu corruption case, see GPYSA; for a general overview of the case, see Preston M. Torbert, *The Ching Imperial Household Department: A Study of Its Organization and Principal Functions, 1662–1796* (Cambridge, MA: Council on East Asian Studies, Har-

vard University, distributed by Harvard University Press, 1977), pp. 136–71; Millward, *Beyond the Pass*, pp. 181–91. Both mention the Muslims' involvement either marginally or not at all.

40. GPYSA, pp. 773–76, doc. 323.

41. Ibid., pp. 373–74, doc. 1, QL43/9/16 (originally from *Junjichu manchu yue-zhedang*).

42. XJZDHB: DG, pp. 163–64, doc. 79, DG15/r6/6 (1835); ibid., p. 173, doc. 87, Fu-xing-a, Fuxing'a gongdu, DG17/10/20 (1837) (originally from *Xilang-a Zougao*).

43. Ibid., pp. 14–16, doc. 11, Nayancheng, Yang Fang, and Wu-long-a's memorial, DG8/6/2. For instance, in 1777, Ūdui and the native officials collected 5,326 *tangga* of *pul* from the urban and rural residents of the oasis on the excuse that they needed to purchase the goods that the Qing *yamen* requested. The beg officials needed to pay not only Ūdui but also the Manchu military governor, Gao Pu. In order to get promoted, in 1783 two sixth-rank beg officials of Yarkand paid four pieces of *yambu* silver and 500 *liang* of silver to the Manchu governor alone (GPYSA, pp. 535, doc. 144; ibid., pp. 773–76, doc. 323).

44. GPYSA, pp. 466–67, doc. 87, QL43/10/6.

45. Ibid., p. 535, doc. 301, QL43/11/21, Gao Pu's servant Chang-yong's deposition.

46. 1 *tahar* = 40 *jin* of rice (in the 1940s). Hori Sunao, "Jūhachi-nijū seiki Uiguru joku no doryōkō ni tsuite," p. 66, fn. 4.

47. Nayancheng, *Na Wenyigong Zouyi*, vol. 77, DG8/8/7; Saguchi Tōru, *Jūha-chi-jūkyū-seiki Higashi Torukisutan shakaishi kenkyū*, p. 186.

48. GZSL, vol. 617, QL25/7/wuwu, Edict; ibid., vol. 691, QL28/7/jiaxu, Edict; XY-WJL, vol. 2, "Yarkand." Ūdui also constantly worked to keep the jade mines open for excavation, presumably because they could be open only when the Qing administration wanted to secure the jade tribute. To do so (in QL 42), Ūdui promised Gao Pu the share of 500 *jin* of jadestones, and to his servant 150 *jin* of jadestones in advance. When Chang-yong asked for silver instead of jade, because he did not know how to smuggle jade, Ūdui gave him 1,000 liang (GPYSA, p. 535, doc. 144, Gao Pu's servant, Chang-yong's deposition).

49. MLZZ, QL50/1/25 (1785), Booceng, converting Alima's property into cash.

50. HJFL, vol. 80, DG9/4/jisi, Nayanchang's memorial; Edward Green Balfour, *The Cyclopaedia of India and of Eastern and Southern Asia*, vol. 2 (London: B. Quaritch, 1885), p. 178. For the use of slaves in Qing Central Asia, see Laura J. Newby, "Bondage on Qing China's Northwestern Frontier," *Modern Asian Studies* 47:3 (2013), pp. 968–94.

51. MLZZ, QL60/2/25, Yungboo's memorial (MW, vol. 202, pp. 379–92). The Qing military governors were correctly worried about the potential social instability that this kind of slave trade could generate in the oasis and mountain society. Therefore, when re-form of Qing rule in the oasis was discussed in the early nineteenth century, the problem of the influx of the Galcha slaves as one of the main problems threatening the security of

its regime came up, and the governors tried to halt the flow. XJZDHB: DG, doc. 117, p. 197 (originally from *Fuxing'a gongdu*, 1838).

52. Hori Sunao, "Kaikyō hankachō [Criminal Records of the Muslim Domain]," *Kōnan daigaku kiyō: bungakuhen* 105 (1997), p. 38.

53. MLZZ, QL53/3/9, Aksu Muslim, Mai-mai-te-xi-li-bu's deposition.

54. Idem, QL49/2/27, Ai-li-ba-nu's deposition.

55. HJFL, vol. 80, DG9 /4/jisi, Nayancheng, Regarding a ban on Muslim households and merchants.

56. Ibid., vol. 47, DG7/6/bingshen; ibid., vol. 43, DG7/5/gengzi, Ush Banshi dachen, Hengqing's report.

57. GZSL, vol. 716, 9/2/1764 (QL 29), Yarkand cancan E'erjing'e's memorial.

58. Wang Shouli and Jinxin Li, *Xinjiang Weiwu'er zu qiyue wenshu ziliao xuanbian*.

59. For examples, see the *waqf* donation documents introduced in the following articles: G. L. M. Clauson, "Eine Kaschgarische Wakf-Urkunde Aus der Khodschazeit Ost-Turkestans. By G. Raquette (Lund Universitets\AA Rsskrift. N.F. Avd. 1. Bd. 26, Nr. 2), 10 × 6½, p. 24, Plate 1. Lund: Gleerup; Leipzig, Harrassowitz, 1930," *Journal of the Royal Asiatic Society* (new series) 63:4 (1931), pp. 908–9; Kim Hodong, "Chung'ang Asia ui Musulim sŏngja sungbae-Turupan ui Alpŭ Ata sungbae rŭl chungsim ŭro [The Cult of Saints in Eastern Turkestan—The Case of Alp Ata in Turfan]," *Chindan hakpo* 74 (1992).

60. Wang Shouli and Jinxin Li, *Xinjiang Weiwu'er zu qiyue wenshu ziliao xuanbian*, pp. 2–3, doc. 003, 8/2/1807.

61. For the dispute during the early twentieth century, see ibid. For Emin Khwāja's descendant becoming a *khalifa*, a manager of a *madrasa* established by Yunus Wang, see ibid., doc. 051 (1902/1/31) and doc. 54 (1904/1/21).

62. Gunnar Jarring, *Materials to the Knowledge of Eastern Turki: Tales, Poetry, Proverbs, Riddles, Ethnological and Historical Texts from the Southern Parts of Eastern Turkestan* (Lund: Gleerup, 1951), p. 11.

63. In 1832, in Du-lai-ti-jiang Bay, a Khoqandian, bought 2 *batman* of dry land in a rural village in Yarkand oasis. He paid 470 silver *yuan* for it (Appendix D-1, case no. 7).

64. Millward, *Beyond the Pass*, pp. 210–11.

65. GPYSA, pp. 466–47.

66. Hori Sunao, "Shindai Kaikyō no suiri kangai: 19–20 seiki no Yaarukanto wo chūshin to shite"; idem, "Shindai Yarkkando no noson to suiro [The Rural Villages and Canal in Yarkand during the Qing Period]," *Kōnan daigaku kiyō: bungakuhen* 139 (2004), pp. 153–91.

67. Idem, "Turufan no ka-re-zu shōkō [Short Study of the Kariz of Turfan]," in *Nairiku Ajia Nishi Ajia no shakai to bunka* [Society and Culture in Inner Asia and Western Asia], ed. by Mori Masao (Tokyo: Yamakawa shuppansha, 1983), pp. 459–80.

68. MLZZ, QL55/4/1, Toktonidazar's and Niyas's memorial.

69. Wang Shouli and Jinxin Li, *Xinjiang Weiwu'er zu qiyue wenshu ziliao xuanbian,* doc. 005, 1817 (JQ 22).

70. GZSL, vol. 798, QL32/11/dingyou, Edict.

71. MLZZ, JQ5/2/7, MW, vol. 210, pp. 88–96, Fugiyūn and Iskandar's memorial. This information was revealed in 1800, when a group of oasis Muslims brought a charge of corruption against Sultan Khwaja's successor governor in Yangi Hissar, Shah Mansur (Manchu Šamangsur). One item of the charge was that he arbitrarily collected grain, cotton, and alfalfa from an oasis farmer. Shah Mansur claimed that he did so because his family's *mazar* formerly received it from the land. Perhaps the oasis farmers accused him because the original donor had died, and thus the *mazar* did not any longer have the right to collect the due from the land.

72. Ibid., JQ 4/12/17 (1799), Yarkand banshi, Qi-feng-e (MW, vol. 210, p. 17). One can translate this sentence as "Akbeg employed the Muslims with his own power/capital (*beyei hūsun*)"; either way, the essence of the translation remains true. Akbeg used his own resources to employ Muslim workers to complete the irrigation.

73. RZSL, vol. 311, JQ20/10/renzi, Yulian's memorial.

74. MLZZ, JQ1/10/22 (1796), Sioi ji's memorial (MW, 206, p. 70).

75. Of course, the above-mentioned beg petition to use the wildland, probably the government's wildland, does not mean that they encroached on it always with the Qing authority's blessing. For a high profile example, in 1824 it was discovered that Ha-di-er, a descendant of a prominent Muslim ally of the Qing conquest (Khwāja Si Beg), who was staying in Beijing at the time, had encroached on government land in a village (*te-yi*) in Aksu/Ush District through the instigation of his "household servants" (*jiaren*). Ha-di-er's nephew also had encroached on government land for years (SYD/DG, vol. 4, pp. 436–37, doc. 525, DG4/11/27; ibid., p. 295, doc. 1015, DG4/7/R23; ibid., pp. 448–49, doc. 1576, DG4/12/5).

76. MLZZ, QL53/10/23, Investigation of the homicide of Duo-la-te.

77. Songyun, *Qinding Xinjiang shilue* [12 Juan] (hereafter XJShL) (n.p., 1821), vol. 1, "Xinjiang shuidao biao [Table of the Waterways of Xinjiang]," p. 287.

78. HJFL, vol. 80, DG9/4/jisi, Nayancheng's memorial. See also XJZDHB: DG, p. 196, doc. 117 (originally from *Fuxing'a gongdu*).

79. *Ye-er-qiang chengzhuang lishu huihu zhengfu gexiang ce* [Register of City, Villages, Distances, Muslim Households, Regular Tax of Yarkand District], c. 1850s.

80. XYTZ; XJShL.

81. RZSL vol. 71, JQ5/7/xinsi.

82. MLZZ, QL51/12/26, Booceng's memorial; ibid.

83. MLZZ, JQ5/2/7, Fugiyūn and Iskandar's memorial (MW, vol. 210, pp. 88–96).

84. MLZZ, QL51/12/26, Booceng's memorial.

85. Ibid.

86. Ibid.

87. Ibid.

88. Ibid.

89. Ibid.

Chapter 3

1. MQSL, vol. 999, p. 1000, "Zhang-ge-er gonci [Jahāngīr's Deposition],"

2. For a recent study on the *khwaja* wars, see Pan Xiangming, *Qingdai Xinjiang hezhuo panluan yanjiu;* Saguchi Tōru, *Jūhachi-jūkyū-seiki Higashi Torukisutan shakaishi kenkyū;* Newby, *The Empire and the Khanate;* Pan Zhiping, *Zhongya Haohanguo Yu Qingdai Xinjiang.*

3. Laura J. Newby, "'Us and Them' in 18th and 19th Century Xinjiang," in *Situating the Uyghurs between China and Central Asia* (Aldershot, England: Ashgate, 2007); idem, *The Empire and the Khanate,* p. 20.

4. Mullā Mūsa Sayrāmī, *Tārīkhi Hāmīdī* [History of Hāmīd] (modern Uyghur edition), trans. Enver Baytur (Beijing: Millätlär näshriyäti, 1986), p. 149.

5. XJZDHB: DG, doc. 203, DG 27/12/9, Sayingʾaʾs memorial (originally from *Sayingʾa Xinjiang Zougao*).

6. The narrative of this event is based on the information given by the following documents: MLZZ, 3004–015, Booceng, QL49/3/26, Reporting the situation of the people Sarimsaq sent; ibid., 3010–009, QL49/4, Sarimsaqʾs letter; ibid., 3019–024, QL49/5, Sarimsaqʾs letter; ibid., 3009–038, QL49/4/1, Cokto, examining Alima; ibid., 3054–007, Booceng, converting Alimaʾs property into cash; ibid., 3092–009, Booceng, QL50/9/30, Sarimsaqʾs situation; ibid., 3011–014, QL49/4/16, Iletu, examining Sarimsaqʾs messengers; ibid., 3026–002.1, QL49/6, Sarimsaqʾs letter.

7. For early attempts to locate and capture Sarimsaq, see ZGEFL, pt. 3, vol. 10, QL26/2/gengxu, Edict to Grand Councilor; ibid., vol. 19, QL27/12/wuxu, Edict; ibid., vol. 21, QL28/3/ququ, Xinzhuʾs memorial. For a detailed examination of a Qing effort at capturing Sarimsaq from 1761 to 1763, see Kwangmin Kim, "Profit and Protection."

8. For an example of the letter, see MLZZ, QL49/4, Sarimsaqʾs letter to Alima.

9. Valikhanov, "O sostoianii Altyshara," p. 149.

10. The Qing tax register of Yarkand from the late nineteenth century, which features the term in the latter sense, used it as a concept opposite that of "regular Muslim households who do cultivation" (*zhenghu chengzhong huizi*). See *Ye-er-qiang chengzhuang lishu huihu zhengfu gexiang ce.*

11. GZSL, vol. 616, QL25/7/gengxu; ibid., QL25/7/jiayin.

12. Ibid., QL25/7/gengxu.

13. ZGEFL, pt. 3, vol. 7, QL25/11; GZSL, vol. 616, QL25/7/gengxu; GZSL, vol. 616, QL25/7/jiayin, QL25/7/jiayin.

14. XYWJL, vol. 3, "Wushi planluan jilue [Summary Description of the Ush Revolt]"; Zhao Yuhai, "Cong Qingdai Manwen dangʾan kan Wushi shijianʾ shimo [The Beginning

and End of the Ush Incident Shown in the Manchu-language Archival Materials]," *Lishi dang'an* (Historical Archive), 2001, p. 94.

15. See the Sultan Yaladin case examined above. MLZZ, QL60/2/25, Yungboo's memorial (MW, vol. 202, pp. 379–92). As for the widespread slave trade and trafficking in this region, see M. N. Shahrani, *The Kirghiz and Wakhi of Afghanistan: Adaptation to Closed Frontiers and War* (Seattle: University of Washington Press, 2002), pp. 29–32; for slavery in the oasis of Eastern Turkestan, see Newby, "Bondage on Qing China's Northwestern Frontier," pp. 968–94.

16. For examples, see MLZZ, JQ14/4/21, Khotan military governor (*bangban dachen*) Sulefang'a's memorial (MW, vol. 224, pp. 175–76); MLZZ, JQ25/9/12, Khotan military governor (*banshi dachen*) Xilinbu's memorial (MW, vol. 240, pp. 283–84).

17. MLZZ, QL53/2/24, Batur Sart's deposition.

18. For examples of the Kirghiz raids on the caravan merchants during the early Qing rule, see GZSL, vol. 627, QL25/12/dingyou, Edict; ibid., vol. 628, QL26/l/guichuo, Edict to Grand Councilors. The Qing governors handled these robberies with unusual severity. They immediately executed the leader of the robbery and cut off the hands of a participant, according to "Muslim law" *(huifa)*. The Qing returned all the stolen commodities to the merchants.

19. Valikhanov, "Ocherki Dzhungarii [Sketches of Zungharia]," in *Izbrannye Proizvedeniia* (Moskva: Izd-vo "Nauka," Glav. red. vostochnoï lit-ry, 1986), p. 283.

20. Beatrice Forbes Manz, "Central Asian Uprisings in the Nineteenth Century: Ferghana under the Russians," *Russian Review* 46:3 (1987), p. 269, fn. 4. Valikhanov notes its meaning as a "merchant" from the oasis, when he relays a Kirghiz chieftain's mention of the following: "I have Sarts (merchants) living with me," to refer to caravan merchants' visits to his camp. Valikhanov, "Ocherki Dzhungarii," p. 281.

21. However, the *manap* themselves seem not originally to have been high-ranking aristocrats. The meaning of the word was "white bones," in contrast to the "black bones of sultans." Valikhanov, "Ocherki Dzhungarii," p. 283.

22. He was also an agriculturalist. Valikhanov ran into Bursuk again at the Djity-Uguz River. The latter had come to the area with his Kadyuk tribesmen to gather a harvest, probably corn, as Valikhanov, while approaching the river, saw half-naked Kirghiz employed in its cultivation. There, the Russian's party (comprising Khoqandian, Bukharan, as well as Kashgarian caravans) hired Buruk as a safeguard against Kirghiz attacks. But later, the group was attacked nevertheless. At that, Bursuk left the caravan without receiving the promised gifts. Ibid., p. 292.

23. Ibid., p. 283.

24. For records on the Galcha, see HJFL, vol. 34, DG6/11/wuzi; ibid., DG6/11/yisi; for a record on E-luo-si, see ibid., vol. 43, DG7/5/gengzi.

25: GZSL, vol. 627, QL25/12/dingyou, Edict; ibid., vol. 628, QL26/l/guichuo, Edict to Grand Councilors.

26. Kwangmin Kim, "Profit and Protection," pp. 615–18.

27. Saguchi Tōru, *Jūhachi-jūkyū-seiki Higashi Torukisutan shakaishi kenkyū*, p. 410.

28. For the importance of the China trade in the rise of Khoqand, see ibid.; Newby, *The Empire and the Khanate*, pp. 45–50; Scott C. Levi, "The Ferghana Valley at the Cross-roads of World History: The Rise of Khoqand, 1709–1822," *Journal of Global History* 2:2 (July 2007), pp. 213–32.

29. A. N. Kuropatkin, *Kashgaria, Eastern or Chinese Turkistan: Historical and Geographical Sketch of the Country, Its Military Strength, Industries, and Trade*, trans. Walter E. Gowan (Calcutta: Thacker Spink and Co., 1882), p. 135. Newby, *The Empire and the Khanate*, p. 47; Indeed, the Qing Empire was willing to intervene in the regional military conflict in the early period of their rule there. In 1763, for instance, a small Central Asian country, Bolor, successfully involved the Qing Empire in the regional military struggle with Badakhshan, and took back a region occupied by Badakshan ruler. See GZSL, vol. 677, QL27/12/guichou, Edict; ZGEFL, pt. 3, vol. 22, QL28/6/gengyin.

30. Susanna S. Nettleton, "Ruler, Patron, Poet: Umar Khan in the Blossoming of the Khanate of Qoqand, 1800–1820," *International Journal of Turkish Studies* 2:2 (1981), pp. 127–40; Newby, *The Empire and the Khanate*, pp. 45–50; Pan Zhiping. *Zhongya Haohanguo yu Qingdai Xinjiang* [Khoqand in Central Asia and Xinjiang during the Qing Period] (Beijing: Zhongguo shehui kexue chubanshe, 1991), pp. 71–80; Saguchi Tōru, *Jūhachi-jūkyū-seiki Higashi Torukisutan shakaishi kenkyū*, p. 388.

31. ZGEFL, pt. 3, vol. 21, QL28/3/renshen. Yonggui's memorial; GZSL, vol. 683, QL28/3/guiyou; ZGEFL pt. 3, vol. 21, QL28/3/guiyou; GZSL 710, QL29/5/guihai, nashi-tong's memorial; Pan Zhiping. *Zhongya Haohanguo yu Qingdai Xinjiang*, pp. 72–73; Saguchi Tōru, *Jūhachi-jūkyū-seiki Higashi Torukisutan shakaishi kenkyū*, pp. 355–60.

32. Saguchi Tōru, *Jūhachi-jūkyū-seiki Higashi Torukisutan shakaishi kenkyū*, p. 388.

33. Nayancheng, *Na Wenyigong Zouyi*, vol. 80 DG8/11/22; HJFL, vol. 4, DG1/10/dinghai; XZSL, vol. 24, Wulong'a's memorial. The Khoqand khanate also used another Kirghiz tribe, the Qartegin, as a source of its standing army; Saguchi Tōru, *Jūhachi-jūkyū-seiki Higashi Torukisutan shakaishi kenkyū*, pp. 361–2.

34. *Tārīkhi Shahrukhī*, 147a, in B. A. Akhmedov, *Iz Istorii Srednei Azii I Vostochnogo Turkestana XV-XIX vv* [From the History of Central Asia and Eastern Turkestan, 15th to 19th Century] (Tashkent: Izd-vo "Fan" Uzbekskoi SSR, 1987), p. 163.

35. Henry Walter Bellew, "History of Kashgar," in Forsyth, *Report of a Mission to Yarkund in 1873*, p. 182; Valikhanov, "O sostoianii Altyshara," p. 150; For the transformation of the Naryn River area, see HJFL, vol. 63, DG8/5/jihai wulong'a memorial.

36. Valikhanov, "O sostoianii Altyshara," 151.

37. The Naqshbandī Order was known for its charity. Much spiritual and political influence could be gained among the Central Asian population through the good deeds of feeding the poor, giving them jobs, and organizing them for land reclamation projects (Manz, "Central Asian Uprisings in the Nineteenth Century"). Jahāngīr Khwaja could

focus the attention of his associates in this regard, particularly on the plight of the up-rooted people in the mountains, caused by the infidel "Chinese" and their beg cohorts, and on the need of their charity.

38. MQSL, gengbian, p. 2004, DG6/5/22 (1826), Ministry of Households, "Copying Imperial Edict for Grand Secretariats."

39. Valikhanov, "O sostoianii Altyshara," p. 149.

40. Ch. Ch. Valikhanov, "Dnevnik poezdki na Issyk-Kul," in *Izbrannye Proizvedeni-ia* (Moskva: Izd-vo "Nauka," Glav. red. vostochnoĭ lit-ry, 1986), p. 46. For the growing opium production and trade in Xinjiang, see David Bello, "Opium in Xinjiang and Be-yond," in *Opium Regimes: China, Britain, and Japan, 1839–1952* (Berkeley: University of California Press, 2000), pp. 127–51.

41. For instance, the khwaja followers transported in and out of the Kashgari-an oasis counterfeit *pul* coins, the quintessential item of the contraband trade; such coin was sought from the donations the *khwajas'* supporters solicited in the oasis. For a discussion of the contraband trade of counterfeit coins in Southeast Asia in the nineteenth century, see Eric Tagliacozzo, *Secret Trades, Porous Borders: Smuggling and States along a Southeast Asian Frontier, 1865–1915* (New Haven: Yale University Press, 2005).

42. The beg would purchase twenty-eight to thirty-two bolts with the silver. He would give Murmet five bolts of satin and keep the rest. MLZZ, QL55/8/21, Itki's memo-rial (MW, vol. 189, pp. 257–62).

43. Valikhanov, "O sostoianii Altyshara," p. 161. As a result, the *khwaja*s generally may have had quite a financial basis underlying their survival, and more. By the time another *khwaja* war (the Wali Khan Khwaja War) took place in 1857, observers were shocked to find the rebels so well armed.

44. Kuropatkin, *Kashgaria, Eastern or Chinese Turkistan*, p. 135.

45. Valikhanov, "O sostoianii Altyshara," p. 151.

46. Ibid.

47. MQSL, "Zhang-ge-er gonci [Jahāngīr Deposition]," *gengbian*, pp. 999–1000.

48. Valikhanov, "O sostoianii Altyshara," p. 154.

49. Pan Xiangming, *Qingdai Xinjiang hezhuo panluan yanjiu*, pp. 115, 120. For this reason, the family and Kirghiz followers of Jahāngīr held a personal grudge toward Ish-āq. However, Mullā Sayrāmī relates that he was courteous in capturing Jahāngīr Khwaja. According to him, Ishāq pursued Jahāngīr from behind in a place called Alai. Realizing the futility of escaping from the Qing troops, the Khwaja asked Ishāq to tie his hands and bring him to the Chinese commander. Ishāq refused, weeping, saying that he could not do it. The Khwaja then tied his own hands with his handkerchief, and asked Ishāq to carry him by holding one end of it. Ishāq followed suit. Sayrāmī, *Tārīkhi āminiyä*, p. 34.

50. Nayancheng, *Na Wenyigong Zouyi*, vol. 78, DG8/10/5.

51. XJZDHB: DG, pp. 41–42, doc. 15, DG8/12/28, Nayancheng and Wulong'a's me-

morial; Saguchi Tōru, *Jūhachi-jūkyū-seiki Higashi Torukisutan shakaishi kenkyū*, p. 459.

52. *Tārīkhi Shahrukhī*,147b–48a, in Akhmedov, *Iz Istorii Srednei Azii I Vostochnogo Turkestana XV-XIX vv*, pp. 163–64; Sayrāmī, *Tārīkhi Hāmīdī*, pp. 148–49; idem, *Tārīkhi āminiyä*, p. 31.

53. For a detailed explanation of Nayancheng's reform measures, see Saguchi Tōru, *Jūhachi-jūkyū-seiki Higashi Torukisutan shakaishi kenkyū*; Newby, *The Empire and the Khanate*; for major primary materials for the Nayancheng reform, see the collections of memorials and reports by Nayancheng and his associated Qing military governors in XJZDHB: DG.

54. XJZDHB: DG, doc.15, DG8/7/3, Nayancheng's memorial.

55. Ibid., doc. 79, p. 164, DG15/r6/6 (1835) (from *Xilang'a Zougao*).

56. Newby, *The Empire and the Khanate*, pp. 138–41; Millward, *Beyond the Pass*, pp. 106–9.

57. Nayancheng, *Na Wenyigong Zouyi*, vol. 77, DG9/1/12; ibid., vol. 79, DG9/2/5; XZSL, vol. 151, DG9/2/wuyin, Edict to Grand Secretariat; Viacheslav S. Kuznetsov, *Ekonomicheskaia Politika Tsinskogo Pravitel'stva v Sin'tsiane v Pervoi Polovine XIX veka* [The Economic Policy of the Qing Government in Xinjiang in the First Half of the Nineteenth Century] (Moscow: AN SSSR, 1973), pp. 136–37; Saguchi Tōru, *Jūhachi-jūkyū-seiki Higashi Torukisutan shakaishi kenkyū*, pp. 374–75.

58. For detailed studies of this trade system, see Newby, *The Empire and the Khanate*, pp. 142–43; Millward, *Beyond the Pass*, pp. 92–101.

59. The reason why the Qing continued to invite the Kirghiz to trade in Kashgar in spite of their participation in the Jahāngīr War, Valikhanov noted, was the high price of livestock, especially sheep. The Qing had to rely on them to bring in livestock continually to stabilize both the cost of livestock and the cost of financing its military. Valikhanov, "O sostoianii Altyshara," pp. 154–55.

60. Ibid., p. 155.

61. Ibid., p. 154.

62. XZSL, vol. 151, DG9/2/wuyin.

63. Ibid., vol. 154, DG9/3/yimao.

64. Nayancheng, *Na Wenyingong Zouyi* [Collection of Memorials of Wenyingong, Nayancheng], vol. 79, DG9/2/5.

65. Saguchi Tōru, *Jūhachi-jūkyū-seiki Higashi Torukisutan shakaishi kenkyū*, pp. 499–504. Khoqand was also expanding south into Sariqol during this time.

66. Ibid., pp. 482–83; Nayancheng, *Na Wenyigong Zouyi*, vol. 79, DG9/2/5.

67. Valikhanov, "O sostoianii Altyshara," p. 156.

68. Ibid., p. 155.

69. *Tārīkhi Shahrukhī*, 43b and 152a, in Akhmedov, *Iz Istorii Srednei Azii I Vostochnogo Turkestana XV-XIX vv*, pp. 166, 168. This document also mentions that the Khoqand ruler obtained the right to collect an "alms tax" (*zakat*) and customs duties (*baj*) from

the Muslim merchants through his own tax agents stationed in Kashgar. However, the negotiation regarding the transfer of the tax right and also the reopening of Kashgar's trade with the Khoqand Muslims did not happen during the war. They began after the conclusion of the war, and will be discussed in more detail in the next chapter.

70. Valikhanov, "O sostoianii Altyshara," p. 155; Bellew, a nineteenth-century British observer, relays that Yūsuf, a peace-oriented *akhund* living in Bukhara, was initially reluctant to participate in the war and later regretted that the Khoqand had disturbed the Muslims in Kashgaria during the Yūsuf War (Bellew, "History of Kashgar," p. 184). For a modern scholarly articulation of this position, see Saguchi Tōru, *Jūhachi-jūkyū-seiki Higashi Torukisutan shakaishi kenkyū*, pp. 480, 482. In particular, Saguchi emphasized the Khoqand khan's commercial motivation to reopen the China trade, and considered the Yūsuf War a mercantilist war.

71. V. P. Nalivkin, *Histoire du khanat de Khokand* (Paris: E. Ledoux, 1889), p. 160.

72. Saguchi, however, dismisses this information, noting that the Yūsuf War broke out only two years after the Jahāngīr War. Therefore, it is doubtful that Yūsuf could have again recuperated his power base, mobilized the "White Cap" Muslims and the Kirghiz, and organized the army of the holy war. Saguchi Tōru, *Jūhachi-jūkyū-seiki Higashi Torukisutan shakaishi kenkyū*, pp. 475, 477.

73. Bellew, "History of Kashgar," p. 184; Valikhanov, "O sostoianii Altyshara," p. 156. During the war, the Khoqandians also seized five hundred Chinese, a large collection of arms, and a considerable quantity of tea and silver.

74. Valikhanov, "O sostoianii Altyshara," pp. 149–51.

75. XJZDHB: DG, p. 107, doc. 55, Changling's memorial (from *Chang wenyang gong banli shanhuo zuoyi*); *Junjichu lufu zouzhe, Waijiao lei, Zhong-E guanxi* (Memorial Copies from the Grand Council Reference Collection, Diplomatic Relations, Sino-Russian Relations), DG12/3/13 (quotation from Newby, *The Empire and the Khanate*, pp. 189–90).

76. Saguchi Tōru, *Jūhachi-jūkyū-seiki Higashi Torukisutan shakaishi kenkyū*, p. 471.

77. XZSL, vol. 180, DG10/11/xinsi, Edict.

78. Valikhanov, "O sostoianii Altyshara," p. 156.

79. For the population growth in Eastern Turkestan, see Hori Sunao, "Jūhachi-nijū seiki Uiguru joku jinko shiron [Population of Uyghurs from the Eighteenth to the Twentieth Centuries]," *Shirin* 60:4 (1977), pp. 111–28.

Chapter 4

1. As for Bellew's and Valikhanov's records on the Zuhūr al-Dīn reign, see Bellew, "History of Kashgar," p. 185; Valikhanov, "O sostoianii Altyshara," p. 157.

2. The study on Qing rule in Eastern Turkestan during the nineteenth century is framed within the narrative of Qing-Khoqand relations. Newby, *The Empire and the Khanate*; Saguchi Tōru, *Jūhachi-jūkyū-seiki Higashi Torukisutan shakaishi kenkyū*. There is no systematic study on the transformation of oasis society during this period. A

major exception to this was the Japanese historian Hori Sunao's studies on the nine-teenth-century social and economic history there. Hori Sunao, "Shinchono Kaikyo tochi ni tsuiteno nisan mondai—Yarukando no ichi shiryo no kento wo tsuite," *Shigaku Zasshi* 88:3 (1979), pp. 273–308, 409–10; idem, "Kaikyō hankachō," pp. 23–43; idem, "Torufan no kaishi dachi," *Kōnan daigaku kiyō: bungakuhen* 109 (1998), pp. 64–84; idem, "Oki bunsho no beku dachi [The Begs Appearing on the Oki Documents]," *Kōnan daigaku kiyō: bungakuhen* 129 (2002), pp. 1–33; idem, "Shindai Yarkkando no noson to suiro [The Rural Villages and Canal in Yarkand during the Qing Period]," *Kōnan daigaku kiyō: bungakuhen* 139 (2004), pp. 153–91; idem, "Turufan no ka-re-zu shōkō [Short Study of Kariz of Turfan]," *Nairiku Ajia Nishi Ajia no shakai to bunka*, ed. by Mori Masao (Tokyo: Yamakawa shuppansha, 1983), pp. 459–80.

3. For recent studies on the agrarian colonies in Xinjiang during the Qing Period, see Hua Li, *Qingdai Xinjiang nongye kaifa shi;* Zhang Anfu, *Xiyu tunken renwu lungao* [The People Who Were Involved in the Development of Agrarian Colonies] (Beijing: Zhongguo nongye chubanshe, 2011); idem, *Qingdai yilai Xinjiang tunken yu guojia anquan yanjiu* [Study on the Agrarian Colonies and the State Security in Xinjiang since the Qing Dynasty] (Beijing: Zhongguo nongye chubanshe, 2011); Zhao Yuzheng, *Sichou zhi lu tunken yanjiu* [Study on the Agrarian Colonies of the Silk Road] (Wulumuqi: Xinjiang renmin chubanshe, 1996); Wang Xilong, *Qingdai xibei tuntian yanjiu.* For a specific study on agrarian colonies in Eastern Turkestan during the post–*khwaja* war period, see Yin Qing, "Shijiu shiji zongye Xinjiang nongkan shiyue de Fazhan [The Development of the Farming and Land Reclamation in Mid-nineteenth-century Xinjiang]," *Xinjiang shehui kexue* 6 (1986), pp. 49–62. Collectively, these studies provide excellent overviews of the *tuntian* system, as well as Qing policy in the implementation of the institution. However, any examination of actual operations of the agrarian colonies in the oasis and the local actors' agency in the process is rare.

4. XZSL, vol. 195, DG11/8/renyin, Edict; idem, vol. 199, DG11/10/renyin, Edict. XJZDHB: DG, p. 93, doc. 47, DG11/11/26, Changling's and Yulin's memorial (from *Chang wenyang gong banli shanhuo zuoyi*). According to the Changling memorial, the Khoqand khan initially proposed the resumption of their trade in Kashgar only to Zuhūr al-Dīn but not to the Qing military governors.

5. XJZDHB: DG, p. 189, doc. 105, DG17 (exact date unknown), Fuxiang'a's letter to Acting Yarkand Cancan dachen Lianjing (from *Fuxing'a Gongdu*).

6. HJFL, vol. 69, DG8/8/dinghai, Nayancheng, Yang Fang, and Wulong'a's memorial; idem, vol. 75, DG8/12/guise, Nayancheng and Wulong'a's memorial. Among them, Nayancheng expelled 108 households immediately, because they had lived less than ten years in the district at that time. Those who had lived more than ten years in Kashgar constituted 607 households, of which Nayancheng expelled 15 immediately. As for the size of an oasis Muslim household, see Hori Sunao, "Jūhachi-nijū seiki Uiguru joku jinko shiron," pp. 111–28.

7. Bichang, *Shoubian jiyao; Ye-er-qiang shoucheng jilue* [Outline Line of Frontier Defense; Record of Defense of the City of Yarkand], 1839.

8. XJZDHB: DG, p. 73, doc. 41, DG11/1/15, Changling's memorial (originally from *Chang wenyang gong banli shanhuo zuoyi*).

9. Forsyth, *Report of a Mission to Yarkund in* 1873, p. 185; Valikhanov, "O sostoianii Altyshara," pp. 156–57.

10. "Customs Duties," *Encyclopædia Iranica*, vol. 6 (London: Routledge and K. Paul, 1982), pp. 470–75. During the 'Ālim Khān (r. 1799–1811), beg officials received a commission from the Andijan merchants and asked the Qing administration for tax exemption on behalf of merchants. Begs reported the Andijans as their underlings in order to do so. Saguchi Tōru, *Jūhachi-jūkyū-seiki Higashi Torukisutan shakaishi kenkyū*, p. 387.

11. This claim prompted scholars such as Joseph Fletcher to thus define this arrangement as the establishment of the first unequal treaty between the Qing and an outside power, anticipating the future Qing-European relations. Within the context of Fletcher's analysis, the Qing Empire became disadvantaged in this arrangement, because they lost the right to tax people within their lawful (imperial) domain. For this interpretation, see Fletcher, "The Heyday of the Ch'ing Order in Mongolia, Sinkiang, and Tibet." For a detailed examination of the Qing-Khoqand agreement on the basis of Chinese sources, see Saguchi Tōru, *Jūhachi-jūkyū-seiki Higashi Torukisutan shakaishi kenkyū*, pp. 488–95; for the most recent examination of the Qing-Khoqand "treaty" on the basis of Central Asian and European sources, see Newby, *The Empire and the Khanate*, pp. 192–206.

12. XZSL, vol. 262, DG/15/1/wuyin, Edict.

13. Valikhanov, "O sostoianii Altyshara," p. 157; Forsyth, *Report of a Mission to Yarkund in* 1873, p. 185; HJFL, vol. 52, DG7/10/yimao, Edict to Grand Councilors; XJZDHB: DG, doc. 47, Changling and Yulin's memorial, DG11/11/26 [originally from *Chang wenyang gong banli shanhuo zuoyi*].

14. Valikhanov, "O sostoianii Altyshara," pp. 129, 157; Forsyth, *Report of a Mission to Yarkund in* 1873, p. 185.

15. Forsyth, *Report of a Mission to Yarkund in* 1873, p. 185.

16. For a few examples, see the case of Ishāq, Zuhūr al-Dīn's predecessor as governor of Kashgar, who donated funds to build an auxiliary Qing military base near the main city of Kashgar in late 1829 (XZSL, vol. 160); see also the case of a timber donation by Governor Mai-ma-te Ma-ha-su-te, for rebuilding the Qing military base and administrative *yamen* buildings of the city of Yangi Hissar in 1832, after the Yūsuf War. In addition to that, he also recruited five hundred Muslim laborers for the project. See XJZDHB: DG, pp. 125–28, doc. 63, Bichang's memorial, DG12/10/13 (from *Bichang Huijiang zougao*). See also the annual donation of 1,200 *shi* of grain by the governor of Khotan, Ismail (Yi-si-ma-yi-er), for food for the Qing soldiers after 1831, following the Yūsuf War; XJZDHB: DG, pp. 96–99, doc. 48, Changling and Yulin's memorial. See also Yarkand Hākim Ismail's son Ma-pu-su's reception of a fifth-rank button and flow-

er feathers, and Sang Beg Yi-bu-la-yi-mu Mai-ma-sa-la's reception of flower feathers because of their contributions in building the city wall and a military camp building in 1845. See XZSL, vol. 415.

17. Valikhanov, "O sostoianii Altyshara," p. 157.

18. XJZDHB: DG, pp. 96–99, doc. 48, DG11/12/11, Changling's memorial (from *Chang wenyang gong banli shanhuo zuoyi*).

19. Hori Sunao, "Shindai shinkyō no kahei seido—furu (pul) chūzōsei," pp. 581–602; Millward, *Beyond the Pass*, p. 61.

20. Kim, "Saintly Brokers," pp. 414–30.

21. Yin Qing, "Shijiu shiji zongye Xinjiang nongkan shiyue de fazhan"; Millward, *Beyond the Pass*, pp. 226–31; Saguchi Tōru, *Jūhachi-jūkyū-seiki Higashi Torukisutan shakaishi kenkyū*, p. 239.

22. XJZDHB: DG, pp. 163–64, doc. 79, Xilang'a's memorial, DG15/r6/6 (from *Xilang'a zougao*); ibid., p. 173, doc. 87, Fuxing'a's letter, DG17/10/20 (from *Fuxing'a Gongdu*).

23. Ibid., pp. 96–99, doc. 48, DG11/12/11, Changling's memorial (from *Chang Wenyanggong banli shanhuo zuoyi*).

24. Hori Sunao, "Shindai shinkyō no kahei seido—furu (pul) chūzōsei," p. 593.

25. Ibid., pp. 592–96.

26. XZSL, vol. 409, DG24/9/dinghai, Edict to Grand Councilors.

27. XJZDHB: DG, pp. 113–16, doc. 56, Changling's memorial, DG8/1/8; XZSL, vol. 130, DG7/11/wuwu, Edict; HJFL, vol. 53, DG7/11/yisi, Changling's memorial; ibid., vol. 55, DG7/12/guiyou, Wulong'a's memorial.

28. Nayancheng, *Na Wenyigong zouyi*, vol. 76, DG8/9/15; XZSL, vol. 145, DG8/10/guiwei, Edict; Nayancheng, *Na Wenyigong zouyi*, vol. 76, DG8/10/17; ibid., vol. 78, DG8/8/12.

29. The *bederege* had previously been involved in the agrarian development of Ili Valley under the Zunghar rulers in the seventeenth and early eighteenth centuries. See Onuma Takahiro, "The Development of the Junghars and the Role of Bukharan Merchants."

30. XJZDHB: DG, doc. 56, Changling's memorial, DG8/1/8 (1828) (from *Changling zougao*); XZSL, vol. 66, DG4/3/jiaxu, Yongqin's memorial.

31. Ibid., p. 36, doc. 77, Nayancheng and Wu-lo ng-a's memorial, DG8/9/15 (1828).

32. HJFL, p. 3688, Nayancheng's memorial. This 3,000 *liang* investment in irrigation development in the *tuntian* in Ush was substantial. For a point of comparison, the Qing administration spent a total of 166,000 *liang* of silver in the entire reconstruction of the infrastructure, including a new fortress, administrative buildings, and other military facilities, in Kashgar, Khotan, Yangi Hissar, and Yarkand after the Jahāngīr War.

33. For an example of the collection rate of the Ush *tuntian,* see Nayancheng, *Na Wenyingong Zouyi,* vol. 76, DG8/4/9; HJFL, vol. 61, DG8/3/yisi; ibid., vol. 64, DG8/5/dingsi. Notably, in contrast to other cases in which the Qing imposed a tax on each

household (*hu*), they did so on each person in the case of the Daheyan *tuntian*. Given that during the Qing Period a household meant an adult male over twelve years old who was supposed to pay tax and corvée for the state, plus his family members, one can assume that the thousand people (*kuo*) on which the 2 *shi* of grain was imposed in 1831 were all adult males; the numbers of women, children, and elderly men may or may not have been included in the figure.

34. HJFL, vol. 55, DG7/2/guiyou, Wulong'a's memorial.

35. XJZDHB: DG, pp. 161–62, doc. 77, Kashgar Banshi lingdui dachen Xilang'a's letter to Yarkand Cancan dachen Xing-de, DG15/2 (1835) (from *Xilang'a Zougao*).

36. Ibid. Zuhūr al-Dīn's payment came from the grain that his *yanqi* produced in the settlement.

37. Ibid. It was not clear from the source how Zuhūr al-Dīn and the villagers apportioned the reduced tax burden between them.

38. Ibid., p. 194, doc. 115, Fuxing'a's letter to the Seal Office clerk (*zhangjing*) Liande, DG18/3/21 (from *Fuxing'a Gongdu*).

39. Ibid.

40. One can synthesize these two statements (the 1835 and 1838 versions), if we are to believe Zuhūr al-Dīn. The land reclamation project in the Cha-la-gen area was abandoned only two years after its beginning in 1828, amid the political instability after the Yūsuf War in 1830. But Zuhūr al-Dīn and the one thousand Muslims had to continue to deliver the 2,000 *shi* from the land until 1835. Consequently, he and his associated merchants wanted to pull back from the area. Thus, in 1835, they blamed bad land quality in order to reduce the tax quota to half the previous amount. In 1838, Zuhūr al-Dīn blamed the Yūsuf War.

41. XZSL, vol. 254, DG28/4/gengwu, Edict.

42. XJZDHB: DG, pp. 471–73, doc. 222, Saying'a, DG29/5/28 (1849), Saying's's memorial (from *Saying'a Xinjiang Zougao*).

43. XZSL, vol. 419, DG25/7/dingchou, Grand Secretariat Muzhang'a's memorial.

44. Ibid., pp. 187–90, docs. 104 and 105, DG17 (exact date unknown), Fu-xing-a's letters (from *Fuxing'a Gongdu*).

45. Ibid., pp. 101–3, doc. 51, Chang-ling's and Yu-lin's memorial, DG 12/2/2, regarding the origin of the Ka-la-he-yi *tuntian*.

46. Lattimore, *Pivot of Asia*, pp. 165–66; Hori Sunao, "Turufan no Ka-re-zu shōkō."

47. Hori Sunao, "Kaikyō Gyokubei Kō [Maize in the Muslim Domain]," *Tōyōshi kenkyū* 52:2 (1993), pp. 254–73.

48. Sanada Yasushi, "Oashisu ba-za-ru no seitaienkyū," pp. 207–20; idem, "Mengyō kara mita Kashugaria oashisu shakai no ichi danmen—1870 nendai ni tsuite [One Aspect of the Oasis Society of Kashgaria: Cotton Textile Industry in the 1870s]," *Chūō daigaku Ajia shi kenkyū* 2 (1978), pp. 29–50; idem, "Toshi, noson yuboku," pp. 108–48.

49. For instance, Ūdui's *tongshi* were frequently appointed to the position of beg officials when he was governor of Yarkand District.

50. XJZDHB: DG, p. 189, doc. 105, 1837 (DG17), Acting Yarkand Cancan dachen Lianjing (from *Fuxing'a Gongdu*).

51. Ibid.

52. For examples of increasing social unrest in the oasis in the 1840s, see the following: for the case of the Kirghiz breaking into the Qing border (1845) (XZSL, vol. 417, DG25/5/renshu, Edict; ibid., DG25/5/yichou, Edict); for Kashgar ironsmith A-wa-si's revolt (1845) (ibid., DG25/15/yisi, Edict); Yangi Hissar Muslim Hu-wan's revolt (1845) (ibid., vol. 419, DG25/7/wuchen, Edict); Kirghiz chieftain Di-wa-nian's invasion of Kashgar (1846) (ibid., vol. 433, DG26/8/bingzi, Edict; ibid., vol. 434, DG26/9/yichou, Edict; ibid., vol. 436, DG26/11/jiachen, Edict).

53. Valikhanov, "O sostoianii Altyshara," p. 158.

54. Ibid., pp. 158–59.

55. XJZDHB: DG, pp. 365–66, doc. 195, DG27, Yishan's memorial (from *Yishan zuogao*); for depositions by the begs under suspicion of collaborating with the *khawaja* rebels, see ibid., pp. 371–74, doc. 196, DG27/10/24, A-bu-du-ka-ha-er's deposition.

56. Kuropatkin, *Kashgaria, Eastern or Chinese Turkistan*, p. 147.

57. XJZDHB: DG, p. 346, doc. 185, DG28/11/6, Yishan's memorial.

58. Ibid., pp. 331–32, doc. 176, DG27/10/24, Yishan's memorial.

59. XZSL, DG9/3/dingwei, Edict; Hori Sunao, "Shinchono Kaikyo tochi ni tsuiteno nisan mondai," pp. p. 289–90.

60. XJZDHB: DG, p. 184, doc. 98, DG17/12/15, Fu-xing-a's letter to the Muslim Affair Office clerk (from *Fuxing'a Gongdu*).

61. Hori Sunao, who first noted this development, faulted the Qing for their decision to ruralize the beg system. In his view, the policy concentrated the new beg positions in rural rather than border areas, from which major threats to the regime supposedly came, thus showing the dangerously inward-looking tendency of the imperial court that resulted in its fall. However, in light of this chapter's finding that the major threat to the security of the Qing regime actually came from the rural hinterlands, made volatile because of the intense agrarian development there, one may have to say that the Qing policy direction was essentially sound. See Hori Sunao, "Shinchono Kaikyo tochi ni tsuiteno nisan mondai."

Chapter 5

1. Sayrāmī, *Tārīkhi äminiyä*, pp. 45–47.

2. Millward, *Beyond the Pass*, p. 61.

3. Ibid., pp. 235–38; Hori Sunao, "Shindai shinkyō no kahei seido—furu (pul) chūzō-sei," pp. 581–602.

4. The imperial court also ordered further expansion of the *tuntian,* a measure that had solved the crisis of military financing in the 1830s, by converting government-owned ranches into *tuntian.* SYD/XF, vol. 4, 199, doc. 605, XF4/R7/20 (from circular to resident soldiers).

5. Hori Sunao, "Shindai Shinkyō no kahei seido—furu (pul) chūzōsei," p. 597.

6. Sayrāmī, *Tārīkhi āminiyä*, p. 48.

7. This story later took a new turn, when Khoqand's Khudayar khan dispatched a messenger and claimed that the trouble this time had actually been planned jointly by Wali Khan Khwaja and a certain Divan Quli, not Yusan Khwaja Ishan. The khan vouched that Yusan did not act together with the Wali Khan Khwaja, and asked that Yusan be released. The Qing responded that if the Khoqand would capture and send the Wali Khan Khwaja and Divan Quli to them, they would release Yusan Khwaja. However, the khan did not do so. It seems that the Khudayar khan's accusation of Wali Khan Khwaja as the real instigator of this 1855 violence was fabricated, an excuse that he used to free one of his associates. After all, he could not substantiate his claim. WZSL, vol. 70, XF2/8/renyin, Edict; ibid., vol. 174, XF5/8/guisi, Zha-la-fen-tai's memorial; ibid., XF5/8/guisi, Edict; ibid., XF5/8/yiwei, Zha-la-fen-tai's memorial. For other examples of the local disturbance in this period, see Kashgar ironsmith A-wa-si's revolt in 1845 (XZSL vol. 417, DG25/5/xinsi, Edict); also see Yangi Hissar Muslim, Hu-wan's revolt in 1845 (XZSL, vol. 417, DG25/5/renxu, Edict; ibid., 432, DG26/7/gengxu, Edict).

8. WZSL, vol. 228, XF7/r5/yisi, Edict; SYD/XF, vol. 7, XF7/r/5/20 and XF7/6/10. For an example of violence in Turfan, see ibid., vol. 2, doc. 1031, p. 332, XF2/9/11, Edict.

9. Manz, "Central Asian Uprisings in the Nineteenth Century, pp. 267–81.

10. XJZDHB: DG, pp. 371–74, doc. 196, 1847 (DG27/10/24), A-bu-du-ka-ha-er's deposition (originally from *Yishan Zuogao*).

11. Since beginning his career with the Qing in his hometown area, Aksu District, in 1827, Ahmad had been involved with local agrarian and mining development projects in the oases. As a sixth-rank beg of Aksu, for instance, he purchased grain for the Qing troops during the Jahāngīr War in 1827. In the same year, he also contributed animal hides to clothe the Qing soldiers in the Qing frontier guard posts. MLZZ, DG7/10/24 (MW, vol. 249).

12. SYD/XF, vol. 6, p. 110, doc. 322, XF6/4/26, Edict. For the development of copper mining and smelting facilities in the neighboring Yarkand District and the award to the begs who contributed to the implementation, see ibid., doc. 926, 11/28/XF6.

13. Wu Yuanfeng, "Qing Qianlong Nianjian Xinjiang Xin Pu'er Qian de Zhuzao Liutong Ji Qi Zuoyong [Minting and Circulation of the New Pul Coins during the Qianlong Period and Its Effects]," *Xiyu yanjiu* [Research on Western Regions] 1 (1997), pp. 41–42, 46.

14. SYD/XF, vol. 8, pp. 315–16, doc. 795, 7/4/XF8, Peng Wenzhang's memorial.

15. MLZZ, *Minzu lei*, vol. 8070, no. 39; quoted from Pan Xiangming, *Qingdai Xinjiang hezhuo panluan yanjiu*, p. 191.

16. Forsyth, *Report of a Mission to Yarkund in 1873*, p. 189; Pan Xiangming, *Qingdai Xinjiang hezhuo panluan yanjiu*, p. 192.

17. SYD/XF, vol. 8, pp. 315–16, doc. 795, XF8/7/4, Peng Wenzhang's memorial.

18. Valikhanov, "O sostoianii Altyshara," pp. 159–64; Pan Xiangming, *Qingdai Xinjiang hezhuo panluan yanjiu*, pp. 186–87.

19. E. Denison Ross, *Three Turki Manuscripts from Kashghar* (Lahore: Mufid-i-am Press, 1908), pp. 6–13.

20. Ibid.

21. XJZDHB: DG, pp. 427–28, doc. 203, 1847 (DG27/12/9), Margilan Muslim, Mamu-te's deposition (originally from *Yishan Zuogao*).

22. Valikhanov, "O sostoianii Altyshara," pp. 160, 163.

23. Ibid., pp. 163–64. For the meaning of *chalgurt,* see Forsyth, *Report of a Mission to Yarkund in 1873*, p. 82.

24. Ibid., p. 161. The khwaja troops were divided into banners, with five hundred men under each, commanded by the *pānsad*s (captain of five hundred).

25. Ibid., p. 164.

26. Ibid. Another reason for the Kashgarian dissatisfaction with Wali Khan Khwaja's regime was its disrespect of Kashgar's "national customs," which were different from Khoqandian customs, particularly those distasteful to the Khwaja. Thus, under his rule, the women of Kashgar were ordered, "in imitation of the Andijans, to cover their hair with a white kerchief and not to venture out unveiled. They were also forbidden to plait their hair, and this was strictly enforced by the police." "The males from the age of six were obliged to wear a turban and to frequent the mosques regularly, to which the Kashgarians were not accustomed." Ibid., pp. 162–63.

27. Ibid., p. 164.

28. Ibid.

29. Ibid., pp. 124–25.

30. *Ye-er-qiang chengzhuang lishu huihu zhengfu gexiang ce* , "Ka-na-ta-ta-er Zhuang." Hori estimates that this document was compiled between 1849 and 1854. Hori Sunao, "Shinchono Kaikyo tochi ni tsuiteno nisan mondai," p. 282.

31. The Japanese historian Hori Sunao suggests such a possibility relating to this record, albeit in somewhat different context. He noticed that the population numbers of Yarkand District listed in the tax register ran virtually identical to its 1770s population tally reported in the Qing record, while the amount of its arable land increased twofold during the same period. He inferred that the lack of increase in the population number was the result of an under-reporting by the village community, and deliberately so, based on a reluctance to pay the poll tax (*alban*) to the Qing. That tax, one crucial component of the Qing tax system, was in origin a non-Islamic tax—a tax collected by infidel Inner Asian nomadic rulers. The Muslims considered it a humiliation to pay it. By under-reporting the Muslim population, the Muslim community anticipated avoiding the payment of this particular tax as much as possible. Ibid., pp. 295–301.

32. For instance, a person named Mullā Ro-zi from the Rawatchi settlement in Yar-

kand District accused in the local Islamic court two fellow villagers of selling 4 batman of his land to a merchant from outside the village, without his permission. The Islamic court decided that this case should be investigated, when the buyer, Shaykh Wa-er, come back from trade trip (Shouli Wang and Jinxin Li, *Xinjiang Weiwu'er zu qiyue wenshu ziliao xuanbian*, p. 5, doc. 7, 6/11/1823).

33. In this regard, the oasis landlords' purchases of dry land are interesting (see Khoqandian merchant Du-la-ti-jan Bay's purchase of 2 *batman* of dry land (Appendix D-1, case no 5) and Samsak Sufi's purchase of 12 *charak* of dry land (ibid., case no. 6). Judging from the environmental conditions of the oasis, the dry land was most likely wildland located outside the irrigation network, one that could be considered as the common resource of the oasis villages. Thus, the sale of the common land by oasis merchants and landlords represented an effort to turn it into private property; they may have planned to make it more productive by extending the waterways to it.

34. GZSL, QL24/7/gengwu, Zhaohui's memorial.

35. Ibid., doc. 655, XF9/5/11.

36. SYD/XF, vol. 8, doc. 794, 7/4/XF8, Edict to Grand Councilors; ibid., pp. 315–16, doc. 795, 7/4/XF8, Peng Wenzhang's memorial.

37. Ibid., doc. 1248, XF8/10/13.

38. Ibid., doc. 378, XF8/4/19; ibid., vol. 9, doc. 1162, 8/20/XF9.

39. WZSL, vol. 321, XF10/6/xinwei, Edict to Grand Councilors; SYD/XF, vol. 10, doc. 1044, XF10/6/9. At this time, Ahmad did not hold any official position. He had been relieved of his former duty as governor of Kashgar because of his failure to defend the district against the forces of Walī Khān Khwaja two years earlier.

40. Ibid.

41. WZSL, XF10/12/jisi.

42. Ibid., XF11/1/renzi.

43. Ibid., vol. 342, XF11/3/13, Edict.

44. Ibid., vol. 354, XF11/6/renshen, Edict to Grand Secretariats; ibid., vol. 346, XF11/3/ yisi, Edict to Grand Councilors. Surprisingly, Mianxing was allowed to serve in Xinjiang temporarily, even after he had been officially relieved of his duty. The extremely unstable conditions in the frontier, small and large local episodes of violence in the oasis, made possible his survival and also that of his associate Ahmad. On the excuse that the Qing local administration should prepare provisions to fight against "rebels/bandits" who had just crossed the border in 1861, Mianxing, again without the Qing court's approval, dispatched Ahmad to devise a way to provide military provisions, and to prepare the oasis for defense. The Qing court could only complain after the fact that Ahmad was not the right person for this task because he could heavily exploit the situation and would not be a help in the defense. The court worried that the Muslim would incite disturbance. See WZSL, vol. 355, XF11/6/bingzi, Edict to Grand Councilors; ibid., vol. 354, XF11/6/ renshen, Edict to Grand Councilors.

45. The same Manchu governor later sold the governorship to the highest bidder, a certain Rustam Beg, in greatest likelihood a wealthy landlord or a sojourner merchant of Yarkand. Reportedly, he "bribed the Qing military governor with eight *charak* of gold" [equal in weight to 160 pounds] to secure the position. Bellew, "History of Kashgar," pp. 201–2. The source of this information for Bellew was "personal observation and enquiry" at the time of his visit to the oasis.

46. The places that gained alternative importance as major trading partners of Eastern Turkestan after the fall of the Qing in the 1860s and 1870s, such as Almati, Khoqand, and British India, did not supply silver in such magnitude as to sustain its circulation in the oasis, to the extent that had been formerly possible under the Qing.

47. Forsyth, *Report of a Mission to Yarkund in 1873*, p. 76.

48. Ibid., p. 35.

49. Ibid., p. 33.

50. Ibid.

51. Relating essentially the same information, Valikhanov, who also visited the oasis around that time, described the oasis agriculture similarly, as being in a "state of decline." Valikhanov, "O sostoianii Altyshara," p. 124.

52. Forsyth, *Report of a Mission to Yarkund in 1873*, p. 63.

53. Ibid., pp. 62–63. The Forsyth Mission's report does not specify which period of "Chinese rule" these numbers represented; however, it stands to reason that they reflected the last stage of Qing rule in the 1850s, whose statistics the Yaʻqūb Beg regime had possession of—probably the same set of numbers from which the Yarkand tax register originated. In this regard, it is notable that Valikhanov, who visited Eastern Turkestan in 1858 and 1859, also reported the same statistics about the population of Eastern Turkestan.

54. Ibid., pp. 481–82, 501–9; Sanada Yasushi, "Oashisu ba-za-ru no seitaienkyū"; idem, "Mengyō kara mita Kashugaria oashisu shakai no ichi danmen"; idem, "Toshi, noson yuboku," pp. 108–48.

55. Forsyth, *Report of a Mission to Yarkund in 1873*, p. 496.

56. Ibid., p. 501.

57. Ibid., p. 482.

58. Ibid., pp. 481–82.

59. SYD/TZ, TZ2/5/24, Edict.

60. Sayrāmī, *Tārīkhi Hāmīdī*.

61. Ibid.

62. Regarding Sayrāmī's *Tārīkhi Hāmīdī*, see Kim Hodong, "Wigurŭ Yŏksaga Sairami (1836~1917) ŭi yŏksasŏsure natʻanan jŏntʻonggwa gŭndae [Tradition and Modernity Shown in the History Writing of Uyghur Historian Sairami (1836–1917)]," *Tongyangsahang nyŏngu* [Research on East Asian history] 57 (1997).

Conclusion

1. Forsyth, *Report of a Mission to Yarkund in 1873*, pp. 474–90.

2. Ibid., p. 482.

3. For the structure of the local administration in the oasis under the rule of Ya'qūb Beg, see Kim Hodong, *Holy War in China*, pp. 103–8.

4. Newby, *The Empire and the Khanate*, pp. 250–57.

5. C. Patterson Giersch. "Borderlands Business: Merchant Firms and Modernity in Southwest China, 1800–1920," *Late Imperial China* 35:1 (2014), pp. 38–76.

6. Idem, "A Motley Throng: Social Change on Southwest China's Early Modern Frontier, 1700–1880," *Journal of Asian Studies* 60:1 (2001), p. 74.

7. Hua Li, *Qingdai Xinjiang nongye kaifa shi*, p. 214.

8. John Robert Shepherd, *Statecraft and Political Economy on the Taiwan Frontier, 1600–1800* (Stanford: Stanford University Press, 1993), p. 8.

9. C. Patterson Giersch, *Asian Borderlands: The Transformation of Qing China's Yunnan Frontier* (Cambridge, MA: Harvard University Press, 2006), p. 185.

10. Idem, "A Motley Throng," p. 74.

11. For some major monographs of the New Qing History scholarship, see Mark C. Elliott, *The Manchu Way: The Eight Banners and Ethnic Identity in Late Imperial China* (Stanford: Stanford University Press, 2001); Crossley, *A Translucent Mirror*; Rawski, *The Last Emperors*; Susan Naquin, *Peking: Temples and City Life, 1400–1900* (Berkeley: University of California Press, 2000); Perdue, *China Marches West*; Millward, *Beyond the Pass*. For a work on the Mongol view of the Qing Empire, see Johan Elverskog, *Our Great Qing: The Mongols, Buddhism, and the State in Late Imperial China* (Honolulu: University of Hawai'i Press, 2006). For a work on the borderland elites in the Yunnan frontier under the Qing, see Giersch, *Asian Borderlands*.

12. The following discussion of the development of "military fiscalism" in northern India in the late Mughal period is drawn from Bayly, *Rulers, Townsmen, and Bazaars*; Burton Stein, "State Formation and Economy Reconsidered," *Modern Asian Studies* 19:3 (1985), pp. 387–413; Perlin, "Of White Whales and Countrymen in the Eighteenth-Century Maratha Deccan," pp. 37–41; Washbrook, "Progress and Problems"; idem, "From Comparative Sociology to Global History: Britain and India in the Pre-History of Modernity," pp. 410–43.

13. Bayly, C. A. *Indian Society and the Making of the British Empire* (Cambridge, MA: Cambridge University Press, 1988), pp. 9–13, 47–48.

14. Washbrook, "Progress and Problems," p. 75. For this reason, the earliest anti-colonial movement by Indians—the pivotal Sepoy Rebellion of 1857—took the form of a peasant rebellion, financially supported by the peasants who found themselves displaced in the new agrarian order of growing capitalist commercial agriculture. In the meantime, even at the height of the rebellion and even in the area where the rebellion

held strong sway, the new commercial elites remained staunch supporters of the British Empire.

15. Helen Dunstan, *State or Merchant? Political Economy and Political Process in 1740s China* (Cambridge, MA: Harvard University Asia Center, 2006); Perdue, *China Marches West*, pp. 350–51, 392, 561.

16. Bayly, *Imperial Meridian*; P. J. Marshall, *The Making and Unmaking of Empires: Britain, India, and America, c. 1750–1783* (New York: Oxford University Press, 2005), pp. 267–68; Washbrook, "Progress and Problems," pp. 57–96.

17. For a recent challenge to this geographical bias against the inland area from the fields of South Asian and Central Asian history, see Levi, *India and Central Asia Commerce and Culture, 1500–1800*.

18. Lattimore, *Pivot of Asia*; Su Beihai and Jianhua Huang, *Hami Tulufan Weiwu'er wang lishi*.

19. Zuo Zongtang, *Zuo Zongtang quanji* [Collection of Zong Zongtang's Writings], vol. 7 (Changsha: Yuelu shushe, 1996), pp. 226–27, doc. 2478, memorial.

Bibliography

Selected List of Acronyms and Abbreviations for Source Materials

GPYSA
  Ye-er-qiang banshi dachen Gao Pu simai yushi an [(Corruption) Case of the Grand Minister Superintendent Gao Pu]. In *Qianlong chao chengban tanwu dang'an xuanbian* [Selected Edition of Archival Materials on the Punishment of Corruption in the Qianlong Period].

GZSL *Da Qing Lichao shilu* [Veritable Records of the Qing Dynasty]: Gaozong [Qianlong] chao.

HJFL *Qinding Pingding Huijiang jiaoqin niyi fanglüe* [The Military History of Campaigns for Terminating and Capturing the Descendant of the Rebels].

HJTZ *Huijiang tongzhi* [Comprehensive Gazetteer of the Muslim Domain].

HJZ *Huijiang zhi* [Records on the Muslim Domain].

HJZL *Huiijiang zeli* [Regulation on the Muslim Territory].

MLZZ *Manwen lufu zouzhe* [Manchu Language Memorial Copies from the Grand Council Reference Collection].

MQSL *Ming Qing shiliao* [Primary Source on the Ming and Qing History].

MW Zhongguo di 1 lishi danganguan, and Zhongguo bianjiang shidi yanjiu zhongxin, eds. *Qingdai Xinjiang Manwen dangan huibian* [Collections of the Manchu Language Archival Materials on the Qing Xinjiang].

MZSL *Da Qing lichao shilu* [Veritable Records of the Qing Dynasty]: Muzong [Tongzhi] chao.

RZSL *Da Qing lichao shilu* [Veritable Records of the Qing Dynasty]: Renzong [Jiaqing] chao.

ShZSL *Da Qing lichao shilu* [Veritable Records of the Qing Dynasty]: Shengzu [Kangxi] chao.

SMFL *Qinzheng pingding shuomo fanglüe* [Military History of the (Kangxi Emperor's) Personal Expedition in the Desert].

SYD/DG *Daoguang chao shangyu dang* [Archive of (Qing) Imperial Edicts: Daoguang Period].

Bibliography

SYD/JQ *Jiaqing chao shangyu dang* [Archive of (Qing) Imperial Edicts: Jiaqing Period].

SYD/TZ *Tongzhi chao shangyu dang* [Archive of (Qing) Imperial Edicts: Tongzhi Period].

SYD/XF *Xianfeng chao shangyu dang* [Archive of (Qing) Imperial Edicts: Xianfeng Period].

SZSL   *Da Qing lichao shilu* [Veritable Records of the Qing Dynasty]: Shengzu [Kangxi] Chao and Shizong [Yongzheng] chao.

SZXZ   *Chongxiu Suzhou xin zhi* [Revised Gazetteer of Suzhou].

WGBZ *Qinding waifan Menggu Huibu wanggong biaozhuan* [Tables and Biographies of Mongol and Muslim Princes].

WGBZXZ
Qinding waifan Menggu Huibu wanggong biaozhuan xuzuan [Tables and Biographies of Mongol and Muslim Princes: Sequel].

WZSL   *Da Qing Lichao shilu* [Veritable Records of the Qing Dynasty]: Wenzong [Xianfeng] chao.

XJQYZL
Xinjiang Weiwu'er zu qiyue wenshu ziliao xuanbian [Selected Editions of the Contract Documents of Xinjiang Uyghurs].

XJShL   *Qinding Xinjiang shilue* [Brief Records on Xinjiang].

XJZDHB DG
Qingdai Xinjiang xijian zoudu huibian: Daoguang chao juan [Collection of the Rarely Seen Memorials and Letters on Xinjiang during the Qing Period: Daoguang Period].

XYTZ   *Qinding huangyu Xiyu tuzhi: (Juan Shou, 48 Juan)* [Maps and Records of the Imperial Domain of the Western Regions].

XYWJL
Xiyu wenjian lu [What I Heard and Saw in the Western Regions].

XZSL   *Da Qing Lichao shilu* [Veritable Records of the Qing Dynasty]: Xuanzong [Daoguang] Chao.

ZGEFL*Pingding Zhun'ga'er fanglüe* [Military History of the Pacification of the Zunghar Mongols].

Primary Sources

Chinese

Bichang. *Shoubian jiyao; Ye-er-qiang shoucheng jilue* [Outline (Narrative) of Frontier Defense; Record of Defense of the City of Yarkand], 1839.

Cao Zhenyong et al. *Qinding Pingding Huijiang jiaoqin niyi fanglüe (80 juan)* (HJFL) [The Military History of Campaigns for Terminating and Capturing the Descendants of the Rebels]. 8 vols. Jindai Zhongguo shiliao congkan [Series of primary source on modern Chinese history]. Vols. 86–93. Taipei: Wenhai chubanshe, 1972.

Changjun. *Dunhuang suibi* [An Essay on Dunhuang]. 2 vols. Ca. eighteenth century. Beijing: Yugong xuehui, reprint edition, 1937.

Da Qing huidian (Yongzheng Chao) [Collected Statutes of the Great Qing Dynasty]. 250 vols. Beijing: Neifu, 1732; Taibei: Wenhai chubanshe, reprint edition, 1995.

Da Qing Lichao Shilu [Veritable Records of the Qing Dynasty]. Gaozong [Qianlong] chao (GZSL). Beijing: Zhonghua shu ju, reprint edition, 1985.

———. Muzong [Tongzhi] chao (MZSL). Beijing: Zhonghua shu ju, reprint edition, 1985.

———. Renzong [Jiaqing] chao (RZSL). Beijing: Zhonghua shu ju, reprint edition, 1985.

———. Shengzu [Kangxi] chao (ShZSL). Beijing: Zhonghua shu ju, reprint edition, 1985.

———. Shizong [Yongzheng] chao (SZSL). Beijing: Zhonghua shu ju, reprint edition, 1985.

———. Wenzong [Xianfeng] chao (WZSL). Beijing: Zhonghua shu ju, reprint edition, 1985.

———. Xuanzong [Daoguang] chao (XZSL). Beijing: Zhonghua shu ju, reprint edition, 1985.

Fuheng. *Huang Qing zhigong tu* [Illustration of the Tributaries of the Qing]. 9 vols. Taibei: Taiwan shangwu yinshuguan, reprint edition, 1972.

———. *Pingding Zhun'ga'er fanglüe* [Military History of the Pacification of the Zunghar Mongols] (ZGEFL). 171 vols.: pt. 1:54; pt. 2:85; pt. 3:32. 1770. Taipei: Taiwan shangwuyin shuguan, reprint edition, 1983.

Fuheng Liu Tongxun, and Yu Minzhong. Preface to *Qinding huangyu Xiyu tuzhi* [Maps and Records of the Imperial Domain of the Western Regions] (XYTZ). 48 vols. In *Yingyin Wenyuange siku quanshu* [Photoprint edition of the complete works of the four branches of literature stored in Wenyuange Pavilion]. 1782. Taipei: Taiwan shangwuyin shuguan, reprint edition, 1983.

He'ning. *Huijiang tongzhi* [Comprehensive Gazetteer of the Muslim Domain] (HJTZ). 12 vols. 1804. Taibei: Wenhai chubanshe, reprint edition, 1966.

Huang Wenwei. *Chongxiu Suzhou xin zhi* [Revised New Gazetteer of Suzhou] (SZXZ). 1737. Qing Daoguang Period (1821–50) edition. Taibei: Taiwan xuesheng shuju, reprint edition, 1967.

Kun'gang, ed. *Qinding Da Qing huidian shili (Guangxu chao)*. Shanghai: Shangwu yinshuguan, 1908.

Liang Fen. *Qinbian jilue* [Record of the Northwestern "Qin" Frontier]. 5 vols. Kangxi Period (1662–1722). Xining: Qinghai renmin chubanshe, reprint edition, 1987.

Lifanyuan. *Huiijiang zeli* [Regulation on the Muslim Territory] (HJZL). Early nineteenth century. *Zhongguo xibei wenxian congshu xubian: xibei shidi wenxian juan* [Collection of the Literature on Northwestern China (Introduction): Literature on Northwestern Geography]. Vol. 5. Lanzhou: Gansu wenhua chubanshe, reprint edition, 1999.

———. *Lifanyuan zeli* [Regulation of Lifan Yuan]. Qianlong Period. Imperial Household Department manuscript edition. In *Qingdai Lifanyuan ziliao jilu* [Collections of primary sources regarding Lifan yuan]. Edited by Zhongguo bianjiang shi di yanjiu zhongxin. Beijing: Quanguo tushuguan wenxian suowei fuzhi zhongxin, 1988.

Nayancheng. *Na Wenyigong zhouhuai Huijiang shanhuo zuoyi* [Na Wenyigong's memorials concerning the Planning of Policy toward the Muslim Domain (after the Suppression of the Local Muslim Rebellion)]. Early eighteenth century. Taibei: Wenhai chubanshe, reprint edition, 1968.

———. *Na Wenyingong Zouyi* [Memorials of Na Wenyigong, Nayancheng]. 80 *juan*. Edited by Zhangjia Rong'an. Taibei: Wenhai chubanshe, 1968.

Qi Yunshi. *Qingchao fanbu yaolüe gaoben* [Summary (History) of Vassal Tribes under the Qing Dynasty: Manuscript Version]. Ca. late eighteenth century. Ha'erbin Shi: Heilongjiang jiaoyu chubanshe, reprint edition, 1997.

Qinding waifan Menggu Huibu wanggong biaozhuan [Tables and Biographies of Mongol and Muslim Princes]. (WGBZ). 1779. Taibei: Taiwan shangwu yinshuguan, reprint edition, 1983.

Qinding Waifan Menggu Huibu Wanggong Biaozhuan Xuzuan [Tables and Biographies of Mongol and Muslim Princes: Sequel] (WGBZXZ). In *Guochao qixian leizheng chubian* [Classified Compendium of Antique Documents of the Dynasty, First Compilation]. Edited by Li Huan. Taibei: Wenhai chubanshe, reprint edition, 1966.

Qishiyi. *Xiyu Wenjian Lu* [What I Heard and Saw in the Western Regions] (XYWJL). 8 vols. 1777. Taibei: Wenhai chubanshe, reprint edition, 1966.

Shangyu Dang [Archive of (Qing) Imperial Edicts] (SYD).

———. *Jiaqing Chao Shangyu Dang* [Archive of (Qing) Imperial Edicts: Jiaqing Period] (SYD/JQ). Di 1 ban. 25 vols. Guilin Shi: Guangxi shifan daxue chubanshe, 2008.

———. *Tongzhi Chao Shangyu Dang* [Archive of (Qing) Imperial Edicts: Tongzhi Period] (SYD/TZ). Di 1 ban. 13 vols. Guilin Shi: Guangxi shifan daxue chubanshe, 2008.

———. *Xianfeng Chao Shangyu Dang* [Archive of (Qing) Imperial Edicts: Xianfeng Period] (SYD/XF). Di 1 ban. Vol. 11. Guilin Shi: Guangxi shifan daxue chubanshe, 2008.

———. Zhongguo di 1 li shi danganguan, ed. *Daoguang Chao Shangyu Dang* [Archive of (Qing) Imperial Edicts: Daoguang Period] (SYD/DG). Di 1 ban. 30 vols. Guilin Shi: Guangxi shifan daxue chubanshe, 2008.

Songyun. *Qinding Xinjiang shilue* [Brief Records on Xinjiang] (XJShL). 12 vols. N. p. 1821.

Wang, Shunan, Yuan, Dahua, and Li, Yushu. *Xinjiang tuzhi: [116 juan]*. Taibei: Wenhai chubanshe, 1923.

Wei Yuan. *Shengwu Ji* [Record of the Military Accomplishments of the Sacred (Qing Dynasty)]. 14 vols. Beijing: Guwei tang, 1846; Beijing: Zhonghua shuju, reprint edition, 1984.

Wenda. *Qinzheng Pingding Shuomo Fanglüe* [Military History of the (Kangxi Emperor's) Personal Expedition in the Desert] (SMFL). Beijing: Neifu 1708; Beijing: Quanguo tushuguan wenxian suowei fuzhi zhongxin, reprint edition, 1993.

Wu Fengpei. *Qingdai Xinjiang xijian zoudu huibian: Daoguang chao juan* [Collection of the Rarely Seen Memorials and Letters on Xinjiang during the Qing Period: Daoguang Period] (XJZDHB: DG). Wulumuqi Shi: Xinjiang renmin chubanshe, 1996.

Ye-er-qiang chengzhuang lishu huihu zhengfu gexiang ce [Register of City, Villages, Distances, Muslim Households, Regular Tax of Yarkand District]. Ca. 1850s. N.p.

Yonggui. *Huijiang zhi* [Records on the Muslim Domain]. Edited by Erde Su. Taibei: Chengwen chubanshe, reprint edition, 1968.

Zeng Cheng and Luji Su. *Dunhuang xian zhi* [Local Gazetteer of Dunhuang Prefecture]. 1831. Qing Daoguang ed. Taibei: Taiwan xuesheng shuju, reprint edition, 1967.

Zhongguo di 1 lishi dang'an guan. *Daoguang chao shangyu dang* [Archive of (Qing) Imperial Edicts: Daoguang Period] (SYD/DG). Guilin Shi: Guangxi shifan daxue chubanshe, 2008.

———. *Jiaqing chao shangyu dang* [Archive of (Qing) Imperial Edicts: Jiaqing Period] (SYD/JQ). Guilin Shi: Guangxi shifan daxue chubanshe, 2008.

———. *Qianlong chao chengban tanwu dang'an xuanbian* [Selected Edition of Archival Materials on the Punishment of Corruption in the Qianlong Period]. Beijing: Zhonghua shuju, 1994.

———. *Tongzhi chao shangyu dang* [Archive of (Qing) Imperial Edicts: Tongzhi Period] (SYD/TZ). Guilin Shi: Guangxi shifan daxue chubanshe, 2008.

———. *Xianfeng chao shangyu dang* [Archive of (Qing) Imperial Edicts: Xianfeng Period] (SYD/XF). Guilin Shi: Guangxi shifan daxue chubanshe, 2008.

———. *Ye-er-qiang banshi dachen Gao Pu simai yushi an* [(Corruption) Case of the Grand Minister Superintendent Gao Pu] (GPYSA). In *Qianlong chao chengban tanwu dang'an xuanbian* [Selected Edition of Archival Materials on the Punishment of Corruption in the Qianlong Period]. Beijing Shi: Zhonghua shuju, 1994.

———. *Yongzheng chao qijuzhu ce* [Qiju zhu of the Yongzheng Court]. Beijing: Zhonghua shuju, 1993.

Zhongyang yanjiuyuan Lishi yuyan yanjiusuo. *Ming Qing shiliao* [Primary Source on the Ming and the Qing History] (MQSL). Taipei,1960.

Zuo Zongtang. *Zuo Zongtang quanji* [Collection of Zong Zongtang's Writings]. 15 vols. Changsha: Yuelu shushe, 1996.

Manchu

Manwen lufu zouzhe [Manchu Language Memorial Copies from the Grand Council Reference Collection] (MLZZ).

———. Zhongguo di 1 li shi dang'an guan, and Zhongguo bianjiang shidi yanjiu zhongxin. *Qingdai Xinjiang Manwen Dang'an Huibian* [Collections of the Manchu Language Archival Materials on the Qing Xinjiang] (MW). Guilin: Guangxi shifan daxue chubanshe, 2012.

Bibliography

Muslim

Ross, E. Denison. *Three Turki Manuscripts from Kashghar*. Lahore: Mufid-i-am Press, 1908.

Sayrāmī, Mullā Mūsa. *Tārīkhi āminiyä* [History of Peace]. 1903. Modern Uyghur edition. Translated by Muhämmät Zunun. Ürümchi: Shinjang khälq näshriyäti, 1989.

———. *Tārīkhi Hämīdī* [History of Hämīd]. Modern Uyghur edition. Translated by Enver Baytur. Beijing: Millätlär näshriyäti, 1986.

Shäh Maḥmūd Churäs. *Khronika*. Moskva: Nauka, 1976.

Tazkira-i Khwāja Muhammad Sharīf [Hagiography of Khwaja Muhammad Sharīf]. Anonymous. In G. Jarring Collection: Prov. 73.

Tazkira-yi Mawalana Arsiddin Wali: uzun nusxasi [Hagiography of Mawalana Arsiddin Wali]. Anonymous. In G. Jarring Collection: Prov. 328.

Wang Shouli and Jinxin Li. *Xinjiang Weiwu'er zu qiyue wenshu ziliao xuanbian* [Selected Editions of the Contract Documents of Xinjiang Uyghurs] (XJQYZL). Translated from Turki to Chinese. Xinjiang: Shehui kexueyuan zongjiao suo, 1990.

English and Russian

Forsyth, Thomas Douglas. *Report of a Mission to Yarkund in 1873, under Command of Sir T. D. Forsyth, with Historical and Geographical Information Regarding the Possessions of the Ameer of Yarkund*. Calcutta: Foreign Dept. Press, 1875.

Haydar, Mirza, Ney Elias, and E. Denison Ross. *The Tarikh-i-Rashidi of Mirza Muhammad Haidar, Dughlat, a History of the Moghuls of Central Asia. An English Version Edited, with Commentary, Notes, and Map*. London: S. Low Marston and Company, Ltd., 1895.

Kashgari, Muhammad Sadiq, Robert Shaw, and Ney Elias. *The History of the Khojas of Eastern-Turkistan Summarised from the Tazkira-i-Khwajagan of Muhammad Sadiq Kashghari*. Calcutta: Asiatic Society, 1897.

Naqshbandi, Ahmed Shah. "Route from Kashmir, Via Ladakh, to Yarkand." *Journal of the Asiatic Society of Great Britain and Ireland* 12:1 (1849), pp. 372–85.

Valikhanov, Ch. Ch. (Chokan Chingisovich). "Dnevnik poezdki na Issyk-Kul' [The Diary of a Travel to Issyk Kul]." In *Izbrannye Proizvedeniia*. Moskva: Izd-vo "Nauka," Glav. red. vostochnoĭ lit-ry, 1986.

———. *Izbrannye Proizvedeniia* [Selected Works]. Moskva: Izd-vo "Nauka," Glav. red. vostochnoĭ lit-ry, 1986.

———. "O sostoianii Altyshara ili shesti vostochnykh grodov Kitaĭskoĭ provintsii Nan-lu (Maloĭ Bukharii), v. 1858–59 godakh [Condition of the Altishar or the Six Eastern Cities of Chinese Province, Nanlu (Small Bukhara), 1858–1859]." In *Izbrannye Proizvedeniia* . Moskva: Izd-vo "Nauka," Glav. red. vostochnoĭ lit-ry, 1986.

———. "Ocherki Dzhungarii." In *Izbrannye Proizvedeniia*. Moskva: Izd-vo "Nauka," Glav. red. vostochnoĭ lit-ry, 1986.

———. *Sobranie Sochineniĭ* (Collected Works). 5 vols. Alma-Ata: AN Kaz SSR, 1961–72.

Valikhanov, Ch. Ch., John Michell, Robert Michell, and Mikhail Ivanovich Venyukov. *The Russians in Central Asia: Their Occupation of the Kirghiz Steppe and the Line of the Syr-Daria: Their Political Relations with Khiva, Bokhara, and Kokan: Also Descriptions of Chinese Turkestan and Dzungaria; by Capt. Valikhanof, M. Veniukof, and [Others]*. London: E. Stanford, 1865.

Wathen, W. H. "Memoir of Chinese Tartary and Khoten." *Journal of the Asiatic Society of Bengal* 4:48 (December 1835), pp. 652–64.

———. "Memoir on the U'sbek State of Kokan, Properly Called Khokend (the Ancient Ferghana) in Central Asia." *Journal of the Asiatic Society of Bengal* 3:32 (August 1834), pp. 369–78.

Yule, Henry. "The Journey of Benedict Goës from Agra to Cathay." In *Cathay and the Way Thither*. Vol. 4. London: Asian Educational Services, 1916.

Secondary Sources

Adas, Michael. "Imperialism and Colonialism in Comparative Perspective." *International History Review* 20:2 (1998), pp. 371–88.

———. *Prophets of Rebellion: Millenarian Protest Movements against the European Colonial Order*. Cambridge, UK: Cambridge University Press, 1987.

Akhmedov, B. A. *Iz Istorii Srednei Azii I Vostochnogo Turkestana XV–XIX vv* [From the History of Central Asia and Eastern Turkestan, 15th to 19th Century]. Tashkent: Izd-vo "Fan" Uzbekskoi SSR, 1987.

Anderson, Fred. *Crucible of War: The Seven Years' War and the Fate of Empire in British North America, 1754–1766*. New York: Alfred A. Knopf, 2000.

Bai Shouyi. *Zhongguo Huihui minzu shi* [History of the Chinese Muslims]. Beijing: Zhonghua shuju, 2003.

Balfour, Edward Green. *The Cyclopaedia of India and of Eastern and Southern Asia*. Vol. 2. London: B. Quaritch, 1885.

Bartlett, Beatrice S. *Monarchs and Ministers: The Grand Council in Mid-Ching China, 1723–1820*. Berkeley: University of California Press, 1991.

Bayly, Christopher Alan. *The Birth of the Modern World, 1780–1914: Global Connections and Comparisons*. Blackwell Publishers, 2003.

———. *Imperial Meridian: The British Empire and the World, 1780–1830*. New York: Longman, 1989.

———. *Indian Society and the Making of the British Empire*. Cambridge [Cambridgeshire]; Cambridge University Press, 1988.

———. *Rulers, Townsmen, and Bazaars: North Indian Society in the Age of British Expansion, 1770–1870*. New Delhi: Cambridge University Press, 1983.

Bellew, H. W. "History of Kashgar." In *Report of a Mission to Yarkund in 1873, under Command of Sir T. D. Forsyth, with Historical and Geographical Information Regard-*

ing the Possessions of the Ameer of Yarkund. Edited by Thomas Douglas Forsyth, pp. 105–213. Calcutta: Foreign Department Press, 1875.

Bello, David. "Opium in Xinjiang and Beyond." In *Opium Regimes: China, Britain, and Japan, 1839–1952,* pp. 127–51. Berkeley: University of California Press, 2000.

Braudel, Fernand. *The Perspective of the World: Civilization and Capitalism 15th–18th Century.* Vol. 3. Translated by Siân Reynold, 1st edition. Berkeley: University of California Press, 1992.

———. *The Wheels of Commerce: Civilization and Capitalism 15th–18th Century.* Vol. 2. Translated by Siân Reynold. Berkeley: University of California Press, 1992.

Brophy, David. "King of Xinjiang: Muslims Elites and the Qing Empire." *Etudes Orientales* 25 (2008), pp. 69–90.

———. "The Oirat in Eastern Turkestan and the Rise of Afaq Khwaja." *Archivum Eurasiae Medii Aevi* 16 (2008/9), pp. 1–28.

———. "Taranchis, Kashgaris, and the 'Uyghur Question' in Soviet Central Asia." *Inner Asia* 7:2 (January 2005), pp. 163–84.

Burton, Audrey. *Bukharan Trade, 1558–1718.* Bloomington: Indiana University, Research Institute for Inner Asian Studies, 1993.

———. "Trending to Unite? The Origins of Uyghur Nationalism." Ph.D. diss., Harvard University, 2011.

Cai Jiayi. *Qingdai Xinjiang shehui jingji shi gang* [Outline of the Socio-economic History of Xinjiang during the Qing Period]. Beijing: Renmin chubanshe, 2006.

Chang Te-Chang. "The Economic Role of the Imperial Household in the Ch'ing Dynasty." *Journal of Asian Studies* 31:2 (1972).

Chaudhuri, K. N. *Trade and Civilization in the Indian Ocean: An Economic History from the Rise of Islam to 1750.* Cambridge, UK: Cambridge University Press, 1985.

Chen Feng. *Qingdai junfei yanjiu* [Study on the Military Expenses of the Qing Period]. Wuchang: Wuhan daxue chubanshe, 1992.

Chen Gaohua. *Mingdai Hami Tulufan ziliao huibian* [Collection of Source Materials on Hami and Turfan during the Ming Period]. Wulumuqi: Xinjiang renmin chubanshe, 1984.

Chen Yuan. *Yun Xiyuren huahua kao* [Sinicization of the Central and Western Asians during the Yuan Period]. 1923. Shanghai: Shanghai Guji chubanshe, reprint edition, 2000.

Chia Ning. "The Li-Fan Yuan in the Early Ch'ing Dynasty." Ph.D. diss., Johns Hopkins University, 1992.

Chun Hae-jong. "Sino-Korean Tributary Relations in the Ch'ing Period." In *Chinese World Order.* Edited by John King Fairbank, pp. 90–111. Cambridge, MA: Harvard University Press, 1968.

Clauson, G. L. M. "Eine Kaschgarische Wakf-Urkunde Aus der Khodschazeit Ost-Turkestans. By G. Raquette (Lund Universitets\AA Rsskrift. N.F. Avd. 1. Bd. 26, Nr. 2), 10

× 6½, p. 24, Plate 1. Lund: Gleerup; Leipzig, Harrassowitz, 1930," *Journal of the Royal Asiatic Society* (new series) 63:4 (1931).

Crossley, Pamela Kyle. *The Manchus.* Oxford: Blackwell, 2002.

————. "Manzhou Yuanliu Kao and the Formalization of the Manchu Heritage." *Journal of Asian Studies* 46:4 (1987).

————. "The Rulerships of China." *American Historical Review* 97:5 (1992), pp. 1468–83.

————. *A Translucent Mirror: History and Identity in Qing Imperial Ideology.* Berkeley: University of California Press, 2002.

Crossley, Pamela Kyle, Helen F. Siu, and Donald S. Sutton. *Empire at the Margins: Culture, Ethnicity, and Frontier in Early Modern China.* Berkeley: University of California Press, 2006.

Di Cosmo, Nicola. "Kirghiz Nomads on the Qing Frontier: Tribute, Trade, or Gift Exchange?" In *Political Frontiers, Ethnic Boundaries, and Human Geographies in Chinese History.* Edited by Don J. White and Nicola Di Cosmo. London: RoutledgeCurzon, 2003.

————. "Military Aspects of the Manchu Wars against Caqars." In *Warfare in Inner Asian History (500–1800).* Edited by Nicola di Cosmo, pp. 337–67. Leiden: Brill, 2002.

————. "Qing Colonial Administration in Inner Asia." *International History Review* 20:2 (1998), pp. 286–309.

————. "State Formation and Periodization in Inner Asian History." *Journal of World History* 10:1 (1999), pp. 1–40.

Duara, Prasenjit. *Rescuing History from the Nation: Questioning Narratives of Modern China.* Chicago: University of Chicago Press, 1995.

Duman, L. I. *Agrarnaia Politika Tsinskogo (Manchzhurskogo) Pravitel'stva v Sin'tsziane v Kontse XVIII Veka* [Qing Government's Agrarian Policy in Xinjiang in the Early Eighteenth Century]. Moskva: Izd-vo Akademii nauk SSSR, 1936.

————. "Feodal'nyj Institut Jan'ci v Vostočnom Turkestane v XVIII Veke [Feudal Institution of Yanci, in Eastern Turkestan in the Eighteenth Century]." Zapiski Instituta Institut vostokovedeniia Akademii nauk SSSR, 3, pp. 87–100.

————. "The Qing Conquest of Junggariye and Eastern Turkestan." In *Manzhou Rule in China.* Edited by S. L. Tikhvinsky, pp. 235–56. Moscow: Progress Publishers, 1983.

Dunstan, Helen. *State or Merchant? Political Economy and Political Process in 1740s China.* Cambridge, MA: Harvard University Asia Center, 2006.

Eaton, Richard Maxwell. *The Rise of Islam and the Bengal Frontier, 1204–1760.* Berkeley: University of California Press, 1993.

Elias, Ney. "Introduction." In *The Tarikh-i Rashidi of Mirza Muhammad Haidar, Dughlat: A History of the Moghuls of Central Asia. An English Version Edited, with Commentary, Notes, and Map.* Edited by Mirza Haydar, Ney Elias, and E. Denison Ross. London: S. Low, Marston, and Company, Ltd., 1895.

————. "Introductory Notices." In *The History of the Khojas of Eastern-Turkistan Sum-*

marised from the *Tazkira-I-Khwajagan of Muhammad Sadiq Kashghari*. Edited by Robert Shaw and Ney Elias. Calcutta: Asiatic Society, 1897.

Elverskog, Johan. *Our Great Qing: The Mongols, Buddhism, and the State in Late Imperial China*. Honolulu: University of Hawai'i Press, 2006.

Encyclopædia Iranica. Vol. 6: "Customs Duties," pp. 470–75. London: Routledge and K. Paul, 1982.

Enoki, Kazuo. "Kenryū-chō no sai'iki chōsa to sono seika: Tokuni sai'iki dōbunshi ni Tsuite [On the Qianlong Court's Investigation of the Western Regions and Its Result: Especially on the *Xiyu Tongwen Zhi*]." In *Chūō Ajia Shi* [History of Central Asia]. Edited by Enoki Kazuo Chosakushū henshū iinkai [Committee on Editing Selected Writings of Enoki Kazuo]. Tōkyō: Kyūko Shoin, 1992.

Fairbank, John King. *Trade and Diplomacy on the China Coast: The Opening of the Treaty Ports, 1842–1854*. Stanford: Stanford University Press, 1969.

Fairbank, J. K., and S. Y. Teng. "On the Ch'ing Tributary System." *Harvard Journal of Asiatic Studies* 6:2 (1941), pp. 135–246.

Fairbank, John King, and Ta-tuan Chen. *The Chinese World Order: Traditional China's Foreign Relations*. Cambridge, MA: Harvard University Press, 1968.

Faroqhi, Suraiya, Bruce McGowan, Donald Quataert, Sevket Pamuk, and Halil Inalcik. *An Economic and Social History of the Ottoman Empire, Vol. 2: 1600–1914*. New York: Cambridge University Press, 1997.

Farquhar, David. "Emperor as Bodhisattva in the Governance of the Ch'ing Empire." *Harvard Journal of Asiatic Studies* 38:1 (1978), pp. 5–34.

Fei Xiaotong. "Zhonghua minzu de duoyuan yiti geju [Multi-origin One-body Structure of Chinese Nation]." In *Zhonghua minzu de duoyuan yiti geju* [Multi-origin One-body Structure of Chinese Nation]. Edited by Fei Xiaotong, pp. 1–36. Beijing: Zhong-yang minzu xueyuan chubanshe, 1989.

Fletcher, Joseph. "China and Central Asia, 1368–1884." In *The Chinese World Order*. Edited by John King Fairbank and Ta-tuan Chen, pp. 206–24. Cambridge, MA: Harvard University Press, 1968.

———. "Ch'ing Inner Asia, c. 1800." In *The Cambridge History of China*, Vol. 10, Pt. 1. Cambridge, UK: Cambridge University Press, 1978.

———. "The Heyday of the Ch'ing Order in Mongolia, Sinkiang, and Tibet." In *The Cambridge History of China*, Vol. 10, Pt. 1. Cambridge: Cambridge University Press, 1978.

———. "Turco-Mongolian Monarchic Tradition in the Ottoman Empire." In *Eucharisterion I*. Edited by Ihor Sevcenko and Frank E. Sysyn. Cambridge, MA: Ukrainian Research Institute, 1978.

———. "Les Voies (Turuq) Soufies En Chine [Sufi Orders in China]. In *Les Ordres Mystiques Dans L'islam: Cheminements et Situation Actuelle* [Mystic Orders in Islam: Progress and Current Situation]." Edited by Alexandre Popovic and Gilles Veinstein. Paris: Ecole des hautes etudes en sciences sociales, c. 1986.

Fletcher, Joseph, and Beatrice Forbes Manz. *Studies on Chinese and Islamic Inner Asia.* Aldershot: Variorum, 1995.

Flynn, Dennis O., and Arturo Giráldez. "Cycles of Silver: Global Economic Unity through the Mid-eighteenth Century." *Journal of World History* 13:2 (2002), pp. 391–427.

Frank, Andre Gunder. *The Centrality of Central Asia.* Amsterdam: VU University Press, 1992.

———. *ReOrient: Global Economy in the Asian Age.* Berkeley: University of California Press, 1998.

Giersch, C. Patterson. *Asian Borderlands: The Transformation of Qing China's Yunnan Frontier.* Cambridge, MA: Harvard University Press, 2006.

———. "Borderlands Business: Merchant Firms and Modernity in Southwest China, 1800–1920." In *Late Imperial China* 35:1 (2014), pp. 38–76.

———. "A Motley Throng: Social Change on Southwest China's Early Modern Frontier, 1700–1880." *Journal of Asian Studies* 60:1 (2001), pp. 67–94.

Gladney, Dru. "The Ethnogenesis of the Uighur." *Central Asian Survey* 9:1 (1990), pp. 1–28.

Green, Nile. *Sufism: A Global History.* 1st edition. Malden, MA: Wiley-Blackwell, 2012.

Greif, Avner. *Institutions and the Path to the Modern Economy: Lessons from Medieval Trade.* New York: Cambridge University Press, 2006.

Gross, Jo-Ann. "The Economic Status of a Timurid Sufi Shaykh: A Matter of Conflict or Perception?" *Iranian Studies* 21:1 (1988), pp. 84–104.

Guo Yunjing. *Qingdai shangye shi* [History of Commerce during the Qing Dynasty]. Shenyang: Liaoning renmin chubanshe, 1994.

Hamada Masami. "Chūō yurashia shi no Shūenka-Higashi Torukisutan [Marginalization of Central Eurasia-Eastern Turkestan]." In *Chūō Yūrashia-Shi* [History of Central Eurasia]. Edited by Hisao Komatsu. Tōkyō: Yamagawa shuppansha, 2000.

———. *Higashi Torukisutan Chagataigo seijaden no kenkyū* [Chagatai Language Hagiography of the Muslim Saints of Eastern Turkestan]. Kyōto: Kyōto daigaku daigakuin bungaku kenkyūka, 2006.

———. "Islamic Saints and Their Mausoleums." *Acta Asiatica* 34 (1987), pp. 79–105.

———. "Jūkyū Seiki Uiguru Rekishi Bunken Josetsu [Introduction to the Uyghur Historical Works of the Nineteenth Century]." *Tōhō gakuhō*, no. 55 (1983).

———. "Moguru urusu kara shinkyō e [From Moghulistan to Xinjiang]." In *Iwanami kōza sekai rekishi* [Iwanami Lecture on World History] 13 (new edition). Tōkyō: Iwanami shoten, 1998.

———. "Satoku Bogura Han no bomyo o megutte [Mausoleum of Satuq Bughra Khan]." *Seinan Ajia kenkyū* [Bulletin of the Society for Western and Southern Asiatic Studies] (Kyoto University) 34 (1991), pp. 89–110.

———. "'Shio no gimu' to 'Seisen' no aidade [Between the 'Duty of Salt' and 'Holy War']." *Tōyōshi kenkyū* [Research on Oriental History] 52:2 (1993).

———. "Supplement: Islamic Saints and Their Mausoleums." *Acta Asiatica* 34 (1987), pp. 79–98.

Hamashita Takeshi. *Chōkō shisutemu to kindai Ajia* [Tribute Trade System and Modern Asia]. Tōkyō: Iwanami shoten, 1997.

———. *Kindai Chūgoku no kokusaiteki keiki: Chōkō bōeki shisutemu to kindai Ajia* [Transnational Moments of Modern China: Tribute Trade System and Modern Asia]. Tōkyō: Tōkyō daigaku shuppankai, 1990.

Haneda Akira. *Chūō Ajia shi kenkyū* [Studies on Central Asian History]. Kyōto: Rinsen Shoten, 1982.

———. "Hsi-ning to Tuo-pa [Hsi-ning and Tuo-pa]." *Tōyōshi kenkyū* [Research on Oriental History] 10:5, pp. 358–64.

———. "Shinchō no Kaibu tōchi seisaku [Qing Policy of Rule over Muslim Tribes]." In *Iminzoku No Shina Tōchi Kenkyū: Shinchō no henkyō tochi Seisaku* [Study on Foreign Rule over China: Qing Dynasty's Frontier Policy]. Edited by Toa Kenkyūjo, pp. 101–213. Tokyo: Shibundō, 1944.

Hori Sunao. "Jūhachi-nijū seiki Uiguru joku jinko shiron [Population of Uyghurs from the Eighteenth to the Twentieth Century]." *Shirin* 60:4 (1977), pp. 111–28.

———. "Jūhachi-nijū seiki Uiguru joku no doryōkō ni tsuite [The Measurement Used by Uyghur People from the Eighteenth to the Twentieth Century]." *Journal of Otemae College* 12 (1978), pp. 57–67.

———. "Kaikyō gyokubei kō [Maize in the Muslim Domain]." *Tōyōshi kenkyū* 52:2 (1993), pp. 254–73.

———. "Kaikyō hankachō [Criminal Records of the Muslim Domain]." *Kōnan daigaku kiyō: bungakuhen* [Kōnan University Bulletin: Humanities] 105 (1997), pp. 24–43.

———. "Mindai no Turufan ni tsuite [Turfan during the Ming Period]." *Machikaneyama ronsō: shigakuhen* [Machikaneyama Collection of Articles: History Edition] 8 (1975), pp. 13–37.

———. "Oki bunsho no beku dachi [The Begs Appearing on the Oki Documents]." *Kōnan daigaku kiyō: bungakuhen* 129 (2002), pp. 1–33.

———. "Shinchono Kaikyo tochi ni tsuiteno nisan mondai—Yarukando no ichi shiryo no kento wo tsuite [Two or Three Questions regarding the Qing Rule in Its Muslim Domain]." *Shigaku Zasshi* 88:3 (1979), pp. 273–308, 409–10.

———. "Shindai Kaikyō no kochimenseki [Acreage of the Muslim Domain during the Qing Period]." *Kōnan daigaku kiyō: bungakuhen* 90 (1993), pp. 16–35.

———. "Shindai Kaikyō no suiri kangai: 19–20 seiki no Yaarukanto wo chūshin to shite [Irrigation in the Muslim Domain during the Qing Period: Case of Yarkand in the Nineteenth and the Twentieth Centuries]." *Journal of Otemae College* 14 (1980).

———. "Shindai Shinkyō no kahei seido—Furu (pul) chūzōsei [The Currency System of Xinjiang during the Qing Period—System of Minting *Pul* Currency]." In *Nakashima Satoshi Sensei koki kinen ronshū* 1 (1980), pp. 581–602.

———. "Shindai Yarkkando no noson to suiro [The Rural Villages and Canal in Yarkand during the Qing Period]." *Kōnan daigaku kiyō: bungakuhen* 139 (2004), pp. 153–91.

———. "Torufan no kaishi dachi." *Kōnan daigaku kiyō: bungakuhen* 109 (1998), pp. 64–84.

———. "Turufan no ka-re-zu shōkō [Short Study of Kariz of Turfan]." In *Nairiku Ajia Nishi Ajia no Shakai to Bunka* [Society and Culture in Inner Asia and Western Asia]. Edited by Mori Masao. Tokyo: Yamakawa shuppansha, 1983, pp. 459–80.

Hua Li. *Qingdai Xinjiang nongye kaifa shi* [History of the Development of Agriculture in Xinjiang during the Qing Period]. Ha'erbin: Heilongjiang jiaoyu chubanshe, 1995.

Ibragimov, S. K., and Arkheologiia Zhăne Ėtnografiia Instituty (Qazaq SSR ghylym akademiiasy), Tarikh, eds. *Materialy po istorii kazakhskikh khanstv XV–XVIII vekov* [Material on the History of Kazakh Khanates in the Fifteenth through Eighteenth Centuries]. Alma-Ata: Nauka, 1969.

Jarring, Gunnar. *Materials to the Knowledge of Eastern Turki: Tales, Poetry, Proverbs, Riddles, Ethnological and Historical Texts from the Southern Parts of Eastern Turkestan.* Lund: Gleerup, 1951.

Jia Jianfei. *Qing Qian Jia Dao shiqi Xinjiang de neidi yimin shehui* [Immigrant Society in Xinjiang: Centered on People from China Proper during Qianlong, Jiaqing and Daoguang Reigns of the Qing Dynasty]. Beijing: Shehui kexue wenxian chubanshe, 2012.

Jiang Shan. "Qianlongdi chengchu Gao Pu sifan yushi shulue [Brief Account of the Qianlong Emperor's Punishment of Gao Pu's Private Jade Trade]." *Lishi dang'an* [Historical Archive], no. 1 (1993), pp. 95–99.

Katanov, N. F., and Karl Heinrich Menges. *Volkskundliche Texte Aus Ost-Türkistan: I–II.* [Ethnographic Texts from East Turkestan]. Leipzig: Zentralantiquariat der Deutschen Demokratischen Republik, 1976.

Kataoka Kazutada. *Shinchō Shinkyō tōchi kenkyū* [Study on the Qing Rule of Xinjiang]. Tōkyō: Yūzankaku, 1991.

Khodarkovsky, Michael. *Russia's Steppe Frontier: The Making of a Colonial Empire, 1500–1800.* Bloomington: Indiana University Press, 2002.

Khodzhaev, Ablat, and B. A. Ahmedov. *Tsinskaia Imperiia I Vostochnyi Turkestan v XVIII v.: Iz Istorii Mezhdunarodnykh Otnoshenii v Tsentralnoi Azii* [The Qing Empire and Eastern Turkestan in the Eighteenth Century: History of International Relations in Central Asia]. Tashkent: Izd-vo Fan Uzbekskoi SSR, 1991.

Kim Hodong. "Chung'ang Asia ui Musulim sŏngja sungbae-Turupan ui Alpŭ Ata sungbae rŭl chungsim ŭro [Muslim Saint Worship in Central Asia: Case of Alp Ata Worship in Turfan]." *Chindan hakpo* [Chindan Journal] 74 (1992), pp. 147–77.

———. *Holy War in China: The Muslim Rebellion and State in Chinese Central Asia, 1864–1877.* Stanford: Stanford University Press, 2004.

———. "Muslim Saints in the 14th to the 16th Centuries of Eastern Turkestan." *International Journal of Central Asian Studies* 1 (1996).

Bibliography

————. "17segi Jungang Ashiaŭi Yŏksaga Sya Mahŭmudŭŭi [p'yŏnnyŏnsa]e Boinŭn Yŏksainshikkwa Hangye [Historical Consciousness Shown in the 17th Century Central Asian Historian Shah Mahmud's Khronika, and Its Limitation]." In *Tongashia Yŏksaŭi Hwallyu* [Reflux of East Asian History]. Seoul: Jishiksanŏpsa, 2000.

————. "Wigurŭ Yŏksaga Sairami (1836~1917) ŭi yŏksasŏsure nat'anan jŏnt'onggwa gŭndae [Tradition and Modernity Shown in the History Writing of Uyghur Historian Sairami (1836–1917)]." *Tongyangsahang nyŏn'gu* [Research on East Asian History] 57 (1997).

Kim, Kwangmin. "Profit and Protection: Emin Khwaja and the Qing Conquest of Central Asia, 1759–1777." *Journal of Asian Studies* 71:3 (August 2012), pp. 603–26.

————. "Saintly Brokers: Uyghur Muslims, Trade, and the Making of Qing Central Asia, 1696–1814." Ph.D. diss., University of California, Berkeley, 2008.

Kishimoto Mio. *Higashi Ajia no "kinsei* [Early Modernity of East Asia]." Tōkyō: Yamakawa shuppansha, 1998.

————. "Higashi Ajia Tōnan Ajia dentō shakai no keisei [Formation of the Traditional Societies of East Asia and Southeast Asia]." In *Iwanami kōza sekai rekishi* [Iwanami Lecture on World History] 13 (new edition), pp. 3–73. Tōkyō: Iwanami shoten, 1998.

————. "Shinchō to Yūrashia [Qing Dynasty and Eurasia]." In *Kōza sekaishi* [Lecture on World History]. Edited by Rekishigaku kenkyūkai [Society on Historical Research]. Tōkyō: Tōkyō daigaku shuppankai, 1995.

Komatsu Hisao, ed. *Chūō Yūrashia Shi* [History of Central Eurasia]. Tōkyō: Yamakawa Shuppansha, 2000.

Kubota Bunji. "Shindai Higashi Torukisutan nogyo mondai ni kansuru ichi kokoromi [Agriculture in Eastern Turkestan during the Qing Period]." *Shichō* [Historical Trends] 71 (1960), pp. 36–48.

Kuropatkin, A. N. *Kashgaria, Eastern or Chinese Turkistan; Historical and Geographical Sketch of the Country, Its Military Strength, Industries, and Trade.* Translated by Walter E. Gowan. Calcutta: Thacker Spink and Co., 1882.

Kuznetsov, Viacheslav S. *Ekonomicheskaia Politika Tsinskogo Pravitel'stva v Sin'tsiane v Pervoi Polovine XIX veka* [The Economic Policy of the Qing Government in Xinjiang in the First Half of the Nineteenth Century]. Moscow: Nauka, 1973.

Lattimore, Owen. *Inner Asian Frontiers of China.* New York: American Geographical Society, 1940.

————. *Pivot of Asia: Sinkiang and the Inner Asian Frontiers of China and Russia.* Boston: Little, Brown, 1950.

Levi, Scott C. "Early Modern Central Asia in World History." *History Compass* 10:11 (November 2012), pp. 866–78.

————. "The Ferghana Valley at the Crossroads of World History: The Rise of Khoqand, 1709–1822." *Journal of Global History* 2:2 (July 2007), pp. 213–32.

————. *India and Central Asia Commerce and Culture, 1500–1800.* New Delhi: Oxford University Press, 2007.

Li Baowen. "'Bo-de-er-ge' Kaoshi [Interpreting 'Bo-de-Er-Ge']." *Xiyu yanjiu* [Research on Western Regions], no. 4 (2009).

Li Yunquan. *Chaogong zhidu shilun* [History of Tribute System]. Beijing: Xinhua chubanshe, 2004.

Lieberman, Victor B. *Strange Parallels: Southeast Asia in Global Context, c. 800–1830.* Studies in Comparative World History. New York: Cambridge University Press, 2003.

Lin Enxian. "Bo-Ke Zhi [Beg System]." In *Qingchao zai Xinjiang di Han Hui geli zhengce* [The Han-Muslim Separation Policy in Xinjiang by the Qing Dynasty]. Taibei: Taiwan shangwuyin shuguan, 1988.

———. *Qingchao zai Xinjiang di Han Hui geli zhengce* [Qing Dynasty's Han-Muslim Separation Policy in Xinjiang]. Taibei: Taiwan shangwuyin shuguan, 1988.

Lin Man-houng. *China Upside Down: Currency, Society, and Ideologies, 1808–1856.* Cambridge, MA: Council on East Asian Studies, Harvard University, 2006.

Lin Yongkuang and Wang Xi. *Qingdai xibei minzu maoyi shi* [History of the Trade of Northwestern Peoples]. Beijing: Zhongyan minzu xueyuan chubanshe, 1991.

Linebaugh, Peter, and Marcus Rediker. *The Many-Headed Hydra: Sailors, Slaves, Commoners, and the Hidden History of the Revolutionary Atlantic.* Reprint edition. Boston, MA: Beacon Press, 2013.

Liu Xiangxue. *Mingchao minzu zhengce yanbian shi* [Development of the Ming Ethnic (Frontier) Policy]. Beijing: Minzu chubanshe, 2006.

Liu Yitang. "Bo-Ke Zhidu Yanjiu [Study on the Beg System]." In *Weiwu'er Yanjiu* [Research on Uyghurs]. Taibei: Zhengzhong shuju, 1997.

Liu Zhengyin and Liangtao Wei. *Weiwu'er yanjiu* [Study on the Uyghurs]. Taibei: Zhengzhong shuju, 1997.

———. *Xiyu Huozhou jiazhou yanjiu* [Study on the Khwaja Families of the Western Regions]. Beijing: Zhongguo shehui kexue chubanshe, 1998.

Luo Xiaorui. "Qingdai Nanjiang Cha-he-tai wen qiyue wenshu yanjiu [Chagatai Contract Documents from Eastern Turkestan during the Qing Rule]." Master's thesis, Xinjiang University, 2011.

Luo Yunzhi. "Bo-ke zhidu [Beg System]." In *Qing Gaozong tongzhi Xinjiang zhengce di tantao* [Research on the Qing Gaozong's Policy concerning the Rule of Xinjiang]. Taibei: Liren shuju, 1983.

———. *Qing Gaozong tongzhi Xinjiang zhengce di tantao.* [Qing Gaozong (Qianlong Emperor's) Frontier Policy]. Taibei: Liren shuju, 1983.

Ma Saibei. *Qing shilu Musilin Ziliao Jilu* [Collection of Primary Sources concerning Muslims from the Veritable Records of the Qing Dynasty]. Yinchuan: Ningxia renmin chuban she, 1988.

Ma Tong. *Zhongguo Yisilan jiaopai menhuan suyuan* [Origin of the Sects and Sufi Orders of Islam in China Islam]. Yinchuan Shi: Ningxia renmin chubanshe, 1986.

Macartney, George. "Eastern Turkestan: The Chinese as Rulers over an Alien Race." London: Central Asia Society, 1909.

Manz, Beatrice Forbes. "Central Asian Uprisings in the Nineteenth Century: Ferghana under the Russians." *Russian Review* 46:3 (1987), pp. 267–81.

Marshall, P. J. *The Making and Unmaking of Empires: Britain, India, and America, c. 1750–1783.* New York: Oxford University Press, 2005.

Mazumdar, Sucheta. *Sugar and Society in China: Peasants, Technology, and the World Market.* Harvard-Yenching Institute Monograph Series 45. Cambridge, MA: Harvard University Asia Center, 1998.

McChesney, R. D. *Central Asia: Foundations of Change.* Princeton, NJ: Darwin Press, 1996.

———. *Waqf in Central Asia: Four Hundred Years in the History of a Muslim Shrine, 1480–1889.* Princeton: Princeton University Press, 1991.

Meng Xianzhang. *Zhong Su jingji maoyi shi* [History of Sino-Russian Commercial and Economic Relations]. Ha'erbin: Heilongjiang renmin chubanshe, 1992.

Metcalf, Barbara D., and Thomas R. Metcalf, *A Concise History of Modern India.* 2nd edition. New York: Cambridge University Press, 2006.

Miao Pusheng. *Bo-ke Zhidu* [Beg System]. Wulumuqi: Xinjiang renmin chuban she, 1995.

Miao Pusheng and Weijiang Tian. *Xinjiang Shi Gang* [Outline History of Xinjiang]. Wulumuqi: Xinjiang renmin chubanshe, 2004.

Millward, James A. *Beyond the Pass: Economy, Ethnicity, and Empire in Qing Central Asia, 1759–1864.* Stanford: Stanford University Press, 1998.

———. "'Coming onto the Map': Western Regions' Geography and Cartographic Nomenclature in the Making of the Chinese Empire in Xinjiang." *Late Imperial China* 20:2 (1999), pp. 61–98.

———. *Eurasian Crossroads: A History of Xinjiang.* New York: Columbia University Press, 2007.

———. "A Uyghur Muslim in Qianlong's Court: The Meaning of the Fragrant Concubine." *Journal of Asian Studies* 53:2 (May 1994).

Millward, James, and Laura Newby. "The Qing and Islam on the Western Frontier." In *Empire at the Margins: Culture, Ethnicity, and Frontier in Early Modern China.* Edited by Pamela Kyle Crossley, Helen F. Siu, and Donald S. Sutton. Berkeley: University of California Press, 2006.

Mindai Seiiki Shi Kenkyūkai. *Mindai Seiiki shiryō: Min jitsuroku shō* [Source on the History of the Western Regions during the Ming Period: Selection from the Veritable Records of the Ming Dynasty]. Kyōto: Kyōto Daigaku Bungakubu Nairiku Ajia Kenkyūjo, 1974.

Nakami Tatsuo. "Chūō Yūrashia shi no shūenka [Marginalization of Central Eurasia]." In *Chūō-Yūrashia Shi* [History of Central Eurasia]. Edited by Hisao Komatsu. Tōkyō: Yamakawa Shuppansha, 2000.

Nalivkin, V. P. *Histoire du khanat de Khokand*. Paris: E. Ledoux, 1889.

Naquin, Susan. *Peking: Temples and City Life, 1400–1900*. Berkeley: University of California Press, 2000.

Nettleton, Susanna S. "Ruler, Patron, Poet: Umar Khan in the Blossoming of the Khanate of Qoqand, 1800–1820." *International Journal of Turkish Studies* 2:2 (1981).

Newby, Laura J. "The Begs of Xinjiang: Between Two Worlds." *Bulletin of the School of Oriental and African Studies* 61:1 (1998).

———. "Bondage on Qing China's Northwestern Frontier." *Modern Asian Studies* 47:3 (2013), pp. 968–94.

———. *The Empire and the Khanate: A Political History of Qing Relations with Khoqand, c. 1760–1860*. Leiden: Brill, 2005.

———. "'Us and Them' in 18th and 19th Century Xinjiang." In *Situating the Uyghurs between China and Central Asia*. Aldershot: Ashgate, 2007.

Nie Hongping. "Jiaqing Chao Xinjiang 'Yu-nu-si an' [Yunus Case during the Jiaqing Reign]." *Zhongguo bianjiang shidi yanjiu* [Borderland History and Geography of China] 17:1 (March 2007).

Onuma Takahiro. "The Development of the Junghars and the Role of Bukharan Merchants." *Journal of Central Eurasian Studies* 2 (May 2011), pp. 83–100.

———. "Promoting Power: The Rise of Emin Khwaja on the Eve of the Qing Conquest of Kashgaria." In *Yūbokusekai to nōkōsekai no setten–Ajiashi kenkyū no atarashitana shiryō to shiten* [Interface between the Nomadic World and Agricultural World: New Primary Source and Perspective for Research on Asian History], pp. 31–59. Tōkyō: Gagushūin daigaku Tōyōbunka kenkyūjo, 2012.

———. "Zaikyo Uiguru jin no kyojutsu kara mita 18 seiki chuo Kashugaria shakai no seiji teki hendo [Political Transformation of Kashgarian Society during the Mid-eighteenth Century Seen from the Depositions of a Uyghur Living in Beijing]." *Manzokushi kenkyū* [Research on History of the Manchu] 1 (2002), pp. 46–61.

Pan Xiangming. *Qingdai Xinjiang hezhuo panluan yanjiu* [Study on the Khwaja Rebellion during the Qing Period]. Beijing: Zhongguo renmin daxue chubanshe, 2011.

Pan Zhiping. *Zhongya Haohanguo yu Qingdai Xinjiang* [Khoqand in Central Asia and Xinjiang during the Qing Period]. Beijing: Zhongguo shehui kexue chubanshe, 1991.

Papas, Alexandre. *Soufisme et Politique Entre Chine, Tibet et Turkestan: Étude Sur Les Khwajas Naqshbandis Du Turkestan Oriental* [Sufism and the Politics between China, Tibet, and Turkestan: Study of Naqshbandi Khwajas in Eastern Turkestan]. Paris: Librarie d'Amérique et d'Orient, Jean Maisonneuve successeur, 2005.

Paul, Jurgen. "Forming a Faction: The Himayat System of Khwaja Ahrar." *International Journal of Middle East Studies* 23:4 (1991), pp. 533–48.

Perdue, Peter C. "Boundaries, Maps, and Movement: The Chinese, Russian, and Mongolian Empires in Early Modern Eurasia." *International History Review* 20:2 (1998), pp. 263–86.

———. *China Marches West: The Qing Conquest of Central Eurasia.* Cambridge, MA: Belknap Press of Harvard University Press, 2005.

———. "A Frontier View of Chineseness." In *The Resurgence of East Asia: 500, 150, and 50 Year Perspectives.* Edited by Giovanni Arrighi, Takeshi Hamashita, and Mark Selden, pp. xii, 354. London: Routledge, 2003.

Perlin, Frank. "Of White Whales and Countrymen in the Eighteenth-century Maratha Deccan. Extended Class Relations, Rights, and the Problem of Rural Autonomy under the Old Regime." *Journal of Peasant Studies* 5:2 (1978), pp. 172–237.

Pomeranz, Kenneth. *The Great Divergence: Europe, China, and the Making of the Modern World Economy.* Princeton: Princeton University Press, 2000.

Qi Meiqin. *Qingdai Neiwufu* [Imperial Household Department during the Qing Period]. Beijing: Zhongguo renmin daxue chubanshe, 1998.

Rawski, Evelyn Sakakida. *The Last Emperors: A Social History of Qing Imperial Institutions.* Berkeley: University of California Press, 1998.

Reid, Anthony. *Southeast Asia in the Age of Commerce, 1450–1680.* New Haven: Yale University Press, 1988.

Richards, John F. *The Unending Frontier.* Berkeley: University of California Press, 2005.

Rosenthal, Jean-Laurent, and Roy Bin Wong. *Before and beyond Divergence: The Politics of Economic Change in China and Europe.* Cambridge, MA: Harvard University Press, 2011.

Rossabi, Morris. *China among Equals: The Middle Kingdom and Its Neighbors, 10th–14th Centuries.* Berkeley: University of California Press, 1983.

———. *China and Inner Asia: From 1368 to the Present Day.* London: Thames and Hudson, 1975.

———. "The 'Decline' of the Central Asian Caravan Trade." In *The Rise of the Merchant Empires: Long-distance Trade in the Early Modern World.* Edited by James D. Tracy. Cambridge, UK: Cambridge University Press, 1990.

———. "Ming China and Turfan, 1406–1517." *Central Asiatic Journal* 16:3 (1972), pp. 206–25.

———. "Ming China's Relations with Hami and Central Asia, 1404–1513: A Reexamination of Traditional Chinese Foreign Policy." Ph.D. diss., Columbia University, 1970.

———. "Muslim and Central Asian Revolts." In *From Ming to Ching: Conquest, Region, and Continuity in Seventeenth-century China.* Edited by Jonathan D. Spence and John E. Wills, Jr. New Haven: Yale University Press, 1979.

Saguchi Tōru. "Higashi Torukisutan hōken shakai josetsu: Hoja jidai no ichi kōsatsu [Introduction to the History of the Feudal Society in Eastern Turkestan: An Examination of the Khoja Period]." *Rekishigaku kenkyū* [Research on History], no. 134 (1948).

———. "Iri no taranchi shakai [Taranchi Society of Ili]." In *Shinkyō minzokushi kenkyū* [A Study on the Ethnic History of Xinjiang], pp. 236–306. Tōkyō: Yoshikawa kōbunkan, 1986.

————. *Jūhachi-jūkyū-seiki Higashi Torukisutan shakaishi kenkyū* [Study on the Eastern Turkestan Society during the Eighteenth and Nineteenth Centuries]. Tōkyō: Yoshikawa kōbunkan, 1963.

————. "Mongoru jin shihai jidai no Uigurisutan [Uyghuristan under the Period of Mongol Rule]." *Shigaku zasshi* [Journal of History] 54:8 (1943).

————. *Shinkyō minzokushi kenkyū* [Study on the Ethnic History of Xinjiang]. Tōkyō: Yoshikawa kōbunkan, 1986.

————. *Shinkyō Musurimu kenkyū* [Studies on the Xinjiang Muslims]. Tōkyō: Yoshikawa kōbunkan, 1995.

————. "Torufan chiiki shakai [Local Society of Turfan]." In *Shinkyō minzokushi kenkyū* [Studies on the Ethnic History of Xinjiang], pp. 116–234. Tōkyō: Yoshikawa kōbunkan, 1986.

————. "Torukisutan no sho han koku [Khanates of Turkestan]." In *Iwanami kōza sekai rekishi* [Iwanami Lecture on World History] 13. Tōkyō: Iwanami shoten, 1971.

Sanada Yasushi, "Mengyō kara mita Kashugaria oashisu shakai no ichi danmen—1870 nendai ni tsuite [One Aspect of the Oasis Society of Kashgaria: Cotton Textile Industry in the 1870s]." *Chūō daigaku Ajia shi kenkyū* [Asia Research of Chūō University] 2 (1978), pp. 29–50.

————. "Oashisu ba-za-ru no seitaienkyū—jūkyū seiki gohan kashugariano baʼai [Static Study of the Oasis Bazaar: The Case of Kashgaria in the Late Nineteenth Century]." *Chūō daigaku daigakuin kenkyū nenpō* [Annual Report of the Graduate School of Chūō University] 6 (1997), pp. 207–20.

————. "Toshi, noson yuboku [City, Rural Villages, and Pastoral Nomadism]." *Kōza Isuramu* [Lectures on Islam] 3, pp. 108–48. Tōkyō: Chikuma Shobō, 1986.

Scott, Bruce R. *Capitalism: Its Origins and Evolution as a System of Governance*. New York: Springer Science and Business Media, 2011.

Scott, James. *The Art of Not Being Governed: An Anarchist History of Upland Southeast Asia*. New Haven: Yale University Press, 2009.

Shahrani, M. N. *The Kirghiz and Wakhi of Afghanistan: Adaptation to Closed Frontiers and War*. Seattle: University of Washington Press, 2002.

Shepherd, John Robert. *Statecraft and Political Economy on the Taiwan Frontier, 1600–1800*. Stanford: Stanford University Press, 1993.

Shimada Jōhei. "Hōja jidai no Beku dachi [The Begs during the Period of the Khoja (Rule)]." *Toho gaku* [Journal of Oriental Studies], no. 3 (1952).

————. "Shindai kaikyō no jintōzei [Poll Tax of the Muslim Territory under the Qing]." *Shigaku zasshi* [Journal of History] 61:11 (1952).

Sinor, Denis. *The Cambridge History of Early Inner Asia*. Cambridge, UK: Cambridge University Press, 1990.

Stein, Burton. "State Formation and Economy Reconsidered." *Modern Asian Studies* 19:3 (1985), pp. 387–413.

Struve, Lynn A. *The Qing Formation in World-Historical Time*. Cambridge, MA: Harvard University Asia Center, distributed by Harvard University Press, 2004.

Su Beihai and Jianhua Huang. *Hami Tulufan Weiwu'er wang lishi: Qingchao zhi Minguo* [History of the Uyghur Kings of Hami and Turfan: From the Qing Period to the Republican Period]. Wulumuqi: Xinjiang daxue chubanshe, 1993.

Subrahmanyam, Sanjay, and C. A. Bayly. "Portfolio Capitalists and the Political Economy of Early Modern India." In *Merchants, Markets, and the State in Early Modern India*, pp. 242–65. Oxford: Oxford University Press, 1990.

Subtelny, Maria Eva. "Centralizing Reform and Its Opponents in the Late Timurid Period." *International Journal of Iranian Studies* 21:1/2 (1988), pp. 123–51.

———. *Timurids in Transition*. Boston: Brill, 2007.

Tagliacozzo, Eric. *Secret Trades, Porous Borders: Smuggling and States along a Southeast Asian Frontier, 1865–1915*. New Haven: Yale University Press, 2005.

Temir, Ahmet. "Ein osttürkisches Dokument von 1722–1741 aus Turfan [An Eastern Turkish Document from Turfan 1722–1741]." *Ural-altaische Jahrbucher* [Ural-Altaic Yearbook] 33:1–2 (1961).

Thum, Rian. *The Sacred Routes of Uyghur History*. Cambridge, MA: Harvard University Press, 2014.

Tian Weijiang. *Gaochang Huihu Shi Gao* [Manuscript History of Gaochang Uyghur]. Wulumuqi: Xinjiang renmin chubanshe, 2006.

Togan, Isenbike. "Difference in Ideology and Practice: The Case of the Black and White Mountain Factions." *Journal of the History of Sufism* 3 (2001), pp. 25–38.

———. "Inner Asian Muslim Merchants at the Closure of the Silk Routes in the Seventeenth Century." In *The Silk Roads: Highways of Culture and Commerce*, pp. 247–63. New York: Berghahn Books, 2000.

———. "Islam in a Chinese Society: The Khojas of Eastern Turkestan." In *Muslims in Central Asia: Expressions of Identity and Change*. Edited by Jo-Ann Gross. Durham, NC: Duke University Press, 1992.

Torbert, Preston M. *The Ching Imperial Household Department: A Study of Its Organization and Principal Functions, 1662–1796*. Cambridge, MA: Council on East Asian Studies, Harvard University, distributed by Harvard University Press, 1977.

Tracy, James D. *The Political Economy of Merchant Empires: Studies in Comparative Early Modern History*. Cambridge, UK: Cambridge University Press, 1991.

———. *The Rise of Merchant Empires: Long-Distance Trade in the Early Modern World, 1350–1750*. Cambridge, UK: Cambridge University Press, 1990.

Viraphol, Sarasin. *Tribute and Profit: Sino-Siamese Trade, 1652–1853*. Cambridge, MA: Council on East Asian Studies, Harvard University, distributed by Harvard University Press, 1977.

Von Glahn, Richard. *Fountain of Fortune: Money and Monetary Policy in China, 1000–1700*. Berkeley: University of California Press, 1996.

Wakeman, Frederic, Jr. "The Canton Trade and the Opium War." In *The Cambridge History of China*, Vol. 10, Pt. 1. Edited by Denis Twitchett and John K. Fairbank, pp. 163–212. Cambridge, UK: Cambridge University Press, 1978.

Waley-Cohen, Joanna. *The Culture of War in China Empire and the Military under the Qing Dynasty*. London: I. B. Tauris, 2006.

———. *Exile in Mid-Qing China: Banishment to Xinjiang*, 1758–1820. Yale Historical Publications. New Haven: Yale University Press, 1991.

Wang Dongping. "Bo-ke ji qi xiangguan falü zhidu [Beg System and the Laws Concerned with It]." In *Qingdai Huijiang falü zhidu yanjiu, 1759–1884 Nian* [Study on the Legal System of the Muslim Domain, 1759–1884]. Ha'erbin: Heilongjiang jiaoyu chubanshe, 2003.

———. *Qingdai Huijiang Falü Zhidu Yanjiu, 1759–1884 Nian* [Study on the Legal System of the Muslim Domain, 1759–1884]. Ha'erbin: Heilongjiang jiaoyu chubanshe, 2003.

Wang Xi. "Lun Qianlong shiqi Yili Hasake maoyi majia, sichoujia yu maoyi bizhi wenti [The Price of Horse and Silk at the Yili's Trade with Kazakh and the Rate of Exchange]." *Minzu yanjiu* [Research on Nationalities], no. 4 (1992), pp. 48–58.

———. "Qianlong shiqi Ka-shi-ga-er de guanfang sichou maoyi [Official Silk Trade in Kashgar during the Qianlong Period]." In *Qingdai quyu shehui jingji yanjiu* [Studies on Regional Society and Economy during the Qing Period]. Edited by Xian'en Ye. Beijing: Zhonghua shuju, 1992.

Wang Xilong. "Hami Da-er-han Bo-ke E-bi-du-la ji qi touqing zhi yingxiang [Hami Da-er-han Beg Ubaid Al-Lah and the Consequences of His Surrender (to the Qing)]." *Guoli Zhengzhi daxue minzu xuebao* [Journal of Nationality Studies of National Zhengzhi University] 23 (1998), pp. 95–116.

———. "Qing qianqi Tulufan Wei-wu-er ren qianju Guazhou di jige wenti [Several Questions about the Uyghur People's Migration to Guazhou during the Early Qing Period]." *Lanzhou Daxue xuebao* [Journal of Lanzhou University], no. 4 (1989).

———. *Qingdai xibei tuntian yanjiu* [Study on the Northwestern Agricultural Colonies during the Qing Period]. Lanzhou: Lanzhou daxue chubanshe, 1990.

Washbrook, David. "From Comparative Sociology to Global History: Britain and India in the Pre-History of Modernity." *Journal of Economic and Social History of Orient* 40:4 (1997), pp. 410–43.

———. "Progress and Problems: South Asian Economic and Social History, c. 1720–1860." *Modern Asian Studies* 22:1 (1988), pp. 57–96.

Weaver, John C. *The Great Land Rush and the Making of the Modern World, 1650–1900*. Montréal: McGill Queens University Press, 2006.

Wei Liangtao. *Ye-er-qiang hanguo shigang* [Outline History of the Yarkand Khanate]. Ha'erbin Shi: Heilongjiang jiaoyu chubanshe, 1994.

Wong, Roy Bin. *China Transformed: Historical Change and the Limits of European Experience*. Ithaca, NY: Cornell University Press, 1997.

Wu Qiyan. "Jianlun qing qianqi neiwufu Huangshang De Xingqi [Brief Discussion on the Emergence of the Imperial Merchants of the Imperial Household Department during the Early Qing Period]." In *Qingdai quyu shehui jingji yanjiu* [Studies on Regional Society and Economy during the Qing Period]. Edited by Ye Xian'en. Beijing: Zhonghua shuju, 1992.

Wu Yuanfeng. "Qing Qianlong Nianjian Xinjiang Xin Pu'er Qian de Zhuzao Liutong Ji Qi Zuoyong [Minting and Circulation of the New Pul Coins during the Qianlong Period and Its Effects]." *Xiyu yanjiu* [Research on the Western Regions], no. 1 (1997), pp. 41–42, 46.

Yin Qing. "Shijiu shiji zongye Xinjiang nongkan shiyue de fazhan [The Development of the Farming and Land Reclamation in the Mid-nineteenth-century Xinjiang]." In *Xinjiang shehui kexue* [Xinjiang Social Sciences], no. 6 (1986), pp. 49–62.

Yu Shanpu and Dong Naiqing. *Xiangfei* [Fragrant Concubine]. Beijing: Shumu wenxian chubanshe, 1985.

Zeng Wenwu. *Zhongguo jingying xiyushi* [History of the Chinese Administration of the Western Regions]. Shanghai: Shangwuyin shuguan, 1936.

Zhang Anfu. *Qingdai yilai Xinjiang tunken yu guojia anquan yanjiu* [Study on the Agrarian Colonies and the State Security in Xinjiang since the Qing Dynasty]. Beijing: Zhongguo nongye chubanshe, 2011.

———. *Xiyu tunken renwu lungao* [The People Who Were Involved in the Development of Agrarian Colonies]. Beijing: Zhongguo nongye chubanshe, 2011.

Zhang Shicai. "Qingdai Tianshan nanbu weiwuer shehui de 'yanqi dimu' [The "Yanqi Land" of the Uyghur Society in the Southern Xinjiang during the Qing Period]." *Xinjiang daxue xuebao* (Zhexue shehui kexue ban), no. 4 (2006).

———. "Qingdai Xinjiang Tianshan nanlu Wei-wu-er shehui jiegou yu bianqian [The Social Structure of Uyghurs in Tianshan Nanlu in Xinjiang (Eastern Turkestan) and Its Transformation during the Qing Period]." In *Xiyu yanjiu* [Research on Western Regions], no. 3 (2012).

Zhang Wende. *Ming yu Ti-mu-er wangchao guanxi shi yanjiu* [The Relations between the Ming and the Timurid Dynasty]. Beijing: Zhonghua shuju, 2006.

———. "Ming yu Xiyu de yushi maoyi [Jade Trade between the Ming China and Western Regions]." In *Xiyu yanjiu* [Research on Western Regions], no. 3 (2007).

Zhang Yongjiang. "Jiben xingzheng moshi zhi san: Huijiang moshi [The Third Basic Administrative Model: The Muslim Domain Model]." In *Qingdai fanbu yanjiu* [Study of Frontier Tribes during the Qing Period]. Ha'erbin: Heilongjiang jiaoyu chubanshe, 2001.

———. *Qingdai fanbu yanjiu* [Study on the Outer Vassals during the Qing Period]. Ha'erbin: Heilongjiang jiaoyu chubanshe 2001.

Zhao Yuhai. "Cong Qingdai Manwen dang'an kan Wushi shijian' shimo [The Beginning and End of the Wushi Incident Shown in the Manchu-language Archival Materials]." *Lishi dang'an* [Historical Archive], 2001.

Zhao Yuzheng. *Sichou zhi lu tunken yanjiu* [Study on the Agrarian Colonies of the Silk Road]. Wulumuqi: Xinjiang renmin chubanshe, 1996.

Zhongguo Xinjiang diqu Yisilanjiao shi bianxiezu, ed. *Zhongguo Xinjiang diqu Yisilanjiao shi* [History of Islam in Xinjiang, China]. Wulumuqi Shi: Xinjiang renmin chubanshe, 2000.

Zhuang Jifa. *Qing Gaozong shiquan wugong yanjiu* [Studies on Qing Gaozong (Qianlong Emperor's) Ten Military Achievements]. Taipei: Guoli gugong bowuyuan, 1982.

Index

'Abd Allāh, 98

Abd al-Rahīm, 68 (table)

'Abd al-Rashīd Khān, 25, 28

Abduriman, 60–61

A-bu-du-ha-li-ke, 145

Āfāq Khwāja, 33–34, 35, 94, 105, 165, 232n15

Afridun Wang Beg, 175–76

Agrarian development: after fall of Qing regime, 177–78; beg administration, 7, 24–25, 62, 65; Chinese colonists, 13–14, 39, 149; commercial, 6, 7–8, 12, 76, 88, 167–68, 172; cotton, 52, 73, 178–79; crops, 5, 168; displaced groups, 91, 95, 98, 125, 189; effects on villages, 7–8, 79–82, 95–96, 125; in Eurasia, 12; harvests, 171, 223–24 (table); irrigation, 5–6, 73, 76, 78–79, 142, 240–41n28; in Khoqand Khanate, 106–7; land under cultivation, 10–11; long-term expansion, 228–29n15; in nineteenth century, 167–68, 172; in northwestern China, 38–41; opium cultivation, 110; Qing investment, 7, 39–43, 237n65; Qing military and, 41, 59; resistance to, 196–98; social tensions, 92–93, 95–96, 149–50, 154–55, 168; of Taiwan, 190; under Timurid rule, 23; by Uzbek rulers, 92; Valikhanov on, 167–68, 172; in Xinjiang

oasis systems, 3–8; in Yarkand Khanate, 28–29; in Yunnan, 189–90; by Zunghar Mongols, 24, 35, 46. *See also* Grain taxes; Land reclamation; *Tuntian*

Agricultural labor: beg control, 40–41; demand for, 38–39, 98; hired, 70–71, 76, 86, 87; for irrigation, 240–41n28. *See also Yanqis*

Agromanagers: begs as, 22–23, 40–43, 48–49, 54, 60–61, 67, 73–75; Sufi leaders as, 22–23, 26–27, 29

Ahmad Wang Beg: as Aksu governor, 138, 174–75; audit of Yarkand District taxes, 174; career, 156, 161, 174, 182, 256n11, 258n39; collaboration with Qing, 182; copper mining and, 161–63; death, 181, 182; as Kashgar governor, 162–63, 174; logistical support for Qing military, 181, 258n44

Akbeg, 76

Aksu District, 108 (map); agriculture, 168; copper mining, 161–62; governors, 130, 138, 174–75, 196; *khwaja* wars, 164; land reclamation projects, 138; military governors, 130, 138, 174; rural villages, 79–81, 80 (fig.); taxes, 174–75

Alahuli, 76

Alima, 68 (table), 70, 93, 95

'Alim Khān, 106, 107

Amursana, 43

Andijan: hired labor, 71; soldiers, 165–66

Andijan merchants: collaboration with begs, 186; expulsions, 118–19; land purchases, 73, 118; residing in Kashgar, 126, 128–29, 131, 133, 150–51, 180; seen as security threat, 150–51; support of *khwajas*, 164–65, 167; taxes, 118–19, 175, 252n10; wealth, 118. *See also* Caravan merchants; Merchants

Artush, 152–53, 160, 162–63

Atantai, 121, 124

A-wa-le-bi, 104

Azziz Khwāja (Manchu: Ashūji), 23

Bai Bursuk, 102, 246n22

Barkul, 24, 190

Batur Sart, 99–102, 100 (fig.), 103, 104, 105

*Bay*s (rich landlords), 72–73

*Bazaar*s, 5, 49–51, 53–54, 179. *See also* Markets

Bederege, 24, 30, 141–43, 144. *See also* Caravan merchants

Beg-Qing alliance: administrative duties, 62–65, 63–64 (table); advantages for Qing, 1, 24, 60, 61, 88–89, 188; agrarian development and, 24–25, 40, 127, 137–38, 144; appointments, 135–36; aristocratic titles, 21, 22, 208–15 (table); autonomy of begs, 21, 48, 51; client relationship, 1, 40, 48, 87–88; collaboration with military, 154; compensation, 22, 24, 56–57 (table), 145, 182; convergence of interests, 7, 60–61, 88–89, 138, 144, 182–83; dependence of begs, 49, 128, 192; economic benefits for begs, 22, 54–57, 58–61, 75–76; fall of regime, 14, 156–57, 187; financial donations, 135; foundation, 22, 24–25, 45–46; global context, 11–13; land

grants, 7, 56–57 (table), 58–59, 61, 73, 74–76, 82–83, 145, 240–41nn28–29; leading families, 20–21; logistical support for military, 20, 24, 37–38, 39, 41, 51–52, 69, 133, 252–53n16; military protection, 49, 128, 153, 240n19; motives of begs, 19–20, 22, 24–25, 36–37, 46, 187; Nayancheng's reforms and, 114–19; Opium War and, 156–59; recruitment, 113; rule of avoidance, 114–15, 134; rural assignments, 154–55, 255n61; submission to Qing, 20, 36–41, 203–7 (table); trade and, 11; *tuntian* development, 136–38, 142–46, 154; wealth created, 7, 44, 47–48, 66–74, 187, 188, 192. *See also* Agrarian development; Military governors; Revenue farming

Begs: administrative hierarchy, 56–57 (table), 62, 241n38; backgrounds, 21–23; from Black Mountaineers faction, 113; former *tongshi* as, 149, 254n49; landholdings, 21, 68 (table), 70, 71, 72, 74–76, 137, 171, 227n8; leadership roles, 6, 21, 23–24; legacy, 182–83; meanings of term, 6, 21, 233n20; migration, 23–24, 25, 42, 44, 45; in new settlements, 144, 145; political power, 1, 12; positions sold, 66–67, 156, 242n43; previous scholarship, 22, 226n5; urban bases, 6, 62; under Zunghar Mongols, 63 (table), 64–65. *See also* Commercial enterprises; Corruption; Kashgar, Muslim governors of; *and individual names*

Begs, economic roles: as agromanagers, 22–23, 40–43, 48–49, 54, 60–61, 67, 73–75; capitalist transformation, 1, 6–7, 9, 10–11, 87–88, 127, 137–38, 185–87; land reclamation projects, 60, 88, 138, 186,

258n33; mining administration, 62, 65, 69, 159, 161–63, 186; trade, 7, 11, 45, 46; *tuntian* and, 127, 136–40, 142–45, 154, 186

Beijing, Muslim aristocrats, 211–12 (table)

Bellew, Henry Walter, 126, 133

Black Mountaineers faction, 33, 91, 113, 232n15

Booceng, 84–86

Borderlands, 1–3, 12–13, 189–92. *See also* Oasis capitalism

Boxing, 137

Braudel, Fernand, 10

Britain, Forsyth Mission, 126, 177–80, 184–85

British Empire, 192–94, 195. *See also* India; Opium War

Bukhara: merchants from, 29, 117–18; military forces, 166; trade, 29, 54; war with Khoqand, 120

Bukhara Khanate, 106

Bukhariyya, 29

Burhān al-Din, 93, 95

Bu-yan-tai, 146

Capitalism: class relations, 9; history of, 3, 9–10, 195; imperial expansion and, 12–13, 192–96; non-European development, 3, 9–10, 195–96; production relations, 10; resistance to transformation, 103; in Yunnan, 189–90. *See also* Commercial enterprises; Oasis capitalism; Trade

Caravan merchants: after fall of Qing regime, 179, 180; cooperation with begs and Qing, 105, 144; groups, 24; landholdings, 105; land reclamation projects, 141–43, 144; migration to Eastern Turkestan, 29–30; military protection, 127; regulations, 117;

robberies, 5, 99, 100–102, 103, 104–5, 240n19, 246n18. *See also* Merchants; Trade

Central Asia: end of Qing rule (1864), 14, 90, 176; Qing expansion into, 1–3, 13, 14–15, 20, 46, 187–89; Russian expansion into, 160; state-building, 92, 165; trade, 29–32, 48–49, 52–54. *See also* Agrarian development; Oasis capitalism; Xinjiang

Changde, 124

Changling, 124, 134–36, 141

Chapman, E. F., 184–85

China: convicts from, 77, 127, 136, 152; merchants from, 53, 73, 194; migration to, 31–32, 33–34; Yunnan, 189–91. *See also* Han Chinese migrants; Qing Empire; Trade with China

Chinggisid Khanate, *see* Yarkand Khanate

Cities, *see* Urban areas

Class relations: capitalist, 9; poverty, 81, 103. *See also* Social tensions

Coins: copper (*pul*), 137, 157, 158, 159, 161–62; counterfeit, 248n41. *See also* Silver

Commercial enterprises: of begs, 66, 68 (table), 69–72, 73–74, 76; markets, 25–26, 33, 34, 117, 177, 179; on military land, 146–51; in Yunnan, 189–91. *See also* Agrarian development; Capitalism; Merchants; Mining; Trade

Copper (*pul*) coins, 137, 157, 158, 159, 161–62

Copper mining, 59, 157, 158, 159, 160, 161–63

Corruption: charges against begs, 42, 49, 83–86, 87, 88–89, 142, 181; of military governors, 65–66, 67, 259n45; reforms addressing, 114–15; in Turfan, 42, 43–44

Corvée labor, *see* Forced labor

Index

Cotton: farming, 52, 73, 178–79; textiles, 24, 52, 173; trade, 149, 178–79, 180
Currency, *see* Coins; Silver

Daheyan, 140–41, 142–43, 253–54n33
Dalai Lama, 236n50
Daoguang emperor, 125, 136, 145–46
Davak, 144
Dawachi Expedition, 37
Ding Guodong Rebellion, 33
Divan Quli, 256n7
Dolan tribe, 59
Duo-la-te, 78

Eastern Turkestan, *see* Xinjiang
East India Company, 193–94
E-luo-si, 104
Emin Khwāja: alliance with Qing, 19, 21, 36–41, 45–46, 87; background, 21, 25–26, 45; battles with Zunghars, 19, 38; career in Qing service, 19; descendants, 19, 25, 132, 175–76; espionage network, 105; logistical support for military, 52; migration to China, 38–41, 45, 237n65; Niyas Sufi and, 43, 44; sons, 42
Eurasia, 2 (map)
European imperialism, 3, 9, 12–13, 29, 195. *See also* British Empire

Falingga, 82–83, 84, 85, 86, 87
Fergana Valley: agriculture, 106–7; climate, 5; local violence, 160–61; merchants from, 130; trade, 179, 180. *See also* Andijan; Khoqand Khanate
Fletcher, Joseph, 187
Forced labor: exemption for begs, 58; under *khwaja* rule, 166; in mining, 69; resistance to, 71, 160; under Zunghar Mongols, 35–36, 37. *See also* Laborers; Slaves

Forsyth Mission, 126, 177–80, 184–85
Frontiers, *see* Borderlands
Fuxing'a, 143

Gadaimet, 21, 60–61, 82, 83
Galcha, 104
Galchas, 70, 104, 242–43n51
Galdan, 34–35
Gansu, 33, 38–39, 194
Gao Pu, 65–66, 67, 242n43, 242n48
Goës, Benedict, 31
Grain taxes: quotas, 54–55, 55 (table), 116, 124, 136; quotas for *tuntian*, 142–43, 254n37; rates, 171–72, 223–24 (table); revenues, 116. *See also* Taxes
Guo-pu-er, 66, 149

Hākim, 1, 21, 27, 58, 62. *See also* Begs
Hami: agricultural colonies, 24; governors, 20, 23; Muslim aristocrats, 208 (table); outmigration, 31–32; Qing investment in agriculture, 39; revolt against Qing, 32–33; trade, 31; Zunghar attacks, 39
Han Chinese migrants: in Taiwan, 190; in Xinjiang, 13–14, 39, 127, 136, 149, 191; in Yunnan, 190
Haqq Quli, Min-bashi, 121
Holy wars, *see Khwaja* wars
Hori Sunao, 73, 255n61, 257n31
Horses, *see* Livestock

Ili Valley: migrants in, 23–24; Qing troops in, 43, 52; *tuntian* (agrarian colonies), 71, 127, 136; Zunghar rule, 35
Imperial Household Department, 59–60, 65–66
Imperialism: capitalism and, 12–13, 192–96; European, 3, 9, 12–13, 29, 195;

military power and, 13. *See also* Qing Empire

India: capitalist development, 12, 192–94; comparison to Xinjiang, 194–95; imperial powers and, 29; revenue farming, 193; Sepoy Rebellion, 260–61n14; trade, 177. *See also* Mughal Empire

Inflation, 137, 157, 159, 171

Irrigation, 5–6, 73, 76, 78–79, 142, 240–41n28

Ishan Khwaja, 197

Ishāq, 115, 141, 142, 248n49, 252n16

Ishāq Walī, Khwaja, 28

Iskandar, 48

Islam: *madrasa*s, 11, 25, 72; Qing Empire and, 13, 14; religious endowments (*waqf*), 11, 23, 27, 72, 75, 220 (table). *See also* Sufi Islam

Islamic leaders: *akhūnd*s and *mullā*s, 1, 19, 72, 73; *fatwa* against *khwaja*s, 164. *See also Khwaja*s; Sufi leaders

Jade: smuggling, 7, 67, 71; trade, 31, 53, 60, 67, 176, 177, 179

Jade mining: beg roles, 69, 242n48; corruption, 65–66, 67; in Khotan, 6, 27–28, 59, 69, 177; output sent to Beijing, 59–60, 67, 69; in Yarkand, 6, 27–28, 59, 65–66, 67, 69

Jahāngīr Khwāja: attacks on Qing military, 109; background, 90, 111; capture, 248n49; charitable deeds, 247–48n37; followers, 109–11, 248n49; miracles, 109, 110–11; as refugee, 111–12; sons and relatives, 151–52, 162

Jahāngīr War, 90, 111–14, 115, 121, 122, 123, 125, 132

Jamal al-Din, 21–22

Jirui, 138

Kangxi emperor, 13, 32

Kashgar: begs, 56–57 (table), 62, 64–65; copper mining, 162–63; depopulation, 152–53, 167; foreign merchants in, 126, 128–30, 131–32, 133, 141–42, 150–51, 180; irrigation, 78; Jahāngīr War, 112, 113–14; *khwaja* wars, 121–23, 124, 151–53, 161, 162–67; *madrasa*s, 72; Manchu fortresses, 112, 133, 151, 152, 163; markets, 117, 179; taxes, 116, 124, 136; Walī Khān Khwāja regime, 163–64, 165–67, 257n26

Kashgar, Muslim governors of: Ahmad Wang Beg as, 162–63, 174; descendants of Emin Khwāja, 132; financial support of military, 252n16; land confiscated from rebels, 60–61; landholdings, 72, 82–83; revenue farming, 115; *tuntian* development, 141, 142–45. *See also* Osman; Zuhūr al-Dīn

Kashgar District, 108 (map); military bases, 133; military governors, 54, 84–86, 143, 147–48, 150, 162; military land, 146–51; Qing troops in, 51–52, 97, 150, 151; *tuntian* (agrarian colonies), 140–45

Kashgarian migrants, *see* Refugees

Kazakhs, 5, 52, 120

Khoqand Khanate: agrarian development, 106–7; collapse, 160–61; expansion, 109; Jahāngīr War and, 113–14, 122; *khwaja*s and, 105–6, 107, 121–24, 128, 164, 250n73, 256n7; merchants, 49, 73, 115, 117, 118, 128, 130; migrants in, 95, 100, 122–24, 167; military, 115, 120, 121–23; refugees from, 92, 107, 119–20; relations with Qing, 106, 115, 117, 121–22, 128, 130–32, 249–50n69; revenues, 119–20, 130–31; state-building, 106–7, 123; taxes, 130, 176; trade embargo on, 115, 117, 119–20, 121–22, 124, 125; trade with Kashgar,

128–32, 180; tribute trade with China, 106, 161. *See also* Muhammad 'Alī Khān

Khotan District, 108 (map); depopulation, 178; jade mining, 6, 27–28, 59, 69, 177; Jahāngīr War, 112; *khwaja* wars, 164; land reclamation projects, 76–78, 144, 146; luxury goods, 52

Khwaja Campaign, 37

Khwajas: coalition opposing, 105–7, 128; followers, 8, 91, 95–96, 120, 125; land confiscated from, 60; merchants supporting, 164–65, 167; mobility, 91; origins, 8; as religious leaders, 91, 162–63; resistance to Qing, 13, 14, 90–91, 96; smuggling networks, 110, 248n43; state-building, 165–67; use of term, 227n9. *See also* Jahāngīr; Refugees; Yūsuf

Khwaja wars: arms, 248n43; captives, 152; coalition, 91, 121, 122, 124, 165–67, 250n72; defense, 148, 152, 258n44; effects, 90, 152–53, 173; of 1857, 162–67; factors in, 8, 125; as holy wars (*jihad*), 14, 91, 92, 111, 113–14, 121, 122, 176; Jahāngīr War, 90, 111–14, 115, 121, 122, 123, 125, 132; Khoqand support, 120, 121–23, 124, 128, 129; legacy, 197–98; opposition to agrarian development, 92–93; previous scholarship, 91; rural support, 112–13; Seven Khwaja War, 151–53, 158, 161, 164; Walī Khān Khwāja War, 163–67, 173, 258n39. *See also* Yūsuf War

Kirghiz: in agrarian settlements, 59; conflicts with Qing military, 110–11; headmen (*bī*), 98–99, 101, 109; hired labor, 71; Khoqand Khanate and, 120; *khwaja* wars and, 124, 152, 165; leaders, 61, 104–5, 106, 124, 152; livestock, 5; political communities, 102; raiders,

99–102, 104–5, 160, 240n19; refugees, 91; slave trade, 98, 100; trade with, 52, 249n59. *See also* Batur Sart

Kucha District, 108 (map); copper mining, 161; *khwajas*, 22; land reclamation projects, 76, 145–46; military governors, 145, 160; Muslim rebels, 181; rural villages, 81, 160

Laborers: from Andijan, 71; Chinese convicts, 77, 127, 136, 152; hired, 70–71, 76, 86, 87; Kirghiz, 71; land reclamation projects, 83, 86, 138, 145–46; miners, 69, 157, 159, 160, 161–62; mobile groups, 23–24, 38–39; slaves, 70, 98, 100, 124, 242–43n51; travel permissions, 71. *See also* Agricultural labor; Forced labor; *Yanqis*

Land: common, 8, 75–76, 82, 86–87, 171, 258n33; confiscated from rebels, 60–61; near urban centers, 148–49; private use of military, 146–51, 147 (table), 153–54; state-owned, 7, 74, 146–51, 244n75; taxes, 174. *See also* Grain taxes; Wildlands

Land grants: by Qing, 7, 56–57 (table), 58–59, 61, 73, 74–76, 82–83, 145, 240–41nn28–29; by Yarkand Khanate, 27–29, 28 (table), 31, 185, 240n27

Land market transactions, 15–16, 71–73, 75, 171, 216–19 (table), 243n63

Land reclamation: beg roles, 60, 88, 138, 186, 258n33; effects on villages, 86–87, 88, 171; labor for, 83, 86, 138, 145–46; projects, 76–78, 77 (table); social tensions and, 146, 171; taxes, 55, 58–59, 116, 172, 175. *See also* Agrarian development

Leaders, *see* Begs; Islamic leaders; *Khwajas*; Sufi leaders

Liu Yunzhong, 146
Livestock: common land for grazing, 82, 86, 171; as customs duties, 239n18; production, 67, 70, 86; Qing military purchases, 41, 52, 54, 117; trade, 5, 24, 53, 239n18, 249n59
Lukchun, battle of, 19

Ma-er-ka-bi, 104–5
Mahomed Yunus Jan, 184
Mai-la-mu, 97
Mai-ma-sa-yi-te, 132
Mamadabula, 58, 76
Manchus, *see* Qing Empire
Manggaliq, 231n6
Manwen lufu zouzhe, 16–17
Markets, 25–26, 33, 34, 117, 177, 179. *See also Bazaar*s; Capitalism; Trade
Mawalana Arsiddin, 26, 30
Mercantilism, 64, 88, 133, 193
Merchants: Bukharan, 29, 117–18; Chinese, 53, 73, 194; expulsions, 115, 118–19, 130, 251n6; from Khoqand, 49, 73, 117, 118, 128, 130; *khwaja*s and, 164–65, 167; landholdings, 73, 141–43, 171; lending, 53, 73; taxes, 118–19, 173–74, 175–76; tax exemptions, 116, 118, 129, 131–32, 252n10; Tibetan, 33. *See also* Andijan merchants; Caravan merchants; Trade
Miad-sharif Liashker, 121
Mianxing, 174, 175, 258n44
Migrants, *see* Han Chinese migrants; Refugees
Mi-la-yin Rebellion, 33
Military forces: of Bukhara, 166; of imperial powers, 13; of Walī Khān Khwāja, 166. *See also* Qing military
Military governors: Aksu District, 130, 138, 174; bribery, 259n45; corruption

charges, 65–66, 67, 259n45; Kashgar District, 54, 84–86, 143, 147–48, 150, 162; Kucha District, 145, 160; oversight of laborers, 71; Qianlong emperor and, 82–83; relations with begs, 51; reports, 16–17; Turfan, 42, 43; Ush District, 98; Yangi Hissar, 82–84, 87; Yarkand District, 174, 176
Military postal relay stations (*juntai*), 65
Ming begs, 58, 62, 84. *See also* Begs
Ming Empire: global trade and, 11; scholarship on, 191–92; tribute trade, 30–32, 33, 38, 46; Yunnan and, 189
Mining: beg roles, 62, 65, 69, 159, 161–63, 186; copper, 59, 157, 158, 159, 160, 161–63; development of, 59–60; gold, 98, 159, 177; labor, 69, 157, 159, 160, 161–62; lead, 59; resources, 4 (map); saltpeter and sulphur, 65; silver, 159. *See also* Jade mining
Mīr Ahmad, 162–63, 165, 166
Modernity, Eurocentric view, 3, 9–10, 195
Modzapar, 21
Moghuls, 26, 27, 30
Mongols, *see* Zunghar Mongols
Mughal Empire: agrarian development, 12; decline, 20, 193; envoys, 30; Yarkand Khanate and, 27
Muhammad 'Alī (Madalī) Khān: death, 160; efforts to tax trade in Eastern Turkestan, 130–32; Jahāngīr War and, 113–14, 122; *khwaja*s and, 92, 123–24; merchants and, 129, 130; migrants and, 122–24; trade with Kashgar, 128; Yūsuf War, 121. *See also* Khoqand Khanate
Muhammad Hasan, 76
Muhammad Khān, 28
Muhammad Shah Khwāja, 21, 23
Muhammad Sharīf, Khwaja, 21, 25–26, 28, 29, 30, 45, 72

Muhammad Yūsuf Khwāja, *see* Yūsuf
    Khwāja
Mu'in Khwāja, 28
Murmet, 110, 248n42
Musa, 137
Muslims: aristocrats, 132, 208–15 (table);
    attacks on Qing military, 97; idle, 96,
    169–71; property-less, 96, 145–46, 149–
    50, 164, 171, 172; revolts against Qing,
    176. *See also* Begs; Islamic leaders;
    Laborers; Sufi leaders

Nalivkin, Vladimir Petrovič, 122
Named Khan, 152, 167
Naqshbandī Sufi Order: begs, 30; Black
    Mountaineers faction, 33, 91, 113,
    232n15; charitable deeds, 247n37;
    in Eastern Turkestan, 30; leaders,
    33–34, 93; revolts against Qing, 20,
    93; trading networks, 29; White
    Mountaineers faction, 8, 33, 91, 95,
    112–13, 232–33n15
Nayancheng: reforms, 114–20, 122,
    124, 125, 129, 134, 150, 251n6; *tuntian*
    development, 141, 142
Newby, Laura J., 16, 91
New Qing History, 187, 191
Ni'ma, 113
Niyas Sufi, 42–44
Nomads: in agrarian settlements, 59;
    horses, 52; nobles, 21, 22; politics, 27;
    trade with, 5, 52. *See also* Kazakhs;
    Kirghiz

Oasis capitalism: after fall of Qing
    regime, 176–80, 187, 196; beg roles, 1,
    6–7, 9, 10–11, 87–88, 127, 137–38, 185–87;
    British views of, 184–85; class and
    production relations, 9, 10–11; collapse,
    157, 176–77, 181; depression, 177–78, 187;

displaced groups, 91, 101, 189; *khwaja*
    wars and, 91; Qing role, 15, 89, 128,
    182–83, 188, 189; refugee communities
    and, 102–3, 186; resistance to, 196–98;
    resuscitation in 1870s, 196–98. *See also*
    Agrarian development; Begs, economic
    roles; Commercial enterprises; Land
    market transactions; Land reclamation;
    Trade
Opium cultivation, 110
Opium War, 156–61, 171, 186
Osman: economic portfolio, 68 (table);
    espionage network, 105; as Kashgar
    governor, 49, 82, 83, 84–86, 93, 96
Ottoman Empire, 12, 20

Pamir, 5, 8, 91, 104
Panthay Rebellion, 191
Poll taxes, 58, 257n31
Pomeranz, Kenneth, 12
Poppies, *see* Opium cultivation
Poverty, 81, 103

Qalandar (Wandering Sufi), 94, 94 (fig.)
Qarashar District, 59, 138
Qianlong emperor: corruption cases
    against begs, 49, 87, 88–89; Emin
    Khwāja and, 41; military governors
    and, 82–83; petitions to, 74, 76; reliance
    on begs, 55
Qian Yiji, 140–41
Qing Empire, 2 (map); administrators, 7,
    13, 16–17, 225–26n4; aristocratic titles,
    21, 22; developmentalist policies, 61;
    end of Central Asian rule (1864), 14,
    90, 176; expansion into Central Asia,
    1–3, 13, 14–15, 20, 46, 187–89; global
    context, 1–3, 11–12; global trade and,
    11–12; indirect rule, 13, 48, 51, 189–90;
    Islam and, 95; multiculturalism,

191–92; reconquest of Xinjiang, 22, 196; revolts against, 20, 32–33, 93, 97–98, 125, 176, 191; scholarship on, 187, 188, 191–92; state-building, 144–45, 172, 194; Taiping Rebellion, 158, 173. *See also* Beg-Qing alliance; Trade with China

Qing military: agrarian development and, 41, 59; buildup in Xinjiang, 13, 114, 115, 126–27, 133–35, 153, 186; collaboration with begs, 154; conflicts with Kirghiz, 110–11; economic impact, 51–54; Ili Generals, 141, 146, 174; Jahāngīr Khwāja's attacks, 109; Khoqand Khanate and, 106; local Muslim attacks on, 97; local rulers and, 51; logistical support, 20, 24, 37–38, 39, 41, 51–52, 59, 69, 133, 252–53n16; mines guarded by, 59; private use of land, 146–51, 147 (table), 153–54; protection of begs' regime, 49, 128, 153, 240n19; protection of trade, 127, 129–30, 132; treatment of robbers, 104–5; *tuntian* development, 138–46; in Xinjiang, 50 (table), 51–54, 194, 238n6. *See also Khwaja* wars; Military governors

Qing military finances: Changling's policies, 135–36; crisis following Opium War, 157, 158–59; donations from begs, 135–36, 252n16; Kashgar governors and, 252n16; monetary devaluation and, 158–59; Nayancheng's reforms and, 114, 115–16; need for revenues, 194; revenues from *tuntian*, 127, 136, 144, 186; silver transfers, 115–16, 135; tax revenues, 51–52, 66, 115–16, 172–76, 186–87

Qing-Zunghar War, 1, 8, 19, 37, 38, 40, 42–43

Qishiyi, 49

Qurbanmät, 71

Refugees: after Seven Khwaja War, 152–53; agriculture, 109–10; alternative economy and polity, 92, 98, 101–4; causes of displacement, 91, 95, 98, 101, 119, 125, 189; communities, 91, 103–4, 106, 109–10, 186; followers of *khwajas*, 8, 91, 109–13, 125, 186; in Khoqand, 122–24; from Khoqand Khanate, 107, 119–20; leaders, 102, 103–4; in mountains, 8, 47, 49, 91, 97, 98–99, 120; origins, 92, 99, 101, 107, 120, 123; public support, 123; relationship to oasis economy, 102–3, 186; resistance to Qing, 189; from Yarkand, 47, 103. *See also Khwaja* wars

Revenue farming: by begs, 62, 69, 115, 186, 194; in India, 193; Nayancheng's reforms, 114, 119; negative impact, 172, 173, 182; offices sold, 66–67; profits, 174–75; to support military, 66. *See also* Taxes

Rural villages: agrarian development and, 7–8, 79–82, 95–96, 125; beg administration and, 62; begs, 154–55, 255n61; common lands, 8, 75–76, 82, 86–87, 171, 258n33; effects of *khwaja* wars, 152–53; effects of land reclamation, 86–87, 88, 171; establishment, 169; growth, 79; headmen, 62, 84, 86; households, 169; Jahāngīr War and, 112–13; landowners, 169; local violence, 196–98; relocations, 79–81, 221–22 (table); security, 155; stability, 79, 80 (fig.), 81 (table), 169; taxes, 82, 119, 169–72, 174–75, 253–54n33; tensions under beg rule, 49, 78–79, 82–87, 95–96, 155; urban areas and, 5, 49; in Yarkand District, 79, 80 (fig.), 169, 221–22 (table)

Russia: expansion into Central Asia, 160; trade, 179

Safavid Empire, 20
Said Khān, Sultan, 27
Saltpeter mining, 65
Salt taxes, 175
Samarqand, 29
Sarimsaq Khwāja, 93–96, 109, 110, 123
Sāyramī, Mullā Mūsa: *Tārīkhi äminiyä*, 22, 156, 158–59, 182; *Tārīkhi Hämīdī*, 15, 113
Setib Aldi, 21
Seven Khwaja War, 151–53, 158, 161, 164
Sha-guan-ji, 47, 103–4
Shah Mansur (Manchu: Šamangsur), 83–84, 244n71
*Shaykh*s, *see* Sufi leaders
Shuhede (Manchu: Šuhede), 54, 97
Si Beg, Khwāja, 21–22, 23, 231n6
Silk Road, 11
Silk trade, 11, 52–53
Silver: devaluation, 137; mining, 159; salaries of begs, 22, 24; thefts, 161; trade, 11, 12, 30, 32, 53; transfers to Xinjiang, 115–16, 135, 137, 157–59, 160–61
Slaves, 70, 98, 100, 124, 242–43n51
Smuggling: counterfeit coins, 248n41; jade, 7, 67, 71; *khwaja* networks, 110, 248n43; tea, 54, 118
Social tensions: agrarian development and, 92–93, 95–96, 149–50, 154–55, 168; economic causes, 156, 157, 164, 186; labor mobilization and, 162; land reclamation and, 146, 171; in rural villages, 78–79, 82–87, 95–96, 155; violence, 14, 159–61, 196–98. *See also Khwaja* wars; Refugees
State-building: in Central Asia, 92, 165; by Khoqand Khanate, 106–7, 123; *khwaja* wars and, 91, 93, 106; local, 165, 181; by Qing Empire, 144–45, 172, 194; Walī Khān Khwāja regime, 165–67

Sucheng, 98
Sufi Islam: Bukhariyya, 29; *dervish*, 235n36; holy men, 15, 227n9; Qadiriyya order, 22, 29; Qalandar (Wandering Sufi), 94, 94 (fig.); shrines and meeting places, 11, 23, 25–26. *See also* Naqshbandī Sufi Order
Sufi leaders: as agromanagers, 22–23, 26–27, 29; descendants as begs, 21–22, 23; fundraising, 93–94, 95–96; migration to Eastern Turkestan, 26–31, 46; migration to Xining, 33–34; tribute trade with China, 30–31; in Yarkand Khanate, 31, 33–34, 40; Yarkand Khanate land grants to, 27–29, 28 (table), 31, 185, 240n27. *See also Khwaja*s
Sulphur mining, 65
Sultān Khwāja, 61, 76
Suranchi, 68 (table), 109

Tailak, 121, 124
Taiping Rebellion, 158, 173
Taiwan, 190
Tāj al-Dīn, Khwāja, 30
Tajiks: agriculture, 5; Galchas, 70, 104, 242–43n51; leaders, 98; slave trade, 70
Tārīkhi äminiyä, 22, 156, 158–59, 182
Tārīkhi Hämīdī, 15, 113
Tārīkhi Sharukhī, 113, 121, 122
Tarim Basin, 5, 6
Tashkent, 121, 123, 179
Taxes: customs duties, 54, 116, 117–18, 129, 130, 131, 239n18; irregular, 172; Nayancheng's reforms, 116, 118–19; new, 172–74, 175–76; paid to military, 51–52; poll, 58, 257n31; on rural villages, 82, 119, 169–72, 174–75, 253–54n33; salt, 175; transit, 173; Yarkand District register, 168–72, 223–24 (table), 257n31. *See also* Grain taxes; Revenue farming

Tax exemptions: for begs' land grants, 58–59, 175; for idle Muslims, 169–71; for merchants, 116, 118, 129, 131–32, 252n10

Tea: plantations in Yunnan, 190; taxes on, 116, 173; trade, 11, 53, 54, 117, 118, 128

Textiles: silk, 11, 52–53; trade, 52–53, 117, 149, 173, 177, 180. *See also* Cotton

Tianshan Mountains, 5, 8, 90, 91, 95, 97, 109, 120

Tibetan Buddhism, 14

Tibetan merchants, 33

Timurid Dynasty, 23

Toktonidza, 74, 75

Tomb compounds, 74, 76

Tongshi interpreters, 148, 149, 254n49

Trade: after fall of Qing regime, 178–80; beg administration, 62, 65, 88; in Central Asia, 29–32, 48–49, 52–54; collapse, 159; customs duties, 54, 116, 117–18, 129, 130, 131, 239n18; global networks, 1, 5, 11–12, 29–30, 45–46, 180, 193–94, 195; in livestock, 5, 24, 53, 239n18, 249n59; maritime, 29, 30; marketplaces, 117; military protection, 127, 129–30, 132; in nineteenth century, 126, 184; Qing regulations, 116–20; Silk Road, 11; in slaves, 70, 98, 100; taxes, 65, 116; in tea, 11, 53, 54, 117, 118, 128; in textiles, 11, 52–53, 117, 149, 173, 177, 180; of Yunnan, 189–90. *See also* Caravan merchants; Commercial enterprises; Smuggling

Trade with China: beg roles, 7, 11, 45, 46; declines, 32, 176; expansion, 11–12; jade, 31, 53, 60, 67, 176, 177, 179; logistical support for military, 37–38; luxury goods, 11, 52–54, 177, 179; in Ming period, 30–32, 33, 38, 46; state-building role, 194; tribute trade, 11, 30–32, 34–35, 46, 53–54, 106, 161; of Yarkand

Khanate, 31–32, 185; of Zunghar Mongols, 34–35

Transoxiana, *see* Bukhara; Samarqand

Transportation: military postal relay stations (*juntai*), 65; roads, 173

Tribute trade, *see* Jade; Trade with China

Tsewang Raptan, 35

Tu-er-du-shi, 42

Tu-lun-tai, 32–33

Tuntian (agrarian colonies): beg control, 127, 136–40, 142–45, 154, 186; development, 127, 136–46, 139–40 (table), 154, 255n4; financial support of military, 127, 136, 144, 186; grain produced for military, 24; grain tax quotas, 142–43, 254n37; in Kashgar, 140–45; labor, 127, 136, 138, 141, 170; taxes, 253–54n33

Turfan: agriculture, 41–43; corruption cases, 42, 43–44; irrigation, 73; *khwajas*, 30; military governors, 42, 43; Muslim aristocrats, 132, 208–10 (table); outmigration, 31–32, 38–40, 41; resettlement by Muslims, 41, 43; revolt against Qing, 32–33; taxes, 173; trade, 31; Zunghar attacks, 19, 36, 37, 38

'Ubayd Allāh, 20, 21, 23

Ūdui: alliance with Qing, 21, 24; background, 21; corruption scandal, 65–66, 67; descendants, 161; economic portfolio, 66–69, 68 (table); jade mining and, 242n48; loans from merchants, 53, 73; logistical support for military, 24, 52, 242n43; movement of settler community, 23–24; *tongshi* interpreters, 254n49; as Yarkand governor, 47–48, 49–51, 65–69, 71

'Umar Khān, 105, 106–7, 109

Uratube, 107, 120

Urban areas: begs, 6, 62; Black Mountaineers faction, 33, 91, 113, 232n15; land near, 148–49; residents, 5, 6, 170–71; rural areas and, 5, 49

Urumqi, 35, 127, 136, 190

Ush District, 108 (map); agrarian development, 23; begs, 58; governors, 74, 98, 137; military governors, 98; Qing troops in, 51; revolts against Qing, 97–98; *tuntian* development, 142, 253n32

Uzbek rulers, 92. *See also* Khoqand Khanate

Valikhanov, Chokan, 16, 95, 102, 110, 111, 117–18, 122, 124, 126, 133–34, 165–66, 167–68, 172, 246n22

Villages, *see* Rural villages

Walī Khān Khwāja, 151–52, 162, 163–64, 165–67, 256n7, 257n26

Walī Khān Khwāja War, 163–67, 173, 258n39

Water: conflicts over, 78–79, 86; irrigation, 5–6, 73, 76, 78–79, 142, 240–41n28; rainfall, 5, 168

Wenyuan, 162

White Mountaineers faction, 8, 33, 91, 95, 112–13, 232–33n15. *See also Khwajas*

Wildlands, 74. *See also* Land reclamation

Wulong'a, 141, 142

Wu-mu-er-bi, 104

Xining, 33–34

Xinjiang (Eastern Turkestan), 2 (map); arable land, 10–11, 202 (table); Chinese migrants, 13–14, 39, 127, 136, 149, 191; climate, 5, 168; geography, 5; mineral resources, 4 (map), 6; outmigration, 152–53, 157, 167, 177–78; political crises, 189, 191; population, 11, 178, 201 (table);

previous scholarship on, 187, 188, 226n5; Qing administration, 19, 21; Qing conquest, 13; Qing reconquest, 22, 196. *See also* Agrarian development; Begs; Oasis capitalism

Xinjiang Shilue, 78

Yangi Hissar: agrarian development, 96; governors, 70, 83–84, 145, 244n71; Jahāngīr War, 112; land held by begs, 83; land reclamation projects, 76; military governors, 82–84, 87; Qing military base, 252n16; Seven Khwaja War, 152

*Yanqi*s: illegally claimed by begs, 7, 82, 83, 84–85; increased number of, 186; provided to begs, 7, 22, 58, 85–86, 144, 182, 226n5; Qing regulations, 85; quotas for begs, 82, 83, 85; rich, 58–59; tax-exempt status, 58–59, 82–86, 87, 88, 175

Ya'qūb Beg, 14, 90, 176, 177, 183, 184

Yarkand: economy, 49–51, 52; irrigation, 73; jade mining, 6, 27–28, 59, 65–66, 67, 69; *khwaja* wars, 112, 152, 163, 164; land reclamation projects, 76; *madrasas*, 25; markets, 117, 177, 179; Muhammad Sharīf in, 25–26; Qing troops in, 51–52; size, 238n5; taxes, 116, 170–71; trade, 184

Yarkand District, 108 (map); agriculture, 168, 223–24 (table); governors, 47–48, 49–51, 52, 76, 175–76, 184, 254n49; military governors, 174, 176; population, 223–24 (table), 257n31; rural villages, 79, 80 (fig.), 169, 221–22 (table); tax collection, 174; taxes, 175–76; tax register, 168–72, 223–24 (table), 257n31

Yarkand Khanate: agrarian development, 28–29; fall of, 35, 185, 187; founding, 27; land grants to Sufi leaders, 27–29, 28 (table), 31, 185, 240n27; political

instability, 27, 31–32; ruling family, 188;
Sufi leaders and, 25, 27–29, 31, 33–34,
40; tribute trade with China, 31–32, 185
Yin-a-wa-ti, 196–97
Yingwen, 174, 175
Yishan, 152, 153
Yi-shan Khwaja (Ishan Khwaja), 197
Yonggui, 53–54
Yongle emperor, 30
Yongzheng emperor, 38–39
Yue Zhongqi, 19
Yunnan, 189–91
Yūnus, 142
Yūnus Wang Beg, 72
Yusan Khwāja Īshān, 160, 256n7
Yūsuf Khwāja, 121, 122, 128, 250n72, 251n70
Yūsuf War: coalition, 250n72; effects, 129,
134, 143; Khoqand role, 121–23, 124, 128,
129, 250n73; Qing defense, 148

Zhang Luan, 53, 73
Zuhūr al-Dīn: career, 132–34; economic
activities, 127, 147–50, 254n36; "just
and liberal rule," 126, 127–28, 134, 154;
as Kashgar governor, 126, 128, 133–34,
136, 140, 152, 154–55; landholdings,
144; support of Qing military buildup,
133–34; trade promoted by, 133, 134;
tuntian development, 142–45, 254n40,
254nn36–37
Zunghar Mongols: agrarian development
by, 24, 35, 46; begs, 63 (table), 64–65;
forced labor mobilization, 35–36, 37;
military strength, 34; Muslim deserters
from, 40; Qing-Zunghar War, 1, 8, 13,
19, 37, 38, 40, 42–43; Sufi leaders and,
34–36, 46; tribute trade with China,
34–35

Milton Keynes UK
Ingram Content Group UK Ltd.
UKHW012217141123
432578UK00003B/57

9 780804 799232